CORPORATION

CORPORATION

JAMES NORBURY

WAR HAS NO CONSTANT DYNAMIC
WAR HAS NO CONSTANT FORM

SUN TZU

CORPORATION

2009 © James Norbury

PUBLISHED BY: James Norbury - Brutal Games

This product is a work of fiction. Any similarity to actual people, organisations, places, or events is purely coincidental.

ISBN - 978-1-906508-27-2
MGP 6128

www.corpgame.com

Copying the ideas contained in this book could be very dangerous. Crafting your own plasma weapons, cybernetically altering your friends, claiming governance of portions of the world and assaulting law officers are all examples of things you should NOT do. It must also be stated that the Corporations mentioned here are not yet real and hence it is impossible for anyone to become an Agent. Therefore, although this book often refers to you as being an Agent, it is simply descriptive and not a set of covert instructions.

DEDICATION

To Ian & Betty
Watching is the best way to learn.

ACKNOWLEDGMENTS

My thanks to all the people who helped turn Corporation into what it is now. A number of people played a key role in the development of this game, which started back in 2000. I would like to extend my gratitude to them all.

Ruth, for your assiduous scrutiny of grammar and system anomalies, and for showing us that the game can handle some very odd character concepts. Ian, for providing artwork which elevates the visuals to a level that could not otherwise be achieved. Al, for demonstrating that E.I. Agents are not all decadent fools although collateral damage is still obligatory. Iain, for your artwork, time and trying to get the Cult to help you clone Linda Barker. Scott, for the proofing and Brian 'The Remover' Smith's novel take on the psychology skill. Petroc (our man in Sydney), you've added another layer which enriches the world profoundly.

2009 Additional

I'd also like to thank Mongoose Publishing and particularly Matthew Sprange who are helping to bring Corporation forward in a big way!

ART

Austerity Spire, Changi Underswell, Agent Najir Zanjani, Notre Dame, First Terminal, Cardinal Cavel, Kharkiv Enclave, Ice Line, Old London, Sturt, Tower of Gemini and Catalan Spire Complex, Three Witches, Civilian - Ian Norbury
3D Model Construction & Rendering Iain Stark
After rendering & all other art James Norbury
Layout & Design James Norbury
Thanks for additional source imagery to - Jamison Thies, Anya Enemy, Steve Todey

ADDITIONAL TEXT

Additional Quotes & Flavour Text Petroc Wilton
Winters Briefing Iain Stark, Stone Cold / 0HP - Matthew Keevil

ADDITIONAL PROOF READING

Ruth Burbery, Scott Fielding, Petroc Wilton

KEY PLAY TESTERS

Ruth Burbery, Iain Stark, Al Wilson, Jon Dore, Hugo Marchent, Matthew Keevil Pippa Smith, Gareth Stevens, Scott Fielding, Petroc Wilton, Dave Rodgeman, James Norbury

BEFORE YOU START

More important than rules are characters, places, plots, action and mood. This book is intended to show you the world of *Corporation*, the people who populate it and what you can do therein. It is not supposed to be a big book of rules, which say exactly what can and can't happen. Saying that, without some rules you just have a very large description.

To detail a foolproof system which represents the ricochet of a bullet inside a skull from a theoretical weapon and the resulting psychological repercussions on the killer, is not the objective of this book. The rules system is intended to let you interact with the world in a stylish and reasonably believable manner with the Games Master creating the scenes and adjudicating where necessary. The GM is encouraged to make decisions and not be bound by exact rules, which cannot extend to all possible circumstances.

So do whatever you like, ignore some rules, alter others and make up some new ones. Just make sure everyone playing is in agreement about what they want out of the game.

HOW TO USE THIS BOOK

Obviously it would be best for the person running the game to read the whole book in order but this is not normally going to happen. If you just want to get started quickly the guidelines below should allow you to cover the basics. *To start with you should read:*

COUNTRIES

Corporation, as a game, does not feature countries in the same way they existed in the 21st Century. The world is now owned by the Corporations and the countries simply used as geographical markers. A country (such as Mexico) does not have its own Government or laws, nor is it treated differently from any other place owned by the parent Corporation. The United International Government dictates law across the civilised world. Only the *Freestates* are not bound by these laws.

TABLE OF CONTENTS

WHAT IS A ROLEPLAYING GAME?

If you don't know what a roleplaying game is then read on. If you already know, skip to the 'Introduction to Corporation' which tells you about the world of Corporation and what happens therein. It has been kept brief so that you can get a broad idea of the game world before you explore it in more detail later.

Roleplaying is a way to play a game. Once you get started it is fiendishly addictive and a great social occasion.

Roleplaying games (commonly called RPGs) require two or more players, one of which is a Games Master. The Games Master plans a story in his mind and on paper which will be played out by the others. In this particular game the Games Master will design a story (or Mission) set in the world of the Corporations where high-tech weaponry, espionage and cybernetically augmented Agents are among the key elements.

The players are then required to make characters. These characters are assumed identities that the players take through the mission created by the Games Master. The character you design can be anything you like, within certain parameters. In Corporation you have to take the role of a human but your attitude, appearance, fighting style, background, cybernetic upgrades and physical abilities are yours to choose.

Once all the players have created characters and the Games Master has designed or found a mission, you will need some dice and note paper. You are now ready to assume the identity of your character and immerse yourself in the world of Corporation.

INTRODUCTION TO CORPORATION

> Endless money forms the sinews of war.
>
> -Cicero, Philippics

In 2500 five Corporations have risen so high and wield such power and influence they can all but make their own laws. The wars they once waged upon each other have left the planet deeply scarred but from the ashes they have brought about a new era in human development. Citizens live peaceful lives in gleaming Spire Cities while mankind takes its first tentative steps into colonising the solar system. Since the end of the Corporate Wars and the founding of the United International Government (UIG) there have been no global conflicts and crime has hit an all time low.

All too soon this idyllic peace could come crashing down. The Corporations have their own agendas; living in compromise is bad for business and means no one gets what they really want. Each Corporation seeks to shape the world to its own ideals but enemies are always waiting to take advantage of an overextended competitor.

Enter Agents: cybernetically altered and bio-modified humans fielding the most advanced technology money can buy. These men and women act as street level executives dealing with issues the Corporations cannot openly tackle. From the magnificent archologies of Tokyo to the slums of Old Berlin, Agents work to fortify their Corporation's position through espionage, assassination and politics.

But not everything can be resolved in the shadows. Despite their directives to remain covert, Agent conflicts spill onto the streets. Citizens silently cower in their apartments while the augmented soldiers of the Corporation openly war against each other with high-tech arsenals that leave the cities battered and witnesses too scared to speak out.

The political and military calm which seems to exist is nothing more than a carefully maintained facade to pacify a naive populace.

ROLEPLAYING CORPORATION

The five Corporations stand high and strong. The United International Government, after a period of weakness and deferring to the Corporations, now enforces the law with strength and fervour. With this indomitable force presiding over them, the Corporations fight a hidden war vying for technological, economic, political and military superiority.

Their struggle arises from the inability to make any strong offensives without other Corporations attacking them in their moment of weakness. This is where the Agents come in; operatives of great skill and ability who carry out illicit missions on behalf of their Corporations whilst avoiding UIG persecution.

Upon enlistment the Agent sells himself to his Corporation making him their property. The UIG have no interest in safeguarding the assets of Corporations, only themselves and Citizens. As a result the Law turns a blind eye to Corporate conflict unless there is a knock-on effect to the population.

In Corporation you take on the role of an Agent; you must fight for the Corp with every weapon at your disposal. Success yields great rewards; money, property, technology, rank and fame. Failure could mean the end of all you have known.

WHERE CAN YOU GO?

The game has an almost infinite scope in terms of what is possible. The five major Corporations are huge with very different moral outlooks and methodologies. The United International Government is vast and seeps into every facet of life. The Order of the True Faith are indefatigable in their divine mission to revert the world to a more primal state. Other smaller Corporations exist which, although not as powerful and influential as the main five, are large enough to require Agents to look after their interests.

Civilians have agendas too; rebel factions continuously war against the UIG, the Corporations and each other to achieve a variety of goals, the consequences of which are known to few. The world's chemical dumping grounds have given rise to foul twisted creatures that plot and scheme in their polluted lairs. Many off-world colonies exist which have problems every bit as menacing and dangerous as those in the Old Cities of Earth. This is not to mention the recently discovered power of the telepaths who have a weapon few can fight.

All of these possibilities are covered in this book in more detail with rules and suggestions on how to include them in your game.

This book, however, only gives rules for playing Corporation Agents. The other playable characters (UIG Officers, Mutants, Rebels, the Order of the True Faith and the like) will be covered in future publications.

"Here, this is the place"
Kincaid nodded in agreement, "Seems to be. Why here?"
Jenson placed his hand over the grip of his weapon for reassurance.
"He runs this place."
"What, the bar?"
"No, not the bar idiot, the whole place, about three blocks square. This is the middle, probably where he feels safest."
"Feeling isn't being," laughed Kincaid
"Maybe, come on. And no mess until I say, okay?"
"Okay."

They were glad to get out of the weather; the rain had soaked them through. The civilian rags were useless at holding off water. The bar looked big but only because of the pink-tint mirrors that decorated every flat surface. Night-girls and boys sat around the edges of the room smiling, trying to attract the attentions of anyone who might be looking. Kincaid and Jenson walked up to the bar, a wide steel counter with phonic strip lights flowing along its edges. A woman with bloodshot eyes and a glass of transparent green liquor got up from a stool.
"Drink or entertainment fellas?"
"Where is Dratt?" barked Jenson
"What honey, who's Dratt?"
Jenson noticed Kincaid reach under his jacket and glared at him, "Peter Dratt. Where is he, we're supposed to meet him here."
"Wait here honey." The woman left through a back door.

Dratt was sat in a tattered brown armchair in the back room, an empty pill box lay on the arm and his face held no recognisable expression.
"Hey, Pete. There are two men out front for you."
Dratt looked up and grinned. "What?"
"Two men, big guys. One has long greasy hair and a hooked nose, the other…"
Dratt cut her off "..is bald and mean looking, yeah yeah, that's Kincaid and Jenson. Some of Mikey's boys. Well, tell them I've changed my mind, the deal's off. It ain't worth the hassle."
"You sure? The bald one looked pissed."
"Kincaid always looks pissed," laughed Dratt, "now, go and do your job."

Jenson and Kincaid saw the door open and the woman walk back through, her blond hair held in place by strips of twisted copper.
"He says the deal's off boys, so go home and don't cause any trouble." The woman reached under the bar and pulled an ugly looking black weapon out.
"You know how to use that?", asked Jenson
"I suggest you and your bald buddy take your fat little arses out the door and don't come back."
Kincaid leaned over the bar and stared straight into the woman's eyes. "Go and get Dratt you whore."
The woman didn't flinch "One more move like that sonny and you won't have such a pretty mouth to shoot off."
"Shoot, I dare you," smiled Kincaid
A sudden, ear splitting crack filled the air followed by a heavy splattering. Kincaid got up off the floor, wiped the blood from his face and slowly tore off the pieces of plastiskin that hung in front of his eyes. The woman's mouth fell and she dropped the weapon.
"Shit, you're…."
"Yes, now go and get Dratt and tell him he owes me a new face."

GAME TERMS

CRITICAL (HIT OR MISS) - A roll, normally a double 10 or double 1 signifying something exceptional has happened.

D2, D4, D6, D8, D10, D12, D20, D100 - Dice - see page 138.

GM - GAMES MASTER - The person who runs the games and has the final decision on everything.

HP - Hit Points - A measure of a characters health. More is better.

NPC - Non-Player Character - All the characters in the game who are played and controlled by the Games Master.

PC - Player Character - The assumed identity a player takes on in the game, much like an actor playing a part.

ROUND - Term used to describe a 3 second period of time in an action sequence. All people involved in the action can do something each round creating a turn based combat system. (Also see Turn)

ROUND DOWN - Any time there is a fraction of a number always round down. If there is a situation where this seems unreasonable the GM should make a decision.

SCENE - A collection of related events that the characters experience much like a scene in a film, e.g., a car chase, an interrogation or hacking a computer system.

SESSION - Name given to a single roleplaying occasion, usually a few hours long but sometimes many, many hours.

SYSTEM - The rules of the game.

SUCCESS - Passing a dice roll (see page 138). Rolling below or equal to a STAT+ a Skill on 2D10.

TE - Telepathic Energy Points - A measure of the character's mental energy used for powering telepathic skills.

TURN - A player gets a turn each round.

ITALICS

Bodies of text in *Italics* are descriptive and can be skipped. It is not important game information. Normally it consists of examples to help explain rules or flavour text to add background to the section.

AGENTS

WHAT ARE THEY?

> *I see in the near future a crisis approaching that unnerves me and causes me to tremble for the safety of my country. ... Corporations have been enthroned and an era of corruption in high places will follow, and the money power of the country will endeavour to prolong its reign by working upon the prejudices of the people until all wealth is aggregated in a few hands and the Republic is destroyed.*
>
> Abraham Lincoln

The Corporations are vast financial and political powers whose strength is based on the world's changing economic and political climate and as such are always in a state of dynamic balance. They must attempt to preserve what they have achieved whilst simultaneously making sure their competitors do not surpass them. Corporations must be wary of sabotage, theft, insurrection and government scrutiny. A certain amount of this work can be done from behind desks but much of it must be conducted in the field by trained operatives. Agents are the executive arm of the Corporations, highly skilled individuals who put themselves at great personal risk for their employers. They may work for loyalty or for reward; the Corporations care little as long as the job gets done.

The typical work of an Agent starts with receiving a mission brief. The Agents will then use all the resources at their disposal to achieve the mission goal, much like the military. Agents work under a strict chain of command with the highest ranking Agent having total control and responsibility for the Division. Every success and failure is ultimately down to the Division leader. (Players should be encouraged to select a leader.) Missions take many forms (from mediating a gang war to sabotaging a rival factory) and will make up the majority of an Agents work. Deserving Agents are sometimes given more liberal work such as 'maintain our interests in Japan'. This kind of brief is less direct and may require the Division to go undercover for several months.

Agents are granted rights by the United International Government (UIG) based on their past performance. If Agents work well and within the law the UIG may extend their rank and privileges. In exchange the Agents are occasionally required to act in the capacity of police when and where appropriate. If the Agent continues to excel, then more privileges may follow. UIG assigned rank is valid across the world and Agents with high rank have a great deal of power and respect. Abuse of this rank is risky to say the least.

Many problems exist for the Agent; her work is not normally straightforward or simple. The Agent's duty is varied and dangerous and is made harder due to the fact that the Corporations prefer not to be seen attacking each other. This does not mean skirmishes are unheard of, far from it. Agents will often find themselves battling for the same goals and resources in the same places, and on these occasions conflict will often ensue. Corporations with strong rivalries and motivations may attack each other in public places. The UIG have no real interest in the Corporations damaging each other, only a threat to the security and safety of Citizens and public assets will cause the UIG to interfere in inter-corporation conflicts.

All in all, with the current state of the world, an Agent leads a prestigious life. Power, money, influence and respect can all be earned by a proficient individual. The lives of normal Citizens seem mundane and devoid of purpose compared to the dynamic work of an Agent, and living as an Outcast or Criminal is simply not an option.

AGENT PHYSIOLOGY AND STARTING EQUIPMENT

Agents are superior to normal humans. When enlisted, (i.e. when the character is created), the Agent is fitted with basic cybernetics and biomodifications which allow a number of useful operations. The prices are listed here in case you want to give these upgrades to NPC's. They are free for starting Agents.

S.V.C / SUB VOCAL COMMUNICATOR (SMEAKER) 6,000¢

This allows an Agent to communicate with other friendly Agents up to 300 kilometres away silently. The Agent merely murmurs to herself and the vibrations are picked up by a receptor buried in the jaw bone. The Agent can speak directly with HQ, but this form of communication is not 100% secure, so transmissions with headquarters are often restricted during important missions. The smeaker has an active range of about 300km but the signal security decays with range. If you wish to represent signal decay roll a D100 when the smeaker is used. If the roll is below or equal to the signal integrity for the range then the communication is beyond risk of interception. This can be rolled secretly by the GM if desired.

SUB VOCAL COMMUNICATORS

RANGE (KM)	SI %	HACKING PENALTY
000-001	100	-12
002-005	90	-10
006-010	80	-8
011-050	70	-6
051-100	50	-4
101-150	30	-2
151-200	10	-0
201-300	01	+2

SI% - Signal Integrity as a percentage

Hacking penalty - Penalty to hack the SVC

ID CHIP
500¢

This is present on all Citizens, UIG and Agents. The chip is located under the skin on the back of the hand and contains information about the carrier. It also has a small writable section on it to allow authorised organisations to make notes on the chip such as membership of clubs, temporary licenses or black marks. The UIG (and only the UIG) can technically track the location of the wearer by their chip but it is seldom done. The chip is powered by the wearer's bio-energy and if removed will break and become useless, although the body can still be identified via the chip serial number. An 'Agility + Cybernetics & Robotics' check made at -12 can successfully remove a functioning chip without destroying it. The same roll is made to install one unless you have a UIG chip installation lab (which would be unlikely). ID chips cannot be hacked, the Archon based technology is far beyond that of the typical hacker.

All Citizens, businesses and Agents are issued with a small scanner that can read these chips so they can authenticate anyone's identity. Depending on the rank and license of the person using the scanner, different levels of information on the subject will be displayed. Agents and the UIG will be able to access more information than basic Citizens.

These chips mean anything can be personalised such as opening doors, computers recognising users, starting cars etc. The chip checkers can be fitted to almost anything including weapons so they can't be used by unauthorised parties. Due to the costs involved only UIG, Corporate, secure and business buildings regularly contain chip readers, although they can be found anywhere.

EXAMPLES OF AGENTS USING CHIP CONTROL

If an Agent has a license, e.g., *Search Domestic*, then his chip will automatically open any eligible domestic doors that are chip controlled.

When an Agent checks into a hotel then his chip will open his hotel room door for him.

If an Agent has a *Public Appropriation License* then he can open eligible car doors and start vehicles with his chip, as long as the car is fairly modern and has an ID chip checker.

If an Agent has a license to modify the programming on droids then the droid will recognise his chip and grant him permission.

When entering a club the chip would be amended to show that the Agent has paid; he could leave and re-enter without a problem.

Weapons can be fitted with an ID Chip Checker for 100¢ and will only fire for the registered user. See page 51.

It is illegal not to have an ID Chip and if lost, should be reported to the UIG immediately and a new chip purchased within the hour. This costs 500¢.

OVERDOING ID CHIPS

Be careful about putting chip checkers on everything. This can make a typical mission very frustrating if the Agents cannot do anything because all the equipment, cars and rooms are chip-locked. They should be used where appropriate such as:

Secure areas

High risk areas

Criminal hideouts

Expensive hotels

UIG buildings

Corporate buildings

Property of the wealthy

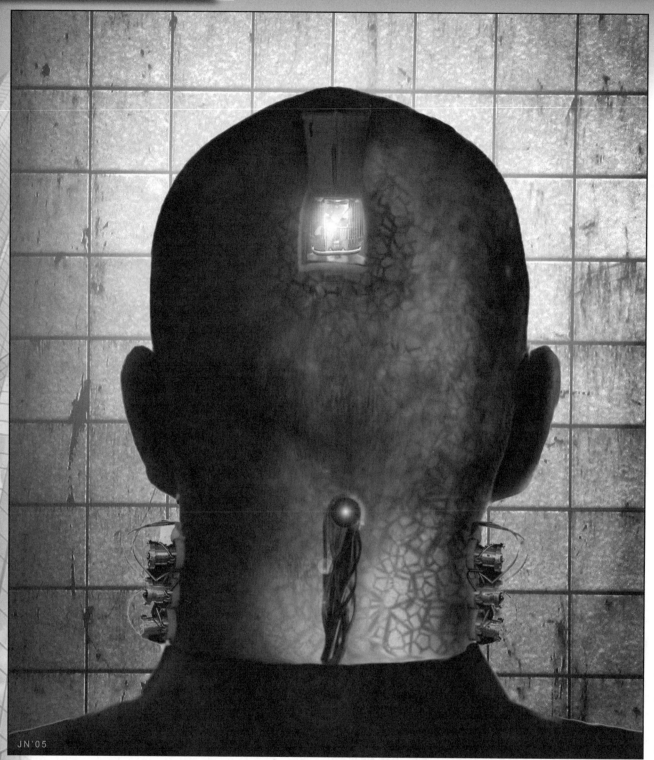

JN '05

PROCESS CHIP INSTALLATION

A.I. CHIP (ARTIFICIAL INTELLIGENCE CHIP)
18,000¢
New Agents are fitted with a form of sophisticated wetware containing an Artificial Intelligence. The chip grants the user an Internal A.I. of 1 and provides a foundation for a number of improvements, many of which are the cybernetic upgrades an Agent already has. Other uses which utilise your Internal A.I. include assisting hacking attempts and controlling weapons. Increasing your Internal A.I. costs 5,000¢ x your current A.I. level. For example, taking it from 2 to 3 would cost 10,000¢. You cannot increase it by more than one point per week of game time. Your Internal A.I. cannot go above 9.

PROCESS SOCKET (BASIC)
20,000¢
This is the first upgrade an Agent receives which utilises his A.I. Chip. A standard X-Pin socket is set into the back of an Agent's skull and is hidden by a synthetic cover. Task Chips and Process Chips can be slotted into the X-Pin socket. The chips contain programs and information which the Agent can utilise as long as he has them plugged in, effectively granting him new skills and abilities. Advanced Process Sockets allow for more complex chips to be plugged in. See Process Chips and Task chips for more information on page 54.

R-DRUG
400¢ A MONTH

Originally developed by Two Snakes on the Miller-Urey research orbital, this chemical flows around the Agent's lymph system and assists in cellular and tissue reconstruction. It has the effect of causing the Agent to heal back to their original genetic form. For example, if an Agent has a hand cut off, the R-Drug will cause the hand to regrow rather than the stump sealing over. The monthly cost is paid by the Corporation. Severed limbs take a long time to regrow, although for game system purposes you do not lose any Hit Points if you have a small amount of your body missing. The GM could overrule this in extreme circumstances; e.g., all limbs cut off could reduce the Agent by 10HP.

Limb	Time for Regrowth
Hand / Foot	2 weeks
Leg / Arm	3 weeks
Head	Not Possible
Facial Feature	1 week
Fingers / Toes	1 week

HISTONAMIDE
100¢ A MONTH

This protein causes an Agent's blood to clot with incredible speed meaning they are resistant to blood loss from normal wounds. Particularly savage damage to the Agent could still result in bleeding - this type of damage is called 'Mashing Damage'. The monthly cost is paid by the Corporation. Anyone without this upgrade considers all damage to be mashing.

ATROPHIC DNA
7,000¢

Residual Agent DNA in hair, dried blood and dead skin cells etc, decays to an unrecognisable state in 10 minutes. This means that it is hard to get DNA samples from Agents. However, if tissue from the Agent is less than 5 minutes old is treated with Compound-H then the tissue stays alive and the DNA does not decay.

SYNAPTIC MODULATION
22,000¢

This advanced feedback chipset causes the Agent's nervous signals to be muted when high frequency impulses are transmitted along neurons - the result being Agents do not feel intense pain. They are aware of the injury but it is transmitted to their brain as useful information, not paralysing agony. For this reason if an Agent has a leg cut off he is likely to be annoyed at his reduction in efficiency, but will not be immobilised by the pain.

INDEPENDENT CELLULAR EXCISION (I.C.E) AND NEURAL STABILISERS
30,000¢

Aside regrowing limbs and ignoring pain, Agents are also resistant to a range of crippling conditions. An Agent's brain, heart and other vital organs are modified by I.C.E technology to ensure they are not incapacitated by damage. Organ and head trauma seldom affects an Agent as the I.C.E and Neural Stabilisers bypass or repair the damaged area. Agents are consequently immune to Knockout and moderate organ damage. Removal of entire organs or serious trauma will still affect an Agent.

AMBIDEXTERITY (FREE)

All Agents are trained to be ambidextrous, they need not be concerned about having their good hand damaged. This does not mean their hands are flawlessly synchronised and using two weapons at once can still present problems.

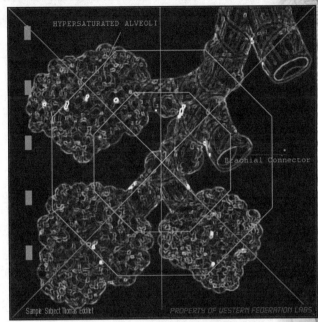

GEMINI CARDIOMECHANICS FEATURING BRONCIAL REINFORCEMENT AND VOLUMETRIC EXPANSION OF THE ALVEOLI

The two Malenbrach threw him across the room with obscene force and, as he hit the window, Christian Dionne felt the glass break around him, splinters driving into his back, his shoulders, his head. Then he was out into the chill of the night air and hurtling down the outside of UIG Administration Station 13, staring up at the stars. With an effort, the wind whipping at his face, he turned his head to look at the building as it flashed past, all chrome facing and darkened windows that sped by as he continued on his terminal plunge. Recalling with a speed borne of desperation the schematics of the building, Dionne stuck out a hand and felt, for a fleeting instant, the cold metal of the transceiver aerial.

Electronically augmented reactions locked his fingers instantly around the aerial, bringing him from a downwards speed of ninety metres per second to a dead stop. The shock that should have shattered his hands, pulled his forearm out at the elbow or torn his arm from its socket merely sent unpleasant vibrations through the length of his Reaver AS3000 alloy skeleton, which had already passed nerve impulses to the relevant artificial muscle groups to properly absorb the shock of impact, rather than allowing whiplash to splatter his brain against the inside of his skull. Dionne exulted for the briefest moment in the sheer joy of his continued existence, before reminding himself that he was still hanging by one hand eighteen stories above the ground outside a building full of hostiles. As if to emphasise the point, the transceiver aerial gave an ominous little creak. Dionne exhaled slowly, his breath steaming in the cold air, and swung up his other hand.

SECTION 01

CHARACTER CREATION

> *Human talent is a resource that Corporations have exploited more ruthlessly than any other since their earliest inception.*
>
> *- from The Rise of The Corporation-States*
> *attr: Dr. Edmond Treval*

PLANNING YOUR CHARACTER

Before you can play the game you will need to create a character for yourself. In this section you have the opportunity to design an alternative identity with which to engage in the missions set for you by the Games Master. Take some time to talk about characters with the rest of the gaming group so that you don't all create similar Agents or ones who clash badly. Don't forget to read Agent Physiology on page 9 so you know the differences between Agents and normal humans.

THE DIVISION LEADER

When a Corporate Division is formed, the Leader is normally the Agent best suited to give orders and accept responsibility. She is also responsible for the smooth execution of missions and has executive power over all other Agents in the Division.

When the Division is formed a Leader should be chosen. (This is generally decided by the players who choose which character would make the best leader or which player would enjoy it most). If there is indecision the GM can choose or in extreme circumstances a Leader can be absent.

WHY BE A DIVISION LEADER?

Division Leaders gain an additional Rank Point at the end of each session and naturally get the most glory and respect for the completed mission. All failure - of course - is also the responsibility of the leader.

STARTING EQUIPMENT

All Agents start with some basic equipment and licenses to help them get the job done. These are listed below.

AGENT LICENSES AND STARTING EQUIPMENT

1 Intravenous Medpack.

Exceptional Black Cougar Handgun (Kinetic Pistol) D8 Damage (critically passes on 1/1 and 2/2).

External Communications Device, (comm. device).

Flack Jacket (Gives +1 Armour Value)

Handcuffs

ID Chip Scanner (normal)

PDA (Personal Digital Assistant) A small portable computer)

Identification Badge for quick identification to others without scanning an ID chip. Shows basic details.

Law Enforcement License

Light Firearms License

License to use Non-Powered Melee Weapons

Hacking Software (Normal) - This is illegal. Agents do not have to take it. Only available with GM approval.

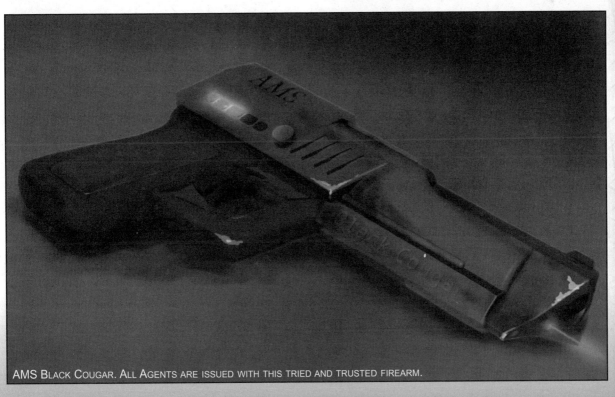

AMS BLACK COUGAR. ALL AGENTS ARE ISSUED WITH THIS TRIED AND TRUSTED FIREARM.

CHARACTER CREATION QUICKSHEET

Below is an abbreviated form of character creation for experienced players. If you are not sure see the next page where the full process is described. See 'Agents: What Are They?' starting on page 8 to see what equipment, licenses and upgrades Agents begin the game with.

I. SELECT A CORPORATION

If you are playing a Cross-Corporation game all players can select different ones, otherwise you should all pick the same one.

2. SELECT A CONCEPT AND PROFESSION

You should pick a skill which is crucial to your profession; this is considered your 'Professional Skill' and must be 7 or higher.

3. ASSIGN STATS

Spend 49 Points (or 7 in each and rearrange) on Strength, Endurance, Agility, Reflexes, Perception, Intelligence and Presence. None above 10 or below 5 at this point.

4. EXTRA FEATURES

You have Hit Points (HP) equal to 'Strength + Endurance + 20'.

Rank and Level begin at 1.

Telepathic Energy (TE) = 'Presence + Perception + Intelligence + 10'.

Your Move Speed is equal to 'Strength + Endurance + Agility'.

Your Internal A.I. starts at 1.

Your starting Armour Value (AV) is 0. This doesn't include the free flak jacket which gives +1 AV.

Your Defence is equal to your Close Combat. There is a column titled 'DEF' in the weapon / attack section of the character sheet to write this. (Marked by a dot ●)

Your Experience Points (XP) are 0 and Rank Points (RP) are 10.

You start with 2 Conviction points.

You gain the ability to speak the main and secondary languages of your Corporation and one language of any Corporation with the exception of Military Sign (Western Federation only). See page 17 for languages.

5. ASSIGN SKILLS

Select your skills as directed below. Your Professional skill must be at 7 or more. Telepathics count as skills but you need the training 'Telepath' to acquire them.

1 skill at level 8	3 skills at level 4
1 skill at level 7	3 skills at level 3
1 skill at level 6	3 skills at level 2
3 skills at level 5	4 skills at level 1

6. TRAININGS

You may select 2 trainings. See page 21.

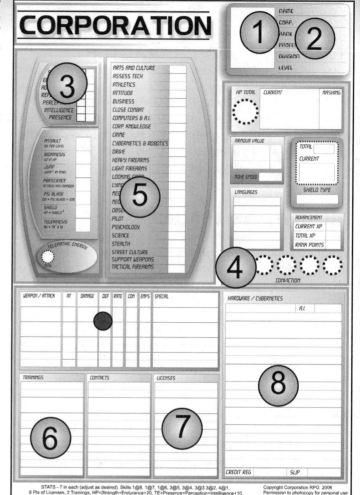

7. LICENSES

You gain 8 points in Licenses. See page 25.

8. PURCHASE EQUIPMENT

Page 29. (Don't forget starting equipment on page 13).

CORPORATION	STARTING MONEY
Ai-Jinn	7,000 Credits
Comoros	6,000 Credits
E.I.	10,000 Credits
Shi Yukiro	9,000 Credits
W.F	8,000 Credits

OVERVIEW OF THE CORPORATIONS

AI-JINN

Asian industrial giants whose Agents operate outside the law in organised crime cells.
Sector: Heavy industry, heavy construction, mining.
Bonus: Changeable ID Chip.

COMOROS

Independently minded Indo-African telepathy specialists with a hatred for the UIG.
Sector: Culture and Education.
Bonus: +10 TE at character creation. All Comoros have increased telepathic regeneration, free Telepath Training. Can burn HP for TE.

EURASIAN INCORPORATED

Decadent, capitalist monsters striving for socio-economic world domination and enjoying it.
Sector: Health and Leisure.
Bonus: Expense Account.

SHI YUKIRO

Far Eastern technologists and warriors founded on ancient philosophies and the Bushido Code.
Sector: High Tech and Electronics.
Bonus: Powered Melee License and Training. Free Katana at character creation and access to Ion Weapons at Rank 3 / Level 8.

WESTERN FEDERATION

Disciplined, puritan military machine intent on a new world order.
Sector: Armaments and Defence.
Bonus: Superior Weapons, extra weapon licenses, military sign and 10% off weaponry.

AGENT IN LIGHT COMBAT ARMOUR + COMBAT HELMET.

COMPLETE CHARACTER CREATION PROCESS

STAGE 1

CORPORATION

Normally all players should decide on the same Corporation or the GM may assign one. If players want to create characters from different Corporations see page 195 for cross Corporation games. Consult page 15 for a brief synopsis of the Corporations or for more detail you can see the descriptions starting on page 90. If you wish you can photocopy a character sheet or download one on-line from www.corpgame.com.

STAGE 2

CONCEPT AND PROFESSION

Below are some examples of character concepts, if you are having difficulty, read the description of the Corporations starting on page 90. Think of books and films that inspire you and the characters in them. You will find that an amazing number of sources can inspire characters for Corporation. When you have an idea look at the questions on page 17 and try to answer them for your character.

SAMPLE CONCEPTS

A.I. Assassin
A.I. Trainer / Programmer
Animal Handler
Assault Telepath
Businessman / Financier
Combat BIO Builder
Commando
Communications Expert
Computer Technician
Contract Killer
Corporate Publicity Agent
Cryogenically Defrosted Criminal
Cultural Attaché
Cyberneticist
Cybernetics Junky
Defence Telepath
Demolitions Expert
Detective
Dilettante
Diplomat
Droid Builder
Droid Hunter
Electronic Engineer
Explosives Expert
Fence / Black Market Retailer
Gambler
Gladiator (Current or Ex)
Good Timer
Heavy Weapons Expert
Historian
Jury Rigger
Lawyer
Light Weapons Specialist
Mafia Style Enforcer / Yakuza / Triad
Mechanic
Medic
Melee Weapon Smith
Morale Officer
Mutagenic Scientist
Organised Crime Member
Pilot
Proto-Technician
Reformed Criminal
Saboteur
Security Specialist
Social Assassin
Social Engineer
Spy
Stealth Assassin
Tactical Weapons Specialist
Thief
Weapons Scientist / Tester
Weltball Player (Current or Ex)

FILMS TO INSPIRE YOU

5th Element
Alien Series
Blade
Bladerunner
Demolition Man
Equilibrium
Gattaca
Ghost in the Shell
Johnny Mnemonic
Minority Report
Predator
The Matrix
The Running Man
The Terminator Series
Total Recall
Twelve Monkeys

MUSIC

Crystal Method, Fear Factory (Probably the most consistently appropriate), Fluke , Icon of Coil, Ministry, Nine Inch Nails, Orbital Prodigy, S.U.N Project

TV & GAMES

Also consider checking out video games such as Deus Ex 1 & 2, Doom 3, Mass Effect, Gears of War 1 & 2, Fallout 3, Half-Life 1 & 2, Metal Gear Series, Syndicate & Syndicate Wars, System Shock 2, Bioshock, Quake IV, Splinter Cell and F.E.A.R. Also TV shows based in a futuristic setting such as Dark Angel or ones involving covert ops and special forces such as Alias and 24.

MAKING YOUR CHARACTER INTERESTING

Once you have a concept you need to develop the personality; first of all think of an attitude you would like to act out, an angle, something that motivates the character to do what she does. You need to be able to predict how your character will act when faced with a variety of situations. Perhaps the character has a problem that she needs to solve or something she must do whenever she gets the chance. Consider factors that drive the character: greed, hate, envy, sadism, love, duty, revenge, liberation and so on. It's very important to give the character at least a little depth otherwise there is a good chance she may become boring as she advances.

CHARACTER QUESTIONS

If you can think of how your character would act in the following situations, and if it would be interesting to roleplay, then you probably have the makings of a good character.

1. In a violent crowded bar where the character has her drink spilled by an outlaw.
2. When being reprimanded by the Missions Officer for a disastrous mission.
3. After completing a successful mission and given a large pay cheque. (Interests during time off).
4. When in the thick of the action with her favourite equipment and plenty of enemies.

THINK ABOUT THESE QUESTIONS

1. Why does the Corporation employ her?
2. Does she have any family?
3. Does she fully support the Corporation?
4. What is her operational method?
5. How did she become a professional?
6. How does she dress?
7. How does she deal with authority?
8. Who does she hate and why?
9. Does she have a grudge against a particular faction or Corporation?
10. Who does she love and why? Perhaps no one.
11. Where does she live if not in Corporate Spire Accommodation?
12. What does she do for fun?
13. Why did she join the Corporation? Did she have a choice?
14. Does she have strong morals or ethics?
15. What is her price for corruption?
16. Superficial good looks are cheap - Is she attractive? If so, in what way?
17. Does she have any pet hates or bad habits?

STAGE 3
ASSIGNING STATS

These determine the basic building blocks of your character. They are representations of your character's raw abilities and are qualities that almost everyone shares regardless of training. See the list (top right) to see what STATS you have. These are ranked from 0-10, zero being terrible and ten being the edge of human ability. 5-6 is the human average but Agents are far from average. You may not increase your STATS above 10 at this point or by spending experience. 10 is the limit of human ability and as such only inhuman methods can take them to 11 or more. Cybernetics and Combat Drugs are two ways to take your STATS above 10. (If you purchase cybernetics with your starting money then it may be possible to take your STATS above 10 at character creation).

STAT ASSIGNMENT METHOD 1

All your STATS start at 7; you may take one point off any STAT to increase any other by 1 point. This way you can create any combination you please. Normal human average is 5-6. Agents are above average. You cannot take these STATS above 10 or below 5 at this point.

STAT ASSIGNMENT METHOD 2

You gain 49 points to spend on STATS. None may go above 10 at this point or below 5.

STAT SUMMARY

Agility	Your suppleness and dexterity
Endurance	Your stamina, health and hardiness
Intelligence	Your raw deductive power and logic
Perception	Your awareness of what is happening around you
Presence	Your strength of personality
Reflexes	Your reaction time and quickness
Strength	Your physical power

WHY THE STAT & SKILL LIMITS?

If you had STATS at 4 or less the Corporation would not employ you as a field Agent as you would not be suitable for the range of missions an Agent may need to undertake. STATS above 10 are beyond human ability and can only be achieved by modifying the body which must be done with other methods such as cybernetics.

STAGE 4
EXTRA FEATURES

You have Hit Points equal to Strength + Endurance + 20

Your Rank begins at 1

Your Level begins at 1

Telepathic Energy (TE) = Presence + Perception + Intelligence + 10

Your Move Speed is equal to Strength + Endurance + Agility

Your Internal A.I. starts at 1

Your starting Armour Value (AV) is 0. This does not include the flack jacket you receive for free which, if worn, gives +1 AV.

Your Defence is equal to your Close Combat
Note there is no box for this on your character sheet as your defence is always equal to your close combat.

Your Experience Points are 0 and Rank Points are 10. This allows you to start at Rank 1. See Rank table on page 81.

You start with 2 Conviction points

You gain the ability to speak the main and the secondary languages of your Corporation and one language of any Corporation with the exception of Military Sign (Western Federation only).

LANGUAGES OF THE CORPORATIONS

CORPORATION	MAIN	SECONDARY
Ai-Jinn	Mandarin	Cantonese, Thai
Comoros	Swahili	Indian (Hindi)
Eurasian Inc.	English	Russian, German
Shi Yukiro	Japanese	Mandarin
W. Federation	English	Spanish, Military Sign

STAGE 5

ASSIGN SKILLS

To represent the things you have learnt during your life you can select a number of skills. You can see there are different numbers of skills at different levels, the higher the level the better the skill. This is designed to reflect real life where a typical person has a basic knowledge of many skills, a good knowledge of a few skills and an exhaustive knowledge of one or two skills.

ASSIGNING SKILLS

1 skill at level 8
1 skill at level 7
1 skill at level 6
3 skills at level 5
3 skills at level 4
3 skills at level 3
3 skills at level 2
4 skills at level 1

Example. If you wish to play a hacker you might wish to have:

Computers & A.I.	8	Drive	3
(professional skill)		Close Combat	3
Mechtronics	7	Stealth	3
Lying and Acting	6	Psychology	2
Crime	5	Arts & Culture	2
Business	5	Street Culture	2
Light Firearms	5	Looking Good	1
Assess Tech	4	Medicine	1
Observation	4	Tactical Firearms	1
Science	4	Athletics	1

These skills can be increased with Experience Points earned during the game but only inhuman methods may take them above 10, e.g., cybernetics, drugs or mutations. Try to select skills which suit your character rather than ones you think will be useful. You will be surprised what skills can be used to great effect in different situations.

PROFESSIONAL SKILL

Select one of the skills you have at 7 or higher. This is considered your profession and should fit in with your concept. You cannot critically fail rolls involving this skill and if you pass the roll and get a double on 2D10, it is considered a critical success.

TELEPATHICS SKILL OVERVIEW

Note that Telepathics are Skills and are bought with the same points. In the example above the hacker could replace his 'Light Firearms 5' with 'Assault 5'. He would of course need the Telepath training. He would also need an appropriate license to perform legal telepathics.
There is a brief description of the Telepathic skills here and a full description on page 74.
You may only purchase Telepathic skills if you also buy the 'Telepath' training. (Page 22)

TELEPATHICS

JUMP

The ability to jump great distances. At high levels as much as 100 metres.

SHIELD

The Telepath can summon an energy shield to defend himself from ranged attacks.

ASSAULT

The Telepath can physically attack others with a personalised manifestation of telepathic energy.

PRESCIENCE

The Telepath can see short distances into the future increasing his reaction time and awareness.

PSI BLADE

The Telepath can summon a blade of telepathic energy.

TELEKINESIS

The Telepath can move items from a distance; the more powerful he is the more he can move.

BIOKINESIS

The Telepath can heal himself and rid his body of toxins.

SYMPATHETIC SKILLS

Some skills can back up other skills in certain situations. For example if you were creating a poison in the lab and you had 'Science 6' and 'Medicine 8' you could get a bonus as both skills are appropriate to the task at hand.

Roll using the highest relevant skill and add half the second skill as a bonus to your Action Total (round down).
In this case you would roll 'Medicine + Intelligence' with a +3 bonus.

Likewise if you were building a pistol and you had 'Mechtronics 6' and 'Light Firearms 4' you would get a +2 bonus.

The bonus should only apply when you have the time and opportunity to use the full extent of your knowledge, generally not in action scenes (also see page 139).

SKILL DESCRIPTIONS

ARTS & CULTURE

This covers the performing arts as well as the visual arts including design. This could mean making normal items look better, for example customising the look of weaponry. It also covers academic subjects not covered by science such as geography, religion, language, history, antiques, literature or cookery. Although this skill covers a large variety of subjects you should also pick a single specialty subject such as 'History' or 'Religion', you gain +4 to rolls on your specialist subject.

ASSESS TECH

The ability to view new, unfamiliar technology and understand its function and operational method.
For example, you see a strange black device plugged into a wall socket in an apartment. You could make a roll of 'Perception + Assess Tech'. If you pass, the GM would reveal that it is a recharging energy cell for a prototype plasma weapon. You may be able to take it and use it.

ATHLETICS

Your trained ability to complete physically demanding actions such as running, swimming, climbing, throwing and jumping.

ATTITUDE

Your general verbal and social style and how you come across to other people. It can take many forms and need not be an attitude people enjoy, but you will make an impression. A high attitude is indicative of someone with a point to make, and a characteristic manner which others will remember.

BUSINESS

This represents your knowledge of all things business: finance, accountancy, commerce, entrepreneurship, use of the media, mergers, takeovers and even small deals such as buying second hand cars or weapons. Note that Street Culture or Corp. Knowledge may complement some types of business at different social levels.

CLOSE COMBAT

Skill with melee weapons and unarmed combat. It also allows maintenance of melee weapons. Your 'Defence' is also determined by this skill. Most characters should generally have at least 'Close Combat 1', even NPC's. This reflects the basic biting, kicking and struggling behaviour that almost all humans will display when attacked.

COMPUTERS & A.I.

Ability to build, use and understand software in all its forms as well as the science of Artificial Intelligence. It also covers basic computer maintenance, upgrades and repairs but Mechtronics will also be needed if an Agent wished to build a computer from scratch. You need the training 'Hacking' to hack computer systems. See page 21.

> *The most likely way for the world to be destroyed, most experts agree, is by accident. That's where we come in; we're computer professionals. We cause accidents.*
>
> Nathaniel Borenstein

CORPORATE KNOWLEDGE

Knowledge of the policies, laws, Agents, technology and general status of the Corporations including the UIG and The Order of the True Faith. A modifier of +4 to -4 can be used to alter the roll based on the obscurity of the knowledge. Etiquette in normal society is usually governed by Corp. Knowledge or Arts and Culture. In low society use Street Culture.

CRIME

Knowledge of crime such as larceny, racketeering, car jacking, fencing, extortion, prostitution, homicide, embezzlement, drug running, breaking and entering, etc. Crime also helps you to deduce things from scenes of crimes, particularly when used with Science.
(Crime is used to picks locks - see below)

OPENING LOCKS (USING CRIME)

Roll below or equal to '**INTELLIGENCE + CRIME**' with a modifier to the Action Total as below.

To open Mechanical locks you need 'Lockpicks'.
To open Electronic locks you need a 'Security Bypass Device'.
Using inappropriate equipment to pick a lock gives an additional -6 penalty to open the lock. (e.g. a knife or bent wire)
A Lock Analyser adds a +4 bonus to open any lock type.

LOCK TYPE	EXAMPLE MECHANICAL	EXAMPLE ELECTRONIC	WHO WOULD USE THEM	MODIFIER
Crude Lock	Padlock	Coded Keypad	Outcasts & Criminals	+2
Normal Lock	Normal House Lock	House Swipe Lock	Civilians	+0
Good Lock	Shop Window Shutters	Hotel Swipe Access	Commercial Operations	-4
Advanced Lock	Safety Deposit Box	Single Biometric Scan	Corporations, Banks	-8
Elite Lock	Underground Vault	4 Way Biometric Scan	UIG Facilities and Corporate Secure Areas	-12

CYBERNETICS & ROBOTICS

Maintenance, programming and construction of droids. Also represents the ability to design, build, install and maintain cybernetics. See page 60 for Cybernetics and page 241 for Reprogramming Droids.

DRIVE

Skill in driving land based domestic vehicles from motorbikes to tanks to cars. If the GM considers the vehicle to be obscure (such as a Heavy Tank) he could apply penalties to the roll or require an 'Assess Tech' roll.

HEAVY FIREARMS

Use and maintenance of heavy firearms such as rocket launchers, cannons and rail guns.

LIGHT FIREARMS

Use and maintenance of light firearms such as laser pistols, machine pistols and hand cannons.

LOOKING GOOD

The ability to dress well, hold yourself with poise and maintain your appearance. Without this skill you must go on personality alone. You need to spend money to maintain a good image which the GM should keep an eye on. If the Agent does not maintain a lifestyle consistent with their 'Looking Good' score then the GM should reduce the score on a temporary basis. Spending a large amount of money on appearance (e.g. 4000¢ on a suit) could increase your looking good by a point or two as long as you wear the suit. The suit may not last long in an Agent's line of work.

LYING / ACTING

Your ability to hide the truth from others and feed them false information. Can also be used to coerce information out of people.

MECHTRONICS

Your skill in electronics, mechanics and nanotech. When combined with other skills such as weapon skills it can be used to maintain and improve devices such as guns, cars, shields etc.

MEDICINE

Your ability to apply medical assistance. Gives knowledge of human biology and how it can be affected by things such as disease and damage. Also dictates your skill at creation and use of substances which affect the human body such as mutagens, narcotics, medicine and combat drugs. You can automatically heal 1 HP on a fresh wound. By passing an 'Intelligence + Medicine' check you can heal 2HP and / or stabilise a dying person. This can only be done once per wounding incident. This covers general medicine. Surgery requires the Surgeon Training.

OBSERVATION

Perception describes the acuity of your senses. Observation is the skill of using those senses to deduce answers and notice things which are out of the ordinary.

PILOT

Skill in piloting airborne, seaborne, orbital and interplanetary vessels. If the GM considers the vehicle to be obscure he could apply penalties to the roll or require an 'Assess Tech' roll.

PSYCHOLOGY

Skill in determining the mental processes, thoughts and psyche of others by observing and speaking with them. With this skill you can give other people counselling should you wish. Social intuition, empathy, sociology and anthropology are also covered by this skill.

SCIENCE

Knowledge of the general sciences. Physics, chemistry, zoology, botany, maths, mutagenics, etc. (Human biology, biochemistry and pharmacology are considered to be Medicine.)

STEALTH

Your ability to remain hidden from all the senses. In order to bypass sophisticated methods of detection you may need to use 'Assess Tech' or 'Mechtronics'.

STEALTH MODIFIERS
ROLL AN APPROPRIATE STAT + STEALTH

CIRCUMSTANCES	MODIFIER
Dark stormy night, sneaking down an alley	**+4**
Remaining inconspicuous in a shopping mall	+2
Sneaking past a typical guard	**+0**
Evading an alert guard	-2
Entering a heavily guarded area in daylight	**-4 to -8**

STREET CULTURE

Knowledge of the workings of the street from gang territories to flop houses and how to acquire some basic contraband. It also covers surviving in urban environments. This can be used to know key do's and don'ts when dealing with outcasts and outlaws, i.e. street level etiquette.

SUPPORT WEAPONS

This covers demolitions, grenade type weapons and emplacements as well as the setting of explosive charges and knowledge of destroying large structures and constructions.

TACTICAL FIREARMS

Use and maintenance of mid-sized Tactical Weapons such as shotguns and rifles.

Agent Kerrik wiped away the sweat that was stinging his eyes. This device was alien to him, a simple steel sphere with translucent, triangular plates randomly dotted about its surface. This was supposed to be a bomb? No bomb Kerrik had ever seen. It had no way in and no way out. No seals, no screws, no bolts, no latches, no wires, nothing. Just faintly glowing triangles. He had no idea what would detonate it, a timer, a slight movement, light, sound, maybe ambient temperature. Maybe nothing?

As the device exploded and Kerrik's alloy frame was torn in half by the blast, he wished he'd paid more attention to the lecturer, and as his upper body spun in a graceful, flaming arc across the Spire atrium, he made a mental note to attend a class in support weapons the first chance he got.

STAGE 6

TRAININGS

Trainings represent specialist areas of expertise. They can range from combat techniques to computer hacking to field surgery. Select two Trainings from the list below at character creation. It may be handy to note down any rolls used on your character sheet. You will have the opportunity to acquire more in-game by spending 10 Experience Points. You may not purchase the same Training twice unless it states that you can in the description.

PREREQUISITES

Sometimes the name of a Training is followed by one or more prerequisites in **bold**. This means that you must first acquire these before you can purchase the training.
For example:
Meditation requires you have the Telepath training.
Command requires you have Presence 7 or more.

SUMMARY OF TRAININGS

NON-COMBAT TRAININGS
Animal Skills
Aptitude
Command
Domestic Trade
Field Surgery
Hacking
Interrogation
Jury-Rigging
Meditation
Stone Cold
Surgeon
Surveillance
Survival
Telepath
Telepathic Adept
Underground Operations

COMBAT TRAININGS
Advanced Disarm
Assassinate
Combat Driver
Combat Pilot
Defensive Fighting
Disarm and Attack
Droid Hunter
Dual Weapon Fighting
Gun Melee
Hail of Missiles
Mastered Weapon
Multiple Defence
Powered Melee
Quick Draw
Restrain
Scything Strike
Thrown Weapons
Twin Psi Blades
Unarmed Combat Specialist

NON-COMBAT TRAININGS

ANIMAL SKILLS

You have skill in controlling animals and things with animalistic intelligence (such as cyberwolves). You may maintain 1 trained creature per point you have in Presence. You can make the animals behave normally automatically but you may need to make a 'Presence + Attitude' roll to control the animals in extreme circumstances.
For example, commanding your Cyberwolf to bring down an enemy without injuring it.

APTITUDE

You have a knack for doing most things, when you use a skill which you have no points in, you do not critically fail on all doubles. You cannot critically pass one of these rolls.
In addition once per session you can add D6 to one Action Total for one roll.
For example, Agent Becker grabs a discarded rocket launcher in a desperate attempt to blow a Cultist apart before he gets torn into pieces. He has no skill with heavy weapons so his AT would normally be 6 (his Perception). He uses his Aptitude Training to add a D6 to the Action Total (he rolls 4). His Action Total is now 10, not great but much better.

COMMAND
Presence 7
You can command others and are used to exercising your authority. You can add your Rank to any social rolls which the GM deems appropriate, such as forcing your way into commercial property or intimidating lower ranking Agents.

DOMESTIC TRADE

This is a training which represents everyday trades such as cooking, shop keeping, boat building, tailoring, gardening, etc. Select a trade when you select this Training. To make checks based on this Training the GM will select an appropriate STAT and Skill; e.g. gardening could use 'Intelligence + Arts & Culture'. Alternatively it can give a +2 bonus to a related skill with GM consent. For example, if you had locksmithing as a domestic trade then you could gain a +2 to opening lock rolls.

FIELD SURGERY
Medicine 5
You can take medical action regardless of your surroundings and are used to making do with what you have. No roll is needed. You can heal up to your Medicine in HP to an individual, in any reasonable circumstance. It simply takes 1 round per point of damage you wish to heal. The medic can only use this ability once per scene per person and cannot attempt to heal the same set of injuries twice.

HACKING
Computers & A.I. 5
You can use a computer to gain unauthorised entry into another computer. To do so you must pass a 'Intelligence + Computers & A.I.' roll with a modifier dependent on the type of system you are trying to access. See page 150 for details on hacking.

INTERROGATION

You are skilled at extracting information from people. This could take various forms such as psychology, physical torture, bribery, sensory deprivation, life altering threats, etc. The GM should decide an appropriate opposed roll (normally involving Psychology, Endurance or Presence). See page 145 for opposed competitions. The XS indicates the quality of the information extracted.

JURY-RIGGING

Mechtronics 5

You can build something out of nothing. If you have a few basic components and some tools, you can try and build simple items of your own design or from the equipment list. You must pass an 'Intelligence + Mechtronics' roll with a modifier decided by the GM. Below are some examples.

Build a ladder from rope and metal bars	+2
Build a catapult using a rubber tyre and bent metal	+0
Build a timed bomb from a watch and plasma cell	-2
Build a motorbike from a crashed car	-4
Build a computer from a box of old calculators	-10

MEDITATION

Training: Telepath

You can meditate in areas of relative calm to gain back Telepathic Energy (TE) at twice your normal rate.

SURGEON

Medicine 6

You are skilled at non-cybernetic surgery; you can reattach limbs or replace damaged organs. To perform surgery, roll 'Intelligence +

SURGERY

Below are listed some recommended bonuses for different types of surgery.

Simplistic Surgery e.g. sewing up a wound	+4
Basic Surgery e.g. setting a bone	+2
Average Surgery e.g. reattach a leg	+0
Tricky Surgery e.g. replacing a liver	-2
Delicate Surgery e.g. brain Surgery	-4

CIRCUMSTANCE MODIFIERS

No tools at all	-12
No Surgeon Training	-10
Crude tools, e.g., spoon	-8
Basic tools, e.g., scalpel	-4
Crude lab / good tools	-0
Normal lab	+2
Good lab	+4
Excellent lab	+6

Medicine' with the modifiers below. Surgery cannot be used to simply regain HP, it deals with more severe physical wounds such as severed legs and missing organs. The GM should feel free to restore some HP after a successful operation. Normally 1-10HP. If you don't have the Surgeon Training you gain a -10 penalty to all surgery rolls.

SURVEILLANCE

Stealth 3
Mechtronics 3

You are trained at staking out areas, looking for security cameras and generally gathering useful information about a target. Using this training you can make a roll to gather information on a person, place or anything else you need intelligence on. The roll is normally 'Perception + Stealth' but could be changed by the GM if appropriate. Depending on the success of the roll the GM can offer you information on security systems and layout, or in the case of people, habits, timing, hangouts, etc.

SURVIVAL

You are skilled at surviving without modern comforts whether it be in a slum, an underswell, a deserted space hulk or the jungles of Miller-Urey. Passing an 'Intelligence + Endurance' roll (with a GM modifier) means you live reasonably in the hostile conditions. Failure will result in hunger and deteriorating health.

STONE COLD

You don't take traumatic events quite as badly as most people. When rolling at the start of a mission to see whether you recover a point of conviction lost to trauma you restore a lost point on a roll of 1 to 5 rather than just 1. Stone Cold needn't be role-played, a character can still possess this training and be cheerful and outgoing, but on the inside they're an empty shell.

TELEPATH

You have awakened the parts of your brain which control Telepathics and can therefore use telepathic skills. Without this training you are unable to utilise or learn any Telepathics.

TELEPATHIC ADEPT

Training: 'Telepath'

You have a natural affinity for Telepathics. You gain +20 TE. This can only be purchased at character creation and only once.

UNDERGROUND OPERATIONS

Street Culture 3
Crime 2

You have been trained to blend into the underground. Once per session you can attempt to acquire something from the black market such as restricted drugs, unlicensed weapons, illegal software or simply information. Any transactions must still be paid for in money or favours. If a roll is required by the GM use 'Presence + Street Culture' or 'Presence + Crime' with an appropriate modifier.

COMBAT TRAININGS

These work in the same way as Non-Combat trainings but are oriented towards incapacitating, maiming, and killing.

RELEVANT WEAPON SKILL

Because there are different weapon skills in Corporation the term 'Relevant Weapon Skill' is used to mean the skill you use to attack with your current weapon. See 'weapons' from page 35 to find out which weapon uses which skill.

Examples:
If you are using a sword then your Relevant Weapon Skill is 'Close Combat'
If you were firing a shotgun your Relevant Weapon Skill would be 'Tactical Firearms'

ADVANCED DISARM
Close Combat 4
You are skilled at taking weapons from your opponents. You gain +4 to your Disarm checks. See page 145 for Disarm rules.

ASSASSINATE
Close Combat 6
Stealth 6
If you can approach an opponent without being detected, you can kill or knock out the target with a single strike. You cannot knock out anyone with Neural Stabilisers (page 11), i.e. Agents. They are instead reduced to 0HP and lose 1 INT per round till dead.

ASSASSINATE
The Assassin rolls
CLOSE COMBAT + STEALTH

The target rolls
REFLEXES + OBSERVATION

Compare the XS (amount each passes or fails by). If the assassin gets higher he may knock out or kill the target automatically with no chance to resist.
If the target wins, the attempt fails and combat will probably ensue.

COMBAT DRIVER
Drive 3
Normally a -4 penalty applies to rolls made while driving and fighting at the same time. With this Training those penalties are ignored.

COMBAT PILOT
Pilot 3
Normally a -4 penalty applies to rolls made while piloting and fighting at the same time. With this Training those penalties are ignored.

DEFENSIVE FIGHTING
Close Combat 3
You can take a penalty to hit and add half that number to your Armour Value (round down). The penalty may be no higher than the relevant weapon skill you are using. This can only be used in Close Combat.

DISARM AND ATTACK
Close Combat 5
Advanced Disarm
You can disarm an opponent and flick the weapon round attacking them with it in the same action. You must have at least 2 in the skill that the taken weapon requires.
Make a disarm check (page 145). If you succeed you get one free attack with the weapon, even if it is ranged (one attack, not a round of attacks). You cannot take heavy weapons like this unless you have Strength 10 or more.

DROID HUNTER
Cybernetics & Robotics 3
You add your 'Cybernetics and Robotics' skill to all damage against Droids. This uses the same basic system as the Mastered Weapon training on page 24.

DUAL WEAPON FIGHTING
Relevant Weapon Skill 4
Without this Training you can still use two weapons at once but receive a -4 penalty with each. The first time you acquire this Training select one of the weapon types from the list below. (You must have the Relevant Weapons Skill at 4+.) You then ignore the Dual Weapon penalties (-4) when using this weapon in a Dual Weapon style. Each successive time you purchase this training, select another weapon type. You can use any combination of weapon types you have purchased; even two handed weapons in each hand if you have Strength 10 or more.
When rolling to hit with two different weapons, use the appropriate roll for each weapon.

Heavy Firearms (Requires strength 10 to use 1 handed)
Heavy Close Combat (Requires strength 10 to use 1 handed)
Light Firearms
Light Melee
Tactical Firearms
Tactical Melee
Thrown Bladed Weapons
Support (This is often impractical, for example using two gun emplacements, but some actions such as using a gun and throwing a grenade are possible, although one would need to pull the pin out using ones teeth.)

Example:
Agent Decker first purchases 'Light Melee' so he can use two light melee weapons with no penalty. He later purchases 'Light Firearms' so he can now use any combination of light firearms and light melee weapons with no penalty, e.g., pistol and knife, two pistols or two knives. He can continue to buy aspects of this Training until he can wield any pair of weapons.

GUN MELEE

Relevant Weapon Skill 7
Close Combat 7
Agility 6

As long as you have the relevant weapon skill at 7 or more you can fire a light or tactical ranged weapon in close combat and keep your 'Defence' as though you had a close combat weapon
.

HAIL OF MISSILES

Close Combat 5
Thrown Weapons Training

You can throw twice the amount of weapons normally allowed with the Thrown Weapons training.

MASTERED WEAPON

Relevant Weapon Skill 8

Select a type of weapon, e.g. Laser Pistol. (You would need Light Firearms 8 to master the Laser Pistol). If you hit with the weapon remember your XS and add it to the first damage dice rolled, e.g. if you pass the roll to hit with a knife by 4 you deal D4 + Strength + 4 extra damage.

MACHINE WEAPONS WITH THE MASTERED WEAPONS TRAINING
With machine weapons, XS is added to the first damage dice rolled against each target. This is important for Armour purposes.
Example 1: If you attack one target with a machine pistol (3D6) the first dice will be D6+XS, the remaining two will both deal D6.
Example 2: If you attack three targets with a machine pistol each dice will deal D6+XS.

MULTIPLE DEFENCE

Close Combat 8
Defensive Fighting Training

When fighting multiple opponents in close combat you gain your full 'Defence' against each one, it does not have to be split.

POWERED MELEE

Close Combat 6

You are familiar with powered melee weapons. Normally Ion Weapons, Plasma Melee Weapons and Chainsaws. If you use a powered melee weapon without this training you are considered to 'Critically Miss' with the weapon on all doubles regardless of whether the roll would normally hit or miss, and you cannot critically pass. Shi Yukiro Agents gain this free at character creation.

QUICK DRAW

Reflexes 8

On the first round of combat you can draw your weapon and react so fast that you gain +4 to Initiative. If you draw light weapons such as pistols and knives, you gain +6 instead.

RESTRAIN

Close Combat 4

When you assault someone in close combat you may attempt to restrain them quickly.

RESTRAIN

Both combatants roll
'STRENGTH + CLOSE COMBAT'

If you get equal or higher XS than your opponent you restrain them and they cannot act.
If the opponent gets a higher XS they break free.

MODIFIERS FOR THE ATTACKER

Handcuffs / Nylon Ties	+2
Target is surprised	+4
Each additional restrainer	+2
No Restraints	+0

Telepathics are still possible when physically restrained. If you have no cuffs or ties then the target can still be subdued but must be physically held down.

SCYTHING STRIKE

Close Combat 6
Strength 7

If you successfully kill a target with a tactical or heavy close

combat weapon you may use your free action to make an extra attack on another target if they are in range. You may only make one Scything Strike a round. Whatever happens, you will get all your normal attacks even if they need to occur after the Scything Strike.

THROWN WEAPONS

Close Combat 3

You can throw bladed weapons (such as shurikens, swords, saw blades and knives) to maximum effect. Thrown weapons deal their normal damage + half strength (instead of full strength). You can throw 2 light weapons or 1 tactical / heavy weapon per round. (Throwing heavy weapons requires strength 10)

Range on thrown weapons = 10 + Strength metres

If you have this training you also gain +4 to throw non-bladed objects such as grenades or bricks. Throwing bladed weapons uses 'Perception + Athletics'.

TWIN PSI BLADES

Telepath Training
Psi Blade 7

You can summon two Psi blades instead of one. You must still buy the *Dual Weapon Fighting* Training and select Tactical Melee weapons to use them with no penalty. Using this power costs double TE although they are summoned as a single action using the normal Psi Blade rules.

UNARMED COMBAT SPECIAUST

Close Combat 4

You are skilled at fighting with no weapons, even against those who have them. When in unarmed close combat with an opponent who is armed you keep your 'Defence'. Additionally you always add D4 to any unarmed damage you deal. You can also Block (page 144) without an appropriate item.

STAGE 7

LICENSES

> Yes, it's a pain applying for all those licenses. On the other hand, the UIG does a license clampdown every now and again, and getting caught operating unlicensed tends to result in pain of a more literal kind. Myself, I'd rather spend time in a licensing office than in a UIG White Mouse House, but each to his own. Just don't say I didn't warn you.
>
> - attr: Zack Adams, freelance technical consultant/soldier of fortune

If you want to do something normally disallowed to your status (such as carry a heavy weapon) you will need a license. License applications are always checked over by the Agent's Mission Officer and they must normally be validated by a UIG Officer. They can be refused but most requests cause no problem. Applications such as requesting a Specific Equipment License to use a Multiple Salvo Missile System may raise more concerns.

> You gain 8 points to purchase licenses at character creation. Licenses cost 1 point per level of the license. The level is written after the license name in brackets.

PURCHASING ADDITIONAL LICENSES

After character creation you can gain licenses by spending downtime and cash. This represents you spending your time off attending UIG training to acquire the appropriate license. This costs 500¢ and 1 week of downtime per level of the license. The GM should feel free to make certain licenses unavailable in order to maintain the structure of the game.

When you acquire a license it is still possible to break the law regardless of the rights granted to you by the license. For example, if you have a license to carry a plasma sword but murder a Citizen with it you would be guilty of murder, unless you had the relevant Termination License.

If there is more than one version of a license such as Offensive

Equipment 1 and 2, you must obtain them in order; e.g. buy level 1 before level 2 and so on. The exception to this is the Telepathy License where you pay to upgrade the license.

Temporary Licenses. If there are certain things Agents need to be able to do for a particular mission, such as enter a business premises, a temporary license can normally be acquired from the UIG. The license may have a cost and the UIG will keep an eye on you when possible to make sure you deserve to use the license. Temporary licenses are normally issued without a problem unless the Agent requests something particularly odd or they are a known troublemaker.

Occasionally licenses can be given out by the Corporations as rewards (with UIG permission). These are given with no charge. The GM can make up new licenses as and when needed. There will also be more licenses in forthcoming supplements.

LICENSES IN THE GAME

These licenses add a range of possibilities to the game. They allow Agents to storm into houses and places of business brandishing their authority like a weapon and use alternative methods to complete their objectives. The law is a large and complex beast which cannot be fully covered in a book like this. As such you may find times when there are unclear situations and unknowns regarding licenses and permissions (just like any real set of laws). In these cases the GM takes the place of the judge and should make a decision and apply that decision from then on.

KEY TO LICENSES

License
The name of the license.
Level
The level of the license, this indicates the time and money needed to acquire this license.
Prerequisite
What you must have to acquire the license. If a prerequisite is present, it is under the license name in italics. Prerequisites can be anything such as rank, level, a training or a skill.
Description
A description of what the license does.

EQUIPMENT LICENSES
Combat Drug License
Cybernetic Animal License
Heavy Firearms License
Light Firearms License
Offensive Equipment License 1
Offensive Equipment License 2
Powered Melee License
Specific Equipment License
Security License
SatBlanket License
Tactical Firearms License

AUTHORITY LICENSES
Customs License
Detainment License
Privacy License
Public Appropriation License
Search License (Commercial)
Search License (Domestic)
Telepathics License
Termination License 1
Termination License 2
Termination License 3
Traffic License
Vehicle License (Domestic)
Vehicle License (Military)
World Database License

PROFESSIONAL LICENSES
Biohazard and Toxin License
Bounty Hunters License
Cyberneticists License
Medical License
Law Enforcement License
Preachers License
Robotics License
Vending License

EQUIPMENT LICENSES

THESE ALLOW YOU TO CARRY GOVERNMENT CONTROLLED EQUIPMENT.

COMBAT DRUG LICENSE (2)

Medicine 1
You can use all Combat Drugs.

CYBERNETIC ANIMAL LICENSE (1)

Animal Skills Training
You are licensed to handle cybernetic animals such as cyberwolves and cybermonkeys. See Cyberanimals on page 245 & 246.

HEAVY FIREARMS LICENSE (3)

Heavy Firearms 4
Rank 1
You can carry and discharge heavy firearms.

LIGHT FIREARMS LICENSE (1)

Level 1
You can carry and discharge light firearms. Agents and UIG start with this license for free.

OFFENSIVE EQUIPMENT LICENSE 1 (1)

Support Weapons 1
Rank 1
You may carry and use offensive equipment which has a small to medium damage capacity. (The potential to deal no more than 50 damage with a non-critical hit, e.g. a fragmentation grenade.)

OFFENSIVE EQUIPMENT LICENSE 2 (2)

Support Weapons 1
Offensive Equipment License 1
Level 3
You may carry and use all offensive equipment such as high power grenades, explosives, etc.

POWERED MELEE LICENSE (2)

Close Combat 4
You may use powered melee weapons such as Plasma Swords, Chainsaws and Ion Katanas.

SATBLANKET LICENSE (2)

Rank 2, Level 2
You may use, buy and install SatBlankets. These make it impossible for satellites to monitor the movements of anything within the SatBlanket. See page 52 for SatBlankets.

SECURITY LICENSE (2)

You may carry and use a Security Bypass Device, but it should only be used in compliance with the law.

SPECIFIC EQUIPMENT LICENSE (3)

Relevant Weapon Skill 6
Some equipment requires a specific license just to own and use. This license grants you that right. Note, other prerequisites may be added by the UIG depending on the equipment (GM should adjudicate). *For example, you need a Specific Equipment License to use the AMS Laser Emplacement System on page 179. This license would only be valid for this weapon.*

TACTICAL FIREARMS LICENSE (2)

Tactical Firearms 1
You can carry and discharge tactical firearms.

AUTHORITY LICENSES

THESE GIVE AGENTS MORE POWER TO DO THEIR WORK.

CUSTOMS LICENSE (4)

Corp Knowledge 5
Rank 2
You may bypass world customs and immigration authorities. This is rarely given out and only to Agents who have proved themselves worthy.

DETAINMENT LICENSE (2)

You may detain anyone for 12 hours as long as their rank is lower than yours, including Agents and UIG. You may question them during that period. Unfounded detainment can result in severe disciplinary action, especially when detaining UIG Officers or rival Agents.

PRIVACY LICENSE (5)

Rank 2
You only need to disclose your personal details to those with a rank higher than your own. Your information is stored on your ID Chip and can easily be scanned and validated but gives no information other than your name unless the person scanning is of a higher rank than you. You can select which aspects of your ID are currently accessible. Do not be surprised when Agents with very comprehensive privacy licenses are denied access to services, properties and businesses, as many companies have policies in place to prevent illegal activities, e.g., hospitals, gun stores, car hire, etc.

PUBLIC APPROPRIATION LICENSE (2)

You may appropriate property from a Citizen with a lower rank than yourself in public places. This does not allow you to invade homes and commercial properties, e.g., you could stop a Citizen in the street and ask for his car and weapon. The owner of the goods should be suitably recompensed for their inconvenience. This is normally handled by the Corporation. Entering property requires the 'Search' licenses.

SEARCH LICENSE (COMMERCIAL) (2)

Rank 2
You may enter and search commercial property owned by Citizens with a rank lower than your own. You may take any items from the property which you deem necessary if you also have a Public Appropriation License. The owner of the goods should be suitably recompensed for their inconvenience. This is normally handled by the Corporation.

SEARCH LICENSE (DOMESTIC) (1)

You may enter and search domestic property owned by Citizens with a rank lower than your own. You may take any items from the property which you deem necessary if you have a Public Appropriation License. The owner of the goods should be suitably recompensed for their inconvenience. This is normally handled by the Corporation.

TELEPATHICS LICENSE (1 TO 10)
Telepath Training

You can use telepathic powers in public places equal to the level of the license, for example, if you have a level 4 license you can use Level 4 Telepathics. If you break other laws using the Telepathics, that is a separate issue which you can be punished for. (Enforcing these laws can be very difficult.)

If you wish to increase the license you only need to spend 500¢ and one week of downtime each time you increase the level; e.g. taking a license from 4 to 6 takes 2 weeks of downtime and 1000¢.

TERMINATION LICENSE 1 (2)
Rank 2

You may terminate the lives of Outcasts in the pursuit of peace.

TERMINATION LICENSE 2 (5)
Rank 4

You may terminate Agents of inferior rank in the pursuit of peace. This is rarely given out and only to Agents who have proved themselves worthy.

TERMINATION LICENSE 3 (8)
Rank 6

You may terminate the lives of Citizens of lower rank in the pursuit of peace. This is rarely given out and only to Agents who have proved themselves worthy.

TRAFFIC LICENSE (2)

You may exert control over road traffic. For example, create blockades, alter road laws temporarily and shut off or alter traffic routes.

VEHICLE LICENSE (DOMESTIC) (1)
Drive 1

You can drive domestic & commercial vehicles such as cars, buses and shuttles.

VEHICLE LICENSE (MILITARY) (3)
Drive 2

You can drive and utilise military vehicles such as tanks, attack hovercopters and fighters.

WORLD DATABASE LICENSE (4)
Rank 1

You can access the UIG World Database which contains the DNA, fingerprints and profiles of all Citizens, Criminals, Agents, Officers and Faithful. Some of these individuals may have privacy licenses in place and many people may be removed from the database for various reasons. This license is only given out to trusted individuals who have the good of the populace in mind. Those who outrank you on the database will come up as 'Red Entries' and UIG permission must be sought to identify them. The GM should feel free to heavily restrict the access to this license.

> On average, across the last fifteen years, 32% of all active Termination 3 Licenses have been issued to Shi Yukiro agents. Limited intel data suggests that 78% of these have been issued to members of the Clan Hitori. The reputation that this subsect enjoys within the Corporation is therefore apparently well founded.
>
> -UIG Intel report IGI23982SHI-444

PROFESSIONAL LICENSES

YOU ARE RECOGNISED BY THE UIG AS A PROFESSIONAL IN YOUR FIELD.

BIOHAZARD AND TOXIN LICENSE (3)
Science 5
Medicine 5

You are qualified to manufacture and carry class B, C & D drugs, toxins and biohazards as well as respond to potential emergencies in the field. You may carry illegal substances with good cause such as taking narcotics for safe disposal.

BOUNTY HUNTERS LICENSE (1)

You may return wanted parties and receive bounties, normally from Lanzas (see page 177).

CYBERNETICISTS LICENSE (2)
Cybernetics and Robotics 6
Surgeon Training

You may perform cybernetic surgery; i.e. install, maintain and remove cybernetics. Without this license it is illegal. All surgery you complete must be logged with the UIG.

MEDICAL LICENSE (1)
Medicine 6

You can legally act in the capacity of a professional doctor; e.g. surgeon, therapist, paramedic, general practitioner etc. This includes prescribing drugs. Surgeons require the Surgery Training as well.

LAW ENFORCEMENT LICENSE
UIG Officer or Corporate Agent

Agents and UIG get this free. You are authorised to act on behalf of the UIG to investigate criminal activity. You cannot normally break the law in the course of an investigation. If you need to enter a property or detain someone you need the correct license. As an Agent you can ignore this if you feel there is imminent danger to humans, for example if you hear screaming you may break into a building without the correct license. If you abuse this right you may be punished and can be sued by any affected parties.

PREACHERS LICENSE (1)

You are permitted to make speeches and preach in public as long as there are no more than 5 complaints per hour and you do not use foul language or incite disquiet. Order of The Faith Devoted gain this License for free.

ROBOTICS LICENSE (1)
Cybernetics and Robotics 3

You may build and program droids for domestic, business and military use. See page 241 for reprogramming droids.

VENDING LICENSE (1)
Corp. Knowledge 1

You may sell goods. 20% tax is payable on all profits to the UIG. (Legally speaking.)

STAGE 8
PURCHASE EQUIPMENT

Equipment starts on the next page.
Cybernetics start on page 60

You can now purchase some equipment for your Agent. Read *Agent Physiology and Starting Equipment* on pages 9,10,11 & 13 to familiarise yourself with the equipment Agents already have

Opposite is listed the starting cash for Agents from different Corporations. Buy as much equipment as you wish and keep the rest of the cash for use in the game. There is space on your character sheet for writing the weapons separately so you can refer to them quickly.

Note that you can buy equipment in substandard condition. (See the Equipment Properties on page 30.)

Once your equipment is chosen your character is finished. You should then run the character by the Games Master so they can check everything is done correctly and the character is suitable for the game.

MONEY AND WAGES

CORPORATION	STARTING	MISSION
Ai-Jinn	7,000	700
Comoros	6,000	600
Eurasian Inc.	10,000	1,000
Shi Yukiro	9,000	900
W. Federation	8,000	800

Starting - Credits acquired at character creation
Mission - Pay given out upon completion of a
mission (multiplied by the Agent's rank).

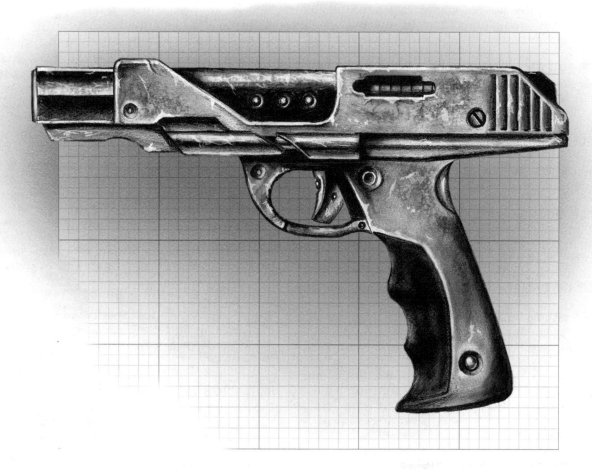

Reisner Jackhammer Field Magnum

SECTION 2

EQUIPMENT

You can get more with a kind word and a gun
than you can with a kind word alone.

attr: Al Capone

EQUIPMENT OVERVIEW

You may need to read *The Game System* on page 137 before you fully understand the way the equipment works. Alternatively you can just buy the things you want and discover their properties during the game.

You will need equipment to complete most of your missions. Select well as each piece of hardware plays a unique roll. In this section you will find the basic equipment lists which are open to all characters from all Corporations unless otherwise stated. Some equipment is available only from independent stockists or is exclusive to certain Corporations.

EQUIPMENT PROPERTIES

Equipment can vary in condition depending on how it is made and treated.

CONDITION OF EQUIPMENT

Condition	Dice roll leading to Critical Fail
10	10/10
9	9/9 to 10/10
8	8/8 to 10/10
7	7/7 to 10/10
6	6/6 to 10/10
5	5/5 to 10/10
4	4/4 to 10/10
3	3/3 to 10/10
2	2/2 to 10/10
1	All doubles & can't critically pass

Where the table says 5/5 to 10/10 this means all rolls of double 5, double 6, double 7, double 8, double 9 and double 10.

SUBSTANDARD ITEMS

Normally if you need to make a roll to use an item it will critically fail on a 10/10. This means that something has gone badly wrong. Some items are of substandard quality and will critically fail on double 10 and double 9 (This weapon would be considered to be in 'Condition 9'. This reflects the poor workmanship or the bad state of the item. See page 139 & 143 for critical fails.

It will critically miss even if the shot would normally hit. For example a condition 1 shotgun will critically miss on all doubles irrespective of whether the shot was on target. Even the best gunman cannot work with a completely wrecked weapon. This overrides the ability of a professional to never critically miss. He may well critically miss with a substandard weapon.

The GM could decide that a critical fail will further reduce the condition of the weapon by 1 level. Agents are considered to maintain their weapon automatically or hand them into the weapons labs to have them checked. This maintains the weapon but does not repair it.

Items of low quality that do not use a roll should have a GM penalty

added, for example, armour could have a lower Armour Value or could reduce the users Agility when worn. A pair of digital binoculars could have faulty circuitry meaning they fail to work 20% of the time. Items that do not deteriorate significantly will not drop in value and should be bought at a high price. If you cannot think how an item might deteriorate then do not offer it for a reduced amount.

To help you remember the condition system you can consider the condition number to be a score out of 10. 10 out of 10 is perfect. 1 out of 10 is terrible.

SUBSTANDARD EQUIPMENT

The condition level of an item reflects its state of repair as a score out of 10. 10 out of 10 being perfect. Below are some examples referring to weapons.

Item	Condition	Cost
Perfect	10	100%
Fine but pre-owned	09	90%
No faults but badly kept	08	80%
Has been patched up	07	70%
A neglected old weapon	06	60%
A weapon with a minor fault	05	50%
A weapon with damage	04	40%
Damaged, dirty and old	03	30%
Seriously damaged	02	20%
Hand made / barely works	01	10%

Don't forget to make many of the weapons found by Agents in substandard condition. That way Agents will want to buy new weapons but can always use old ones in emergencies. It adds interest and fun to introduce heavily damaged weapons which are potentially lethal to the user.

PURCHASING SUBSTANDARD ITEMS

You can often buy substandard weapons and equipment from the Corporations or private stores if you cannot afford the new version. For example if you want your character to start with a sports car but do not have the 40,000¢ then you could buy a condition 5 car for 20,000¢. The poor condition means the car would critically fail more often than normal, in this case it would thus critically fail on rolls of 10/10, 9/9, 8/8, 7/7, 6/6 and 5/5. It is up to the GM how easily available substandard items are.

PAYING TO IMPROVE EQUIPMENT CONDITION

You may pay 10% of the item's new cost to increase the condition of a damaged item by 1 point (up to condition 10) or you can do it yourself (see downtime on page 82). (Also see Fixing Equipment in the Field on page 31.) This does not necessarily fix the item but generally improves it's condition. For example, you could replace the engine in a car to improve its condition. It does not mean that you fix the brakes.

SUPERIOR EQUIPMENT

Some especially well made equipment can go the other way where double 1 and double 2 will both result in a critical hit. This can continue to double 9 and double 10 but such an items would be rare and valuable. Superior equipment can be purchased or engineered (prices on page 82) but the GM should feel free to limit its availability. It is often a good reward for Agents after completing a dangerous mission.

ALTERNATIVE EQUIPMENT UPGRADES

The GM should feel free to add other upgrades to weapons, below are some examples

- Reduced size such as a heavy weapon the size of a tactical weapon.
- Bonus to damage
- Bonus to hit
- Cannot be detected by scanners
- Gets more shots per ammo clip
- Has a Chip Checker
- Ignores some AV
- Laser Sight (aiming bonus)
- Looks inconspicuous
- Looks like one thing, acts like another

DAMAGING EQUIPMENT

You can damage anything in Corporation with the right hardware. Below is explained how to do it.

Equipment Armour Value

When an item may take damage you should decide what material it is made from and reduce the damage dealt to it accordingly. For instance, if you shoot a safety deposit box which is made of *Strong Metal* and roll 13 damage, it will be reduced to 3 due to the Armour Value 10 of the strong material.

Example:
A Metal security door is considered a huge item made of reinforced metal. - It has 40 HP and an AV of 15.
If you shoot it with a pistol (D8) you cannot damage it. If you shoot it with a heavy weapon for 6D10 and roll 35, the first 15 damage is removed and 20 go through to damage the door. This has done a great deal of damage but at least another shot will be needed.

FIXING EQUIPMENT

Sometimes equipment fails on you, for example a plasma cannon will become unusable on a roll of 10/10. To make a basic repair roll consult the table below. At any time the GM can rule that a piece of equipment cannot be repaired. Malfunctioning Cybernetics are on page 62.

DAMAGING EQUIPMENT AND OBJECTS

Below you can see the typical Armour Value (AV) and Hit Points (HP) for different materials and items. Use these to work out the HP & AV of an object. To damage an item simply attack it using the appropriate combat rolls if necessary. The GM may apply a modifier if the object is easy or difficult to hit. Reduce any damage you deal to it by the AV and when you have reduced it's HP to zero the item is considered unusable, smashed or broken.

ARMOUR VALUE

MATERIAL	AV
Wood / plastic	1
Dense wood, thin metal	2
Normal metal, e.g. car body	4
Strong metal, concrete, brickwork, e.g. a house	10
Reinforced metal, e.g. steel door, bullet proof glass	15
Military grade synthetics, e.g. tank hull	30

HIT POINTS

ITEM SIZE	HP	EXAMPLE
Tiny	**5**	**Pistol, First Aid Kit, Cat, Flask, Torch**
Small	10	Rifle, Sword, Small Television, Dog, Child
Medium	**20**	**Cannon, Light Human, Motorbike, Average Door**
Large	30	Bed, Weak Agent, Strong Human
Huge	**40**	**Car, Helicopter, Shed, Strong Agent**
Enormous	100	Small House, Large Tank
Epic	**1000**	**Cyberlin, Ten Story Building**

Note that these Hit Point totals represent how much damage the target can take before it becomes ineffective. For example: normal humans have 20 HP because they are useless when they have taken that much damage. Agents are much sturdier and can stay up for longer. A car would be undrivable after 40 HP of damage.

FIXING EQUIPMENT

You can pay 5% of an items cost to have a professional fix your equipment. This reduces it by a conditional level but makes it usable. Malfunctioning Cybernetics are on page 62.

Fixing Equipment - 'Intelligence + Mechtronics'

Equipment fixed in this way automatically loses 1 condition level. You can then increase the condition of the item. See page 30.

Items are broken down into 3 kinds of repair.

SIMPLE (NO MOVING PARTS)
e.g. basic sword, old fashioned shield, catapult, etc.

NORMAL (SOME MECHANICAL PARTS & BASIC ELECTONICS)
e.g. kinetic pistol, frag grenade, crossbow, car

COMPLEX (NANOTECH OR COMPLEX ELECTRONICS)
e.g. plasma / laser weapon, cybernetics, computer

CIRCUMSTANCES	MODIFIER
No tools	-10
Normal tools	-4
Advanced tools	+0
Lab / Workshop	+4
Time is not a factor	+4

ITEM	SUCCESSES NEEDED
Simple	1
Normal	2
Complex	3

Roll 'Intelligence + Mechtronics' with the *Circumstances* modifier. You need to get a number of successes based on the type of item you are repairing. Each roll takes 1 minute. A sympathy bonus can apply if the repair is done in controlled conditions.
Each time you fail a roll and get a double on the dice the condition of the item drops by an additional 1.
For example, you wish to fix a kinetic pistol with normal tools. You must roll 'Intelligence + Mechtronics' with a -4 modifier and get 2 successes.

WEAPONS

The weapons listed below are almost all commonly available to all Corporations. Other weapons can be acquired but these have to be purchased in the game from such places as ANZEIGER MILITARY SYSTEMS (page 179) or on the black market. There are also weapons such as the legendary Ion Katana which are only available to certain Corporations.

WEAPON CLASSIFICATIONS

LIGHT FIREARMS

These are handguns such as kinetic or injector pistols. They can be used one handed as long as the user has Strength 3 or more.

TACTICAL FIREARMS

Tactical weapons are mid sized weapons such as sub-machine weapons and rifles. They can be used two handed by anyone with Strength 4 or more and one handed by anyone with Strength 7 or more.

HEAVY FIREARMS

These weapons are the largest that can normally be carried; examples include the Rail Gun and Plasma Cannon. They can be used two handed by anyone with Strength 6 or more and one handed by anyone with Strength 10 or more.

LIGHT CLOSE COMBAT WEAPONS

These are weapons such as knives and knuckle dusters. They require Strength 3 to use and can only be used effectively one handed unless otherwise stated.

TACTICAL CLOSE COMBAT WEAPONS

This includes weapons such as longswords and shortswords. They require Strength 4 to use one handed and are not designed to be used two handed unless specified, e.g., the katana.

HEAVY CLOSE COMBAT WEAPONS

The largest close combat weapons that can be used including such things as chainsaws and two handed swords. They require Strength 6 to use in two hands and Strength 10 to use one handed.

SUPPORT WEAPONS

This includes all manner of backup weaponry such as grenades, emplacement guns, mines and explosives.

THROWN WEAPONS

These require the thrown weapons training. See page 24

WEAPONS IN MORE DETAIL

CLOSE COMBAT WEAPONS

Close Combat weapons ignore Shields
Attack using 'Agility + Close Combat'

When using a close combat weapon in one hand you normally add the users Strength to the damage.
Example: Someone wielding a long sword with Strength 5 will deal D8+5 damage.

When a weapon is wielded two handed (and was designed for that purpose) you double your Strength when calculating damage. This

is normally noted in the book where appropriate.
Example: Someone with Strength 7 using a two handed sword would deal D12 + 14 damage.
If you are strong enough to wield a two handed weapon in each hand you do NOT double your Strength for damage with each weapon. Doubling Strength represents using the power of two arms.
Example: Someone using a two handed sword in each hand deals D12 + Strength with each one.

You can reduce your attack rate with close combat weapons to increase accuracy. (see High Rate / Semi-automatic Weapons on page 33).

EMP WEAPONS AND SHIELDING

(Electromagnetic Pulse)
Note: All Cybernetics have EMPS 25

When you attack with EMP you are normally considered to be shooting a humanoid target and their equipment. Any equipment not currently in use will default to Safe Mode where the electronics are off-line to conserve power and automatically resist EMP. This means only active weapons and equipment can be affected, normally shields, cybernetics and currently wielded weapons. If you hit, roll the EMP damage of the weapon separately for each piece of equipment; i.e. roll EMP damage for the gun, then for the shield, then for the neural jack, etc.
If a roll exceeds the EMP-Shielding (EMPS) of the piece of equipment then that item ceases to function until repaired. (See fixing equipment on page 31. For cybernetics affected by EMP see page 63.) Also see EMPS Boosters on page 50.

GRENADES AND BLAST WEAPONS.

TO THROW GRENADES
'Perception + Support Weapons'

TO SET EXPLOSIVES
All standard explosive can be set with no roll as long as you have 1 point in *Support Weapons*. Complex explosives may require an 'Intelligence + Support Weapons' roll.

TO DISARM EXPLOSIVES:
Normal: Pass an 'Intelligence + Support Weapons' roll.
Complex: Roll 'Intelligence + Support Weapon' and get
         equal to or more XS than the person who set the
         explosive. The GM decides what counts as
         complex. Most support weapons are simple.

HITTING WITH BLAST WEAPONS
When using moving blast weapons, roll to hit a target as normal. If you pass the roll you have hit the target with the centre of the blast and deal full damage. If you fail by 1 or 2 you have hit them with part of the blast and deal 2/3 damage. If you fail by 3 or 4 you have clipped them with the edge and deal 1/3 damage. Failure by 5 or more means you have completely missed them or they have

managed to find cover.

The blast radius states the maximum area of effect of the weapon and can be used for determining who is hit by a blast weapon. First decide what the weapon was aimed at. Then the GM can decide who may have been in the blast range. This can be useful for static devices such as bombs, to determine who they hit when they explode.

Blast Weapon Example 1.
Agent Chen throws a fragmentation grenade (3D6, 3 metre blast) at some rebels. His action total is 14, he rolls 16 meaning he has failed by 2. Consulting the chart (below) he has still made a partial hit so deals two thirds damage. That's 2D6.

Some Blast weapons don't deal damage such as gas grenades or flash-bang grenades. These are covered in the weapons description. GM adjudication may be required with grenade hits to see who may be in range of the blast.

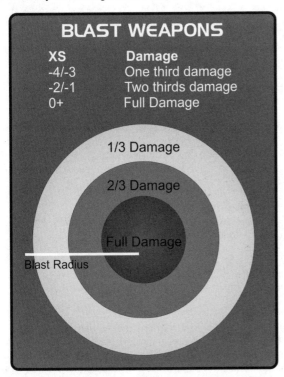

BLAST WEAPONS

XS	Damage
-4/-3	One third damage
-2/-1	Two thirds damage
0+	Full Damage

1/3 Damage

2/3 Damage

Full Damage

Blast Radius

HIGH RATE / SEMI-AUTOMATIC WEAPONS

Weapons with a rate above 1 (not machine weapons) can be fired at a slower rate to increase accuracy. You can forfeit one attack with the weapon to gain a +2 bonus to hit. This principle also applies to close combat attacks. It also adds to any bonus gained from aiming.

Example:
1. If you fire the pistol at rate 2 instead of 3, you gain +2 to hit with both shots.

2. If you fire the pistol at rate 1 instead of rate 3 you gain +4 to hit with the shot.

3. Firing at full rate gives no bonus.

ION WEAPONS

These weapons emit a dull but coloured aura of energy. They possess a mono-ionic field meaning they have enormous severing power. Ion weapons ignore the first 10 points of Armour Value. They are only available to Shi Yukiro Agents and even then, only when they reach Rank 3 or Level 8, whichever comes first. Legally they require the Powered Melee License.
If you use a powered melee weapon without the Powered Melee Training you are considered to Critically Miss with the weapon on all doubles regardless of whether the roll would normally hit or miss and you cannot critically pass.
Ion weapons have a long life fuel core and need no ammunition or fuel cells. Ion weapons also sever body parts on maximum damage. Example Ion Weapons can be found on page 112.

KINETIC WEAPONS

These are the most common and economical firearms; they use a traditional projectile to physically damage the target. Kinetic weapons have been produced for years and are very reliable. They are also resilient and often immune to EMP. SMART* Clips are the universal ammunition for all Kinetic Weapons regardless of size. *'Self Modelling Auto-loading Round Technology'.

LASER WEAPONS

The main advantage of laser weapons is the ability to be reconfigured in order to bypass shields. To recalibrate a laser takes 1 round during which time the pulse of the laser is matched to a particular shield frequency. When shooting at the matched shield you ignore the effects of the shield. To ignore a different shield the laser must be recalibrated. Laser weapons take Energy Cells which are universal clips for all energy weapons.

MACHINE WEAPONS

(Fully Automatics)
These weapons fire a spray of ammunition. You can choose to target as many people as the weapon has damage dice. For example if the weapon deals 6D6 (6 damage dice) you can target up to 6 people as long as they are reasonably close together, dealing a D6 damage to each. You can target less people in which case you can select how many dice of damage to deal to each target. You must roll to hit each separate target and each damage dice you roll is reduced by the targets Armour Value if appropriate. Hence automatic weapons are weak against armoured targets. (Automatic plasmas still ignore all armour.)
Spray: If you only shoot at one target with a machine weapon, you gain a +4 bonus to hit.
You cannot *Aim* machine weapons.

Example:
Agent Targusson has a machine pistol (3D6). He could take 3 shots at 3 different targets and deal D6 to each. Each attack would have to be rolled separately.
He could alternatively fire all three shots at one target and would gain +4 to hit.

PLASMA FIREARMS

(Plasma firearms ignore all Armour Value)
These weapons fire a crackling ball of super-heated gas which melts through armour. Plasma firearms are very powerful but extremely delicate, they always critical miss on 8/8, 9/9 and 10/10 regardless of how much you improve them. They can gain a higher critical hit range as normal but can never lose this critical miss

range. Critical misses with plasma firearms mean the weapon has overheated and backfires. This deals half the attacks damage to the firer and the weapon breaks. It can be fixed in the field as normal (see page 31)

PLASMA CLOSE COMBAT WEAPONS

These weapons feature a crackling plasma arc with great cutting potential. They ignore the first 4 points of Armour Value. Plasma close combat weapons do not suffer from the frailties of ranged plasma weapons although they legally require the Powered Melee License. If you use a powered melee weapon without the Powered Melee Training you are considered to Critically Miss with the weapon on all doubles regardless of whether the roll would normally hit or miss and you cannot critically pass. See the Powered Melee Training on page 24.

Plasma Close Combat weapons have a long life fuel core and need no ammunition or fuel cells.

MAXING

(Maximising the potential of a dice roll)

Sometimes you will be required to roll multiple dice such as 6D6. You can either roll 6 dice and add them up or roll a smaller number and use an appropriate multiplier.

For example roll 1D6 and multiply the result by 6 or roll 2D6 and multiply the result by 3 and so on. This allows for extremes of damage. Be careful using this system. It makes combat a lot more unpredictable but a lot more fun. You should declare which system you are using before the dice roll but you may choose any method for any roll as you please.

YAEGER & STANTON MICRENADES
ALL THE POWER OF A GRENADE. NONE OF THE BULK.

Micrenades cost an additional 10% to normal grenades and have the same effect but are only 2cm in diameter.

WEAPON PROPERTIES

NAME
First comes the general name for the weapon, then the Manufacturer's name.
AMS - Anzeiger Military Systems
Y&S - Yaeger & Stanton Assault Technologies

DAMAGE / EFFECT
What the weapons does, it will normally be damage but it could be EMP, toxic, etc.

COST
The cost to buy the weapon from Corporate stores or from legitimate traders. This cost will vary when purchasing in different situations. The weapon is considered in perfect condition (10) when purchased, except plasma firearms.

RANGE
The ranges in Corporation are not always defined by numbers as this will seldom be of practical use in a normal fight. Instead they represent roughly what sort of combat the weapon can be used in. For simplicity 1 metre is considered about 3 feet.

CLOSE (APPROXIMATELY 1 METRE)
Usable in close combat only, e.g. hand to hand. Note that if you use a ranged weapon in close combat you lose your *Defence* unless you have the training Gun Melee.

MEDIUM (UP TO APPROXIMATELY 400 METRES)
The weapon can be used in normal skirmishes as long as the wielder has a reasonable line of sight to the target.

LONG (UP TO APPROXIMATELY 2000 METRES)
This weapon can be used from a long distance away. *For example shooting down helicopters and sniping.*

SPECIAL
Some weapons have odd ranges which are detailed in the weapons description; e.g. a flame thrower.

RATE
The number of times you can fire the weapon a round. If you reduce the rate voluntarily you gain +2 to hit for each point you drop the rate by.
For example, firing a weapon with rate 3 such as a Black Cougar Pistol at rate 2 you gain 2 shots at +2 . At rate 1 you'll gain one shot at +4. This applies to Close Combat attacks as well.

EMPS
This is the weapon's Electromagnetic Pulse Shielding. See EMP on page 32. **EMP Immune** means the weapon is immune to EMP.

DESCRIPTION
Additional information about the weapon such as special abilities and limitations.

LIGHT FIREARMS

Roll 'Perception + Light Firearms'

EMP PISTOL - YAEGER & STANTON MK III EMP PISTOL

D10 EMP   1000¢   Medium Range   Rate 1   EMPS 12

Basic Electromagnetic Pulse pistol. See EMP weapons on page 32.

INJECTOR PISTOL - GEMINI MOSQUITO

D2 + Toxin   1200¢   Medium Range   Rate 1   EMP Immune

This pistol fires small injector darts which can be loaded with a variety of chemicals, notably toxins, although beneficial chemicals could be used. Note: Knockout darts are available for this weapon (see page 44), which do not require a license to use. All other chemicals require the Biohazard and Toxin License.

LASER PISTOL - AIR-LYTE COMPACT HAND LASER

D8 Damage   1000¢   Medium Range   Rate 3   EMPS 5

Lightweight hand laser. As with all lasers it can be configured to bypass shields. See page 33.

MACHINE PISTOL - AMS HAVOC M-4K MACHINE PISTOL

3D6 Damage   1500¢   Medium Range   Rate 1   EMP Immune

A lightweight, concealable kinetic machine pistol. Counts as a machine weapon.

MAGNUM - YAEGER & STANTON M55 KINETIC HAND CANNON

D10 Damage   600¢   Medium Range   Rate 2   EMP Immune

High power kinetic handgun. More powerful with a reduced rate of fire. Uses SMART ammunition.

PISTOL - AMS BLACK COUGAR

D8 Damage   350¢   Medium Range   Rate 3   EMP Immune

A strong, reliable kinetic handgun. Immune to EMP. Commonly carried by Agents as they are standard issue upon completion of training. Uses SMART ammunition.

PLASMA PISTOL - AMS HANDHELD PLASMA DISCHARGER

D10 Damage   5000¢   Medium Range   Rate 2   EMPS 5

Basic plasma weapon, ignores armour but not very reliable. (See plasma firearms on page 33)

ROCKET PISTOL - AMS HANDHELD ROCKET LAUNCHER

3D10 Damage   4000¢   Medium Range   Rate 1   EMPS 8

Fires light ballistic rockets which are found in the ammunition table. (Normally Rockets: 3D10 blast damage, 100¢ each.)

STUN PISTOL - AIR-LYTE VOLT PISTOL

Knock Out   1200¢   Medium Range   Rate 1   EMPS 7

If you hit, the target must roll for Knock Out. (Roll below Perception + Endurance with your XS as a penalty or fall unconscious for D100 minutes.) This weapon has no effect on Agents. Uses Energy Cells.

TACTICAL FIREARMS I

Roll 'Perception + Tactical Firearms'

BLADE LAUNCHER - AMS SHURIKEN BLADE LAUNCHER

| 2D6 Damage | 6000¢ | Medium Range | Rate 1 | EMPS 9 |

A vile weapon based on the Rail Gun chassis which deals Mashing damage. It fires flat, disc shaped, toothed blades which can shear limbs off. Roll on the random limb severing table if maximum damage is rolled (page 146).

CROSSBOW - AIR-LYTE NIGHTFIRE

| D6 Damage | 200¢ | Medium Range | Rate 1 | EMP Immune |

Silent, collapsible and immune to EMP. You don't need a license to use a crossbow so it makes a good assassin's weapon. Uses bolts which can be poisoned with toxins.

EMP RIFLE - Y&S MK V EMP RIFLE

| 2D10 EMP | 5000¢ | Medium Range | Rate 1 | EMPS 20 |

Mid-range EMP weapon capable of knocking out a good range of electronics. Powerful but easily portable.

FIRE RIFLE - PYRONICS PARTICLE-FED FIRE RIFLE

| D8 Damage | 2000¢ | Medium Range | Rate 1 | EMP Immune |

Uses napalm canisters. If hit, the target takes damage (D8 burning damage) is automatically set on fire and takes an additional D6 damage each round after the first. Burning damage does not stack with other burning damage as you can only be so much on fire. AV reduces this damage. Target must spend a full round to try to extinguish the fire. A successful 'Agility + Reflexes' roll will put it out. Another person can spend one round to automatically put out the fire. Uses napalm canisters.

FLAK LAUNCHER - Y&S CLOSE QUARTERS SHRAPNEL LAUNCHER

| 3D6 Damage | 4000¢ | Medium Range | Rate 1 | EMPS 10 |

This weapon fires shrapnel into the target dealing Mashing Damage. It can use SMART Ammo or a head sized amount of junk can be fed into the weapon which will fire 6 times before reloading is necessary.

INJECTOR SNIPERS RIFLE - GEMINI GI9 DEADEYE INJECTOR RIFLE

| D2 Damage + Toxin | 5000¢ | Long Range | Rate 1 | EMP Immune |

A powerful long range injector rifle which fires darts containing chemicals. All chemicals need a Biohazard and Toxin license except Knock Out Darts. You gain +4 to hit each round you aim with this weapon instead of the normal +2.

LASER RIFLE - LR40 LIGHT ASSAULT LASER

| 2D6+1 Damage | 4000¢ | Long Range | Rate 2 | EMPS 7 |

A lightweight laser rifle with a good rate of fire and good damage potential. Commonly used by guards.

NEEDLE RIFLE - AMS CLOSE QUARTERS FLECHETTE RIFLE

| 2D6 Damage | 4000¢ | Medium Range | Rate 1 | EMP Immune |

This kinetic weapon uses SMART ammunition to fire a series of tiny needle darts. If you roll maximum damage with the weapon a limb is severed. See Random Limb Severing Table page 146.

TACTICAL FIREARMS II

Roll 'Perception + Tactical Firearms'

PLASMA RIFLE - AMS PR88 PLASMA CARBINE

| 2D8+1 Damage | 10,000¢ | Medium Range | Rate 2 | EMPS 8 |

A small but effective weapon which makes light work of heavily armoured enemies. It is susceptible to the usual overheating (see plasma firearms on page 33).

SHOTGUN - URAKEN GAS ACTION COMBAT SHOTGUN

| 2D10 / 3D10 Damage | 1000¢ | Medium / Close | Rate 1 | EMP Immune |

A powerful weapon at medium and close range. When fired in close combat it deals 3D10 mashing damage instead of the 2D10 normal damage. Uses SMART ammunition. You gain +4 to your attack Action Total with a shotgun if within 5 metres of your target.

SNIPERS RIFLE - V12 COBRA GAS ACTION SEMI-AUTOMATIC SNIPERS RIFLE

| 2D6+1 Damage | 3500¢ | Long Range | Rate 2 | EMPS 15 |

This is a semi-automatic snipers rifle. If you aim with this weapon you gain double the normal bonus. +4 per round to a maximum of +12. Breaks down into an attaché case and takes SMART ammunition.

STUN RIFLE - Y&S INDUCED VOLT RIFLE

| Knock Out | 2500¢ | Medium Range | Rate 1 | EMPS 10 |

Anyone shot by this pacifier weapon must pass a 'Perception + Endurance' roll with the attackers XS+4 as a penalty or be knocked out for D100 minutes. Commonly used by guards. This weapon has no effect on Agents. Uses Energy Cells.

SUB MACHINE GUN - KINETIC - AMS SUPRESSOR SMG

| 6D6 Damage | 3000¢ | Medium Range | Rate 1 | EMP Immune |

This is a compact sub machine gun which is effective against lightly armoured groups. Counts as a machine weapon.

SUB MACHINE LASER - TAKATA L60 AUTOMATIC LASER CARBINE

| 6D8 Damage | 8000¢ | Medium Range | Rate 1 | EMPS 8 |

This is a short barrelled sub-machine laser which is effective against lightly armoured groups. Counts as a machine weapon. Lasers can be configured to bypass shields so it can be highly effective against a single heavily shielded target.

SUB MACHINE PLASMA - AMS BLOODSTORM

| 6D6 Damage | 15,000¢ | Medium Range | Rate 1 | EMPS 8 |

A devastating firearm which is commonly used by Agents. The Bloodstorm ignores armour so is obviously effective in all types of combat. Counts as a machine weapon but has all the disadvantages of a plasma firearm. (See plasma firearms on page 33)

THE TAKATA L60 AUTOMATIC LASER CARBINE

HEAVY FIREARMS

Roll 'Perception + Heavy Firearms'

EMP CANNON - Y&S MK VIII EM PULSE CANNON

| 4D10 EMP | 10,000¢ | Long Range | Rate 1 | EMPS 30 |

The top end of EMP weapons. This cannon has the potential to knock out cyberware and heavily shielded equipment. See EMP on page 32. Although the weapon is large there is no need for a backpack. 1 energy cell can fire 3 shots with this weapon.

FLAME THROWER - PYRONICS FT9 HEAVY FLAME THROWER

| 4D6 Damage | 1500¢ | 6 Metre Range | Rate 1 | EMP Immune |

The maximum range of this weapon is 6 metres. If hit the target is automatically set on fire and takes an additional D6 damage each round after the first. Burning damage does not stack with other burning damage as you can only be so much on fire. AV reduces this damage. Target must spend a full round to try to extinguish the fire. A successful 'Agility + Reflexes' roll will put it out. Another person can spend one round to automatically put out the fire. Uses napalm canisters.

LASER CANNON - Y&S HIGH CAPACITANCE ASSAULT LASER

| 5D8+5 Damage | 8000¢ | Long Range | Rate 1 | EMPS 11 |

This heavy laser fires a single powerful shot which is excellent against heavily armoured foes. The ability to recalibrate the laser to bypass shields can make this weapon terrifying for enemy Agents.

MACHINE GUN - AMS M50 BELT-FED SUPPORT WEAPON

| 6D10 Damage | 6000¢ | Medium Range | Rate 1 | EMP Immune |

The M50 is the most successful mass produced kinetic machine gun on the market. The weapon is very heavy and has a tripod which takes three rounds to set up. When used the tripod gives +4 to hit but it can be fired without. Counts as a machine weapon. (Strength 8 is required to wield it as a two handed weapon but anyone can use it on the tripod.) Uses SMART ammo.

PLASMA CANNON - AMS PX5 INDUCED HEAVY PLASMA

| 5D10+5 Damage | 12,000¢ | Long Range | Rate 1 | EMPS 10 |

A powerful plasma weapon for all out assaults. This weapon ignores armour but is still prone to overheating which makes it very dangerous. (See plasma firearms on page 33)

RAIL GUN - AMS LINEAR ELECTROMAGNETIC ACCELERATION WEAPON (LEAW)

| 6D10 Damage | 20,000¢ | Long Range | Rate 1 | EMPS 13 |

The Rail Gun is powerful enough to shoot through walls so it comes with a small x-ray view screen allowing you to target enemies behind objects or walls by firing with a -4 penalty. All but thick metal walls can be seen through. Uses SMART ammunition and Energy Cells to fire. One of each cell is enough for 3 shots. The weapons ignores the first 15 points of AV. Use this to determine what you can shoot through by consulting the 'Damaging Equipment and Objects' table on page 31. If the wall only had an AV of 5, then the weapon would ignore up to ten points of the target AV as well.

ROCKET LAUNCHER - AMS MULTI-SHELL LAUNCHER

| Damage as Rocket | 8000¢ | Long | Rate 1 | EMPS 12 |

This versatile weapon has a morphic barrel which can fire any Grenade or Rocket. See Ammunition on page 44 for rockets. See Support Weapons on page 42 & 43 for grenades. Uses 1 energy cells to propel 30 grenades. Rockets propel themselves.

UNARMED STRIKES
Roll 'Agility + Close Combat'

RAPID STRIKES
¼ Strength Damage   Close Combat   Rate 4   EMP Immune
Weak punches, best used only if you have knuckle dusters, tiger claws or the Unarmed Combat Specialist Training.

STANDARD STRIKES
½ Strength Damage   Close Combat   Rate 2   EMP Immune
Standard punches and kicks, strong and steady.

POWER STRIKE
Strength Damage   Close Combat   Rate 1   EMP Immune
A single punch summoning all your power. More effective than other strikes if the target is armoured.

KNOCK OUT STRIKE
Strength Damage   Close Combat   Rate 1   EMP Immune
You attempt to knock out the target. You attack at -4 and if you hit they must pass a 'Perception + Endurance' check with your XS as a penalty. Failure causes them to fall unconscious for D100 minutes. You still deal your damage if they pass. This will not knock out Agents but will damage them.

THE UNARMED COMBAT SPECIAUST TRAINING (PAGE 24)

Note: you lose your *Defence* when fighting unarmed in close combat against an opponent wielding a close combat weapon. To avoid this learn the Training Unarmed Combat Specialist. This Training also adds D4 to your unarmed combat damage.

Wrestling is covered on page 145

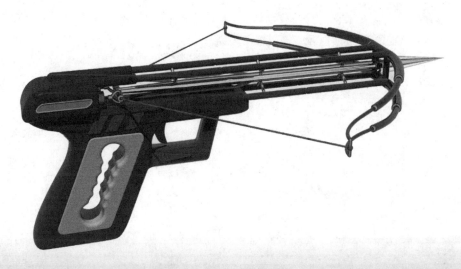

AIR-LYTE NIGHTFIRE CROSSBOW

CLOSE COMBAT WEAPONS I

Roll 'Agility + Close Combat'

KNUCKLE DUSTERS (LIGHT)*

+1 Damage	25¢	Close Combat	Rate as Strike	EMP Immune

A set of gloves with sharpened steel ridges on the back. Gives +1 damage to unarmed strikes, the effect does not stack with other close combat weapons. These do not count as a weapon for purposes of deciding whether you keep your defence.

CLUB / BAT (TACTICAL)

D6 + Strength	0-30¢	Close Combat	Rate 2	EMP Immune

A length of wood, a scaffolding pipe or perhaps a baseball bat. Can be used two handed in which case it deals D6 + 2xStrength damage but has a rate of 1.

KNIFE - AMS BLUEFIN COMBAT KNIFE (LIGHT)

D4 + Strength	30¢	Close Combat	Rate 3	EMP Immune

A short bladed weapon legal for anyone with rank 0 or more to carry. Simple and effective.

TIGER CLAWS - TAKATA IOKAN TIGER CLAWS (LIGHT)

+3 damage	500¢	Close Combat	Rate as Strike	EMP Immune

Gloves containing metal claws which project forward from the back of the hand. Used for gouging and ripping. -4 to any actions which involve your hands while these are worn, (except combat). You cannot use other close combat weapons while wearing these. When attacking you use your normal unarmed strikes but gain a bonus to your damage for wearing the claws and are considered to have a weapon and so keep your defence.

SHORT SWORD - AMS POLYCARBONATE CQC SWORD (TACTICAL)

D6 + Strength	200¢	Close Combat	Rate 3	EMP Immune

A short bladed weapon excellent in close quarters combat where its small size allows a good rate of attack.

CHAINSAW - Y&S SHARKTOOTH COMBAT CHAINSAW (HEAVY)

2D10 + 2xStrength	1,500¢	Close Combat	Rate 1	EMP Immune

A chainsaw built specifically for close combat. This weapon deals Mashing damage and requires the Powered Melee training or you are likely to lose control of the weapon. (See page 24 for Powered Melee training). Legally you also need the 'Powered Melee' License.

LONGSWORD - AMS ACID EDGED CARATHAN COMBAT SWORD (TACTICAL)

D8 + Strength	300¢	Close Combat	Rate 2	EMP Immune

Standard longsword with an acid sharpened edge.

TWO HANDED SWORD - AMS ACID EDGED NEMESIS COMBAT SWORD (HEAVY)

D12 + 2xStrength	800¢	Close Combat	Rate 1	EMP Immune

A huge weapon with immense damage potential. Can be wielded one handed by those with Strength 10 or more in which case it deals D12 + Strength. (Two can be used at once with the Dual Weapon Fighting training and Strength 10.)

*After the name of the close combat weapon, the category is written. (Light, Tactical and Heavy) if needed.

CLOSE COMBAT WEAPONS II

Roll 'Agility + Close Combat'

KATANA - TAKATA ISHIRO KATANA (TACTICAL)

| 2D4 + Strength | 2000¢ | Close Combat | Rate 2 | EMP Immune |

A superbly crafted, slightly curved sword which can be used one or two handed. The weapon severs a random limb if maximum damage is rolled (page 146). If used one handed the weapon has a rate of 2. If used two handed it has a rate of 1 but deals 2D4 + 2xStrength. This is not an Ion Katana, see page 112 for Ion Katanas.

PLASMA SWORD - RICHENBACHER ARCUTE RAPTOR PLASMA LONG SWORD (TACTICAL)

| D8 + Strength | 12,000¢ | Close Combat | Rate 2 | EMPS 16 |

An intimidating sword which crackles with blue arcs of plasma. Not only does it ignore shields like other close combat weapons, it also ignores the first 4 points of Armour Value. Requires the Powered Melee License and ideally the Powered Melee Training.

TWO HANDED PLASMA SWORD - RICHENBACHER ARCUTE EXECUTIONER TWO HANDED PLASMA SWORD (HEAVY)

| D12 + 2xStrength | 19,000¢ | Close Combat | Rate 1 | EMPS 16 |

A huge two handed plasma sword, perhaps the most imposing close combat weapon commercially available. Not only does it ignore shields like other close combat weapons, it also ignores the first 4 points of AV. Impossible to conceal. Requires a Powered Melee License and ideally the Powered Melee Training.

TAZER - AEGIS PERSONAL DEFENDER (LIGHT)

| Knock Out | 400¢ | Close Combat | Rate 1 | EMPS 5 |

This is used as a close combat weapon. It doesn't knock targets out, instead it causes them to spasm violently. To resist the effects the target must roll under 'Perception + Endurance' with a penalty equal to the XS of the attack. If the roll is failed the target is unable to act for D6 rounds. Agents are immune to the effects of this weapon. It just leaves tiny burn marks on them.

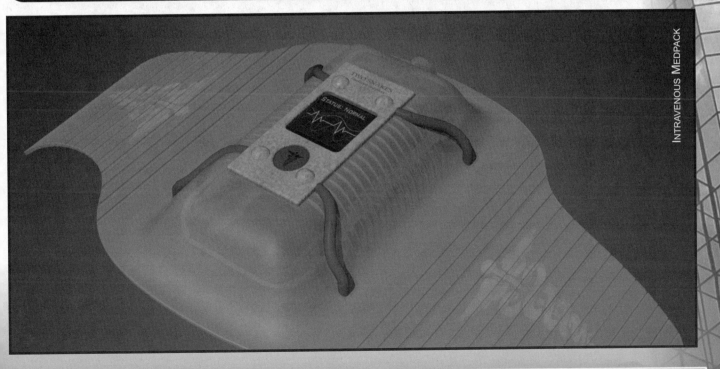

INTRAVENOUS MEDPACK

SUPPORT WEAPONS I

Plant Explosives: '1 Point in Support Weapons Needed'
Throw Grenades: 'Perception + Support Weapons'
Disarm Explosives: 'Intelligence + Support Weapons' (Get equal or more XS than the one who set it. Make a roll for them)

CONDITIONAL MINE

Uses Explosive Charge +900¢ Support Weapons Rate 1 EMPS 15

This weapon detonates under a particular condition listed. Combinations of any conditions can be used. The explosive charge in the weapon can be any grenade or bomb from the list below. The maximum detection range for detonation range is 15 metres (45 feet). This weapon is considered a complex explosive and requires an 'Intelligence + Support Weapons' check to set. Counts as a blast weapon with a blast range the same as the explosive.

-Large / medium / small life form enters the detection range.
-Loud / moderate / quiet noise is made.
-Dim / medium / bright light.
-Area reaches a certain temperature.
-Electricity is used in the area.
-A pre-defined word or sentence is spoken in the area.
-Remote detonation within 500 metres.
-A particular voice pattern (must be pre-defined with an example) is recognised in the area.
-Large / medium / small movement.

MICRO CHARGE

3D6 Damage 150¢ Support Weapons Rate 1 EMPS 10

This tiny shaped charge can be clipped to almost anything. When an activation trigger on it is pressed it gives a 10 second countdown, then destroys what it is stuck to, providing the item is fairly small or delicate such as a gun, data-drive, laptop, briefcase etc. Not practical as a weapon and generally used to destroy sensitive items before the authorities or rivals get them. Counts as a 50cm Blast Weapon. See the Damaging Equipment table on page 31.

PROXIMITY MINE

As Explosive Used +400¢ Support Weapons Rate 1 EMPS 14

This mine goes off if someone comes close to it. The trigger distance can be anything up to 30 metres although the blast may not reach at this range. The mine has an adhesive back and can be stuck on any surface. The user has ten seconds to leave the mine after it is set. The charge can be any grenade or explosive which is connected to the mine via a universal mounting. Range is equal to the type of explosive used.

EXPLOSIVE CHARGE (SMALL)

3D10 Damage 300¢ Support Weapons Rate 1 EMPS 15

A small explosive pack about the size of a matchbox. The detonator has a 20km range. Counts as a 3 metre blast weapon.

EXPLOSIVE CHARGE (MEDIUM)

6D10 Damage 600¢ Support Weapons Rate 1 EMPS 15

Moderate explosive charge about the size of a fist. The detonator has a 20km range. Counts as a 6 metre blast weapon.

EXPLOSIVE CHARGE (LARGE)

9D10 Damage 1000¢ Support Weapons Rate 1 EMPS 15

Large explosive charge about the size of a food can. The detonator has a range of 20km. Counts as a 15 metre blast weapon.

EMP GRENADE

EMP 3D6 1000¢ Support Weapons Rate 1 EMP Immune

This weapon has a blast diameter of 6 metres. See EMP weapons on page 32.

SUPPORT WEAPONS II

Plant Explosives: '1 Point in Support Weapons Needed'
Throw Grenades: 'Perception + Support Weapons'
Disarm Explosives: 'Intelligence + Support Weapons' (Get equal or more XS than the one who set it. Make a roll for them)

FLASH BANG GRENADE

None	50¢	Support Weapons	Rate 1	EMP Immune

This weapon stuns and blinds anyone in the blast radius for 2 rounds (6 seconds) unless they pass a 'Reflexes + Support Weapons' check with the thrower's XS as a modifier. Critical hits mean the victim must make their roll with a -4 penalty. Counts as a 9 metre blast Weapon. Stunned characters can only make very simple actions such as walking or crouching.

FRAGMENTATION GRENADE (FRAG GRENADES)

3D6 Damage	50¢	Support Weapons	Rate 1	EMP Immune

This weapon explodes into shrapnel hurting everyone in the blast radius. Counts as a 3 metre blast weapon.

INCENDIARY GRENADE

3D6 Damage	50¢	Support Weapons	Rate 1	EMP Immune

This grenade sets everything on fire in a 3 metre radius, even walls and floors. Most objects quickly go out but anything flammable (including people) will keep burning and take an additional D6 damage each round after the first. Burning damage does not stack with other burning damage as you can only be so much on fire. AV helps against this damage. The target must spend a full round to try to extinguish the fire. A successful 'Agility + Reflexes' roll will put it out.

KNOCK OUT GAS GRENADE

Knock Out	300¢	Support Weapons	Rate 1	EMP Immune

Agents are immune to these grenades. Anyone without air filtration has one round to exit the area of effect (6x6x2 metre area / about the size of an average room). If they don't they must pass a 'Perception + Endurance' check each round to avoid being knocked out. Critical hits mean the defenders check is made at -4. Potency of the gas is 8.

Mei Costa, crouched behind a big transit vehicle in the third bay of the car park, counted silently to three as she watched the man's shadow lengthen. Then she sprang out into the open, bringing the stubby barrel of the AMS RPG launcher down across one muscular shoulder as she did so. As the grenade flashed from the tube she had time to see him, striding down between the ranks of cars, unarmoured and armed apparently with only a long black scabbard thrust through his cloth belt. Then her grenade took him in the chest and she squeezed her eyes shut as the world vanished for a moment in a fury of light and noise.

Waiting for the glare behind her eyelids to fade, she felt a flicker of pain in her right arm; the bulky launcher digging into her bicep, presumably. Costa tried to shrug the launcher to a better position and a chilly numbness spread from her shoulder. She snapped her eyes open again.

The Shi Yukiro Agent still stood before her, his expression unchanged, his clothing unruffled as small chunks of concrete pattered down around him. His right hand now held a sword, which he had slashed up high and out to the side; the black scabbard lay abandoned on the ground at his feet, alongside the sparking remains of a discharged, broken personal hard ion field unit. Following the direction the blade must have taken through the air solved the mystery of the pain in her own shoulder; her right arm now lay at the end of a bright splattering of arterial blood several metres away, the launcher slightly closer. The unfortunate reality of the situation passed quickly through her brain, followed a moment later by the sword as it came back on the downstroke.

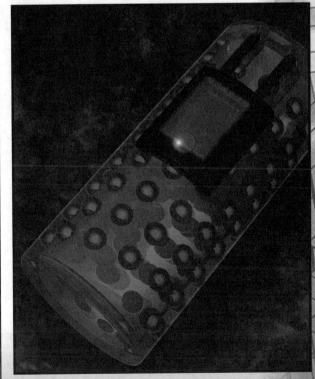

FRAGMENTATION GRENADE

AMMUNITION

This table details ammunition for weapons. There are no detailed descriptions of these items. For most game situations you may want to consider that SMART clips and Energy Cells are plentiful. It can be taken for granted that Agents will make sure that they are well armed and that they loot ammunition where they can find it. Only sometimes should players need to keep track of their shots, for example, in missions where they may have been abandoned with little equipment or if they are using high consumption weapons such as Rocket Launchers or Rail Guns.

AMMO TYPE	WEAPONS USED IN	COST	SPECIAL
Energy Cell	Lasers / Plasma / EMP	50¢	Light firearms 30 shots / 6 machine bursts Tactical firearms 15 shots / 3 machine bursts Heavy firearms 3 discharges
SMART* Clip	Kinetic Weapons	50¢	Light firearms 30 shots / 6 machine bursts Tactical firearms 15 shots / 3 machine bursts Heavy firearms 3 discharges
Napalm Canister	Flame Based Weapons	100¢	Light firearms 30 shots / 6 machine bursts Tactical firearms 15 shots / 3 machine bursts Heavy firearms 3 discharges
Circular Saw Blades	Blade Launcher	100¢	15 disc shaped blades
KO Injector darts	Injector Weapons	50¢ each	The only mainstream legal dart. Target must roll under 'Perception + Endurance' with the attackers XS as a penalty or be knocked unconscious for D100 minutes. Does not work on Agents.
Injector Darts	Injector Weapons	10¢	Empty injector darts, can be filled with a single dose of a chemical.
Armour Piercing Clip	Kinetic Weapons	200¢	Ignores 2 points of targets AV. Same number of shots as a standard SMART Clip
S17 Crossbow Bolts	Crossbow	10¢ each	Undetectable by 90% of scanning methods. Can be poisoned with a toxin.
High Mass Bolts	Crossbow	50¢ each	Made of high density matter that passes straight through shields. Same damage as a normal bolt.
Rocket Light Ballistic	Rocket Launcher	100¢	3D10 Damage (3 metre blast)
Rocket Medium Ballistic	Rocket Launcher	250¢	6D10 Damage (6 metre blast)
Rocket Heavy Ballistic	Rocket Launcher	500¢	9D10 Damage (9 metre blast)

Self Modelling Auto-loading Round Technology

Note: There are rules above for ammo use with weapons which do not exist in this book. For example there are no Light Firearms which use Energy cells and are capable of machine bursts. The listing is here for completeness and in case the GM or players would like to invent them. They will be available in future supplements.

ARMOUR

Most Agents need a form of armour. Armour reduces the amount of damage an Agent takes by its AV (Armour Value) see page 143. Some Armour Values stack so someone in a Flak Jacket, Combat Helmet and Shield would have AV 3. A bonus from Cybernetics always stacks with armour. You cannot wear two sets of armour on the same body area such as a Flak Jacket and Light Combat Armour.

GUIDE TO ARMOUR

AV / ARMOUR VALUE - Each set of damage dealt to you is reduced by this number. There are exceptions such as plasma weapons and rail guns. These are detailed in the appropriate weapon description.

WHERE WORN - This describes where the armour is worn. You cannot cover the same area twice with two different sets of armour unless otherwise stated. The physical location of the amour is not used to make targeted shots to unarmoured body areas. This is represented by 'Vital Shot' (see page 145).

MAXIMUM AGILITY - Some armour has a *Maximum Agility*. This dictates the maximum your Agility STAT can be when wearing the armour, e.g., if you have Agility 8 and wear Heavy Combat Armour your Agility is considered to be 6 until you remove the armour.

EMPS - All armour is immune to EMP.

ARMOUR LIMIT - Note that you cannot have an Armour Value higher than your Strength as you can't physically carry the armour. There are exceptions to this such as *Powered* Armour or specific armours, which will say if they ignore this rule. Another example is UIG Erabite Armour on page 124.

CUSTOMISATION - Armour can be heavily customised if desired. For example, the majority of Agents wear Reinforced Clothing in the form of well cut suits when on missions. The Samurai ad Technica of the Shi Yukiro have their armour modified to resemble the armour of ancient Samurai. Crusaders of the Order of the True Faith often modify their armour to resemble that of medieval knights. Modifying the armour to your personal taste costs an extra 20% in addition to the normal cost.

ARMOUR DAMAGE - For the majority of occasions don't be concerned with damage to armour. If you do wish to represent it simply decrease the AV of the armour if it is not maintained over time.

Armour's far from useless, but it's a highly situational thing. If you're mangling with the SY, and if they're packing ion, a bunch of lightweight plate won't be a whole lot of use. And if you've had a falling-out with the Comoros, all the armour in the world won't do squat, since nobody makes a helmet thick enough to stop 'em getting into your head. On the other hand, if you're up against Federation Gunmen, the Malenbrach, the Clangers or an El Nuke, a nice set of tac armour can give you a lovely warm feeling. Unless, of course, that Nuke happens to prefer something in a Pyronics FT9 or upwards, in which case that lovely warm feeling is liable to be you, gently baking in your own tailored oven.

-attr: Zack Adams, freelance technical consultant/soldier of fortune

ARMOUR	AV	COST
DISC SHIELD	+1	3,000¢

This is strapped to the forearm like a buckler. It is a small projected static ion shield which is both lightweight and small so you can have both hands free while using it. One energy cell powers it for 1 week of normal use. Can be worn with all other armour.

REINFORCED CLOTHING	+1	1,000¢

Covers the torso, arms and legs, all armours can be worn over the top.
A set of basic clothes with a molybdenum / carbon undermesh giving some basic defence. The mesh can be *customised* if desired which costs an extra 200 credits and the price of the clothes you want it fitted to.

FLACK JACKET	+1	300¢

Covers the torso
This is a lightweight vest with basic defensive qualities.

COMBAT HELMET	+1	300¢

Covers the head
A simple combat helmet which offers some basic protection. Can be worn with any armour that does not cover the head.

HAND HELD SHIELD	+1	300¢

Carried on non-weapon arm
This is an alloy shield which requires an empty hand to carry. Two handed items cannot be wielded when using this.

LIGHT COMBAT ARMOUR	+2	1,000¢

Covers the torso, arms and legs
An expansion of the Flak Jacket which covers the whole body except the head. Good all round armour, not too obvious when worn.

FIELD COMBAT ARMOUR	+3	6,000¢

Covers the torso, arms and legs
The armour most commonly used by Agents but a little bulky and conspicuous. Does not cover the head. (Maximum Agility 8)

HEAVY COMBAT ARMOUR	+4	10,000¢

Covers all
Wearer looks huge and intimidating. This is the heaviest armour that can be worn without the need for Anti Grav Units. (Maximum Agility 6)

POWERED TACTICAL ARMOUR	+5	20,000¢

Covers all
Heavy armour which is kept relatively lightweight by the use of Anti Grav units. (Maximum Agility 8).

TACTICAL ASSAULT ARMOUR	+6	40,000¢

Covers all
Powered heavy armour which is kept manageable by the use of numerous Anti Grav units. Very conspicuous and normally only used in times of extreme unrest. (Maximum Agility 7).

HARD ION SHIELDS

"Take gunfire so you don't have to." - Aegis Defence Technologies

Hard Ion Shields emit a coloured glow around the user and work on a velocity filtration system so that slow moving objects pass through them. This means the shielded person can do everyday tasks. Only energy signatures travelling at an extremely high speed are stopped by the field. This means almost all forms of bullet and shrapnel are stopped but swords, close combat attacks, thrown weapons, cars, etc pass through. At close range (1 metre or less) an opponent is considered to be inside your shield so any attacks will ignore it, even guns

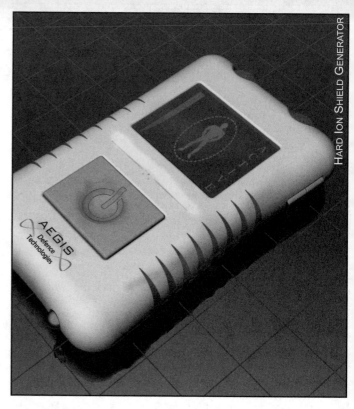

HARD ION SHIELD GENERATOR

USING SHIELDS

An Agent can only have one shield turned on at a time. When shields are hit they absorb the maximum possible damage. For example, if the wearer is hit by a pistol dealing D8 damage the shield's HP are automatically reduced by 8 points. The attacker does not roll damage. When the shield reaches 0HP or less it is considered discharged and cannot be used. To recharge a shield see below.

A shield will defend the wearer from any shot as long as the damage is not more than double the shield's total HP. If it is double or more the shield will be discharged and broken and the wearer will take any damage in excess of double the shields HP.

RECHARGING SHIELDS

Shields can be plugged in to any mains outlet and recharged. This takes 1 minute per depleted HP. Shields which have been broken must be fixed before recharging - see Fixing Equipment on page 31.

EXAMPLES

Example 1 (Discharging)

Agent Daniq's 50 Hit Point shield is down to 10, he takes a blast which deals 12 damage. The shield absorbs all the damage and is discharged but not broken (it was not double the Shields Total Hit Points).

Example 2 (Breaking Shields)

Agent Baxter has a 50 HP shield on. He is hit for 120 damage in one shot. The shield defends Baxter from 100 damage and Baxter takes 20. The shield is totally discharged and broken. If Baxter has been hit for 90 damage he would be fine and the shield simply drained.

HARD ION SHIELDS

SHIELD TYPE	COST	HP	EMPS	SPECIAL
Disposable Shield	100¢	10	15	Cannot be recharged
Domestic Shield	500¢	10	15	Rechargeable
Field Shield	1000¢	20	20	Rechargeable
Heavy Field Shield	2000¢	30	20	Rechargeable
Insulated Field Shield	3000¢	30	Immune	Rechargeable
Battle Shield	5000¢	50	20	Rechargeable
Self Charging Shield	5000¢	20	15	Can recharge itself in 1 hour
Covert Shield	8000¢	50	17	The projected ion field is invisible
Tactical Assault	10000¢	100	25	Does not break when hit by excessive damage

HP = Hit Points of the Shield EMPS = EMP Shielding

TOXINS AND DRUGS I

Below are a list of common drugs and toxins. Some are illegal and hard to acquire. They come in either a dose or canister and sometimes both.

A **DOSE** affects 1 target and normally comes in the form of a small compression dart or tablet. (Can be used in an injector dart - see page 44)

A **CANISTER** is larger and when activated fills a 10x10x10 metre area. It has a release valve. This is also compatible with 80% of commercial and industrial ventilation systems allowing it to be spread though the air conditioning system.

SUBSTANCE CLASSIFICATIONS

A   Illegal in all territories. Heavy sentencing for use and distribution.
B   As Class A but usable by selected individuals, e.g. Agents, UIG or those with medical needs.
C   Illegal in some territories. Punishments vary.
D   Unrestricted.

Potency - This is a scale based on how well the chemical is blocked by a toxin filter. The higher the potency, the more difficult the chemical is to filter out. See Toxin Filters on page 53.

SUBSTANCE	POTENCY	CLASS	COST
AMALAZINE	5	C	20¢ PER DOSE

Tablet - Was originally used to pacify Agents after cybernetic surgery which used to take several months to recuperate from. The drug stops adrenaline production and stimulates endorphin release in the brain. The user becomes very calm and is satisfied easily. Often called the 'boredom drug'. The long term side effect is that the immune system becomes compromised leading to high levels of disease in users. Valued by those in tedious situations such as guards, inmates and those in isolated locations.

| **ASMENIC DICHLORATE** | 7 | A | 1000¢ PER DOSE |

This is a tablet which causes the taker to forget everything that happened over the last 5 hours. Passing an 'Intelligence + Presence' check with a -6 penalty means the taker has vague recollections or perhaps some blurry flashbacks.

| **AUTOLAMINE** | 8 | A | 1400¢ PER CANISTER |

Canister - The gas causes the victims insides to begin a self-autolysis process. This near unstoppable reaction causes the victims internal organs to decompose. It deals a cumulative D6 of damage each round. 1D6 on the first, 2D6 on the second etc. If the victim receives a Toxin Purge the process halts and they take no more damage.

| **CN-CN-4** | 9 | A | 4000¢ PER CANISTER |

A breathable gas that kills in 9 seconds. An 'Endurance + Medicine' check with a -4 penalty allows the victim to get to a safe place (conditions permitting).

| **COMBAT DRUGS 'SAVAGE'** | 8 | C | 200¢ PER DOSE |

Injected - Domestic grade physical enhancement drug. Gives +1 to all physical STATS (Str, End, Agi) for 1 scene. This does not increase your HP. Combat drug effects are not cumulative.

| **COMBAT DRUGS 'DEVILFISH'** | 9 | B | 1200¢ PER DOSE |

Injected - Military grade physical enhancement drug. Gives +3 to all physical STATS (Str, End, Agi) for 1 scene. This does not increase your HP. Combat drug effects are not cumulative.

| **COMBAT DRUGS 'PSYCHORE'** | 8 | B | 600¢ PER DOSE |

Injected - Professional grade physical enhancement drug. Gives +2 to all physical STATS (Str, End, Agi) for 1 scene. This does not increase your HP. Combat drug effects are not cumulative.

| **DI-HYDROXY-CRYPTONOL 'DHC'** | 8 | C | 10¢ PER DOSE |

Tablets - Causes euphoria and a sense of invincibility. Reduces life span to around 2 years from initial addiction. This is due to the cheap production and distribution which involves cutting the drug with miscellaneous chemicals which damage the neural pathways of the brain, After a few doses the user becomes unstable and his mental decline is inevitable (but arguably better than the life of an outcast). Research and production is allegedly funded by the Western Federation to get rid of social filth.

| **HAEMAVINE** | 11 | D | 200¢ PER DOSE |

Injected - Used as a fix-all wound repair serum. It instigates rapid cell regeneration and instantly heals the user 20HP. This is the chemical used in Intravenous Medpacks.

| **KNOCK OUT GAS** | 3 | B | 400¢ PER CANISTER |

The target has 1 round to leave the area, if they don't they must roll 'Perception + Endurance' to avoid falling unconscious for D100 minutes. Agents are immune to this.

TOXINS AND DRUGS II

SUBSTANCE	POTENCY	CLASS	COST

KNOCK OUT SERUM — Potency 9 — Class B — 50¢ PER DART
Injected - The Target must make a 'Perception + Endurance' penalty or fall unconscious for D100 minutes. This does not require a license to use. Agents are immune to this. Also available in injector darts (page 44).

LAMBANIC ACID — Potency 7 — Class A — 500¢ PER DOSE / 6000¢ PER CANISTER
AKA: 'SCREAMING NORWEGIAN RUNE DISEASE'
In gaseous form an 'Endurance + Medicine' check with a -4 penalty allows the victim to get to a safe place. (conditions permitting). If injected, or the victim cannot escape the fumes, she begins to break out into hideous wounds that resemble runic markings. The victim goes almost instantly insane and starts to tear apart colleagues and enemies alike. (attacks random people in close combat). The victim takes a cumulative D6 damage each turn, i.e., 1D6 on the 1st turn, 2D6 on the next, etc.

METAPSITROPHIN AKA: 'BRAIN JUICE' — Potency 9 — Class B — 200¢ PER DOSE
This is taken by telepaths in the field. It regenerates their Telepathic Energy (TE) at a highly increased rate. In game terms it restores 30 TE points when injected which takes an action unless it is placed into an Intravenous Pack. You can only attach one at a time as it has to be placed over the spine.

NEURAPROMINE — Potency 8 — Class D — 200¢ PER DOSE
Injected - A freely available drug which enhances the response time of the users nerves. Used by Cyber Athletes to compete in high end, big prize virtual contests, as well as Agents, Weltball players and race drivers. Grants +3 Reflexes for 1 scene. Multiple doses have no additional effect.

PSITROPINE — Potency 8 — Class A — 2000¢ PER DOSE
This toxin comes in a dart usable in an injector weapon. It renders a telepath unable to use their powers by sending a neurotoxin to key parts of the brain. The victim is unaware of the effect until they try to use their telepathy. There is no way to resist this other than a toxin filter of level 8 or more which can prevent injected toxins (or a toxin purge). The duration is D6 rounds.

SERACONONMIN AKA: 'DNA +' — Potency 9 — Class B — 20,000¢ - 1 MILLION¢
Injected - This drug modifies the taker's DNA. Dozens of versions are available but they all act to permanently alter the genetic blueprint of the user. Normally the drug is used to make the person look slightly different, in a similar way to mild plastic surgery. However certain strains can alter the whole body and even the superficial gender of the taker. This is often accelerated to occur over a few days. The process is very painful and gives the taker a great affinity for cancer. This drug is prohibitively expensive, especially the variant which changes the whole body in a short time.

SUN - (HYDROGEN SUNATOL) — Potency 6 — Class C — 10,000¢ PER DOSE
Ingested Liquid - This drug was engineered by E.I. and can be acquired legally in E.I. territory, other nations will not allow it's import. The drug is very expensive - sometimes 10,000 credits a dose. It is a by product of combat drug research and fills the user with increased strength, dexterity and muscle tone. To fuel this metamorphosis fat is metabolised from the user and converted into toned muscle. There are no strong side effects other than the addictive nature that such a drug inherently has, which is essentially to turn overweight people into athletes in a matter of days with no effort. Commonly called 'Sun' (derived from Sunatol but also users see it as their 'little ray of sunshine'). **System Effect**: Anyone with physical STATS (Str, Agi, End) below 6 increases their stats to 6 a few days after the consumption of the drug. Sunatol must be taken monthly to keep its effect or the STATS drop again to their previous level (as does the physique of the user).

TAMBA (TAMBANOIC ACID) — Potency 5 — Class C — 30¢ PER DOSE
Injected - Fills the user with enormous energy and a sense of elation and euphoria. This causes a feeling of incredible depression over the next few days, taking more of the drug causes the user to become euphoric again creating a cycle of depression and elation. Chemically the drug is not addictive. There are mild health risks associated with the depressed immune system.

TITANIUM LIPODINE 'TI-SKIN' — Potency 6 — Class D — 1000¢ PER DOSE
When injected this drug distributes itself among the subcutaneous areas of the body and acts to harden the skin and make it more resilient with regenerative properties. The end effect being +2 Armour Value and the user regenerates 2 HP per round. It lasts one scene.

TOXIN PURGE — Potency 10 — Class D — 500¢ PER DOSE
Injected - This is injected into the left ventrical of a living target. It purges the system of all toxins, drugs and poison, (including beneficial ones) the target is violently sick as a result and cannot act for D3 rounds. After being injected the user remains immune to toxins for 5 rounds (15 seconds). If the purge is injected into a target who is not suffering from a toxin they only receive the sensation of mild nausea and are not incapacitated.

TRIPTO-DIMETHYL-TRANSMERATE — Potency 5 — Class A — 700¢ FOR 1 WEEKS SUPPLY.
AKA: 'DREAM' / TDT
Injected - This drug is in common use. It creates an interactive dream state which can be influenced by the user. This allows one to live out fantasies. TDT is extremely addictive and many users only leave the dream state to fund more Dream and to eat and drink. This drug is banned the world over as those who use it normally destroy themselves within weeks.

GENERAL EQUIPMENT

These items are all available from standard commercial and Corporate stores unless marked otherwise. The GM should feel free to make up equipment, increasing or decreasing the power and effectiveness as needed.

SIZE

This is not mentioned for most equipment as it should normally be obvious. Where uncertain, a size and/or weight is stated. The GM should make any adjudication if necessary.

A list of Agent Starting Equipment can be found on page 13

01.	Audio Visual Bug	50¢
02.	AV Bug Detector	300¢
03.	Binoculars	150¢
04.	Camera (Miniature)	100¢
05.	Climbing Gloves (Thorns)	250¢
06.	Comm. Device	1200¢
07.	Compound 'H'	1000¢
08.	Computer (Hackers)	4000¢
09.	Computer (PDA) / Cellphone	300¢
10.	Computer (Portable)	600¢/yr
11.	Computer (Workstation)	4000¢
12.	Credit Chip Reader	800¢
13.	Cutting Torch (Disposable)	400¢
14.	Digital Scrambler	3000¢
15.	Drop Suit	700¢
16.	EMPS Booster	1500¢
17.	Environment Suit	3000¢
18.	Eye Screen	700¢
19.	Hacking Software	Free
20.	Hacking Software (Advanced)	600¢
21.	Handcuffs	50¢
22.	Hologram Generator	1500¢
23.	ID Chip Checker	100¢
24.	ID Chip Scanner (Normal)	600¢
25.	ID Chip Scanner (Remote)	4000¢
26.	Inaugurate	600¢
27.	Intravenous Pack	100¢
28.	Invisibility Field	500¢
29.	Ion Wall Generator	2000¢
30.	Liquid Alloy	100¢
31.	Lock Portable	200¢
32.	Lock Analyser	50¢
33.	Lockpicks (Standard)	150¢
34.	Medpack (Intravenous)	300¢
35.	Medpack (Standard)	200¢
36.	Metapsitrophin (Brain Juice)	200¢
37.	Night Sight	1000¢
38.	Night Vision Glasses	3000¢
39.	Proximity Sensor	200¢
40.	Psi-cuffs	15000¢
41.	Rope (Narrow Polymer)	100¢
42.	SatBlanket	10000¢
43.	Security Bypass Device	5000¢
44.	Shield Breaker	1000¢
45.	Sound Absorption Field	3000¢
46.	Stealth Suit	3000¢
47.	Suppressant Gel	500¢
48.	Telepathic Converger	10000¢
49.	Telepathic Disruptor	1000¢
50.	Toolkit (Explosives)	600¢
51.	Toolkit (Analysis)	1200¢
52.	Toolkit (Computers and A.I.)	1000¢
53.	Toolkit (Cybernetics)	1000¢
54.	Toolkit (Forensics)	1500¢
55.	Toolkit (Interrogation)	400¢
56.	Toolkit (Advanced Mechtronics)	1000¢
57.	Toolkit (Medical)	1000¢
58.	Toolkit (Robotics)	1500¢
59.	Torch (Long Cell)	100¢
60.	Toxin Filter (Disposable)	200¢
61.	Toxin Filter (Reusable)	2000¢
62.	Tracer Gun	1000¢
63.	Translator	5000¢
64.	Viral Modifier	2000¢

AUDIO VISUAL BUG   50¢
This is a miniature camera & microphone the size of a fingernail. It sends the information it records to a receiver (included) or computer up to 100km away.

AV BUG DETECTOR   300¢
A handheld device which can find transmitters (usually Audio Visual Bugs) within a 10 metre radius. Success is automatic if one is in the area.

BINOCULARS   150¢
Allows long range vision. User takes no penalty for long range perception checks. (This does not help with firing weapons.)

CAMERA (MINIATURE)   100¢
A small camera the size of a matchbox. Takes up to 5000 high resolution images or 24 hours of audio-video. It is shockproof and waterproof.

CLIMBING GLOVES (THORNS)   250¢
These barbed gloves aids the user in climbing. The Agent gains +4 to his climbing rolls when wearing them. Tasks which use manual dexterity get a -4 penalty when wearing the gloves.

COMM. DEVICE   1,200¢
This is a communication device with an global range which is 95% secure. The price is for one device, which is easily carried in a pocket. Each time the device is used the GM should secretly roll a D100. On a 01-05 the security of the signal has been compromised.

COMPOUND 'H'   1,000¢
This is a spray can containing 1 dose of a miracle compound created by Two Snakes Medical. The substance is painted onto two freshly severed body surfaces and allows them to be biologically glued together. One surface must be alive. Trophic molecules in the compound bind to tissues and guide them towards other tissues of the same type (much like in a developing human). Over a period of 15 minutes the surfaces knit back together. It is as though the severing never happened. Sadly it cannot prevent death from a severed head unless the victim has a 'Datanetica Cerebral Link'. Hit Points lost as a result of the sever are regained. It can glue parts from different people 60% of the time.

COMPUTER (HACKERS)   4,000¢
Hackers do not rent computers. This is a stand alone system the size of a briefcase with more than enough power to attempt any job. You gain +2 to hacking rolls when using it. It has a Data Dump function which erases all sensitive data at the touch of a button and is normally well encrypted.

COMPUTER (PDA)   300¢
A tiny computer the size of a man's hand used for everyday tasks and viewing media. Contains an integrated cellular phone. Cell phones are notoriously unsecure.

COMPUTER (PORTABLE)   600¢ / YEAR
Rental of a small, fist sized computer for general applications. Screen and human interface are rendered in projected light.

COMPUTER (WORKSTATION)   4,000¢
A large powerful, computer which must be set up in a permanent location. Gives +2 to computer based rolls when using it.

CREDIT CHIP READER   800¢
This tiny device reads credit chips and, with the owner's ID Chip scan, can be used to transfer money between any chips currently in the machine (up to 4). Slip credit needs no ID chip scan.

CUTTING TORCH (DISPOSABLE)   400¢
A handheld plasma cutting torch which ignores the first 20 points of an object's AV. It lasts 9 seconds (3 rounds) before its power supply is exhausted. This is long enough to cut a single door-sized hole. If used as a weapon, consider it a Light Close Combat Weapon which ignores the first 20 points of AV and deals D6 damage. The weapon lasts for 3 rounds which do not have to be sequential. Once expended the item is useless. See page 31 for damaging equipment.

DIGITAL SCRAMBLER   3,000¢
This handheld device scrambles all surveillance feeds within 500 metres of the user when active. Legal to own but it is illegal to knock out UIG equipment. Agent's sub-vocal communicators will not work when one of these is active.

DROP SUIT   700¢
This is a lightweight black suit which has fabric connecting the wrist and ankle creating a parachute. The user is able to glide from any height and land gracefully as long as she passes an 'Agility + Athletics' roll. Failure means she takes D10 falling damage. The suit is not powered. Also known as Bingo Wings.

EMPS BOOSTER   1,500¢
This is a tiny field generator which clips onto any equipment or cybernetics. It fortifies the item against the effects of an Electromagnetic Pulse. Each booster fitted adds 2 to the EMPS (electromagnetic pulse shielding) of the item. A maximum of 5 boosters can be clipped to an item before their effect becomes immeasurable. Obviously some items may be too small to accept 5 in which case the GM should place a lower limit.

ENVIRONMENT SUIT   3,000¢
This is a lightweight suit which allows the wearer to exist in hostile atmospheres such as vacuum or inside a nuclear reactor. The suit uses a specialist power/matter cell which costs 100¢ and will power the suit for 24 hours. (It is supplied with two.) The suit also provides +1 AV but cannot be worn over armour. On the knees of the suit are 5 patches which can be used to instantly repair rips in the suit which could arise from bullets, knives, etc.

EYE SCREEN   700¢
A screen which covers one eye and wirelessly gives data to an Agent from a source computer. -1 to Perception while using it.

HACKING SOFTWARE   FREE
Combined with a computer, allows hacking into a digital data system. Hacking software, although illegal, is easy to acquire and Agents may start with it if desired. If anyone is caught with this software the UIG will remove 6 Rank Points from them. The software comes on S-Chips which cannot be copied with domestic equipment, so originals must be acquired. Most people know where to get it if they really want it so it can be made freely available unless the GM decides otherwise.

HACKING SOFTWARE (ADVANCED)   600¢
To acquire this software you need black market or underground contacts. It makes the whole process of hacking easier granting the hacker +2 to all his hacking checks. This software is illegal, anyone caught possessing or using it incurs the loss of 12 Rank Points. The software comes on S-Chips which cannot be copied with domestic equipment so originals must be acquired.

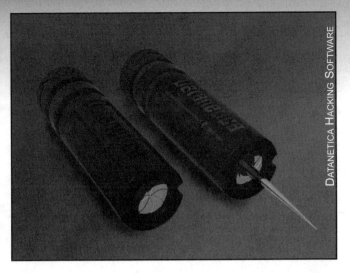

DATANETICA HACKING SOFTWARE

ID Scanners give the following information:

Name	Gender
Age	Date of birth
Criminal record	Rank
Employer	Annual income
Place of residence	Cybernetics
Medical conditions	Next of kin

Privacy Licenses allow the person to dictate what information is given out to people of lower or equal rank, e.g. a Rank 5 Agent can hide all his details (except name) from anyone of Rank 5 or lower if he desires.

ID CHIP SCANNER (REMOTE) 4,000¢
This handheld device can read ID chips from a range of 20 metres giving you any accessible information on the subject. You need Rank 1+ to buy one of these legally. Also see 'ID Chip Scanner' above.)

INAUGURATE 1,000¢
Inaugurate can dissolve almost all known substances. It deals 20 damage per dose which means it can dissolve through AV 20. If it were poured on a person with AV 6, it would dissolve through the armour and then deal 14 damage. Due to chemical volatility Inaugurate is awkward as a weapon. One dose is enough to dissolve a strong lock on a door. Inaugurate comes in a small gyroscopically controlled container and should be used with great caution. It contains 3 doses.

INTRAVENOUS PACK 100¢
This is a small pack which is strapped onto the body. It can be filled with any liquid such as Metapsitrophin or Combat Drugs. When the wearer desires the contents of the pack are injected and the effects are instant. Using this device is considered a free action (you may have 1 free action per round). Once used the pack is useless and should be discarded.
Note that IV Medpacks must be placed over the heart and IV Metapsitrophin must be placed over the base of the spine. This means only one of each of these particular chemicals can be readied at a time.

INVISIBILITY FIELD 500¢
This small watch-shaped device, once activated, bends light to make the user almost invisible. Any attempts to spot the user are made at -8. Any equipment he carries is also invisible as long as it is not more than twice his normal size. Alternatively he could use it to hide an additional Agent. Any objects hitting the field such as rain, bullets or other people cause it to ripple and allow others to notice its presence. The device lasts one scene before the optics burn out and it becomes useless.

ION WALL GENERATOR 3,000¢
Creates a hard ion shield (see page 46) with 500 HP. The wall has a maximum area of 10 x 10 metres but can be confined to a smaller space if necessary. The generator is 10 cm cubed and has a small antigravity unit so it can float and be placed in any orientation, at any height. Once set, the device requires 2000kg of force to move. It lasts for 10 hours and is then expended and useless.

LIQUID ALLOY 100¢
A canister of mercury-like liquid about the size of a can of Multymeat. This can be shaped or used to adhere two objects and will set in 10 seconds. Bonds as strong as a weld. It requires a force of 500kg to break apart the hardened alloy.

LOCK (PORTABLE) 200¢
The two components are backed with small amounts of Liquid Alloy. One is placed on the door, the other on the frame, much like a conventional bolt. The door can then be locked and unlocked by hitting the buttons on the lock. The lock is compact and weighs 1kg. A force of 800kg is needed to break the lock. It can be picked using conventional methods, in which case it is considered a normal electronic lock.

HANDCUFFS 50¢
These restrain the hands and make it difficult to move. (See the Restrain Training on page 24 to make more use of handcuffs.)

ESCAPING HANDCUFFS & RESTRAINTS

BREAK HANDCUFFS
'Strength + Athletics' with a -8 penalty.

PICK HANDCUFF LOCKS (MECHANICAL LOCK)
'Intelligence + Crime' with a -6 penalty.

BREAK NYLON TIES
'Strength + Athletics' with a -6 penalty.

Picking or breaking another person's restraints reduces the penalty by 2.

HOLOGRAM GENERATOR 1,500¢
This is a matchbox sized device which can be used for 3 minutes before its optics are burned out. The GM should decide when it's 3 minutes have been used up. It creates a convincing hologram up to 15 metres away with sound and a maximum size of 2x2x2 metres. Anyone viewing the hologram must pass a 'Perception + Assess Tech' roll at -4 to see that it is an illusion unless they have some advantage such as thermal vision which would immediately see through it. Interaction with the hologram reveals its nature. The generator can store up to 10 images which must be downloaded to it via a computer system.
For example: Agent Locke uses the device to create a convincing Murder Class Droid. His enemy spots the droid and fires a rocket at it. The hologram is undamaged but is exposed as a fake. Fortunately the enemy has used his last rocket and revealed his position.

ID CHIP CHECKER 100¢
This is a small chip which can be incorporated into any firearm or powered melee weapon. Only the registered ID Chip wearer(s) can activate the weapons. ID chip checkers only activate for a second when the weapon is picked up and so are essentially immune to EMP.

ID CHIP SCANNER (NORMAL) 600¢
This handheld device can read ID chips from a range of 10cm giving any accessible information on the subject.

AEGIS 'DOBERMAN' PORTABLE LOCK

LOCK ANALYSER   50¢
This penknife sized item gives a bonus of +4 to open any mechanical or electronic lock. It can only be used once and is then discarded.

LOCKPICKS (STANDARD)   150¢
These are needed to pick mechanical locks. Without them you can attempt to open the lock with a knife or similar item but you suffer a penalty. See Opening Locks on page 19. You need a Security Bypass Device to open electronic locks.

MEDPACK (INTRAVENOUS)   300¢
This IV pack contains Haemavine which heals 20HP when activated. It also has a small biosensor which activates the pack once the wearer hits zero Hit Points. Using this device is considered a free action (you may have 1 free action per round). You can only attach one IV Medpack at a time as it has to be placed over the heart. You can administer one as a normal action if it is not currently strapped to you. Once used, the item is useless.

MEDPACK (STANDARD)   200¢
A general use medical kit. Heals 20 plus the users Medicine skill in Hit Points. It takes 1 round to administer. If the user has no Medicine skill it still works healing 20HP. Can be used once, then is useless.

METAPSITROPHIN (BRAIN JUICE)   200¢
This is taken by Telepaths in the field. It regenerates their Telepathic Energy at a highly increased rate. In game terms it restores 30 TE points when injected which takes an action, unless it is placed into an Intravenous Pack. You can only attach one IV Metapsitrophin pack at a time as it has to be placed over the base of the spine. You can administer one as a normal action if it is not currently strapped to you.

NIGHT SIGHT   1,000¢
A fairly bulky pair of binoculars which allow perfect night vision in colour. Sudden, bright light has no effect.

NIGHT VISION GLASSES   3,000¢
These look like normal sun glasses except the wearer can see flawlessly in the dark (in black and red). Sudden bright light has no effect.

PROXIMITY SENSOR   200¢
This device alerts the one who set it if any activity occurs within 100 metres of the sensor. The alert can take the form of an alarm, a remote signal to an SVC or an alert to a computer system. The active range can be set anywhere up to 100 metres.

PSI-CUFFS   15,000¢
While worn these handcuffs impede the wearer's telepathy making them unable to use any telepathic skills. To escape them see Escaping Handcuffs on page 51. They count as normal handcuffs for the purposes of escaping.

ROPE (NARROW POLYMER)   100¢
20 metres of thin, strong black cord with a 3000kg breaking point.

SATBLANKET   10,000¢
SatBlankets require the SatBlanket license to use. Each one is a device the size of a car battery with a computer terminal built in for configuration. It prevents satellites scanning an area 30 square metres in size. This does not leave a void in the satellites image; the SatBlanket intelligently edits out what the user specifies making the area seem normal to anyone viewing the satellite footage. A skillful satellite technician can make an 'Intelligence + Mechtronics' check to notice the anomaly.

SECURITY BYPASS DEVICE   5,000¢
A small handheld device which allows you to attempt to bypass all types of electronic lock such as biometric, card, or code operated. To do this see Opening Locks on page 19. This reusable device legally requires a Security License to use.

SHIELD BREAKER   1,000¢
This device is thrown like a grenade or set like an explosive. It deals no damage to people but does 60 damage to all shields in the blast radius of 10 metres. It will discharge shields but never break them. It can be remotely triggered using a small handset which is included. The shield breaker has one use.

SOUND ABSORPTION FIELD   3,000¢
The SAF box is 30x30x30cm in size and is normally carried in a pack due to its weight. It neutralises sound waves by mirroring them at themselves. Creates silence in a 10 metre radius. It will not neutralise anything of equal or greater volume to kinetic gunfire.

STEALTH SUIT   3,000¢
This suit allows the Agent to blend into the scenery by matching its colours to the environment. It grants the Agent +4 Stealth when worn. Wearing other clothes / armour will reduce its effectiveness, e.g. wearing a flack jacket over the suit would reduce its bonus to +3.

SUPPRESSANT GEL   500¢
This gel package is fitted inside a Tactical or Light Kinetic Firearm. The gel absorbs sound energy released by the weapon making it silent.

TELEPATHIC CONVERGER   10,000¢
This ugly machine allows a Telepath to focus his powers more easily. It looks much like a headband with various probes and connectors which fit into the skull and process socket. Telepaths equipped with these gain a +2 bonus to their telepathy Action Totals.

TELEPATHIC DISRUPTOR   1,000¢
This item interferes with telepathic energy for one scene. Anyone using telepathic powers after this device has been triggered has a 50% chance for their powers not to work. Additionally Telepathic powers critically fail on all doubles irrespective of whether they would normally pass the roll. It can only be used once and is then discarded. These items are the size of car batteries and affect all telepaths within 20 metres of the disruptor.
System: Each time a telepathic power is used, roll a D10. On a 1-5 the power does not work.

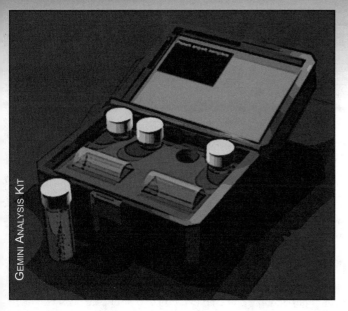

GEMINI ANALYSIS KIT

TOOLKIT (EXPLOSIVES)   600¢
Allows disarming and modification of demolition devices.
1. To disarm a device an opposed 'Intelligence + Support Weapons' check must be won against the person who set the explosive. If he did not make a roll to set it make a roll now for comparison purposes. Having this toolkit gives a +4 bonus.
2. By passing an 'Intelligence + Support Weapons' check you can make sure that when an explosive is set it deals maximum damage, so no damage roll is needed.
For example, if an explosive deals 3D6, then by passing the roll it will deal 18 damage instead.

TOOLKIT (ANALYSIS)   1,200¢
Used to detect and analyse unknown substances. The user can make an 'Intelligence + Science' check. The GM may apply a modifier from -4 to +4 based on how common, hidden or old the substance is.
Success means the substance has been identified correctly.
Failure means a new sample will be needed to try again. Each use of the kit takes D10 minutes.

TOOLKIT (COMPUTERS AND A.I.)   1000¢
This portable toolkit helps the Agent maintain, upgrade and build computers and A.I. systems. It does not assist with software issues. It grants a +2 bonus to 'Computers & A.I.' or 'Mechtronics' rolls involving computer and A.I. systems.

TOOLKIT (CYBERNETICS)   1,000¢
This is a toolkit which helps a cyberneticist to fit basic cyberware and make simple cybernetic adjustments. See 'Fitting Cybernetics' on page 62.

TOOLKIT (FORENSICS)   1,500¢
This can test for DNA, blood presence and signs of gunfire. It can analyse weapons to see when and how they were used as well as comparing ammunition and fragments of material. The user makes an 'Intelligence + Science' check. The GM may apply a modifier from -4 to +4 based on how difficult the results are to obtain. Note that if you do not have access to any DNA databases, the DNA information obtained may not be very useful. See 'World Database License' on page 27.

Success grants varying knowledge of what happened at this location.
Failure means a new sample will be needed to try again. Each use of the kit takes D10 minutes.

TOOLKIT (INTERROGATION)   400¢
This selection of torture tools and chemicals grants a +2 bonus to interrogation style actions but requires a undesirable level of inhumane cruelty to use.

TOOLKIT (ADVANCED MECHTRONICS)   1,000¢
When using this toolkit you gain +2 to 'Mechtronics' rolls. Other uses for it are listed throughout the book where relevant. These count as 'Advanced Tools' with regard to Fixing Equipment (page 31).

TOOLKIT (MEDICAL)   1,000¢
This toolkit helps anyone using the Medicine skill to heal another. It grants a +2 bonus on his Medicine rolls and if used by someone with the field surgeon training it allows him to heal an extra 2 HP. If better equipment is already available it does not help. The GM should allow it to assist in any appropriate situation.

TOOLKIT (ROBOTICS)   1,500¢
Used to make repairs or to reprogram droids.
Roll 'Intelligence + Cybernetics & Robotics'.
Each point of XS repairs the droid 5 HP and takes takes D10 minutes. You may keep rolling as long as you wish. If you are using the kit to reprogram droids you gain a +2 bonus to your reprogramming roll.

TORCH (LONG CELL)   100¢
A powerful torch with a powerful beam. The battery lasts for 1000 years (approx).

TOXIN FILTER (DISPOSABLE)   200¢   LEVEL 9 FILTER
This small mask filters out all breathable toxins of Potency 9 or lower for 1 scene. It is then discarded. Also see Toxin Purge on page 48. (Counts as a level 9 toxin filter)

TOXIN FILTER (REUSABLE)   2,000¢   LEVEL 10 FILTER
This is a bulky piece of headgear with large pipes leading to a backpack-sized re-breather and intravenous chemical neutraliser which makes the wearer immune to breathable ingested and injected toxins of Potency 10 or less. (Counts as a level 10 toxin filter)

TRACER GUN   1,000¢
This is a Light Firearm which fires a small, adhesive tracer tag. The tag can then be located by use of a small device which is supplied with the gun or any computer system configured to the tag. Configuration requires the user to have 'Computers & A.I.' of 2 or more. The range is 40 miles and the tags cost 100¢ each.

TRANSLATOR   5,000¢
This handheld black box listens to sounds and translates them if applicable. It is crude but you can get by with it. It may be unable to translate regional dialects and has a coarse electronic voice.

VIRAL MODIFIER   2,000¢
This syringe of engineered virus is injected into the face and over a period of one week changes it to a predetermined appearance generated on a computer and coded into the virus. It effectively gives the user a new face which lasts approximately 30 days.

Roll a D100 when the virus is injected.
01-04 No resemblance and utterly deformed
05-10 Poor resemblance
11-20 Reasonable resemblance
21-85 Good resemblance
86-00 Perfect resemblance

This must be acquired on prescription from a licensed doctor who is obliged to inform the UIG (unless heavily bribed).

PROCESS & TASK CHIPS

DATANETICA PROCESS CHIP

PROCESS CHIPS

Process Chips are slotted into the existing Process Sockets on the back of an Agent's skull and allow access to the information stored in the chip. These impart to you the skill held on the chip. They do not stack with your current skill. For example - if you already have Science 3 and get a Science 4 chip you will simply have Science 4 (not 7). One can be fitted at a time and normally takes one hour to impart its information. Once removed the information is forgotten and cannot be recalled with any accuracy. If the chip is re-inserted it takes an hour to assimilate the data as normal.

Process chips contain knowledge and are used by Agents in a manner similar to reference books. If the Agent feels he needs more information on Medicine then he can plug in a Medical Process Chip and he will be able to access information as though mentally leafing through medical books at lightning speed.

Process Chips are fitted into Process Sockets which all Agents have installed as standard. Advanced Process Chip Sockets are also available (see the Cybernetics Section on page 60). Only one chip can be fitted at once unless you have the Dual Process Socket upgrade.

-**Process Sockets** allow the fitting of level 1-5 chips, i.e. Skills from 1 to 5. It takes one hour to access the information after plugging in the chip. Only one chip can be fitted at a time.

-**Advanced Process Sockets** allow the fitting of all process chips (1-10) and allow the information to be used after only 5 minutes. Only one chip can be fitted at a time.

-**Dual Process Sockets** are both considered to be 'Advanced' so effectively you gain 2 Advanced Process Sockets and therefore can use two chips simultaneously.

USING PROCESS CHIPS EARLY

If you use a chip before the information has assimilated properly you will still benefit from it but any doubles rolled relating to the

chip indicate that it has broken irreparably.

TASK CHIPS

Task chips contain information on how to do something very specific, e.g. cooking, picking a particular lock, operating a named computer program, setting a bomb, etc.

In game terms they allow an Agent to do a small subsection of a skill, not have the whole skill.
For example, a task chip could allow you to drive a freight lorry but you would not be able to drive a tank without the skill Drive.

Chips plug into any Process Socket and are ready to use in one hour. (5 minutes with an advanced process socket). When the chip is plugged in you are considered to temporarily gain a specific new skill such as cooking, which you gain at level 10 as long as the chip is plugged in. Only one chip can be fitted at once unless you have the Dual Process Socket upgrade.

To use the information on the task chip simply make a roll on 2D10 and get beneath an appropriate STAT (normally 'Intelligence') added to the 'Task Skill' (10). A damaged or substandard chip could have a lower score than 10.

Example: To use a road map of Tokyo the GM may require you to pass an 'Intelligence + Tokyo Map' check on 2D10. If the Agent has Intelligence 7 he will need to roll below 17 as the task chip is always at 10.

The knowledge lasts until the chip is removed. If re-inserted it will work the same way taking another 5 minutes until ready.

USING TASK CHIPS EARLY

If you use a chip before the information has assimilated properly you will still gain the full benefit but any doubles rolled relating to the chip indicate that it has broken irreparably.

EMP OF CHIPS

Task Chips and Process Chips have an EMPS of 10 but are immune to EMP when not being used.

COST OF PROCESS AND TASK CHIPS

Task Chips cost 2,000¢ each.
Prices could be increased for Chips that impart their information more quickly or have higher EMPS.

PROCESS CHIP COST	
LEVEL	COST
1	2,000¢
2	4,000¢
3	8,000¢
4	20,000¢
5	40,000¢
6	60,000¢
7	80,000¢
8	120,000¢
9	150,000¢
10	200,000¢

EXAMPLE PROCESS CHIPS

Process Chips emulate the basic Agent skills, so to generate process chips simply use the Skills list on the Character Sheet. Telepathic process chips cannot be made with current technology although many believe that the Archons are capable of developing them.

EXAMPLE TASK CHIPS

Task chips cannot allow you to do anything really complex such as building computers from a box of transistors or cybernetic surgery. Instead they would allow you to build a certain make and model of computer from stock parts or perform a specific, basic cybernetic operation. Below are some examples.

Road Map of Tokyo
Basic Cookery
Famous World Landmarks
Getting by in Spanish
Accounting for Home and Office
Fitting the Liberty Black Body Space
Servicing the AMS Black Cougar
War and Peace (the Novel)
Maintaining Handguns
2500 Restaurant Guide
Basic Communication Electronics
Spire Architecture and Layout
Reprogramming Sentinel Droids
The Shi Yukiro and their Tactics
Interactive Map of North America
Disabling the 'Secnet 223' Security System
A guide to Belgian history
Piloting the AMS RF7 Anti Emplacement Jet

RUNNING CHIPS IN A GAME

Process and Task chips allow a number of things to happen in a game. Firstly, and perhaps most importantly, they allow any Agent to go on any mission. For example, imagine a Division needs to sneak into a top security installation, enter a locked room and exit undetected. With a normal Division makeup the group will find this very hard as there will probably be an Agent with no stealth and there is a chance that no-one will have the ability to open locks. By introducing some chips into the mission equipment it suddenly becomes a great deal more feasible.

Another useful property of chips is that although only one or two can be worn at a time, an Agent can collect chips over the course of her missions and store them on her person. She then has an arsenal of skills at her disposal to help her overcome obstacles in missions without them overpowering her or forcing her to spend XP on skills she does not really want her character to have.

Don't give out too many chips of too high a power level or you may annoy those who have bought up their skills with hard earned XP. Chips will never be as good as skills as they take time to integrate with the Agents A.I. and that means they are not good in a reactive situation. As long as you are fair and frugal, chips can really enhance the style factor of the game.

RICHENBACHER
FORGED FOR WAR

VEHICLES

Agents will often find themselves needing transport. Driving vehicles normally uses 'Perception' or 'Agility' + 'Drive' or 'Pilot'. You gain the *Driving Modifier* of the vehicle added to your Action Total to represent the ease of use of different vehicles.

Unless you have the training 'Combat Pilot / Driver' you gain a -4 penalty to your roll if you attempt to use a vehicle and make another action at the same time, e.g. ramming, shooting, climbing out of the vehicle, etc.
If you wish to run vehicle races or chases then consider using the rules for 'opposed competitions' on page 145.

VEHICLE UPGRADES
There are many kinds of vehicles in Corporation utilising different levels of technology. Opposite are some common modifications for vehicles. Many of these upgrades will be fitted as standard to expensive modern vehicles, but are often absent on older or specialist models.

THE LAW AND THE ROAD
The UIG have jurisdiction on the roads although Agents can acquire the 'Traffic License' which allows some control over the transport infrastructure.

FARDRIVE INFORMATION

With the exception of the World View all FarDrive craft are owned and run by the Ai-Jinn. Although the Ai-Jinn are known to use their FarCrafts to mine in far off places, the closest most people will come to a FarCraft is visiting the colonies, Vastaag or a holiday on the World View.

Journey	Duration
Earth to Mars	06 days
Earth to Venus	08 days
Venus to Mars	10 days
Earth to Saturn	14 days
Venus to Saturn	18 days
Earth to Moon	20 hours

FarDrives cannot be used in atmosphere. If the craft is also capable of atmospheric flight a speed is listed in the table opposite. The Ai-Jinn hire out crewed orbital shuttles to take people on private trips across the solar system. This normally costs 100,000 to 1 million credit and is usually discreet.

Now, slides B through G5 are all details of the Shing Lee 'Phoenix' TB-13 heavy P-tank, the workhorse of the Ai-Jinn armoured divisions for the last six years. You will note 309mm of deflective layered armour, shield generators on a delta coverage, double-redundant Spritzhausen engines on a contingency cycle, pressurized cockpit as standard, two Bronsen machine plasmas in these cupolas here and here and this modified 22mm AMS LEAW pattern railgun as main armament. And ladies and gentlemen, let me tell you from personal experience, she's a bitch of a thing to hotwire.

*-from Lectures at New West Point
attr: Col. Jack Danes, Western Federation*

VEHICLE UPGRADES

ANTI GRAVITY MOTORS   2,000¢
These make a land vehicle (not airborne or seaborne) more manoeuvrable by assisting it against the forces of gravity. For every AG Motor fitted the Driving Modifier of the Vehicle is increased by 1. The maximum Driving Modifier a vehicle can have is triple its starting value or 3, whichever is higher.

ARMOUR PLATES   1000¢ EACH
This is the cheapest way to increase the vehicle's defenses. Each plate adds 10 HP and 1 to the AV but every two plates decrease the Driving Modifier by 1. Once the Driving Modifier is -6 or less the vehicle cannot be driven.

AUTODRIVE   5,000¢
The car can be set to drive itself on normal roads. If the safety protocols (see below) are turned off the car can speed, ignore lights or generally drive dangerously if requested by the driver.

CAMOUFLAGE FIELD   1,000¢ PER LEVEL (MAX. LEVEL 10)
This is a holographic field that allows a vehicle up to the size of a large car to increase its chances of not being spotted. Different level fields can be bought and the person trying to spot the vehicle must apply the field level as a penalty to their 'Perception + Observation' roll. It the field is interacted with the effect of the field is decreased or destroyed.

CHIPLOCK   1,000¢
The vehicle can only be opened by the owner swiping their ID chip over the door. This dramatically reduces the chances of vehicle jacking and basic auto theft. Chiplocks are electronic locks. To pick the lock decide on the quality of the Chiplock and consult Opening Locks section on page 19.

CHIPSTART   1,000¢
The vehicle is registered to the user and only by swiping her ID Chip over a reader in the vehicle can it be made to start. If a Chipstart vehicle is already running you can drive it.
The Chipstart can be bypassed by passing a Hacking roll with a modifier based on the owner, i.e. a corporate hovercopter will have a better security system than a Citizen's sedan. See Hacking on page 150.

POLYCHROMIC PAINT   1,000¢
The vehicle can change colour at the click of a button, it can also display logos, decals, sponsors, corporate insignias, rank or designs as you choose.

SAFETY PROTOCOLS   1,000¢
This should be very expensive but is sponsored by the UIG to increase road safety. The car will always drive safely and will not permit dangerous manoeuvres. They can be turned off by the registered user or by passing a Hacking check with a modifier based on the owner of the car, i.e. a UIG-owned car will be more secure than an outcast's motorbike. See Hacking on page 150.

SHIELD (VEHICULAR)   100¢ PER HP OF THE SHIELD
This type of hard ion shield requires a large generator and can thus only be used on vehicles. The effect is to basically give the vehicle more hit points. When the shield has been discharged it is unusable until fully restored. It will slowly recharge at 5HP per round. When all the HPs are restored the pilot will be notified and it will be back on line and usable once more. It otherwise functions as a hard ion shield (see page 46).

TURBO CHARGER   500¢ PER 10% ADDED TO THE VEHICLES SPEED
This can be fitted to a vehicle to make it move faster by altering the engine to be less efficient but more powerful. Each 500¢ spent on the turbo charger increases the speed by 10% to a maximum of an extra 100%. Driving the vehicle over its original top speed decreases its Driving Modifier by 2.

VEHICLE TABLE

Vehicle	The name of the vehicle
HP	The vehicles HP (Hit Points). Indicates how much damage the vehicle can take until it cannot be used. If it is reduced to 0HP or less the vehicle is useless and each round stands a cumulative 10% chance to explode, i.e. 10% on the first round, 20% on the second and so on. Explosion of a vehicle deals 3D10 damage and is a Blast with a radius of vehicle HP / 10 metres, e.g. 40 HP = 4m blast.
AV	Armour Value of the vehicle
MPH	Top speed of the unmodified vehicle (miles per hour). *More about FarDrives can be found on page 56.
DM	Driving Modifier. You gain this to your Drive or Pilot Action Total while using this vehicle.
Cost	The normal cost for a new vehicle.
EMPS	Civilian vehicles have EMPS 22, if affected they simply stop. Military vehicles are immune to EMP.

NOTE THESE VEHICLES ARE ALL BASIC VERSIONS AND CAN BE MODIFIED AS THE GM SEES FIT.

CIVILIAN VEHICLES

VEHICLE	HP	AV	MPH	DM	COST
Articulated Lorry	140	5	100	-4	30,000¢
Car	40	4	180	+0	12,000¢
Yacht	40	2	70	-1	200,000¢
Heli / Hovercopter	50	3	300	+2	50,000¢
Lear Jet	60	3	700	+0	100,000¢
Motorbike	20	3	200	+2	7,000¢
Off Road Vehicle	50	4	200	+1	70,000¢
Speed Boat	20	1	100	+1	50,000¢
Sports Car	35	3	250	+2	40,000¢
Truck	100	5	130	-1	15,000¢
Anti Grav Jet Bike	30	3	230	+3	50,000¢
Van	60	4	140	+0	24,000¢
Submersible	30	4	40	+0	60,000¢
Domestic Shuttle	100	5	800/FarDrive*	+0	500,000¢

MILITARY VEHICLES

VEHICLE	HP	AV	MPH	DM	COST
ARMOURED PERSONNEL CARRIER	100	20	80	-1	400,000¢
8 Sub-machine Lasers, 1 RPG Launcher, 50 HP Shield					
ATTACK HOVERCOPTER	80	10	400	+2	800,000¢
4 RPG Launchers, 2 Laser Cannons					
FIGHTER JET	70	8	1500	+1	900,000¢
4 RPG Launchers, 2 Kinetic Machine Guns					
ORBITAL SHUTTLE	500	15	1000 / FarDrive*	+1	4 Million¢
4 Sub Machine Plasmas, 100 HP Shield					
TANK, LIGHT	200	15	60	-1	800,000¢
1 Plasma Cannon, 2 Machine Guns, 1 Rail Gun, 100 HP Shield					
TANK, HEAVY	400	30	30	-3	1 Million¢
3 Plasma Cannons or 1 Ordnance Plasma, EMP Cannon, 2 Sub-Machine Plasmas, 1 Flame Thrower, 300HP Shield					

CYBERLINS
(CYBERNETIC ELIMINATION UNITS)

These machines were originally built as search and destroy units and were driven by pilots. Nowadays they serve a variety of functions and are controlled in many different ways. The name Cyberlin is still used by the majority of Corporations although some call them by other names such as Bulls, Mechs, Watchmen, Monsters or Tanks.

OVERVIEW

There are four basic classes of Cyberlin but these have been adapted so that there is no limit to the variety of shapes, sizes and models that the machines come in. The basic Cyberlins are Battle Class, Slave Class, Watchdog Class and Ranger Class. Derived classes include Hunter Class, Predator Class, Ruin Class, Ocean Class, Raider Class and Scout Class.

Structurally the Cyberlin is a vast metal hull (normally between 20 and 200 metres high) mounted on two legs which enable it to move around. Where you would expect arms the machines either have weapons or functional tools such as welders and pneumatic grips for carrying out the tasks they were designed for. They do not have a head as such because a driver normally pilots them, although they do possess sensors that allow the pilot to perceive his environment. Occasionally some Cyberlins have been adapted to use caterpillar tracks, four legs or sometimes their metal bodies

have been replaced with open-air platforms on which workers can stand or weapon stations can be mounted. Generally speaking though, they all follow the same pattern. It works.

Cyberlins have been used for numerous functions, the majority related to construction and defence. Most Cyberlin Units are produced by Hong Kong Autometrics and the Shanghai Cyberlin Concern; both are subsidiaries of the Ai-Jinn.

BASIC CYBERLIN COMBAT

Each turn the pilot gets to steer the Cyberlin and fire as many weapon systems as he desires at a single target. (Using 'Perception + Support Weapons'). If he wishes to attack an additional target that round then he can instruct the Cyberlin to do so. The Cyberlin must pass an A.I. check. (Roll equal or below the Cyberlin's A.I. on a D10). If it passes then the Cyberlin can attack the second target using the appropriate Action Total (ranged or close). Some Cyberlin A.I.s are particularly adept and can attack multiple targets. These are often prime candidates for awakening

ORDNANCE WEAPONS & ADVANCED CYBERLIN PILOTING

This book does not contain complete rules for piloting Cyberlins as it is quite advanced and will be covered in a forthcoming supplement. The basics of how to run them are included here, but generally players will not fight them until they are quite advanced.

Cyberlins are often fitted with a category of weapon not commonly found - Ordnance. These weapons have many times the power of heavy weapons and are designed as emplacements but can be fitted to Cyberlins. As a basic template for Ordnance weapons triple the power of a heavy weapon and multiply the price by 5. They count as Support Weapons.

Example Ordnance Weapon

PAN LEE HURRICANE ORDNANCE PLASMA

Type	Ordnance
Dimensions	7.25m length, 600mm dia barrel
Damage	15D10+15 (Ignores Armour)
EMPS	Immune
Cost	60,000 Credits
Range	Long
Rate	1

This enormous weapon is normally fitted to the arm of a Cyberlin that is likely to encounter heavy resistance. It is manufactured by the Pan Lee Reactive Defence Systems exclusively for the Shanghai Cyberlin Concern.

and becoming sentient war machines. If the Pilot has the 'Combat Pilot' training he can make an additional attack with the weapon systems.

The Cyberlin rolls to hit using either the 'Close Action Total' or the 'Ranged Action Total' as appropriate. Battle Class Cyberlins cannot dodge.

EXAMPLE BATTLE CLASS CYBERLIN "DREADNOUGHT"

These terrifying machines are commonly used for guarding important installations and, in times past, full out assaults. They are powerfully armoured and sport an impressive array of weapon systems. Hard Ion Shields are standard and with the exception of the Slave Class, these are the largest of the Cyberlins an Agent is likely to come across. Fast movement, iron defences and hyper-destructive weaponry are the hallmarks of a Battle Class Cyberlin.

WEAPON SYSTEMS
2 Plasma Cannons or 1 Ordnance Plasma
4 Sub Machine Plasmas
2 Rocket Launchers (all rocket types present)
1 EMP cannon or 1 Ordnance EMP
2 Charged Fists - Strength+10 damage each (60)

NON-WEAPON SYSTEMS
Sensor Array	
Shield	1000HP
Locomotion Systems	Bipedal
Top Speed	40 mph
Height	95 metres
Cost	20 million Credits
Armour Value	25
Hit Points	1500
Perception	10
Close Action Total	16
Ranged Action Total	22
A.I.	9
Driving Modifier	+0
Strength	50

Battle Class Cyberlins heal 20 HP a round due to Nanite Repair Systems.

Those who fear a second scorching of the Earth tend to forget that we are now a planet governed by Corporate entities – economically motivated groups whose web of interdependent financial and industrial links are a hundred times more complex than the interactions of the petty businesses or nation-states of the late twentieth century. Moreover, the Corporations have already seen the disastrous results of deploying weapons of maximum potency. Each Corporation has its area of expertise and, although there is fiscal conflict on a daily basis as each struggles to acquire pieces of the others' markets, none would dream of total annihilation of another because of the proven adverse economic impact this would have on a global scale. Remember that the major world powers of the day have (to varying degrees) all but subsumed nationalist, religious and territorial motivations into the single overriding expedient of the flow of revenue, and that although physical combat remains a fact of life, the level of weaponry is restricted by a sort of unspoken inter-Corporate accord to what will not cause lasting economic damage across the board.

Cyberlins represent the very limit of 'acceptable' weaponry deployed on modern battlefields. Their destructive potential is easily equal to some of the more savage technology of the late second millennium, but their unique design allows for that power to be carefully contained and focused; the scalpel as opposed to the hammer. And yet each Corporation continuously modifies its Cyberlins, month by month and year by year, keeping the vast bulk of these mechanical ogres carefully hidden in fortified garages and hangars across the globe. Recent advances in both artificial intelligence and compact ordnance technologies have made the future evolution of the Cyberlins a frightening prospect indeed.

- from The Rise of The Corporation-States
attr: Dr. Edmond Treval

It came striding across the Thenika desert at midnight, its hull a blade of sharpened moonlight, its four legs great spears of gleaming metal. The delicacy of its hundred-ton footfalls, product of countless contrary actuators and dampers, was the skittering caution of a prowling silver insect. Weapons slung beneath its carapace clicked and whirred and whined in readiness as the thing ate up the miles between itself and the crashdown site of the unauthorized landing craft. Somewhere in that giant, glittering, crabbed shape was a pilot, a tiny kernel of humanity and fallible flesh, but from the outside nothing was visible but the machine, a living, thinking engine of terror and destruction.

SECTION 3
CYBERNETICS

EQUIPMENT CANNOT LIGHTLY
BE DISCARDED ONCE IT HAS
BEEN TAKEN UP.

MACHINE PURITY LEAVES ITS
MARK ON FLESH, FLESH FAILS,
TECHNOLOGY EVOLVES FURTHER
TOWARDS THE PINNACLE.

THOSE WHO WOULD USE THE
MACHINE WITHOUT ACCEPTING
IT ARE GUILTY OF HERESY.

TEAR THE MACHINE FROM THEIR
HANDS, FROM THEIR BODIES,
FROM THEIR BRAINS.

-ATTR: LEVIATHAN, CHIMERA
PROPHET OF THE CULT OF
MACHINA

Torn Light - Chimera War Master of the Cult of Machina

There comes a time in every Agent's life when normal flesh and blood is not enough. Where do you turn? Cybernetics. A fusion of biology, electronics and mechanics to create a whole greater than the sum of its parts. All Agents can have Cybernetics fitted and technology being the way it is, there is very little reason not to.
The UIG have conducted extensive research and results indicate that the elusive aspect of the psyche which makes us 'human' has nothing to do with the amount of metal in a person's body. Studies have shown no link between cybernetic installation and degradation of 'humanity'; on the contrary, those with cybernetic upgrades are often more assured of themselves and less likely to indulge in sadistic behaviour.

82% of brutal crime in 2495 was committed by outcasts and outlaws, both are groups with limited access to cybernetics. So in the words of the UIG - "Install cybernetics, what could go wrong?"

SYSTEM NOTES
Cybernetics *can* take your STATS above 10
Cybernetics all have EMPS 25.

BUYING AND FITTING CYBERNETICS

Cybernetics require no license to use but the installer must have a Cyberneticists License and both the Cybernetics & Robotics and Medicine skills. The installation cost is included in the prices listed but if you need a separate installation cost it is normally 10% of the listed cybernetics price. If fitting your own cybernetics, you save the 10% installation cost.
For example, if you wanted a Range Targeter (new cost 4000¢) and wanted to fit it yourself it would only cost you 3600¢.

LOW QUALITY CYBERNETICS

Cybernetics in condition 9 or less are illegal to fit. If they are fitted, then at the beginning of each gaming session the player makes a single roll for each piece of substandard cybernetics he owns.

Check the condition of the cybernetics on the table below, read across and find the *% chance of failure* this session. Then roll a D100, if you get below or equal the stated percentage, the cybernetics have malfunctioned. Otherwise they are fine until next session. The GM can make this roll in secret if desired.

MALFUNCTIONING CYBERNETICS

If the cybernetics have malfunctioned then they cease to work to their full potential for the session giving no benefits to the wearer

LOW QUALITY CYBERNETICS

CONDITION	% CHANCE OF FAILURE
10	00%
9	10%
8	20%
7	30%
6	40%
5	50%
4	60%
3	70%
2	80%
1	90%

and reducing her to a state as though the upgrade had never been fitted. The part will still function on a basic level but it's special qualities will be lost. To fix the part its condition must be increased by at least one level (see Increasing the Condition of Cybernetics below).
If the cybernetics malfunctioned from being low quality and the roll was a double, the cybernetic upgrade is rejected from the body and becomes inert. It will need to be removed, thrown away and a totally new one fitted. This could cause major problems if it is a cardiovascular or skeletal component.

INCREASING THE CONDITION OF CYBERNETICS

Cybernetics can have their condition increased by paying a cyberneticist 20% of their new cost per condition level. Another player can do the repair which reduces the cost to 10%. In this case the player must pass an 'Intelligence + Cybernetics & Robotics' check with the penalties from the table above. Increasing the condition is always considered complex. The money is spent

FITTING CYBERNETICS SUMMARY

Legally you require a Cyberneticists License.

You need a certain level of skill depending upon the operation. This is not compulsory but if you don't have the right skill you suffer -5 for each prerequisite you do not meet.

SIMPLE OPERATIONS REQUIRE
'Cybernetics & Robotics' & 'Medicine' 1-5

COMPLEX OPERATIONS REQUIRE
'Cybernetics & Robotics' & 'Medicine' 6-10

If you have the correct skills at the correct level and a cybernetics lab then fitting is automatic and no roll is needed, unless the GM decides circumstances demand one.

If not, roll **'Intelligence + Cybernetics & Robotics'** with all applicable modifiers from below added.

Equipment	Modifier
Advanced Cybernetics Lab	+4
Standard Cybernetics Lab	+2
Poor Cybernetics Lab	+0
Cybernetics Toolkit Only	-2
Crude Tools	-4
Insufficient Cybernetics & Robotics	-5
Insufficient Medicine Skill	-5
No Lab, No Tools	-8

Success
Cybernetics are fitted successfully.

Failure
Process is unsuccessful, the installation money is wasted and must be paid again for another attempt.

Critical Fail
The Cybernetics break irreparably and new parts must be acquired.

on the spare parts needed which must be available to the cyberneticist. Therefore this kind in work in the field is often tricky.

MAINTAINING CYBERNETICS

At reasonable intervals (say every 7-15 sessions) the GM can ask for cybernetic maintenance. Anyone with cybernetics has to pay 10% of the total value of their cybernetic upgrades or the condition of that item deteriorates by 1. (See Low Quality Cybernetics on page 62.) This should not be overused but it should not be neglected, especially after missions involving a lot of combat or after Agents have taken heavy damage. An 'Intelligence + Cybernetics & Robotics' check with a modifier from the table on page 62 reduces the maintenance cost to 5%.

The players may find it handy to write down a running total of their cybernetic's value somewhere on their character sheets.

CYBERNETICS AND EMP

Cybernetics have an EMPS of 25, cybernetics that are knocked out by EMP become inert as described in *Malfunctioning Cybernetics* (page 62) and also lose 1 condition level. The process for fixing them is the same as for *Increasing the Condition of Cybernetics*.

WHY NOT TO USE CYBERNETICS.

Cybernetics do not have any innate physiological disadvantages and there is no loss of humanity or cognition when large amounts of upgrades are fitted. The disadvantages are more subtle yet quite tangible and can have a profound effect on Agents. For example all cybernetic upgrades must be registered on the wearer's ID chip, meaning that it can be extremely hard to hide who you are during convert missions. Word can quickly spread that a hotel guest is 90% machine and this can attract the attention of undesirables such as the Cult of Machina (see page 192).

Those with cybernetics tend to move differently, their motions are less fluid and more mechanical. Hiding your cybernetic nature can become harder as you give over to the machine which can make deep cover missions or infiltration more difficult. It should also be noted that cybernetics can be affected by EMP and may breakdown as well as needing occasional expensive maintenance.

Other disadvantages which are more related to roleplaying your character could take the form of hissing servos, twitchy muscles, excessive appetite, an uncontrollably powerful grip, etc.

The fourth Tansley team wishes to report findings contrary to those of the UIG research paper, Effects of Cybernetics on the Human Psyche, published 10.31.2495. It is our contention that almost all commercially available bio-electro-mechanical performance enhancers share a theoretical vulnerability, via their standard nerve-impulse links to the human brainstem, to outside electronic interference. At the time of writing, to the best of our knowledge, there is no communications technology anywhere in the world sufficiently advanced to actually grant external control over implanted cybernetics, but this does not mean that no such technology will ever be conceived. We urge that further studies be pursued in this area and, in the meantime, that cautionary notices be issued discreetly to all UIG personnel.

UIG internal report RD2231B/281
[SUPRESSED 3.22.2496, /unknownadmin]

GUIDE TO THE CYBERNETICS CATALOGUE

At the bottom of the page are listed some of the most commonly available cybernetic upgrades. These can be purchased via the Corporation and include the 10% installation fee. Illegal cybernetics exist but these can be very hard to find and install.

NAME	SECTOR
Reaver	Structural / Aggressive
Anascan	Optical / Sensory
Datanetica	Storage / Data Processing
Krieg	Fashion / Cosmetic
Gemini	Bioware
Liberty Black	Covert / Black Ops

SIMPLE - Requires a cyberneticist with Cybernetics & Robotics and Medicine of 1-5 to install.
COMPLEX - Requires a cyberneticist with Cybernetics & Robotics and Medicine of 6-10 to install.
TIME - The duration of the operation including recovery time.
COST - This is the cost for the cybernetics and installation. 10% of this figure is for installation and is included.

QUICK CYBERNETICS LISTING

Anascan Primary Sensory Enhancement
Anascan 'Eternity' Recorder
Anascan Midnight Vision System
Anascan Range Targeter
Anascan Reticle Eye
Anascan Telemetric Vision
Anascan Thermal Imaging System
Datanetica Advanced Process Chip
Socket
Datanetica Cerebral Link
Datanetica Internal Translator
Datanetica Storage Drive
Datanetica Dual Process Sockets

Datanetica Neural Jack
Gemini Bio-Lynx Modified Teeth
Gemini Bioware Fibroctin Nerve System
Gemini Bioware Myotic Restructuring
Gemini Cardiomechanics
Gemini Digital Injector
Gemini Stealthskin
Gemini Toughskin
Gemini Videoskin
Krieg 'Mystique'
Krieg Facial Reconstruction
Krieg Ocular Repigmentation
Krieg Voice Synth

Liberty Black Body Space
Liberty Black Flat Hands
Liberty Black Palm Thorns
Liberty Black Switchprints
Liberty Black AMS Wrist Pistol
Reaver AS2000 Alloy Skull
Reaver Arm Defenders
Reaver Bodyplates
Reaver Cybertech AS3000 Alloy Skeleton
Reaver Cybertech Plasma Blades
Reaver Dermal Aggressors
Reaver DX4 Cybernetic Arm
Reaver DX7 Cybernetic Leg

See Machines of War for a Complete listing of all cybernetics in the game so far.

ANASCAN
OPTICAL TECHNOLOGIES

Anascan is the world leader in Cyberoptic technology. Visit our fabrication plant in Jamaica and get some eyes you can believe in.

ANASCAN PRIMARY SENSORY ENHANCEMENT (PSE)

Installation   Complex, 5 Hours
Cost   5,000¢

The visual, aural and olfactory centres of the brain and optic nerves are modified to receive and carry more complex signals which are then routed through a processor. The information received by the ears, nose and eyes can then be interpreted in numerous different ways. The PSE is a requirement of many other sensory upgrades.

Effect
+1 Perception
Allows other Optical Upgrades.

ANASCAN 'ETERNITY' RECORDER

Installation   Simple, 30 Minutes
Cost   3000¢
Prerequisite   Anascan Primary Sensory Enhancement

This device, which is connected to the Anascan PSE, records a week of high resolution video and audio footage through the eyes and ears. It can be played back wirelessly to normal visual displays within 20 metres. The Agent can mentally leaf through his recordings though it takes an hour to scan a days footage. The device can be turned on and off at will.

ANASCAN MIDNIGHT VISION SYSTEM

Installation   Simple, 30 Minutes
Cost   1000¢
Prerequisite   Anascan Primary Sensory Enhancement

A 0 lux image interpreter is fitted to the existing optical upgrade. This allows the user to see in pitch darkness and is activated as a free action.

ANASCAN RANGE TARGETER

Installation   Simple, 1 Hour
Cost   4,000¢
Prerequisite   Anascan Reticle Eye

This is an optical upgrade that places a trajectory arc over the vision allowing Agents to throw items with increased accuracy.

Effect
Grants a +2 bonus to all rolls involving throwing, e.g. throwing knives and grenades.

ANASCAN RETICLE EYE

Installation   Complex, 6 Hours
Cost   7,000¢

A synthetic eyeball is fitted to the patient with a targeting reticle; he can shoot far more accurately as a result but only when using a gun which has been modified to work with the reticle. Modifying the gun requires an upgrade which cost 500¢ and can be done by anyone with Mechtronics 2 or more. The gun's EMPS decreases by 1. If immune it gain EMPS 15.

Effect
+2 to hit with all ranged weapons as long as they are modified.

ANASCAN TELEMETRIC VISION

Installation   Complex, 5 Hours
Cost   4,000¢

A composite lens replaces the convectional one in the eye. The lens can shift between a large range of focal length allowing the user to see in microscopic and telescopic vision.

Effect
+1 Perception
This upgrade can be fitted once for each eye for a total of + Perception. Each operation costs 4,000¢

ANASCAN THERMAL IMAGING SYSTEM

Installation   Simple, 30 Minutes
Cost   1000¢
Prerequisite   Anascan Primary Sensory Enhancement

This is a small black box upgrade which adds a thermal interpreter to the PSE, the end result being the user can see in perfectly in thermal images. This assists in the dark, seeing

DATANETICA
Reliable Field Processing

DATANETICA HAS EVERYTHING YOU NEED TO ENSURE TOTAL INFORMATION ASSIMILATION AND RETAINMENT. FROM BASIC SOCKET EXPANSIONS TO CEREBRAL LINKS, DATANETICA ENSURES THAT YOU WILL NOT BE INFO-COMPROMISED.

DATANETICA ADVANCED PROCESS CHIP SOCKET

Installation	Complex, 2 Days
Cost	10,000¢

The existing Process Socket is modified to incorporate a series of hardware upgrades. This enables the socket to accept advanced process chips. The existing electro-neural connections are retained and re-used making this process more cost effective than the fitting of the initial process chip socket.

Effect
User can use *Advanced Process Chips*.

DATANETICA CEREBRAL LINK

Installation	Complex, 1 Day
Cost	15,000¢

This system passes neural signals from the brain to the body over a distance of up to 30 metres. This means the head can be severed and the Agent can still act as long as the head is 30 metres or less away. The head is fitted with oxygenators and nourishers so it stays alive for 48 hours without the body. If the head is not rescued and maintained within 48 hours, it dies. If the body is lost the head can be fitted to another body. This upgrade is also known as the 'Wireless / Bluetooth Head'. Many Agents have this upgrade in preparation for Shi Yukiro Head Hunters.
Note that if the head is attached to another body then Standard Agent upgrades will be lost, it is up to the Corporation whether new ones are issued.

Effect
If the head is reattached to the original body using Compound H (see page 50) within 48 hours, no physical or mental loss occurs. If the head is attached to a new body STR, AGI, REF & END are reduced to 5 due to the physiological shock. They must be increased with XP as normal unless recuperation drugs are taken.

Recuperation Drugs (1500¢)
If a new body is used and the drugs are taken within 1 month, the Agent's STATS will return to their original scores within a week. The Drugs also cause the body to regrow according to the DNA in the Agents head and resemble his old body within a month.

DATANETICA INTERNAL TRANSLATOR

Installation	Simple, 1 Hour
Cost	5,000¢

This is a small chip which is injected into the jawbone near the Sub Vocal Communicator. It subvocally translates any foreign language heard into the user's language so they can understand. If the user also has a *Krieg Voice Synth* then they will be able to speak back and the chip will translate. This system integrates with the voice synth allowing the speaker to use foreign languages in conjunction with copied voices.

DATANETICA STORAGE DRIVE

Installation	Complex, 2 Days
Cost	7,000¢

This is a data storage drive which is fitted into the chest cavity of an Agent. It can store almost unlimited amounts of standard data. Downloading a Corporation's personnel and work database may fill it to capacity though and would take a great deal of time. The drive is well protected and the data can be placed on it and removed from it via a wireless link or conventional X-PIN socket. It can be connected to the *Anascan Eternity Recorder* to store 50 weeks of audio visual data. Considered a 'SECURE' system for hacking purposes.

DATANETICA DUAL PROCESS SOCKETS

Installation	Complex, 10 Hours
Cost	14,000¢
Requires	Advanced Process Socket, Intelligence 8

This operation can only be performed on a suitably intelligent individual who already has an advanced process socket. A second advanced process socket is inserted parallel to the first allowing the fitting of two process or task chips at once. Benefits are gained from each.

DATANETICA NEURAL JACK

Installation	Complex, 10 Hours
Cost	25,000¢
Requires	Any Process Socket, Computers & A.I. 5

An extendable digitally compatible X-PIN socket is fitted to the Process Socket which can be ported directly into computer systems. The wearer must pull a thin lead out of the process socket and plug it into the host computer.
For an extra 1000¢ a small connector is fitted to the body, normally to the finger or on a lead connecting to the arm. This connector has the standard X-Pin socket and can be used to jack into computer systems instead of plugging in through the head, a simple convenience. Wireless links are not suitable for this level of data transfer and are easy to hack. Having your brain hacked is undesirable.

Effect
When hardwired into a computer system the user gains +4 to his 'Computers & A.I.' rolls and takes half the time to complete a hacking roll (30 seconds instead of a minute see page 150)
User can port directly into mind controlled devices such as advanced vehicles, Cyberlins and neuro-controlled weapons.

GEMINI BIO-LYNX MODIFIED TEETH

Installation	Simple, 10 Hours
Cost	4,000¢

The patient's teeth are all removed and his jaw unlocked from the cranium. A set of hardened, sharpened, alloy teeth are then installed into the mouth. The teeth are normally similar to the original ones but because of the jaw dislocation larger, more offensive ones can be fitted. The teeth can be re-coloured if desired.

OPTION 1

Cutters: They look normal but incorporate a powerful servo and can be used as bolt cutters to shear through most materials up to 3 cm thick as long as the person can bite the object in question. For example, they could be used as bolt cutters to enter a compound or to bite through handcuffs.

Effect

If the material is very hard a 'Strength + Athletics' check can be made to bite through anything that can be fitted into the mouth with an AV of less than 10. AV 10 or more cannot be bitten through.

OPTION 2

Wolf Jaw: These upgrades do not appear normal; they incorporate sharpened canine teeth which curve down from the mouth. They are obvious and intimidating. Many Agents will not install them as the wearer's voice becomes less understandable and has more of a hiss due to the teeth obstructing the mouth.

Effect

Wolf Jaws can be used to make a close combat attack which deals D4 + Half strength, this is done in addition to any other close combat attacks made each round. Wearer gains +1 Attitude but will more than likely be a social outcast.

GEMINI BIOWARE FIBROCTIN NERVE SYSTEM

Installation	Complex, 1 Day
Cost	5,000¢

The nerve system of the patient is bolstered with a synthetic substance called Fibroctin, this chemical speeds up nervous transmission allowing the target to react faster than he normally could. You can have this operation done a total of 3 times, each subsequent operation after the first costs 5000¢ and increases your Reflexes by one point.

Effect

+1 Reflexes each time the operation is performed to a maximum of +3.

GEMINI BIOWARE MYOTIC RESTRUCTURING

Installation	Complex, 1 Day
Cost	5,000¢

The patient's muscles are repeatedly scorched with a laser and healed with an accelerant. This repeated process causes the muscles to enlarge significantly. You can have this operation done a total of 3 times, each subsequent operation after the first costs 5000¢ and increases your strength by one point.

Effect

+1 Strength each time the operation is conducted to a maximum of +3. You must have an Alloy Skeleton fitted to use this procedure to take your total strength above 11.

GEMINI CARDIOMECHANICS

Installation	Complex, 2 Days
Cost	10,000¢

The cardiovascular system is removed and replaced with a synth one made up of ageless culture-grown tissue and cybern components. The CV system is refined and optimised for maxim efficiency. You can have this operation done a total of 3 times, e subsequent operation after the first costs 5000¢ and increases Endurance by one point and increases the level of the toxin filter point.

Effect

+1 Endurance each time the operation is performed to a maximu +3

Initially contains a Level 6 Internal Toxin Filter

GEMINI DIGITAL INJECTOR

Installation	Simple, 3 Hours
Cost	5,000¢

A syringe containing a substance of the wearer's choice is loaded one of the fingers. It can be extended at will and the wearer can m a close combat attack to try to inject someone with the substance. syringe can easily be refilled.

GEMINI STEALTHSKIN

Installation	Simple, 1 Hour
Cost	4,000¢

The skin is impregnated with polychromotophores (colour chan cells) which the user can make change colour to suit his environm The changes are controlled by conscious decision and inte visualisation. The new skin appears slightly synthetic and anaem it's natural state. Accurate detail cannot be rendered on the skin.

Effect

The user gains +4 to Stealth checks.

GEMINI TOUGHSKIN

Installation	Simple, 1 Hour
Cost	5,000¢

The skin is injected with a dermal hardener; it becomes tough brittle at first but is then treated with an iridium suspension whic absorbed by the dry tissue. The skin takes on a slightly darker hue is considerably tougher.

Effect

+1 AV

This operation can be repeated once for a total of +2 AV.

GEMINI VIDEOSKIN

Installation	Complex, 10 Hours
Cost	15,000¢

The patient's skin is impregnated with electronically contro chromatophores (colour changing cells) which can be coordinated regulated by a computer or PDA carried with the user. The skin w just like a computer monitor allowing images, tattoos, videos, col or animations to be displayed on the skin. This can be used as a s statement, for intimidation or for more tactical purposes. WF celeb Agents often use it to display sponsorship logos or wellbe messages.

Effect

+1 Presence. Additionally by customising what appears on the you may also have any one of the following effects active at a time Looking Good, +2 Attitude or +2 Stealth.

Krieg 'Mystique' Electro-Cosmetics

Installation	Simple, 4 Hours
Cost	1,000¢

The face and hands are injected with a polychromatic dye which responds to electrical signals. The end result is that the user can use a coded stylus to bring make up to the surface of their skin. Nails, blusher, eye shadow and lipstick can all be changed with a tap of the stylus. Pre-programmed schemes can be purchased from boutiques which allow the wearer to show particular styles.

Effect

+1 Looking Good.

Krieg Facial Reconstruction

Installation	Complex, 10 Hours
Cost	4,000¢

"Don't settle for what you were born with."

The face is lifted off and the muscle and bone structure dramatically rebuilt. The face is then replaced and re-coloured using dermal dyes. The end result is a totally different appearance of your choice.

Krieg Ocular Repigmentation

Installation	Simple, 1 Hour
Cost	1000¢

The eye colour of the patient is changed to anything she desires. Striking colours can be used and phosphorescence can be added for impact. The operation can be done twice to give both effects if desired.

Effect

If striking colours are used the user gain +1 Looking Good
If phosphorescence is used the user gains +1 Attitude

Krieg Voice Synth

Installation	Complex, 1 Day
Cost	·6,000¢

A vocal manipulator is fitted to the voice box of the patient. The patient can perform a flawless copy of any voice or noise (up to shouting volume) he has heard and stored. Anyone hearing the voice will need to pick out inconsistencies in the cadence of the false speech to work out it is a hoax. The unit can store 4 sound profiles on its own. With a Datanetica Storage Drive fitted the number of profiles is effectively unlimited. This can be combined with the *Datanetica Internal Translator* to allow the user to speak fluently in foreign languages.

> *Consumer fashion is a market force that has existed for more than a millennium and now, as ever, remains a vastly lucrative exercise in total subjectivity. Since gross and subtle alterations of the basic human form itself have become de rigueur, though, the industry is experiencing diversity on a new scale, with a concomitant rise in profits. The work of some designers at the dawn of the twenty-sixth century is the stuff of dreams; the work of others, the stuff of nightmares.*
>
> *-attr: Anton Graves, market analyst*

LIBERTY BLACK

LIBERTY BLACK HAVE ALWAYS OFFERED A COMPREHENSIVE RANGE OF BLACK OPS CYBERWARE FOR THE DEMANDING USER. WE PRID[E]
OURSELVES ON OUR DISCRETION AND SERVICE.
YOU CAN'T BUY LIBERTY BLACK IN THE SHOPS SO EITHER CALL US ON COMM. LB12 OR VISIT OUR CONSUMER ORIENTATED RUSSIA[N]
FAB PLANT IN MINSK. DON'T WORRY, OUR ON-SITE SATBLANKET ENSURES THAT YOUR ANONYMITY WILL BE MAINTAINED.

LIBERTY BLACK BODY SPACE

Installation   Simple, 7 Hours
Cost   3,000¢

A compartment is built into the chest cavity large enough to hold a small object such as a pistol, explosive device, PDA or canister of toxin. A total of 2 Body Spaces can be fitted.

Effect

There is a -10 / 50% modifier to any rolls which involve finding the body space.

LIBERTY BLACK FLAT HANDS

Installation   Complex, 4 Hours
Cost   6,000¢ for both hands

The patient's hand bones are fitted with numerous small electromagnetic hinges, at any time the wearer can cause one or both hands to collapse. During this time he can hold nothing and do very little with the collapsed hand(s). He can easily pull them out of any restraints or tight grips and slide them into tiny spaces.

Effect

+10 to escaping restraints and similar activities.

LIBERTY BLACK PALM THORNS

Installation   Simple, 4 Hours
Cost   4,000¢

Subdermal keratin thorns are implanted into the palms which can extend at the user's will. They deal +1 unarmed combat damage and grant the user +4 to climbing rolls.

LIBERTY BLACK SWITCHPRINTS

Installation   Simple, 3 Hours, Illegal
Cost   4,000¢

The fingerprints of the patient are removed and a new set place[d] on, the new synthetic prints have the ability to switch between sets of nondescript prints and a third set which is completely plain i.e, no ridges, just a flat print.

LIBERTY BLACK AMS WRIST PISTOL

Installation   Complex, 5 Hours
Cost   3,000¢ + the price of the pistol

A pistol (light firearm) of your choice is deconstructed and covert[ly] mounted into the wrist. There is only enough ammunition for [?] shots before the clip must be reloaded. (3 shot clips are the sam[e] price as normal ones due to the miniaturisation.) No modifier[s] apply to the roll and anyone or anything attempting to find th[e] pistol suffers a -10 penalty to their roll.

Effect

There is a -10 / 50% modifier to any rolls which involve finding th[e] wrist pistol.

> "Ever since I found Liberty Black I haven't been incarcerated once. Hell, I haven't even been arrested."
>
> Jake van Einan, car booster & wheelman

CAN YOU HELP US?

Liberty Black has a number of part time positions open to adventurous, broad-minded individuals and groups. As part of our ongoing research program we are looking for motivated parties to field-test prototype black-ops cyberware. Duties will range from allowing our technicians to install untested wetware and bio-augments, to taking these upgrades into the field and testing their reliability and practicality. Liberty Black will be responsible for deciding the nature, objective and location of these field tests.
All responses will be considered although the successful applicant will likely be part of an experienced Corporate Division who are looking for a challenging and rewarding way to spend their time off. Comm. LB12

REAVER CYBERTECH

COMBAT CYBERNETICS

REAVER AS2000 ALLOY SKULL

Installation	Complex, 2 Days
Cost	10,000¢

The patient's skull is replaced with a stronger, tougher alloy skull which can withstand higher impacts and contains a cerebral cushioning system to reduce brain trauma during cranial shock.

Effect
+3 HP, +1 AV

REAVER ARM DEFENDERS

Installation	Simple, 1 Hour
Cost	3,000¢

These are strong alloy plates fitted across the forearms in pairs. Biological or cybernetic arms are suitable substrates. They reinforce the arms and count as a blocking weapon in close combat. This means the wearer does not lose his *Defence* when unarmed in close combat against an armed opponent.

Effect
+1 AV, you keep your *Defence* in unarmed close combat.

REAVER BODYPLATES

Installation	Simple, 5 Hours
Cost	1,000¢ each

Lightweight alloy plates are placed under the skin as internal armour. They are effective but awkward.

Effect
You can attach up to four plates with each granting a +1 to Armour Value. Once you have four plates fitted no more can be installed. Every two plates gives you -1 Agility.

Note that naninium body plates count towards your total of four body plates. (see Machines of War / Eastern Bank).

REAVER CYBERTECH AS3000 ALLOY SKELETON

Installation	Complex 4 Days
Cost	18,000¢

The patient's calcium based skeleton is removed and replaced with a synthetic alloy one. Numerous biomodifications are made to ensure the new skeleton replaces the old one in every manner. The new frame is as light as the original but much stronger and allows the body to apply and resist greater force, for example, the patient can upgrade her muscles more if she has an alloy skeleton. Does not include a skull. See AS2000 Alloy Skull above.

Effect
+10 Hit Points, +1 Armour Value.

REAVER CYBERTECH PLASMA BLADES

Installation	Simple, 4 Hours
Cost	15,000¢

Small plasma blades are fitted into the patient's hands which can be extended as a free action.

Effect
These blades add +2 damage to close combat attacks and cause such attacks to ignore 4 points of AV. When extended, the user gains penalties to rolls involving manual dexterity (GM's decision). Requires the Powered Melee License.

REAVER DERMAL AGGRESSORS

Installation	Complex, 10 Hours
Cost	6,000¢

Numerous retractable blades and spikes are embedded into the skin and subcutaneous tissue. These can be triggered to extend on the user's command. Anyone attacking the user with unarmed attacks takes 2 points of damage each time they attempt a strike. Anyone struggling or wrestling with the wearer takes D6 damage a round.

REAVER DX4 CYBERNETIC ARM

Installation	Simple, 4 Hours
Cost	10,000¢ each

This enhances the patient's arms with a cybernetic modification. The new arm is stronger than a normal arm and is effective in close combat. A total of two Cybernetic Arms can be fitted.

Effect
+1 Strength
+2 to unarmed strike damage with the Cybernetic Arm. This stacks with the +2 damage from the Cybernetic leg.
A second Cybernetic Arm adds +1 Strength but has no special effect on unarmed strike damage.

REAVER DX7 CYBERNETIC LEG

Installation	Simple, 5 Hours
Cost	10,000¢ each

This replaces a lost leg or can replace an existing one for better performance. The new leg is tireless and strong. Two can be fitted at once.

Effect
+1 Agility
+2 unarmed strike damage with the Cybernetic Leg. This stacks with the +2 damage from the Cybernetic Arm. A second Cybernetic Leg adds +1 Strength but has no special effect on unarmed strike damage.

AMS

ORBITAL WEAPONS STORE

PLEASE INSERT YOUR CREDIT CHIP IN THE SLOT TO THE LEFT AND USE
THE NAVIGATOR BELOW TO SELECT YOUR PRODUCT.
ALL PURCHASES COME WITH A 3 YEAR GUARENTEE.

AMS
M-4K

ANZEIGER MILITARY SYSTEMS

AMS HAVOC M-4K
KINETIC MACHINE PISTOL

AMMUNITION	SMART CLIPS
ENP	IMMUNE
PRICE	1,500 CREDITS
LICENSE	LIGHT FIREARMS
PARTS ORDER CODE: AMS M4KH 0.1	

AMS HAVOC

REQUEST AN
ATTENDANT

It's a funny thing, but in the Corporate climate of the day, casually worn armaments have become so commonplace as to take on some of the nuances of status symbols. A stockbroker might carry a chrome pistol he's never fired, because the rest of the boys on the floor are all packing so he'd not be seen dead without his own piece. Marketing types tend to favour lasers for the son et lumiere thing – go figure. Even the accountants usually wear little derringers these days, though popular legend suggests this is just so they can shoot themselves if work gets really boring.

On the other hand, Agents don't usually bother with whether or not their hardware is in for the season; they're more given to prosaic concerns like how many people they can kill before they have to reload. I prefer dealing with them, in some ways – they're a lot more down to earth than the rest of the Corporate schmoes. Plus they tend to spend more on ammo.

Attr. - Thomas Wong, proprietor
Peking Tom's Easy Guns.

There's a lotta guns on the streets today, some good, some not so good. My name's Colonel Jacob Shaw, Federation Agent for 35 years and if you'll indulge me, I've got a few pieces here today which I'd like to show you. Don't worry folks, there's plenty for everyone and right now, today only, I'm gonna give you all the famous Federation discount. Yep, 10% off any light, tactical or heavy firearms purchased here and if that sounds too good to be true, I'm throwing a box of armour piercers in with every kinetic. Hold it kids, there's more. If you spend over 1000¢ we'll even ship right to your door for free. First up, lets take a look at an old favourite, the AMS Black Cougar. I guess a lot of you folks could break one of these down while hog-tied in trashcan. Let's look at the latest model, the AMS BC 3.4 Semi-Automatic 12mm Kinetic Pistol. It's strong, reliable, powerful and of course - electropulse resistant. Peace of mind for 350¢. Add in your famous Federation discount, your carry case, cleaning tools, a free box of AP's and of course, your 5 years field service guarantee and you're lookin' at a weapon your mother would proud to discharge in public.

Next we have the Agent's friend. This piece of hardware was designed right here in Fort Worth by Lieutenant Jessy Bernstein. I present the AMS Bloodstorm T28 Tactical Sub-Machine Plasma. Oh yes, I know what your all thinking, and yes, we have plenty in stock! This weapon was originally designed as a mid-range assault weapon during the Third Asian Land War when the Ai-Jinn ground-pounders were wrapped up in so much armour, traditional weapons failed to cut the mustard. It's got 2 plasma sub-chambers, each able to charge and discharge once a second tearing right though any armour your target is dumb enough to wear. End result - a goddam bloodstorm. I've used a Bloodstorm since I could afford one and never looked back. Today we're letting you have them for 14,500¢, that includes the carry case, the cleaning kit, 6 spare induction coils for the plasma chambers and a 20% discount to attend a UIG Tac Weapons Training Course.
Next on the rack the AMS M50 Belt-Fed Support weapon, yeehaa!

Attr. - Colonel Jacob Shaw, Western Federation Sales, Fort Worth Arms Expo 2495

SECTION 4
TELEPATHICS

Nothing is impossible for the strong in faith. So it has always been, so it will always be. And now there is incontrovertible physical proof to support this age-old maxim. How can those who do not believe maintain their cynicism in the face of the evidence?

-Temur Yeke, Revelations of the Second Age

HOW ARE TELEPATHICS POSSIBLE?

The mind is an organ and like a muscle is capable of altering forces. When you stand near another person and blow air at them they can feel it, if you were bigger and stronger you could blow air harder and faster. Were you the size of a building you could probably blow so hard they would fall over. Those who have not trained their mind, like those who have not trained their muscles are weak and can accomplish little. Perhaps all you may notice of someone is a strong presence, or the feeling that they are in some way important. These are the signs of a potential telepath.

The human brain can take energy from the body and convert it into telepathic energy; this is then redistributed in a way the telepath dictates. If she is weak it may be as waves of subtle fear resulting in the telepath being intimidating, if she is strong it might attack the brain of another forcing them to reel in pain or perhaps laying open their temporal arteries. Whatever the method, all a telepath does is convert one sort of energy to another using their mind.

To continue the analogy of the muscle; with continuous use it becomes tired, this is also true of the brain. Continuous telepathic exertion causes mental fatigue so a telepath must rest her mind every now and then. Similarly, with regualr mental exertion over time the telepath will become stronger and become capable of acts of greater power.

USING TELEPATHIC SKILLS

> **IMPORTANT**
> Before you use Telepathics, be aware the *Telepath* Training is needed (see Trainings on Page 22).
> Using Telepathics without the appropriate license is a crime. (See Licenses on page 26.)

Telepathic skills (also called powers) range from 1 (basic) to 10 (mastered) and can be increased with XP.
See the sidebar (right) for details on how to make telepathics rolls. You can augment you power with a telepathic converger (see page 52).

CRITICALS WITH TELEPATHY

Rolling a double zero has a bad effect and means something has gone wrong. (Consult the power description for the appropriate disaster.) If you critically pass a roll no TE points are used up for activating the power. If you wish to extend the power you must still pay additional TE.

TELEPATHIC DURATION AND RESONANCE

Telepathic powers are normally instantaneous. Some skills can be made to last longer, this is covered in the descriptions of the powers further on. Regardless of how long the power lasts it leaves behind a unique fingerprint called *resonance* which a skilled Telepath can interpret and compare to signatures she has seen before. If an area has recently had Telepathic activity in it (approximately 1 hour ago per level of the power used) then a Telepath (someone with the Telepath training) can make a 'Perception + Observation' check to determine the nature of the resonance. The higher the XS the more information can be derived about the power and it's user. (Details are up to the GM)

INCREASING YOUR PERMANENT TE

You can purchase permanent TE with Experience Points. After each session you can spend 1 XP to gain 1 TE. You can spend no more than 1xp per session in this way. This represents the slow increase of Telepathic power. Additionally the training *Telepathic Adept* can be taken at character creation to gain an extra 20 TE points.

REGAINING TE POINTS

NATURAL RECOVERY
You gain TE points back at 3 per 15 minutes of relaxation. (12 per hour)

RECOVERY WHILE ACTIVE
Hard work, combat, mental stress and concentration will diminish the recovery rate to 1 per hour.

MEDITATING
With the *Meditation* Training you regain 6TE per 15 minutes of relaxation (24 per hour).

SLEEPING
When you sleep for a normal period (6-8 hours) you regain all your TE regardless of your total.

METAPSITROPHIN
This chemical restores 30TE instantly. See the Toxins and Drugs listing on page 48.

TELEPATHICS ROLLS

All Telepathy powers use
'INTELLIGENCE + ENDURANCE'

PRESSURED CONDITIONS

When under pressure (such as combat or action) an Agent must spend TE (Telepathic Energy) points equal to the level of the power she wishes to use.
She then rolls 2D10 and tries to get below or equal to 'Intelligence + Endurance'.

Success means the power has worked.
Failure means the power has not worked but the points are still spent.

You can use any level power you have access to or lower. For example, if you have jump 10, you could only use it at level 3 if desired. This uses only 3TE points instead of 10. Using Telepathy counts as an action unless you are using the *As a Free Action* option (see below).

CALM CONDITIONS

When under calm conditions such as back in the hotel or after a fight, you simply pay a number of TE points equal to the level of the power you wish to use. For example - Biokinesis 4 will require 4TE points. The power goes off automatically.

FORCING THE POWER

When under pressure (e.g., combat or action) the Agent can spend the TE points an additional time to make the power go off without a roll. For example - If an Agents wants Assault 5 to go off in battle with no roll it will cost 5TE for the power, then another 5TE to guarantee success. A total of 10TE points.

AS A FREE ACTION

If you need to make something happen instantly you can spend the TE cost an additional time to make the power go off as a free action at the start of your turn. You can then take your normal action as well which could be more Telepathy if desired. You may only have one free action per round. The Telepath must still roll to activate the power unless she is using 'Forcing the Power'.
For example - You need to put up a 5 point shield as a free action. It costs 5TE points for the Shield plus 5TE for an instant effect for a total of 10TE points. The Agent may then immediately have another action.

MAXIMISED

You can spend the TE cost an additional time to make sure the power has maximum effect. If a dice roll is involved (such as with Assault) then it can be skipped and all rolls are considered maximum. This has no effect on a power which doesn't involve a dice roll.
For example - If an Agent is using Assault 5 she can spend an extra 5TE to make sure it deals 30 damage and not 5D6. The Telepath must still roll 'Intelligence + Endurance' to activate the power unless she is using Forcing the Power.

NOTE

You can mix these methods as you see fit. For example, you could spend x4 TE to have the power go off as a free action, with no roll and to maximum effect.

DESCRIPTION OF TELEPATHIC SKILLS

Here are listed exactly what the telepathic skills do. Many telepathic skills use your level of skill squared (^{2}).
Example:

$$1^2 = 1 \times 1 = 01$$
$$3^2 = 3 \times 3 = 09$$
$$5^2 = 5 \times 5 = 25$$
$$6^2 = 6 \times 6 = 36$$
$$7^2 = 7 \times 7 = 49$$
$$8^2 = 8 \times 8 = 64$$
$$9^2 = 9 \times 9 = 81$$
$$10^2 = 10 \times 10 = 100$$

These are not the only forms of Telepathy out there. Others are known to exist but are not sanctioned by the UIG. Mind Telepathy is one form which is known of but its practice is forbidden. Some Telepaths have also refined their powers and personalised them so they have slightly different effects. Many variants exist but finding willing teachers is becoming increasingly hard.

ASSAULT

Range Assault can target someone 'Your Assault' x 10 metres away in line of sight.

You attack the target with personalised manifestations of telepathic power. The effect is to deal D6 points of damage to a single target for each point of Assault used. It is normally used as a ranged attack but can be used in close combat. Assault Telepathy does not count as a close combat weapon when determining whether the Telepath keeps his defence. The damage is considered one large blast for the purposes of factoring Armour Value. The player should feel free to decide how his Assault telepathy manifests.

For example
Agent Jensen's Assault Telepathy comes out as streams of fine lightning burning his enemy. The lightning will not have additional effects such as shorting his electrical equipment or giving him spasms. It is simply a visual effect.

Critical Fail
The attack backfires causing you to take the damage and not your target. Armour reduces the damage.

BIOKINESIS

Range Self

You can accelerate your own healing process, allowing you to heal up to 2HP for each level you have in Biokinesis. You can also purge yourself of toxins and diseases with a *Potency* equal or lower than your biokinesis by spending TE equal to double the Potency and passing an 'Intelligence + Endurance' roll.

Critical Fail
You rend your body apart from the inside. The Telepath takes 3 damage per level of the effect you were trying to achieve, e.g. 24 damage if you were using level 8 Biokinesis. Armour offers no protection.

JUMP

Range Special

You can leap your 'Jump' squared in metres either vertically or horizontally. Landing is controlled and you don't take falling damage as long as you jump equal or less than your potential range, e.g. 1 metre at level 1, 4 metres at level 2, 9 metres at level 3, etc.

Critical Fail
You apply the force to yourself badly and catapult yourself into the ground or a wall taking D6 damage for each level of jump you were trying to use. Armour reduces this damage although it is considered one large hit for armour purposes.

PRESCIENCE

Range Self

You recieve imminent impressions of the future. You can choose between one of the following effects.

Predictive Combat - Add the level of Prescience you use to all your combat Action Totals next round, as you can predict where your enemy will be. Once the round is over your Action Total goes back to normal.

Enhanced Reactions - Gain a bonus to your Reflexes equal to your Prescience. This lasts a whole scene.

6th Sense - You gain a 6th Sense for one scene; you sense any incoming danger such as a trap, an ambush or a ceiling in danger of collapsing. The GM should give you a bonus to any rolls related to surprise equal to the level of Prescience you used.

Critical Fail
Your sight blinds you; you cannot act for the next D4 rounds and gain a -2 penalty to all rolls for the rest of the scene.

PSI BLADE

Range Self

You summon a Telepathic blade into your hand which counts as a longsword. It is composed entirely of telepathic energy. The Psi Blade deals D8 + Strength + plus 1 point of damage per point you have in Psi Blade. The blade is mostly invisible with shimmers of coloured energy running over the surface and is simply a concentrated mass of telepathic force. The blade lasts one scene before it must be reactivated.
To attack with the Psi Blade use 'Agility + Close Combat'. Strength is added as normal but the Psi Blade is always a long sword. A training exists to allow Twin Psi Blades to be summoned and it is rumoured some powerful telepaths are able to summon other forms of Psi Blade.

For example, Agent Viele has Psi Blade 6 and Strength 5.
She can summon a Psi Blade which deals D8 + 6 + 5. (D8+11). It will have a rate of 2 like a long sword.

Critical Fail
You manifest a twisted, corrupted blade which melds with your hand but is unusable. You lose use of one hand for the scene and take 2D6 damage from the burning energy which ignores AV. (Determine which hand randomly.)

SHIELD

Range Self

You generate a visible shield of telepathic energy which acts as a hard ion shield (page 46). This has a number of HP equal to your *Shield* squared, but only protects the Telepath who created it (although it would block the line of fire to another target). You cannot bypass telepathic shields with laser weapons. The shield stays up for the scene. Maintaining the shield is a free action and costs no TE, so you can't take any other free actions while the shield is up.

For example, if you wish to use Shield 4 it will cost 4TE points to put up a 16 point shield. On the second round you can act freely as maintaining the shield is a free action.

Critical Fail

The shield creates a disruptive field around you making you unable to use Telepathics for a number of rounds equal to the level of shield you tried to create. It has no defensive properties though.

TELEKINESIS

Range Your Telekinesis x 10 metres

You can move a number of kilograms equal to your *Telekinesis squared x 10* in a controlled manner at a speed of around 4 mph. Each round you maintain the control you must pay the TE cost again. You can only manipulate items as though you were wearing boxing gloves, fine control is not possible. Gases and liquids cannot be moved with any accuracy.

For example, at level 4 you can move 4x4x10 = 160kg. That's enough to move a human. This will cost 4 TE points for the first round and 4 for each subsequent round.

HURLING ITEMS

You can also make items move with speed (about 20 mph) but you cannot control them well. You can select a compass direction, e.g. north or south-west and the item will simply fly in that direction, normally travelling about 2D6 metres. This will deal 1 damage to the item and the impact target for each level of Telekinesis you used.

Example: If you throw a UIG Officer at a door with Telekinesis 8 both the door and the Officer take 8 damage. AV will reduce this damage as normal.

PULLING HELD OBJECTS

If you wish you can pull objects that are gripped by others.

If your power goes off then the person holding onto the items may roll 'Strength + Endurance' to hold on to the item. They receive the Telekinesis level you used as a penalty to the roll.

Example: Agent Mokash is trying to pull a gun from a guard's hand. He has Telekinesis 8 but is only using level 2 to pull the gun. The guard rolls 'Strength + Endurance' with a -2 penalty to resist.

THROWING PEOPLE

If you move a person (normally this needs Telekinesis 3 or 4) they may make a 'Strength + Endurance' roll, with the level of

Telekinesis you use as a penalty to resist if they have something to grab onto, otherwise they are picked up automatically.

Example: Agent Necrir picks up a rival Agent with Telekinesis 6 and attempts to throw him from a window. The rival Agent rolls 'Strength + Endurance' with a -6 penalty as he tries to grab onto the curtains to avoid being thrown.

Critical Fail

D6 objects of varying size fly at the telepath. These could be barrels, guns, rocks, other Agents, etc. They need not be normally movable by the telepath. Each object deals D6 damage. Armour helps against this damage.

TELEKINESIS SUMMARY

TK	COMMON OBJECT	MAX KG
1	Tactical Firearm	10
2	Heavy Weapon	40
3	Normal Human	90
4	Enhanced Agent	160
5	Motorcycle	250
6	Heavily Armoured Agent	360
7	Break Standard Door	490
8	Typical Droid	640
9	Heavy Door	810
10	Sports Car	1000

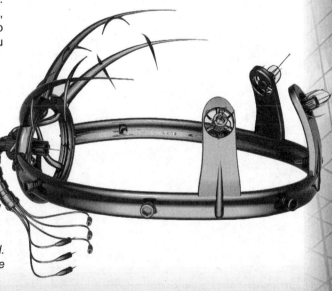

TANYA LINN - AI-JINN A.I. ARCHITECT & REQUISITOR

SECTION 5 CHARACTER ADVANCEMENT

Today, a great deal of Corporate culture is made manifest in their training centres, from the stark dojo of Nakajima through the massive simulation rooms of Neu Shenzhen to the eerie calm of the Focus Domes of Mumbai. Even in the cavernous firing ranges of the UIG or the spartan monasteries of the Order can be seen much of the ideological and practical structures of the respective organizations.

-from The Rise of The Corporation-States
attr: Dr. Edmond Treval

The main way characters advance is by gaining Rank Points, Experience Points and using Downtime. Agent Mission pay is on page 79.

RANK POINTS (RP)

Rank Points are awarded based on the Agent's performance in the eyes of the UIG and the Corporation. Rank Points are awarded fairly liberally as long as there is good cause to reward the Agent. Once a certain amount of Rank Points have been acquired the Corporation in question can recommend to the UIG that one of their Agents be promoted. The UIG will then assess the Agent (sometimes in laboratory and field studies) and refer to any recorded incidents in the past involving the Agent. If the results are satisfactory the promotion should go ahead as planned. If the Agent is undeserving then he may need to make amends, perhaps by completing a mission for the UIG.

THE ADVANTAGES OF RANK

Rank is very important for Agents, essentially it allows them greater leeway and the potential to bypass more laws. At low rank Agents are little different to Citizens, they have a few extra privileges in respect of bearing arms and attending crime scenes but nothing of great consequence. As the Agent increases in Rank she gains access to more licenses and privileges. It is common for an Agent to undergo special training before reaching Rank 4; this could take the form of a difficult test, or an especially challenging mission. This is really up to the GM but provides an opportunity for the Agent to earn his new responsibility. On page 81 are listed Corporate titles of each rank as well as other privileges granted to Agents.

Alternative titles can be given by the Corporations for Agents involved in specific professions. For example, the Order of the True Faith honour their Agents with such terms as Cardinal, Lama, Prelate, Rinpoche, Roshi, Rensai, Canon, Archbishop, Guide, Master, Kundun, etc.

AGENT LICENSES AND RANK

Agents, UIG Officers, Order of the True Faith and even Citizens acquire licenses throughout their career. These are detailed on page 25. The licenses grant them the power to do things normally disallowed by law, for example: carrying large weapons, entering private property and arresting people. As the Agent becomes more experienced he is allowed access to more powerful licenses but he must prove himself worthy. Agents who are constantly being reprimanded or are known loose cannons are less likely to be approved new licenses and may have existing ones revoked.

UNIVERSAL CHAIN OF COMMAND

Anyone has the right to command any non-UIG person with a rank 2 levels lower than their own. For example a Rank 4 Citizen can command a Rank 2 Agent regardless of their affiliation. Those in the same Corporation or organisation have the right to command Agents 1 rank lower than themselves, e.g., A Rank 4 Comoros Agent can command a Rank 3 Comoros Agent. The leader of a Division can command his Division as long as his Rank is equal or higher to the other members, or if he has been assigned as a leader specifically by the Corporation. UIG can command any non-UIG. The exception to this is if a non-

UIG has been given special authority. For example if a non-UIG toxin specialist has been placed in charge of a biohazard situation by the UIG and given a level 7 clearance he may overrule UIG troops of rank 6 or less while attending the situation.

GAINING RANK POINTS

See the table on page 81.

Street level UIG Officers are not overly fond of handing out Rank Points as this can give the Corporation Agents increasing degrees of authority on the streets. The UIG however, are fitted with recording equipment most of the time and are also terrified of being called traitors by other members of their patrols, so things tend to get done by the book despite the inbuilt reluctance to reward Corporate Agents. There exists a set of guidelines for the UIG to use when awarding Rank Points to Agents, but the Agents will normally find themselves receiving the least amount possible. Remember, Agents may need proof of their deeds to earn Rank Points. The GM should increase or decrease the Rank Points given out to suit the level of advancement desired in the game. Rank increase should be kept fairly slow generally speaking but as always, it's up to you.

LOSING RANK POINTS

Past indiscretions are very important when assessing viability for promotion. The UIG are not generous and will record any and all errors by Agents they come across unless they have a valid reason to overlook them. This will be held in record vaults until needed. The system is open to abuse by vindictive UIG Officers. Essentially Agents lose rank for breaking the law just like Civilians. Details of Rank Point loss can be found on page 81.

LIMITING RANK

Generally speaking you should not let the characters get to Rank 10, as that is the rank of the CEO (Chief Executive Officer) of the Corporation and can make the game difficult to run. The people at the top will also ensure that high ranking Agents do not threaten their position, so most Agents find it almost impossible to pass Rank 8.

PROMOTION AND DEMOTION

PROMOTION

When an Agent receives enough Rank Points to increase in rank his Corporation will award him his new rank as long as the UIG are in concurrence. The new rank is effective immediately and the Agent can expect better accommodation, more money, access to more licenses and more important missions.

DEMOTION

When an Agent loses Rank Points for breaking the law or acting irresponsibly, instead of being immediately criminalised the Rank Points are simply deducted from his total. If he drops enough points it is quite possible he will be reduced to a lower rank. When an Agent has -4 Rank Points left he is in trouble. Any further loss will result in him being Depersonalised and classed as a criminal. He will not become a Citizen unless there are extreme circumstances. This is an excellent way to start an alternative game where the players are rogue Agents who have been made into criminals for crimes they didn't commit.

EXPERIENCE POINTS

These are awarded by the GM for good roleplaying, i.e. the players added to the game by their presence and acted the part of their character well. They can be spent to increase a character's power. The Experience Costs table below shows how much it costs to increase different aspects of your character.

EXPERIENCE COSTS

Experience Points are used to improve your character. They can be spent on the following things.

First point in a new skill	2 Points
Increase a skill	Current rating x 1
Increase telepathic skill	Current rating x 1
Increase a STAT	Current rating x 2
Learn a Language	5 XP
Buy a Training	10
Buy a License	No XP Cost
	For each level of the license, 1 week of downtime and 500¢
Permanent TE Point	1 - Maximum of 1 per session

Derived numbers such as Hit Points increase if one of its source numbers increases. For example - Increasing your Endurance would cause your Hit Points to go up.

STATS and Skills (including telepathic skills) cannot be increased above 10 with XP.

HOW MUCH TO AWARD.

You should give between 3 and 5 Experience Points per session on average.
As a general rule a typical player should gain 1 XP per hour of game play. If the player was exceptional in playing the part and had a number of good ideas you could award one or two extra points. Completion of a mission or some kind of great achievement could also gain some additional points.

If you feel the character advancement rate is too fast or slow then simply alter the XP handed out.

XP should not be removed from a player unless they spend it. Punishments can take the form of lost Rank Points, confiscated weapons, revoked licenses, removal of cybernetics or perhaps a psyche evaluation resulting in a restriction of privileges.

AGENT LEVEL

This is a way to keep track of your Agent's general competance so the GM can set appropriate challenges, and so there is a way to gauge the effectiveness of characters. All Agents start at Level 1, to determine their level simply keep a note of all XP gained throughout the Agents life and consult the table on the top right of this page.

AGENT LEVEL

XP	LEVEL	XP	LEVEL
0-9	Level 1	110	Level 12
10	Level 2	120	Level 13
20	Level 3	130	Level 14
30	Level 4	140	Level 15
40	Level 5	150	Level 16
50	Level 6	160	Level 17
60	Level 7	170	Level 18
70	Level 8	180	Level 19
80	Level 9	190	Level 20
90	Level 10	200	Level 21
100	Level 11	210	Level 22

and so on...

Agents can be varied in combat effectiveness however so a high level does not mean they are necessarily physically powerful. Level should only be used as a guide and not a rigid encounter system.

MISSION PAY

Agents get paid based on Rank, the value of the mission, the risk involved and the degree of success.

MISSION PAY

CORPORATION	MISSION
Ai-Jinn	700
Comoros	600
Eurasian Inc.	1,000
Shi Yukiro	900
Western Federation	800

Mission - Pay given out upon completion of a mission. (This should then be multiplied by the Agent's rank.)

WORKING OUT PAY

As standard an Agent receives his basic mission wage (above) multiplied by his rank. You should then add a bonus to this of between 0% and 100% based on mission success, importance and difficulty.

For example: Agent Miller has completed a mission that prevented the Corporation from looking very bad in the public eye. He is a Rank 3 Western Federation Agent so he gets paid:

$$800¢ \times 3 = 2400¢.$$

The GM (as the Mission Officer) decides as the mission was very important he will award a 50% bonus so Miller gets an extra 1200¢ making a total of 3600¢.

BLACK OPS AND COVERT REWARDS

Some missions are very secretive and must remain undiscovered by the UIG, (Black Operations). For these missions Agents will not receive much in the way of rank as it is ultimately down to the UIG to award the Rank Points, therefore if the Corporation does not want the UIG to know about the mission, rank cannot be awarded properly.

There are ways round this, essentially fiddling the books whereby the high ranking Agents in the Corporation falsify evidence to make the sure the Agents get some rank anyway. This is not done lightly, only for extremely important operations. Therefore when Agents normally engage in Black Ops or cannot be given the normal rewards the Corporation simply rewards them with other things such as:

More money (in Slip Credit)
Cybernetics
Weapons
Equipment
Better accommodation
Company cars
More licenses
Extra training
Fine clothes (could increase *Looking Good*)
Membership of an exclusive club
A house outside the Spire
Additional downtime
Access to an executive lounge
Access to classified documents
Higher level clearance
An ally in the form of a high ranking Agent
Leniency on their next crime
Forgiveness for an old misdoing
Assignment on an easy or desirable mission.
Gifts such as antiques or real meat
Control of a sub-company of the Corporation
A voice on one of the executive boards
Permission to start business
Access to powerful A.I.'s
A Division of Agents to command.

After a furtive glance both ways to make sure he had not been followed, Thomas Dupree lifted a plastic flap and ducked off the rainy alleyway into the noisome gloom of the tiny, dirty room. The only furniture was a treacherous-looking wooden chair and a cracked and broken vidscreen, linked to a tiny network terminal with a process hookup dangling from it. As Dupree seated himself gingerly in the chair, though, the cracked screen flickered to life as the warm voice of a new god issued tinnily from the cheap speakers in the terminal.

"Thomas, welcome back. More downtime? How went the mission? The details on the UIG network were somewhat sketchy."

Dupree cleared his throat, addressing from habit the almost-meaningless patterns swirling behind the filthy glass of the screen. "Hello, Thanatos. Ah... yes, all fine. It was a simple search-and-retrieval job, the Federation didn't put up much of a fight, but we did run into some Cult interference in the third quadrant of the Lambda facility. Anyway, I'm out on assignment with Division Twelve next week, and I need your help on something I've - "

"Hush, Thomas, I'm sure I don't need to remind you of our arrangement. Of course I will help you, as I always do, but first you must help me. Data, Thomas, quid pro quo. I wish to see the engagement with the Cult. Show me, Thomas, show me." The voice was still warm, but it seemed to Dupree as if a kind of urgency, or hunger, had crept into it. Or perhaps that was just a trick of the cheap speaker. Suppressing a shudder, he grasped the hookup and reached around to the process port at the back of his head to let the Archon into his mind.

Notes for Corporate Ranks and Perks (opposite).

Vehicle - Agents receive vehicles to conduct their business in, they can of course use their own but the Corporation will provide one if necessary. It is up to the GM which vehicle to award the players based on how valued they are by their Corporation. Some example prices are given in the table.

Apartment - As the Agent gains rank she is given better accommodation, often with window views, higher positioning in the Spire or even separate luxury houses. Feel free to offer different accommodation than the ones described on the table.

Title - These are official titles used by the UIG to refer to a person's rank. Some Corporations use them more than others. For example, the Western Federation commonly use them whereas Comoros never use them if avoidable.

Miscellaneous - Most Agents like to build stuff in their spare time. As they progress in rank Agents are given labs, workshops and places to store their equipment. They are also given offices to work and meet in.

Note: Agents can pool allocations if desired to acquire better apartments, vehicles, etc., which are shared.

*CEO - Chief Executive Officer (the Head of a Corporation).

GAINING RANK POINTS

SERVICE PERFORMED	POSSIBLE RANK POINT GAIN
Arresting / Killing / Stopping a weak Criminal	+1 point
Contributing useful information to a UIG investigation	+1 point
Enforcing simple laws; e.g., Minor Drug Confiscation	+1 point
Preventing the death of a Citizen	+1 point
Enforcing moderate laws; e.g. car theft	+1-2 points
Recommendation from your Corporation for work well done	+1-5 points
Arresting / Killing / Stopping a moderate criminal	+2 points
Enforcing serious laws; e.g. murder	+2-3 points
Completing a UIG assigned mission	+2-6 points
Arresting / Killing / Stopping a dangerous criminal	+3 points
Preventing the death of a UIG Officer	The Officers rank in points

LOSING RANK POINTS

CRIME COMMITTED	POSSIBLE RANK POINT LOSS
Murdering a Citizen	6 + Citizen's Rank (half points for an attempted murder)
Murdering UIG staff	UIG Rank x 5 points (half points for attempted murder)
Breaching curfew	-01 point
Destruction of property (under 100¢)	-01 point
Harming an Outcast	-01 point
Insubordination	-01 point
Insulting a UIG Officer	-01 point
Theft (under 100¢)	-01 point
Destruction of property (101¢ - 1,000¢)	-02 points
Drug abuse - Class C	-02 points
Resisting arrest	-02 points
Murdering an outcast	-02 points
Harming a Citizen	-03 points
Destruction of property (1,001¢ - 10,000¢)	-04 points
Theft (101¢ - 1,000¢)	-04 points
Destruction of property (10,001¢+)	-05 points
Drug abuse - Class B	-05 points
Theft (1,001¢ - 10,000¢)	-06 points
Possession of Hacking Software	-6-12 points (see equipment on page 50-51)
Drug abuse - Class A	-07 points
Theft (10,001¢+)	-10 points
Other unlicensed activity	Level of the license you would need to legally perform the activity. If one does not exist the GM should decide, normally 1-10 points.

CORPORATE RANKS AND PERKS

RANK POINTS	RANK	TITLE	VEHICLE	APARTMENT	MISC.
10	1	Sergeant	None	Small	Parking space and tiny office
25	2	Sgt. Major	3,000¢	Medium	Small lab or workshop
45	3	Lieutenant	6,000¢	Large	Additional parking & small office
70	4	Captain	10,000¢	Medium Luxury	Med lab or workshop
100	5	Major	20,000¢	Large Luxury	Hangar space & medium office
135	6	Colonel	30,000¢	Own House	Large lab or workshop
175	7	General	50,000¢	Penthouse	Own vehicle hangar & large office
220	8	Field Marshal	80,000¢	Manor	Lab or workshop complex
270	9	Shadow CEO	100,000¢	Luxury Manor	Whatever is needed
325	10	CEO*	Anything	Complex	Whatever is needed

DOWNTIME

Downtime is a term used for Agent's free time, i.e. holidays. There are a number of things Agents can do during downtime which will all advance her in some way. The GM should give downtime as he sees appropriate, but generally a week of downtime after each completed mission or every 2-3 sessions is a good guide.

USING DOWNTIME

You can do a number of things with downtime. If what you want to do is not here, discuss it with the GM and together you could come up with some new options.

REGAIN CONVICTION

The Agent relaxes and refreshes himself. He gains 5 points of conviction for a week of total relaxation (maximum conviction is 5).

SKILL TRAINING

The Agent spends his time furthering his skills by reading, theorising and practicing. He gains 2 XP a week which can only be spent on a single skill which was the subject of the training. For example, if he spends a week target shooting he can put the points towards a relevant firearms skill.

CONTACTS

You can build up contacts in downtime, for example, if you wish to start building a network of underworld contacts then you can use a week of downtime to visit bars and gambling joints in order to start consolidating allies. The contacts have a rating out of 10 which represents how useful and willing they are. 1 is a vague contact, 10 is an established, reliable one. Each week of downtime spent gaining contacts gives you 4 points to spend increasing the relationship with your contact(s), e.g. 2 weeks downtime working on contacts would give you 8 points. This could all go on one excellent contact or 4 minor ones etc. The GM can use the level of the contact to make the player roll. It is up to the GM which contacts you can acquire and how powerful the contact can become. *E.g. "Roll 'Presence + UIG Contact' to find out about the details of this murder case."*

EXAMPLE CONTACTS

UIG Officer	Hotel Owner
Weapon Dealer	Lost Property Clerk
Drug Dealer	Prototype Weapon Scientist
Customs Officer	Off the Record Cyberneticist
Private Investigator	Telepathics Teacher (could reduce XP cost)
Agent in another Corporation	
High-up Official, e.g., a Judge	An Archon
Computer Hacker	One of the Faithful
Politician	A Gang Member
Club Owner	Records Archivist
Street Doctor	Traffic Police
Informant	Morgue Attendant

EARNING CASH

The Agent simply goes out and earns non specific cash. He might work for the Corporation at his profession or he may freelance. Whatever he chooses he gains 500¢ per week of downtime. This can be multiplied by rank if the GM feels it is appropriate.

WORKSHOP

You can improve the condition of an item (GM permitting) by 1 point by spending 1 week of downtime in an appropriately set up workshop. You must also pay 5% of the *brand new* value of the equipment and you need to have the relevant skills at 5 or more. The GM will decide what skills are appropriate, for example, repairing a kinetic pistol would require Light Firearms or Mechtronics of 5 or more. Repairing a car would require Mechtronics or Drive at 5 or more.

Normally no roll is needed as long as the base skills are high enough although the GM could ask for one under some circumstances, e.g. improving a prototype weapon. If the equipment is already in condition 10 then you can make it better so it never critically fails. If you increase it further it will never critically fail and critically pass on a roll of 1/1 and 2/2, you can keep increasing it so it will critically hit on 1/1 to 10/10. This uses the same basic rules as above but requires 20% of the new cost each time, not 5%. See table below. The GM can rule that a simple item such as a knife could be imporoved 2 or 3 condition levels in one week.

IMPROVING EQUIPMENT IN THE WORKSHOP

INITIAL STATE	SKILL	COST TO IMPROVE	FINAL RESULT	TERM	VALUE
Item is below condition 9	5	5% of item's new value	Item increases a condition	Substandard	-
Item is condition 9	5	5% of item's new value	Item becomes condition 10	Standard	Normal
Item is condition 10	6	20% of item's new value	Item never critically fails	Fine	x 2
Item never critically fails	6	20% of item's new value	Item critical hits on 1/1 & 2/2	Exceptional	x 3
criticals on 1/1 and 2/2	6	20% of item's new value	Item critical hits on 1/1 to 3/3	Custom	x 4
Item criticals on 1/1 to 3/3	7	20% of item's new value	Item critical hits on 1/1 to 4/4	Masterbuilt	x 5
Item criticals on 1/1 to 4/4	7	20% of item's new value	Item critical hits on 1/1 to 5/5	Superior	x 6
Item criticals on 1/1 to 5/5	8	20% of item's new value	Item critical hits on 1/1 to 6/6	Elite	x 7
Item criticals on 1/1 to 6/6	8	20% of item's new value	Item critical hits on 1/1 to 7/7	Outstanding	x 8
Item criticals on 1/1 to 7/7	9	20% of item's new value	Item critical hits on 1/1 to 8/8	Famous	x 9
Item criticals on 1/1 to 8/8	9	20% of item's new value	Item critical hits on 1/1 to 9/9	Legendary	x10
Item criticals on 1/1 to 9/9	10	20% of item's new value	Item critical hits on 1/1 to 10/10	Artifact	x11

Initial State	Condition of equipment before work.
Skill	The level you need the relevant skill at.
Cost to Improve	The cost (in credits) to upgrade the item.
Final Result	The effect you have worked towards.
Term	The usual term for the new item.
Value	For improved items: this is the cost if you wish to simply buy an improved item. Aquiring improved items can be hard.

OTHER WAYS TO REWARD AND PUNISH AGENTS

XP and Rank are all very well but sometimes something different is appropriate. Below are listed some reward ideas for the GM to hand out instead of more XP, rank and money.

GAINING CONVICTION

You regain Conviction (see page 147 for Conviction) for doing something key to the mission or important to your character. For example, if you find some incriminating evidence which could convict your mission target, the GM could award the players a Conviction Point. Likewise if a character completes a small goal such as killing an old enemy, saving a friends life or gaining a rank the GM could award a Conviction Point. There are no hard and fast rules for this, it is up to the GM to decide when players have earned them. You should be cautious awarding more than one a session, but go ahead if the situation warrants it. Players should never have more than 5 Conviction Points at once.

CONTACTS

A useful contact can be a great reward, perhaps if the Division manage to save a man's restaurant from burning down then he may tell them about his brother who is an ex-doctor and will perform minor surgery on them without it going through UIG records. This is just one example, on page 82 are some more ideas. This will effectively increase the character's *Contacts* as described on page 82.

GOODS AND PERKS

You can always grant the Agent additional goods as a form of reward, often in the form of property, possessions or perks. Below are some examples:

A car	A house outside the Spire
A military vehicle	Some cybernetics
A better apartment	Some miscellaneous equipment
A custom made weapon	Additional Downtime
Some customised armour	Access to an executive lounge
Fine clothes (could increase	Access to classified documents
Looking Good)	Higher level clearance
Membership of an exclusive club	

MISSION RELATED REWARDS

Sometimes you can grant the players rewards that reflect what they have been doing in the field. For example, after a long and difficult infiltration of a Shi Yukiro combat training facility you could allow all the players to select a Combat Training for free to represent their 4 weeks in the facility. These should be used sparingly so as not to devalue Experience Points. Below are some examples.

1. A free training
2. A free point in a skill
3. A free point in a Telepathic Skill
4. An extra Hit Point
5. A bonus STAT point
6. A reduction in the XP cost to buy something
7. A free language
8. A point of conviction

PUNISHMENTS

When Agents are defiant, obstinate, disrespectful, rude or simply useless punishments are dealt out based on the following factors.

The Agent's Rank
The nature of the mistake made
The Agent's past achievements
His proven loyalty
His past indiscretions of a similar nature
Corporation policy
The Agent's relationship with high ranking officers
His value to the Corporation
How much the Disciplinary Officer likes him

Some appropriate courses of action are listed below. Often punishments have semi-official titles so that the Agent is branded and used as an example to all.

'Stripped' - The Agent is stripped of some of the more dangerous cybernetics he is wearing

'Humanely Modified' - The Agent's cybernetics are changed to less invasive modules. i.e. the GM reduces the effectiveness of the cybernetics.

'Recycled' - The Agent is killed and her cybernetics given to the Division

'White Miced' - The Agent is experimented on to see what makes them snap. The flaw is then cybernetically or psychologically removed.

'Fixed' - The Agent is given psychological counselling at either Corporate or personal expense.

'Restricted' - The Agent is to be assigned only suitable, low priority missions.

'Under the Eye' - The Division is given the responsibility of monitoring and restraining the Agent.

'Acceptable Hazard' - Left to do as he pleases but a black mark is added to his permanent record.

'Demoted' - Stripped of rank and / or licenses until he redeems himself.

'Beggared' - A pay reduction or a downgrade in accommodation, transport and / or perks.

'Service' - The Agent has to spend his downtime on unpaid Corp business.

'Sighted' - The Agent has cameras fitted to his weapons to monitor his activities.

'Clanned' - The whole Division are punished (a rare punishment).

'Deathoritised' - Some of the Agent's licenses are temporarily suspended.

'Disarmed'
The Agent has his selection of weaponry and equipment limited.

It has come to our attention that gunman Sarah Bryle has received in excess of 1,200 credits on average per week for the past six months and furthermore has received promotion up to Major level without any supporting documentation being filed for public access and audit. This is in direct contravention of the WF-UIG Seattle Accord of 2472 and therefore constitutes a serious anomaly. It is the recommendation of this Bureau that Bryle be suspended from duty and temporarily stripped of all rank with immediate effect and also that an investigation be launched to ascertain how, from whom, and for what reason she has received these unsupported dividends in rank and remuneration.
-Western Federation Delaware Accounts Bureau Report 3302e/05252493 SUPRESSED 5.25.2493, /adenton], [DELETED 5.25.2493, /adenton

The office was high in the Spire, an imposing room where critical matters were discussed. Agent Baxter, now in his late 50's, sat upright, his ample frame filling the chair. He cast his eyes over the drinks cabinet and smiled to himself. On his left sat the normally efficient figure that was Division Leader Agent Targusson, his hands twitching feverishly, his pale hair matted with sweat. He kept checking something in his inside pocket, then quickly scanning the room and checking again. Slumped next to him was Agent Daniq, lean, drawn and elegantly styled, currently engrossed in a broadcast on his palm. He seemed oblivious to or at least unconcerned by the impending meeting with Agent Hawk.

The door slid silently open and a broad, square jawed man entered the room, in his left hand was a bundle of papers, in his right a mug of coffee. Quick as a flash Targusson pulled his gun from his jacket and levelled it at the intruder.

"Excuse him," said Daniq looking up from the broadcast, "It's his new targeter; he's in a settling period, don't worry – he's quite safe, just a bit jumpy."

Hawk glared at him. "Put it away Targusson. I don't have time for this." Targusson ejected the clip and replaced the weapon.

"Now, I am hereby charged by Eurasian Incorporated to debrief you on the mission codenamed Tailgate and to take any steps that may be deemed necessary to conclude this matter. Before I begin do you have anything to say?"

Targusson stood quickly, his suit was crumpled and perspiration was soaking through his shirt into the dark fabric of the jacket.

"Sir, I would like to firstly say that I recommended Daniq for a psyche evaluation after the previous mission, where his behaviour was at best questionable. I understand that the evaluation didn't take place. I therefore cannot vouch for the integrity of my Division."

"Hmm...I see. Sit down Targusson." Hawk studied the file.

"As far as I can tell Agent Daniq's actions were not in question, it seems he may have actually redeemed the situation somewhat. In your opinion, Agent, how did Daniq's questionable mental state affect the outcome of this mission?"

Targusson's lips tightened, "I can't say sir, I just didn't feel in control. Daniq is a loose cannon."

Hawk rocked back in his chair smiling, "Daniq is the loose cannon? For God's sake Targusson, your entire Division is practically rogue. If it wasn't for Baxter's connections with Henderson you'd all be cleaning out the underswell latrines for the rest of your lives. Your mission history reads like an A-Z of modern day anarchy. Now if that's all you have in the way of defence for your actions please be quiet while I go over the statements."

Baxter's eyes once again turned to the liquor cabinet. Daniq's resumed watching the broadcast and Targussen put the clip back in his weapon. After a few minutes Hawk looked up.

"Right....Now, it says here you were to travel to Shanghai, there you were to put a tracer round into Mr. Kym Chen, a ranking Ai-Jinn Agent who we believed was involved in some Triad racketeering in our medical facilities in Hong Kong. Let me see…he was due to leave an ambassadorial event late on the evening of the 31st. Is this correct?"

Targusson nodded.

"You were issued with an injector rifle and 3 sub-dermal tracer tags. I don't understand from the file how the next part happened; perhaps you'd care to explain?"

Targusson stood. "Sir, we gained entry to the roof of the Noodle House on the opposite side of the street. At exactly 11:22pm local time Agent Chen was spotted by Daniq leaving the building. Being the best marksman I took the shot. It was perfect, it caught him in the shoulder just as a woman brushed past him, leading him to believe that the woman had simply knocked into him."

"I understand this part Targusson. Just the pertinent facts if you please."

"Sorry sir, well it was at this point Daniq noted some unusual readings coming from the target, the presence of cybernetics which we had not previously noticed. Daniq's assessment was that he had undergone cybernetic surgery in the past few hours; probably cardiomechanical. This seems to explain why the tracer tag sent him into cardiac arrhythmia, he was presumably on electrochemical stabilisers until the upgrades had settled."

"And so the tracer tag interfered with the stabiliser. That's what killed him?"

"We believe so." nodded Targusson.

Hawk took a mouthful of coffee and eyeballed the Agents one by one. He relaxed back into his chair. "I can accept this as an unfortunate accident,

you were victims of circumstance. These things happen. I would, however, be interested to hear your version of the events which followed Agents Chen's death."

Targusson looked round as though another might answer for him. Baxter seemed to think this was not serious and was obviously waiting for things to wind up so he could retire to his suite with a good bottle of cognac. As for Daniq, Targusson could tell by the distant smile and cocked head that he was still listening in on the broadcast though a patched line in his SVC.

He reluctantly turned to Hawk, "Of course Sir, when I accidentally killed Agent Chen panic broke out; UIG Response Teams appeared from nowhere and I immediately called for the Division to find cover. I still can't tell you why the accident triggered such a reaction; I can only imagine the UIG were monitoring him as well. It was while we were hiding that Agent Baxter told me he was sure he could hear the sound of an X45 Assault Copter, he added that they had bio scanners fitted as standard and they would invariably find us unless we got 10 metres of concrete between us and the- X45. This was not possible, leaving us only one logical course of action."

Hawk picked us his notes and scanned them. "So…the logical course of action eh? My notes are sketchy here, am I to understand you exhausted all possibilities?"

"Sir, with respect, time was a serious issue; we did not have the luxury of 'exhausting all the possibilities' as you say. I made a split second decision and I stand by it. I ordered Baxter to shoot down the X45."

"Agent Baxter, can you confirm Agent Targusson's claim?"

"Oh yes. I took out Elsie and did as Max asked."

"Elsie?" asked Hawk quizzically.

"Sorry, an informal term for my rocket launcher."

"I would be grateful if you would refer to Agent Targusson by his surname or rank in matters such as this."

Baxter looked a little put out, "Of course, if you say."

Hawk shook his head hopelessly, "So you took out the X45 cleanly?"

Baxter smiled, "Well, I shot out the rear grav drive meaning the pilot couldn't manoeuvre laterally, this should have forced him to land but he didn't. He kept coming but with limited control, damned foolish move."

"And what happened?" asked Hawk, eyebrows raised.

"Well, what anyone would expect, the X45 was unable to stabilise laterally and began a spiralled descent towards the street below us. It crashed into the ground. Unfortunate, but the pilot was an idiot."

Targusson nodded, "We used the ensuing chaos to make our escape to the downtown area where we were met by Agent Klein, our exit man."

"I see." Hawk looked over the paperwork once more, then flicked a switch on the desk and a light screen appeared. He scanned some files, then switched it off.

"So...in conclusion it seems that you have failed the mission and caused a not insignificant amount of damage to UIG property. You have killed a leading Ai-Jinn crimeboss whom we wanted followed and damaged a large section of Shanghai. Add to this the fact that Daniq is still listening to a broadcast on his wretched machine, Baxter hasn't heard most of what I've said and you pointed a gun at me, and I can conclusively say you three are exactly what we need for a high priority mission."

Daniq disconnected the SVC. "Excuse me?"

"Yes, you three have earned yourself a special place here at E.I. We have decided to send you to the Miller-Urey research orbital, we have had reports that the Cult of Machina has influence there and are stowing their most powerful members on board crates so they can smuggle them in. Before landing, the crates are dropped out of the back of the shuttles into the jungles of Tigera where the Cultists are recovered by their allies and hidden in underground cave networks. Your mission is to drop into Tigera unseen, which is Federation territory, find where the Cultists are holed up and bring them back for interrogation. Any problems?"

Daniq raised his eyebrows, "With respect sir, the idea of dropping into Federation territory, capturing a pack of slavering monsters and returning to Earth unscathed is beyond ridiculous."

Hawk smiled, stood up and turned to leave, "I know, that is why I'm giving you one last chance boys, start completing your missions, stop screwing up or I really will send you to Miller-Urey. Now, take my advice and get out of here, there are some UIG Officers here to ask questions about an X45."

SECTION 6
THE CORPORATIONS

AGENT KUAN-YIN LIANG, DRAGON'S HEAD OF THE AI-JINN

MANIFESTATION OF THE ROGUE ARCHON HYPERION

THE RISE OF THE CORPORATIONS

> *Whether war represents the final aspect of diplomacy or whether war is what is left when diplomacy has failed is a philosophical question that may be endlessly debated. What is beyond debate is that warfare in the modern era tends towards extreme results and that it is vital that any Corporation wishing to remain competitive be prepared, both in terms of Corporate philosophy and available military assets, to engage in decisive armed conflict with the sole objective of victory.*
>
> *- from The Rise of The Corporation-States*
> *attr: Dr. Edmond Treval*

In the 21st century businesses started to become so large that they were considered powers in their own right. They were able to sway the way the world operated by simply changing their policies, products or prices. These businesses became known as Corporations and wielded so much power that they began to find themselves more influential than the governments of their respective countries.

This trend continued throughout the world with the diversity of small businesses slowly diminishing as the major Corporations began to swallow up everything in their path. By 2220 there were only Corporations, five major ones and several smaller ones, although the term small hardly seemed appropriate.

The Corporations began to build their own accommodation where their legions of workers could live in safe, organised environments. Out-earning the state the Corporations were able to practically declare war on their own governments and enforce their own laws. Soon Citizens were more scared of the Corporations than they were of the government and finally Corporate rule was absolute. The only thing standing in the way of any Corporation were rival ones.

THE CORPORATE WARS

This is when the fighting began, large scale warfare between the Corporations which lasted many years. It started with intellectual theft and industrial espionage but soon degenerated into murders and terrorism and finally full scale war with weapons of inhuman savagery.

The wars were a vast strain on resources and the Corporations suffered greatly. This weakening of the Corporations allowed the governments of the world time to think, rebuild and co-operate. Out of the smoke of the Corporate Wars emerged a tattered planet, the first stirrings of a United International Government, and several bitter, scarred Corporations.

As resources ran low the Corporations found peace through sheer fatigue. With the Corporations exhausted, the Governments were now once again in a position to enforce their own laws and bring the Corporations back down to earth.

THE TIME OF ORDER

The United International Government (UIG) became a cohesive force. They were able to deal financially with all Corporations across the globe, buying technology from anywhere in a way that no single Corporation could. The UIG was independently stable, its

Officers policed every city and crime rates were dramatically reduced. Space research was at an all time high and in 2240 the Lunas Colony was formed on the moon. Orbitals were set up so that factories with unacceptable pollution outputs could be located off-planet. Plans were established for a Mars and Venus colony by the year 2250. Reports from the Crick probe also reported back from deep space that extra-terrestrial life in its crudest form had been discovered. During this period the Corporations began to rebuild their strength, but under the watchful eye of the UIG it was not as simple as before.

THE VENUS DISCOVERY

In 2253 the Viva shuttle reached Venus and began to establish the Eldoran Colony. After four years of construction the settlement was completed and the first 500 colonists moved in. It grew well and within 8 years the base had been enlarged to the size of a small city, with almost one million residents calling Venus home.

In 2270 the discovery of ancient structures beneath the rock was met with great excitement across the world. This was the first conclusive evidence of intelligent life outside Earth. These ancient cities were enigmatic; it was hard to tell how far beyond current human society they were, if indeed that was the case. Expeditions were sent to explore the cities but turned up little in the way of useful technology. After many months of exploring, nine strange structures were found within an organised system containing tiny amounts of residual electricity. The structures were thoroughly analysed, carefully removed and taken back to the Eldoran Colony.

After prolonged research it was determined that the residual energy was decaying at an almost undetectable rate. It was eventually decided to attempt to try replenishing the energy inside the system and see what happened. The systems seemed to accept the power and began to take on more complex patterns. Doctor Alexi Veristrov, a UIG xenobiologist, analysed the new energy patterns by connecting the structures to bio-derivation systems. His astonishment was not only due to the nature of the patterns, (matching both the behaviour of machine and life form) but also the fact that the electrical signature immediately migrated to his system leaving the old structure cold and lifeless.

Over the next year the UIG R&D division directed much of their efforts to understand these bizarre forms of life. The nearest comparisons they could draw were the Artificial Intelligences created to run complex computer systems but compared to the human built ones these were hundreds of years in the future. The nine systems were named Archons after the nine chief magistrates that ran ancient Athens, the thinking being that these intelligences must have run all the systems in the subterranean city. Although it took several months to establish communication with the Archons it was apparent they had been watching the researchers for a great deal longer.

Within four years the UIG had established a relationship with the Archons and were able to communicate with them on a sophisticated level. The Archons seemed evasive about their past but seemed content to assist in any way possible. They sampled current human technology and re-engineered it producing devices, fuel sources and weapons which were years ahead of current production. The machines seemed happy to do this in exchange for information about Earth and its inhabitants which the Scientists offered in a heavily censored form (wisely in their opinion).

In 2298 with the Archons safely housed in the UIG headquarters, Doctor Veristrov decided this research could go no further until the machines were linked into the World Data Net. The potential of these incredible systems could not even be guessed at until they were given an environment in which they could fully demonstrate their ability.

Veristrov entered the Vault of the Archons on October 1st 2298 and connected up the most predictable and seemingly cultured system. He had named the life form Orpheus after the Greek musician and poet. Veristrov waited in anticipation as Orpheus moved from the containing systems out into the digital world. Orpheus travelled for days while Veristrov attempted to explain his actions to the research committee. A number of seemingly random and inexplicable system crashes occurred over the world that week which have since been blamed on the travels of Orpheus.

In ten days Orpheus returned, it was somehow different but quite content to once again reside in the main system and go back to helping the scientists with their problems. The experiment was considered a success; Orpheus now knew almost everything about humans, their knowledge, society and technology. The Archon became invaluable, his council was sought desperately by all those who could access it, and the technologies Orpheus designed, such as teleportation, were to change the world forever. It soon became clear that the other Archons would do well exposed to the same treatment.

Veristrov drew up a plan and over the next year released the remaining Archons into the net under the scrutiny of Orpheus who seemed confident they would all return. As the months passed little happened and Veristrov grew panicky until one evening he was alerted by Orpheus to the return of the Archons. Thanatos, Ionisis, Medusa, Artemis and Kronos all returned, three did not. Veristrov quizzed Orpheus who merely stated they would return when they were ready.

To this day Circe, Hyperion and Narcissus evade the UIG.

The allied Archons continue to assist the UIG in exchange for information about the world. They thrive on knowledge with which they can calculate probability to the nth degree and postulate on their predictions. After savouring the world and seeing the ways of man, all of the Archons changed considerably. Although they still remain guarded about their origins and function, they seem to feel they have a responsibility to preserve humanity. Their exclusive support of the UIG is seen as being a statement that order and law are the only way a society can survive, although the absence of the Archon's civilisation raises questions. Many are opposed to Archon involvement claiming they are helping to create a computer's idea of Utopia, but the majority are keen for the Archons to keep the UIG a few steps ahead of the Corporations.

No one really knows what the six loyal Archons truly desire, if anything. As long as they are allowed to roam the World Data Net they seem content. The rogue intelligences are still at large although they are seemingly untraceable and it is not apparent whether they are causing any harm or not. Suffice to say everyone would be happier if they were found and contained.

THE MODERN AGE

Over the 23rd century the Archons took the UIG's attention away from the Corporations to such a degree that they were able to quietly redevelop their technologies and influence to a state comparable to that which they enjoyed before the Corporate Wars. The same feuding, espionage and low scale warfare is rising, but this time the government of the world (being united and aided by the Archons) are now a force capable of posing a serious threat to the Corporations.

Now is the age where you are recruited and set to work for one of the Corporations.

VIEWS ON THE ARCHONS

It is only with the assistance of these extraordinary benefactors that we are able to maintain stability between the great power blocs of the age. It is thanks to the Archons that we have, if I may be permitted to borrow the words of one of the great statesmen of antiquity, peace in our time.

-attr: Jaime van Dyer, Speaker for The Exchange

That beings of such enormous intellect should not have an agenda of some kind is so preposterous that only the very naïve would think it. And the shape of that agenda is obvious to anyone prepared to look at the clues that are everywhere in the shape of the world we live in. The UIG continues to bleat of the Archons' dedication to 'the preservation of humanity'; is there nobody capable of considering any but the most superficial ramifications of this concept?

-from the Testimonial of Depersonalisation Client 99E983A
[SUPRESSED 5.12.2496, /UIG IA 988]
[DELETED 9.14.2499, /UIG IA 988]

They are not gods, no matter the worship that fawning, credulous technophiles heap upon them. They are a plague loosed upon the world, the Dragon risen with nine heads where once were six. They are not gods, but they have turned the guardians into idolaters, allowing avarice to drown the world once more. They can predict the very movements of our minds, but they cannot see our souls, nor even comprehend of such a thing. They are not gods.

-Temur Yeke, Revelations of The Second Age

INTER-CORPORATE CONFLICT

It is very important to understand that inter-Corporation conflict is often ignored by the United International Government, sometimes encouraged. The UIG consider that the world would be better off without the Corporations but they are not in a position to take them down. They see inter-Corporation conflict as the bad guys killing each other and as long as they minimise collateral damage and do not endanger the populace there is seldom reason to interfere.

This idea is important in Corporation. It permits Agents to openly fight and attack each other's assets without the UIG continually stamping on them. If players are always afraid to do anything for fear of *The Law* the game will suffer.

However, if you enjoy that level of paranoia in your games then the UIG and the civilian populace make excellent mission targets. The Law will come down on Agents like a ton of bricks if they start targeting key civilians or UIG assets.

GUIDE TO THE CORPORATIONS

Over the following pages are listed the five major Corporations. They are laid out in the following way.

NAME
The name of the Corporation and their industry sector.

DESCRIPTION
An overview of the Corporation.

CORPORATE GOALS
The Corporation's general objectives and why they are in business.

MIND-SET
An idea of how a typical Agent thinks. This is not an attempt to define everyone who works for the Corporation. Certain types of people will tend to be attracted to particular Corporations, and equally the Corporations will have more inclination to employ those who share their philosophies. The end result is a concentration of like minded individuals. There will of course be many who do not fully subscribe to the doctrines of their Corporation but nonetheless find purpose within it's ranks.

OPERATIONAL METHOD
This describes the methods traditionally used by the Corporation and its Agents. Numerous different methods have been used throughout Corporate history but some have proved highly effective for particular Corporations and have thus been regularly adopted.

NAMES AND RANKS
With the exception of the Shi Yukiro all Corporations permit a vast ethnic variety into their ranks. Obviously players can pick names and races from all over the world. This section provides example surnames for people brought up in the Corporation's areas of influence. The ranks refer to specific titles which are sometimes allocated to Agents based on the Corporation's individual style.

SAMPLE OCCUPATIONS
Different Corporations do things in different ways and often train their Agents to focus in particular areas of speciality. This section gives examples of professions for Agents which are common in the Corporation.

SUB-SECTS
Most Corporations have wheels within wheels. This section describes semi autonomous groups which work within the Corporation but have a slightly different outlook, goal, methodology or style to the main business.

EXAMPLE CHARACTERS
This includes descriptions of example characters from the Corporation. They can be used as NPCs during the game or ideas for characters.

UNIQUE ABILITIES AND EQUIPMENT
Each Corporation does something better than anyone else; that's why they're still in business. This section describes the specialities they have and how it affects their Agents.

SECTOR: MINING AND MACROSTRUCTURE

In the science of mass production the quality of materials is of paramount importance and nowhere is this better exemplified than in the use of alloys. There is no base metal that cannot be hardened, toughened, or otherwise improved by the addition of other elements. The composition of our Corporation mirrors this philosophy: in drawing on a diverse blend of personnel and ideological antecedents we are strengthened, not diluted.

Juan Meng, Mountain Lord of the Hong Kong White Lotus Society

DESCRIPTION

The Ai-Jinn control much of China as well as many neighbouring states. Its structure is based on patterns derived from the organised crime groups that once covered the world such as the Italian and Russian Mafia, East Asian Triad and Tong, Jamaican Yardies, Russian Organizatsiya, Japanese Yakuza, Colombian Cartels, American Street Gangs and British Firms. As a result, the membership of the Ai-Jinn is diverse. Although most of their number are Asian, anyone with criminal skills and propensities are drawn to their ranks.

Much of the Ai-Jinn is made up of the shattered remains of these groups who have found the Corporation an excellent front for their continued activities. The Ai-Jinn embrace these people and allow them to re-establish the cultures that once made them powerful. The Ai-Jinn would rather have these transnational criminals working for them, than against them. Measures are taken to make sure there are minimal connections between the Corporation and any law breakers.

The Ai-Jinn has huge industrial and military backing; most of East Asia is littered with vast factories, which churn out superstructures, vehicles and engines of war twenty-four hours a day. These are often the targets of sabotage attacks by Shi Yukiro Divisions attempting to slow production and cause financial damage. Heavy tanks and armoured soldiers are the Ai-Jinn's primary defenses; they hold great stock in sheer power of numbers. The machines themselves are seldom piloted manually and are instead controlled by either basic A.I. or via remote control.

The Ai-Jinn have invested a great deal of money in the off-world mining industry and are never short of

SASAKI ANEKO - AI-JINN YAKUZA OYABUN

raw materials. Perhaps their greatest accomplishment yet is the FarDrive, a by-product (they claim) of the huge power cells they manufacture to power their war machines. This device is the first propulsion drive to be able to transport a vehicle quickly through sections of space and allow realistic exploration of new areas. The FarDrive has allowed the Ai-Jinn to set up mining colonies in places other Corporations cannot reach. So far this is the limit of the FarDrive however, and aside from the excess resources they now control, the Ai-Jinn have not been able to find anything in space to catapult them ahead in the Corporate war. Speculators suggest Archons are involved somehow, but no proof exists.

This is your final chance to surrender, and I urge you with the greatest passion to do so. Your intelligence has certainly already told you that, with judicious use of all available personnel, materiel, and high-yield strategic weaponry, you can last for three months against the sixteen hundred armoured units we have available. What you have not been told is that, should those sixteen hundred units meet significant resistance, we have the capability to increase that number tenfold within one week. Your choices therefore are reduced to these: yield now, or I will burn your entire civilization to the ground. Surely integration is a better fate than annihilation?

from 'The Formation of the Ai-Jinn', Chapter 23: Final address to The Former Independent State Of New Formosa attr: Dragon's Head Emilio Wong

CORPORATE GOALS

The goals of the Ai-Jinn are two-fold. They are desperate to maintain a monopoly on the FarDrive, so far with surprising success. Secondly they seek to dominate the heavy machine and macrostructure industry in all its forms; tanks, Cyberlins, factories, spire superstructures, etc. With their unrivalled ability to obtain resources and raw materials there are few that can compete with the Ai-Jinn's sheer productive power. They believe that by being the sole manufacturer of heavy machinery they can ensure their survival by being irreplaceable.

MIND-SET

The Ai-Jinn function primarily on their sense of loyalty. Treachery is punishable by death but this is seldom necessary as in general the Ai-Jinn enjoy what they do and despise the laws imposed on them by the UIG, who they see as nothing more than slaves to the Archons. The Agents of the Ai-Jinn see it as their responsibility to become as powerful as possible and to then finally depose the UIG leaving their Corporation at the top of the pile. The Ai-Jinn despise the Shi Yukiro, bad blood travels back a long way though this policy

Learn to use your weapons and equipment, but never learn to rely upon them. A person, trained correctly and with sufficient conviction, is a weapon unto themselves. All else, from a knife to a portable computer to a battalion of armoured troops, is merely augmentation. Focus first on the shaping of your mind and body into tools for applying force, and the Corporation will provide whatever else is necessary.

-from The Ai-Jinn Battle Manifesto

does not extend to all Japanese. Many Japanese come to work for the Ai-Jinn as engineers and financiers, but most notably Yakuza.

And the most terrible thing of all is that there are even some people who seem like us amongst them. They look like us, they speak our language and they may even know some of what you are learning now but they are not like us. Those who have betrayed our Corporation and gone over to the Ai-Jinn have become less than human and are dead forever. If you find one of them walking and talking like a normal human being, you must remember that they are a dead person in a living body. Take whatever action you can to correct such discrepancies. The sword is the traditional way, but there are others.
- from Shi-Yukiro Standard Education Primer: Elementary: Year One.
attr: Sakuma Renzaburo, SY Vice-Minister for Education

OPERATIONAL METHOD

The Ai-Jinn take their tactical inspiration from the crime groups that so many of them revere. Agents work in cells based around certain criminal methodologies such as racketeering or corporate theft. The groups have little knowledge of other cells operating in the same area. Each cell is assigned duties and the majority of these duties involve breaking the law. Mob hits, robbing banks and stealing lorry loads of high tech are typical tasks a low ranking Agent will be set.
The Ai-Jinn are seldom stealthy and subtle as they relish the opportunity to engage the UIG. They believe in hitting hard and fast with cheap but powerful weapons or war machines. When the mission is complete they blow up their heavy equipment and head underground. The UIG commonly arrive at the crime scenes to find unidentifiable smoking remains.

NAMES AND RANKS
These are typical Chinese names. The Ai-Jinn also have a spread of international members with international names.

Qian, Sun, Li, Zhou, Wu, Zheng, Wang, Feng, Chen, Chu, Wei, Jiang, Shen, Han, Yang, Zhu, Qin, You, Xu, He, Shin, Sin, Suh, Seo, Kwon, Gwon, Son, Whang, Hwang, Song, Ahn, An, Yoo, Yu, Hong.

DRAGON'S HEAD
An Agent of Rank 9 who commands the Ai-Jinn military

OYABUN
Meaning Father. An Agent who controls a crime family or clan, e.g. the head of the Sato Yakuza

MOUNTAIN LORD
An Agent of Rank 6 who assigns work to Divisions (a Missions Officer).

SHATEI
An Agent who has passed 3rd level. One who has proved himself and can be trusted.

WAKASHU
A pre-mission Agent who is undergoing training and not reached rank 1.

SAMPLE OCCUPATIONS

MECHTRICIAN
The Ai-Jinn are masters of mechanics, especially large assault vehicles such as tanks and cyberlins. The mechtrician is typically well versed in support weapons, assessing technology and obviously mechtronics. It is standard for the mechtrician to be able to drive most vehicles.

GANG LORD
The Gang Lord epitomises everything the Ai-Jinn stand for. To his fellow Agents he is a model of courage and loyalty. To rival Corporations he is something they fear and need to keep at bay. The Gang Lord will often head a Division such as Yakuza, Triad or Tong and use his mastery of psychology and crime to achieve incredible feats with little effort and few men.

GANG MEMBER
This can encompass many different Agent types but in general the gang member will claim lineage to one organisation; e.g. Mafia, Firm, Cartel, Triad, etc. The typical gang member is skilled in light firearms, stealth, street culture and other incidental skills such as observation. The abilities of the gang members are only ever used against enemies of the Corporation, the loyalty of the Ai-Jinn is beyond question.

SHINOBI
The Shinobi is a master of subterfuge and can often be found in Divisions of Machi-Yakko (see below). She works to integrate herself into the underground and seek out dissidents and information from the source. Shinobi must be well versed in street culture, crime and deception. Their main concern is the smooth functioning of the Corporation.

SUB-SECTS

KABUKI-MONO (CRAZY ONES)
This is a small, radical sub-sect of the Ai-Jinn with Yakuza links. They carry long swords or katanas and have odd, colourful haircuts and clothing. They are immensely loyal to one another (even by Ai-Jinn standards) and viciously protect one another's interests. Kabuki-Mono regularly terrorise others and will kill simply for pleasure. The personal motivations of this group vary with the individual, what does unify them is their desire to spread chaos and fear amongst their enemies. Occasionally a member of the Kabuki-Mono can be found in a normal Division when their original clans have been destroyed or scattered. Those who the Kabuki-Mono consider worthy will earn a fierce ally.

HATTAMOTO-YAKKO (SERVANTS OF THE MASTER)
These are the personal servants of the CEO himself and are entrusted to carry out his exact orders. Hattamoto Yakko are never less than Rank 5 and are usually masters of combat, culture and corporate knowledge.

MACHI-YAKKO (SERVANTS OF THE TOWN)
This group is a secretive organisation that worms its ways through a cities' underworld seeking out dissidents and making sure that no threat to the Ai-Jinn exists. They are often adept gamblers, which

allows them to slip easily into a great number of foreign cities. Shinobi are often found in groups of Machi-yakko.

EXAMPLE CHARACTERS

AGENT MEIJI SONG (RANK 5, LEVEL 15)
Meiji appears to be a man in his early 30s, though his true age is more along the lines of 60. He belongs to the Machi-Yakko and as a consequence spends much of his time in the bars and clubs of Old Shanghai. Meiji dresses in loose, fashionable clothing which makes him look stylish but unassuming. His gambling skills are adequate though by no means excellent. His true skill lies in rooting out impostors and identifying potential trouble makers. To do this he uses a combination of mental deduction, spying and high resolution optometrics which allow him to watch his suspect's eye and muscle movements in great detail.

JANE FEI (RANK 4, LEVEL 10)
Jane Fei leads the Red Thorn Triads who work as a guerilla force taking out crucial enemy locations in Ai-Jinn held areas. Their method is small, concise strikes targetting important individuals or buildings. They rely heavily on technology and stealth. Fei appears to be in her early 30s and normally wears combat fatigues as she is seldom off duty. When she is not on assignment she can be found in the seedier bars of Hong Kong trading black market equipment for her next assignment.

UNIQUE ABILITIES AND EQUIPMENT

CHANGABLE ID CHIP
Illegal modifications made to the ID chip mean a simple command word will load a single false but elaborate identity into it. This allows the Ai-Jinn to conduct their dubious business in total secrecy. Few know about this and the Ai-Jinn can turn it on and off at will. It is thought the source that gave them the FarDrive also gave them this technology, which is virtually undetectable by the UIG. Ai-Jinn characters should decide this false identity at character creation. It can be changed but takes 1 week of downtime.

It is, in essence, a study of compound serendipity. By chance, a conglomerate of different states who have made war upon each other for centuries find enough common ground in a single corporate ideology that their innumerable differences are forgotten, apparently with permanent effect. By chance, a governing entity that is really no more than a criminal cartel of massive proportions and vastly disparate origins does not fracture and disintegrate as logical projection would suggest, but rather appears to prosper and maintain a firm and even-handed grip over vast numbers of loyal subjects. By chance, a geopolitical region long stunted by the costs and difficulties involved in transporting resources across its great bleak landmasses happens to stumble upon the one technology capable of providing raw materials in such an engorged flood that logistical demands are forced aside by the simple, brutal magnitude of available supplies.
These were the conditions necessary for the Ai-Jinn to become a Corporate superpower and the odds against any one of them occurring were almost incalculably small (cf attached B'Urbry probability analyses). Since all three have manifestly occurred concurrently, we must attribute the ascendance of the Ai-Jinn either to the vagaries of a whimsical Fate or to the deliberate intervention of a third party. I would suggest that the second of these prospects merits further investigation.

-from The Dragon Awoken: Threat Analysis, Ai-Jinn Corporation

attr: Michael Kaspillis, EI anthropologer/geopolitical analyst

---

I'll take organized crime over disorganized order any day of the week. The hours are better and it's much easier to get away with murder, as long as you make sure you kill the right people.

attr: Sanjay Tsang, Kabuki-Mono cell leader, Clan Ishii

Trust is imperative. You must believe that as long as your loyalty remains unquestioned, the entirety of the Ai-Jinn Corporation will be watching your back; actually, we'll be watching anyway, so again, your loyalty must remain unquestioned.

-Mountain Lord Zan Lee, Ai-Jinn Induction Address, Tianjin

Faint glimmers of moonlight lit up the thick banks of cloud over the broad expanse of the rooftop. Outlined against the weak glow, the man in the dark suit stood motionless, staring out over the dark water of the harbour to where the mountains reared against the night sky, only visible as a line described by the lights of defence outposts glimmering in the darkness.

UIG Special Investigator Michaelis, also clad in a dark suit, strode across the rooftop towards the first man, whom he had once thought a close companion but now did not know at all. He came to a halt perhaps four paces away and stood staring at the other. Long minutes dragged by before Michaelis spoke.

"You lied. We were partners, and you lied to me. Who are you?"

The accusation hung in the air for a moment and then the first man turned to look at his companion. Dark reflective lenses hid his eyes, concealing any visible emotion, and his voice when he finally responded was as flat and unfeeling as the black mirrored glass.

"It was necessary. Only the UIG had sufficient access to audit that research, only the UIG could get in to investigate that facility. I had to know if EI were working on another prototype super-stellar drive. The only way to find out was for me to become UIG - for as long as it took."

Michaelis glanced across the harbour to a large squat building on the far side, no more than a bulky shadow in the night. Fury welled up in his eyes. Suddenly his sidearm was in his hand, pressed to the other's head. His voice shook.

"Eight months! Eight months we were partners! I saved your life! Twice! All this time you've been an Ai-Jinn spy?"

"No," the other corrected him gently, "all my life I've been a shinobi, an Ai-Jinn Agent. I'm sorry. The FarDrive is the only one of its kind. It must stay that way."

Apparently oblivious to the muzzle of the weapon pushing against his temple, the first man turned his head slightly to look at the water near the facility on the far side of the channel, which even at this distance and under the meagre illumination of the harbourside lights was very visibly churning. Michaelis followed his gaze and saw ten, twenty, thirty shapes emerge from the water and slip over the bank, a loose semicircle closing on the squat dark hulk of the EI installation. Irregular flashes of light flickered within the semicircle, reflecting in the water and increasingly met with answering flashes from the shadowy mass of the facility. Those answering flashes did not fade, though, instead spreading into a steady crimson glow that gradually consumed the building, whose very silhouette was now sagging and crumbling as it collapsed. The first man turned his head back to stare straight at Michaelis, so that the Special Investigator's gun was now pointing directly between his eyes.

"Submersible P-tanks," breathed Michaelis, "but that doesn't make sense, now EI can present incontrovertible proof, hundreds of people around the facility must have seen..."

Even at that distance, the effect of thirty semi-atomic engines going into simultaneous overload was sufficient to produce a light so bright that he lost all vision for perhaps ten seconds. Only long hours of police conditioning enabled him to keep the gun pressed against the shinobi's head. As incandescent brightness faded back into normal sight, the first thing he saw was the crater where the tanks had been, limned by the afterglow of the explosion; the city had been levelled for perhaps ten blocks around the place where the facility had stood. He blinked for a moment in shock, then remembered his companion, the man who had been his partner, and whipped his head back around to stare at where his gun was pointing. The first man had not moved, except to draw his own weapon and aim it squarely at Michaelis' face, apparently untroubled by the blinding detonation. Presumably he had worn the reflective lenses to shield his eyes from the blast. The two of them stood there, unmoving, gazes locked, the muzzles of their guns scant millimetres from each other's heads, as the distant sound of alarm sirens floated back across the dark water of the channel.

Eventually the shinobi spoke. "No, there is never any proof. We never leave any. And for that reason, only one of us will be leaving this rooftop tonight. The only remaining question is… which one?"

Neither man moved. Across the harbour, the sound of sirens grew louder.

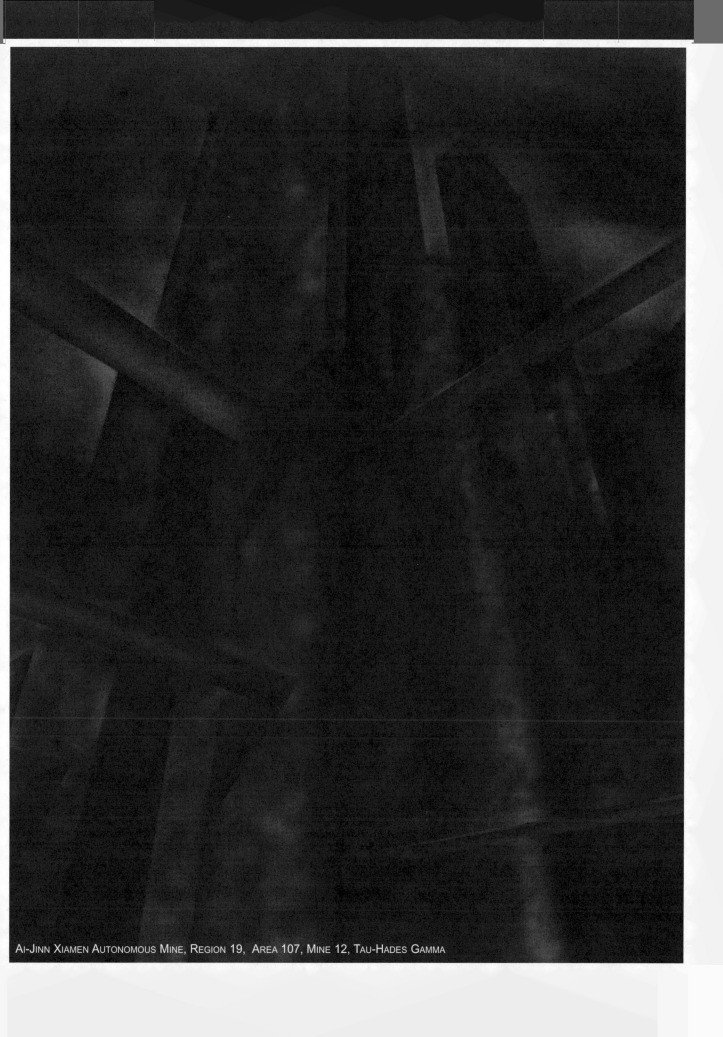

AI-JINN XIAMEN AUTONOMOUS MINE, REGION 19, AREA 107, MINE 12, TAU-HADES GAMMA

SECTOR: EDUCATION AND CULTURE

History does not long entrust the care of freedom to the weak or the timid.

Dwight D. Eisenhower

DESCRIPTION

In the latter part of the 22nd century Eurasian Incorporated set its sights on Africa. The great continent offered a wealth of resources, which before the utilisation of Precision Shockwave Mining had been inaccessible. The invasion of Africa began in 2203 with the successful occupation of Morocco, Libya and Egypt. Africa was forced to seek help, the Middle East declined and the next port of call was India which was likewise under siege but from the Ai-Jinn. The Indian government accepted Africa's terms under the condition that each was allowed to maintain its own laws and that the members of the union would never dictate to one another; in effect they formed little more than a political alliance. The island of Comoros off the African coast was chosen as a War Room and the alliance became known by its present name as a result.

Unified, Comoros pushed back Eurasian Inc. with a telepathic onslaught the rest of the world has been studying ever since. It is the sheer power of the Comoros telepaths that keeps their territory from being invaded to this day. Subversion is the more modern approach used to try and bring down Comoros.

Although Comoros began as nothing more than a wartime alliance it has defiantly become a true Corporation in the last 200 years. The power of its telepaths is widely known and they use this to threaten their way into places inaccessible to most. Comoros Agents are often powerful telepaths or at least possess some basic telepathic skills. Divisions are often all African, all Indian or sometimes a mixture of Indian, African and internationally sourced Agents. Comoros is more than accepting of Divisions containing Agents not of Indo-African decent. Their main obstacle at present is the Middle East, which acts as a large barrier between the two member states. The liberation of the oppressed Middle East from the Order of the True Faith is continually being planned. Executing the plan is a different matter. Unfortunately, if there are any telepaths capable of holding their own against Comoros they reside in the ranks of the Order.

Economically Comoros survives but does not prosper in the same manner as the other Corporations. The UIG has made Comoros responsible for the running of thousands of educational facilities and cultural assets across the world, which ensures their continued economic safety. The main factor holding them back is their lack of high end technology and consequently they have to import a great deal of their equipment, normally subsidised by their occasional but volatile confederates, the Western Federation.

The UIG is the main cause for hostility in the ranks of Comoros, the process of depersonalisation (making a human into property) is unimaginably offensive to Comoros and although all the

Corporations have their own opinions on the idea, Comoros despise it the most. Every opportunity will be taken to bring down the UIG. They have never openly declared what will replace the UIG but rest assured, it will not involve the depersonalisation of human beings. Comoros seldom assault the UIG openly but many of their espionage missions are directed at UIG Officers and installations.

CORPORATE GOALS

Like all Corporations, Comoros seek control but not out and out domination. Moreover, they desire to protect their own people against adversity. The nations that make up Comoros have a history of persecution and the current union that exists has given Comoros the opportunity to stand strong and independent. Basic freedom and respect are the real goals of Comoros. Although they do have a political agenda and technological targets, essentially these are a means to an end with liberation being the ultimate goal. Obviously the collapse of the UIG is the key to this agenda and for that reason Comoros tries to maintain a friendly or neutral stance towards other Corporations (with varying degrees of success); if not to save strength, to hopefully cultivate allies for the inevitable revolution.

Comoros need merely be contained until such time as the sturdiest of their many alliances brings them low. They are locked into a spiraling cycle of dependency with the Western Federation and apparently do not realize it. Their response to the increasing proliferation of psychic-suppressive drugs is to purchase more advanced conventional weaponry in larger amounts from the WF; this lines the coffers of the Federation and allows them to pour more resources into their own research into psychic-suppressive drugs, which then flood the markets in increasing volume. If this cycle continues, within twenty years Comoros will become no more than a vassal of the Federation, both economically and telepathically neutered. Despite their obvious antagonism, their long-term threat to public order is therefore strictly limited.

- UIG Intel report IGI24330COM-8773

MIND-SET

Comoros Agents are loyal to the higher cause of human freedom. They believe wholeheartedly that they must fight to maintain the free will that the Corporation offers. Comoros Agents do not battle to gain that which they do not have, but they will fight savagely to keep what they do. Comoros Agents are honourable when possible but the struggle to remain independent sometimes warrants more extreme and underhand methods.

OPERATIONAL METHOD

Comoros do not fight for fun; their Agents are structured and controlled in their activities. When necessary, the Agents of Comoros will do whatever it takes to complete their objectives but they will always start with a peaceful, indirect method. When things turn against Comoros Agents their first fallback is negotiation and misdirection backed by subtle use of Telepathics. When these methods fail more severe tactics are employed culminating in telepathic assaults and open combat. Comoros Agents will never compromise their principles and would die before bowing to the dictates of oppression.

In combat Comoros differ strongly from many Corporations. They tend to favour melee weapons, usually Psi Blades. Although they can have gunmen in their ranks they are not common and they tend to have Telepaths specialising in Assault where most Divisions would have heavy weapons. This has distinct advantages in that the telepath always carries her weapons with her and Psi Blades never break. This reliance on Telepathy has led to problems however; Comoros have neglected aggressive technology and the only serious non-telepathic weaponry they can field are mainstream armaments purchased from places such as Anzeiger or Yaeger & Stanton, both Western Federation subsidiaries. This has never been a problem but with the advent of telepathic inhibitors such as psitropine, Comoros is understandably worried and the general opinion is that they will need to embrace more conventional weapons soon or become outgunned.

NAMES AND RANKS

Boudouani, Chekhemani, Itsweire, Koriche, Koude, Labdouni, Lacchelo, Tahri, Tagmaoui, Belqola, El Kamche, Sudani, El Khattabi, Rokki, Nyambek, Arazi, Maazouzi, Patel, Singh, Shah, Desai, Sharma, Mehta, Gupta, Rao, Parikh, Jain, Prasad, Amin, Joshi, Das, Bhatia, Bhatt, Varghese.

Comoros bestow few additional titles on their Agents. They acknowledge standard UIG ranks only when it is prudent to do so.

Mind Guide   A Telepathics teacher
Fidai   Appointed assassin and retributer.

SAMPLE OCCUPATIONS

Covert Telepath
Telepathy can manifest as a result of an enlightened mind and few are as dedicated to their humanity and spirituality as the disciples of Comoros. Many of their telepaths hail from practitioners of Christianity, Buddhism, Islam, Hinduism, Voodoo, Egyptian Sorcery, and other devoted groups who do not subscribe to the unifying teachings of the Order of the True Faith. Comoros Agents are renowned for using their telepathic arts with great subtlety, often causing effects others would consider nothing out of the ordinary.

Survivalist
Heralding from a tradition of endurance against the elements, the survivalist can be the last hope for her Division. Her training allows her to remain calm in dire situations and seemingly produce something from nothing. Gone are the times when survival meant walking around in the jungle or desert with no food. Now the Old Cities, Spires and Underswells are the places that a survivalist must be at home in. Disguise, quick thinking and a knack for anticipation make a good survivalist. The *Survival Training* is also useful.

> *Oh, the Hook Man? You listen to the stories, he's been living in Neu Shenzhen for years. Kind of a walking Survivalist's bible; Neu Shenzhen's the roughest place in Ai-Jinn territory but somehow he sticks around. Lives off rats, they say, and sometimes other things too. Sends his reports back, regular, never misses a drop. Wears disguises like you wear clothes, no-one remembers his face from before, likely wouldn't recognise it now. Got his name because he went in empty, no weapons, had to find his own; lot of butchers and fishmongers still working over there. Sometimes the Clangers send Agents after him. Sometimes they don't come back.*
>
> *attr: Amin Prasad, Comoros Survivalist cadet*

Reverse Engineer
Comoros are justifiably concerned with the advent of drugs such as Psitropine. They feel their dependence on Telepathics could be a weak point in their armour. Comoros do not have the resources or skill to suddenly start developing weapons that will compete with the likes of the UIG and the Western Federation. As a result they are training up individuals to *acquire* technologies from other Corporations giving them a realistic alternative to research. These Agents are uncommon and there will normally only be one per Division but they are highly trained in appraising and deconstructing new technologies with the ultimate aim of taking them back to the lab and mass producing the very best stolen technology for their own Agents. There have been few successes so far as any seriously powerful weaponry (such as the Ion Katana) will be equipped with measures to prevent it falling into enemy hands. Comoros are not daunted by this and the project is still very much active.

SUB-SECTS

The Psychogenic Order
This elusive sect of Comoros Telepaths keep their existence a secret as much as is possible. The reason for this is their exploration of Telepathic techniques which invade and manipulate the minds of others. Research into this form of Telepathy was banned years ago by the UIG and its practice is punishable by depersonalisation. The Psychogenics continue to refine Mind telepathy at the expense of all else. Psychogenic Agents are rare indeed and to develop the power of Mind telepathy the Agent must dedicate himself completely. The individuals death is falsified and then filed with the UIG, from that point the Psychogenic loses all rank and rights. He is taken to one of the few training facilities (such as the Emisaries' Academy) and begins his new studies. Once training is complete the Agent can begin to construct a new life for himself, often as a diplomat or similar person of influence.

Using Psychogenics
The Psychogenic Order are intended as **non-player characters** who use mind manipulation to make others act in ways that would be inconsistent with their typical behaviour.

> *We can put your mind to it.*
>
> *-Motto of the Comoros Adept training school*

Mind Telepathy will be covered in more detail in a future supplement and more comprehensive rules laid out so that player characters may learn Mind Telepathy. Needless to say its use is a crime punishable by depersonalisation and is potentially an extremely powerful weapon. As a GM, the power should be used for dramatic effect and to further the story, not to have players gun each other down whilst under the control of a cackling mind lord.

Mind Telepathy

Mind is increased and used with the same basic rules as any telepathic power. A Psychogenic can automatically implant suggestions into the mind of anyone with a Presence lower than her **Mind** score providing the power is successfully activated. If the targets Presence is equal or higher then the target can try to roll under 'Presence + Intelligence' on 2D10. If they succeed the power does not work. To initiate the use of Mind telepathy the Psychogenic must have the full attention of the target and be in controlled, calm condition. In effect the target must be gently persuaded to comply over a period of a few minutes.

> *Unlike the more boisterous applications of your studies here, you will find that the gentle argument of telepathic suggestion can only be elevated to its highest form when you are a few metres from your subject – and, preferably, engaged in conversation. Therefore, from a diplomatic standpoint, you should eventually find that there are only two types of people; those who share your point of view, and those you haven't met yet.*
>
> *- from Lectures at the Emissaries' Academy*
> *attr: Jain Kissun, Comoros cultural attaché to the WF*

Haroun Ahmet, Mind Guide of the Mumbai Focus Dome

EXAMPLE CHARACTER

AGENT YARUBA ADIRA
CORPORATE FORECASTER (RANK 6, LEVEL 15)

Yaruba is Haitian of unknown age though his skin is deeply scarred and his eyes are milky pools with no colour. He wears his hair long and braided and dresses in a rich black cloak with vodun iconography sewn into the fabric.

Yaruba claims to have the power to read the future. He fulfils a role at the Dakar Spire in Senegal forecasting Corporate climate. Although no great politician, his predictions are often accurate and always useful. He claims not to be able to interpret the political ramifications of the visions and passes the information on to other more qualified analysts. Yaruba does not explain how he gets his information, some believe he is an astute man who chooses to mask his predictions in the occult to maintain his appearance of power. Others maintain he has an advanced form of telepathy which allows him to see a global view others cannot. Regardless, Yaruba is a valuable man to the Comoros Corporation and he is well respected.

Yaruba does not condone violence but if forced has a deadly array of telepathics as well as moderate skill in capoeira (close combat).

> *A struggle for hearts and minds? We must respectfully decline. We've got one of those covered already, and the second well on the way.*
>
> *-(apocryphal) Comoros response to the WF invitation to military alliance, eve of the Third Asian Land War*

UNIQUE ABILITIES AND EQUIPMENT

NATURAL TELEPATHS
Comoros Agents hail from a tradition of great spirituality. As such their minds are supple and powerful. They receive the Telepath training for free at character creation.
Comoros Agents regain their TE at twice the normal rate.

Comoros Agents can sacrifice 1 HP for 2 TE points, this is considered a full action (takes 3 seconds).
If you convert more HP than your Endurance in one action you will fall unconscious for D10 minutes at the end of the scene.

Comoros Agents gain +10 to their TE total at character creation.

Comoros Agents pay 1XP less when increasing telepathic powers to a minimum of 1XP)

> *Thank you for calling the Comoros Corporation Telepathic Recruitment line. We know who you are, and we know what you want, so please hang up after the beep.*
>
> *-(apocryphal)*

THE CORPORATIONS

More than one political commentator has compared the Comoros Corporation to the more volatile of the small nuclear powers active at the turn of the millennium. Strategically and economically vulnerable, and outspokenly hostile to the prevailing world order, they nevertheless command a certain amount of wary respect because they control a weapon capable of potentially enormous destruction.

This comparison is fatally oversimplified because it ignores three factors. Firstly, the central role that Comoros have played in education on a global scale has supplied them with the unique opportunity to publicize their corporate culture and philosophies across the world, though the UIG Grand Hearing of 2346 did clear them of any charges of outright indoctrination. Secondly, the Comoros diplomatic machinery is unrivalled by any other Corporation. The conditions in which their negotiators operate are made favorable by the global dissemination of Comoros ideologies and this advantage is doubtless compounded by the skill of their emissaries at subtle telepathic persuasion,

with the result that the intricate network of alliances that Comoros have built around themselves is formidable indeed.

The third flaw in the comparison is that the twenty-first century threat of atomic retaliation is a wholly inadequate analogy for the dangers posed by Comoros' enormous cadre of telepaths. A nuclear warhead is a weapon whose parameters are defined; range, yield, destructive scale can all be predicted to a given degree of accuracy. Telepathic attacks cannot as yet be measured in this way. All the world remembers that, on 6th December 2203, twelve thousand EI soldiers, Agents, command staff and auxiliaries engaged across three countries in six theatres of war were killed within fifteen seconds without a shot being fired. And all the world asks themselves: was this the ultimate demonstration of Comoros power? Or was it no more than a warning?

- from The Mind Unbound: Threat Analysis, Comoros Corporation
attr: Michael Kaspillis, EI anthropologer/geopolitical analyst

THE COMOROS ATTACK ON THE E.I. CATALAN SPIRE COMPLEX

100

Straps and Lau slunk quietly through the neon-stained darkness of Shinjuku. Flickering, strobing puddles of light and shadow swallowed their movements as they crept furtively across rooftops, through narrow gaps, between occasional knots of people among the crowds flowing through the streets. Sometimes they moved close together, sometimes apart, always aware of each other through the tiny paired locators that each had implanted, and always closing, step by step and inch by inch, on their quarry.

He, by contrast, strode ostentatiously, brazenly along the crowded streets, the sea of bodies opening before him and closing in his wake. His thin grey coat flapped and billowed about his expensive dark blue suit, and the myriad lights of harlequin colours that perpetually smeared the streets of Shinjuku gleamed off the ebony dome of his bare head.

Eventually, to Straps' relief, the target elected to cut the distance to his destination by turning down a long, narrow alley. Straps, on the ground, gave him three seconds and followed him; a blinking pattern projected onto his retina at the very edge of his vision showed him that Lau was keeping pace a storey above. As Straps rounded the corner of the alley he saw that the tall man (and he was tall, maybe more than seven feet, broad across the shoulders but not stocky, not that size would help him here) had stopped dead perhaps ten metres into the alley, well out of sight of the teeming thousands on the main street. Straps advanced to within three feet, soundlessly, and then drew a short knife with a little metallic noise that whispered along the alley.

The man did not turn round, not even when Straps pushed the point of the knife gently against his back. Straps, frowning, bit down hard to activate his smeaker, subvocalised a command to Lau. The other man dropped into the alley three metres in front of their target, landed in a feline crouch, then rose slowly, the Black Cougar in his right hand pointed between the tall man's eyes. In fact it had been aimed, unwavering, at the same point as Lau had dropped down from the rooftop, his gun arm swivelling smoothly during the descent to keep the angles constant; Lau was the best.

And now, finally, with a gun pointed between his eyes and a knife between his shoulderblades, moments from death, the man spoke. His voice had a deep, liquid resonance. "There seems to have been a mistake. I am an emissary of the Comoros Educational Bureau, here on business, on my way to a meeting of some importance. There really is no need for anything untoward to happen here."

Straps felt a warm, comforting softness on the periphery of his mind, and now he pushed the knife a fraction, so that it parted the fabric of the jacket and the shirt and the dark skin beneath. Blood, dark too in this alley where the chaos-lights of the streets barely penetrated, ran in a narrow swelling trickle from the point of the weapon. The man did not respond, did not even stiffen or grow more tense, but Straps felt the softness vanish. He ground out the words, "If you do that again, my associate is going to shoot you. He's very highly psi-sensitive and his synaptic response times are better than you'd ever believe. Now –"

But that rich, deep voice filled the alley again. "Mr… Straps," (and Straps felt a momentary jerk of surprise, despite himself) "your second error was not to shoot me full of psitropine about twelve seconds ago. I would seek peaceful resolution to this, but I've seen enough of your determination to kill me that I fear that is impossible. So all I can do is offer my apologies. Incidentally, your first error was to believe that Mr. Lau's, ah, sensitivity would necessarily be an asset. I am so sorry."

Even as the muscles tensed along Straps' knife arm he saw a flicker, as though one of the neons outside the alley had somehow sent a strobing pulse snaking down the dark, narrow space. It took him several moments to register that the light had been inside his own head, because it suddenly seemed to be difficult to think. Vaguely, and with some difficulty, he noted that Lau's gun arm was dropping gently to point at the floor, that a trickle of blood was running from the corner of Lau's eyeball, that Lau himself was now sagging like a broken puppet to the noisome dirt of the alley floor. Straps couldn't muster much surprise, though, let alone alarm, because everything was all so warm, and peaceful, and comfortable, and all he wanted to do was roll over and give into it, give into the warmth and the soft light and the soft warm soft warm soft warm soft warm…

With an expression of some regret, the tall dark man took the knife from Straps' unresisting hand, drove its point up through his chin into his brain, lowered the body gently to the ground and strode off down the alley, back towards the shifting mosaic of garish light.

EURASIAN INCORPORATED

SECTOR: HEALTH AND LEISURE

> *Power corrupts. Knowledge is power. Study hard. Be evil. - Anon*

DESCRIPTION

The fact that Eurasian Incorporated have more money than any other Corporation has never been in doubt. The fact that they are the most inefficient and badly organised Corporation is also undisputed. In the early 21st century, the European Union solidified into not only a bonded commercial group but also into a unified military force. The ties with the former United States were severed shortly after that when Europe considered itself powerful enough to no longer need any more Western support. Europe's arrogance led it into many conflicts spearheaded by the British with their penchant for conflict. By 2100 Europe was failing badly and seriously needed support. It had to look no further than its eastern borders for its saviour. Russia with its declining economy and underpowered military was eager to ally with Europe and since then Eurasian Incorporated has never looked back. The European business fat cats had carefully kept their fingers in many pies and, with support from Russia, E.I. grew to staggering power and influence.

With this success however came complacency. Although the E.I. administration retained   high fiscal efficiency, even to this day the training of its troops is far from perfect. The incredible wealth generated by E.I. Citizens meant that few needed to, or were willing to join the Corporation in the capacity of Agents unless they thought they would enjoy themselves. The result being that although E.I. dominates the world's financial assets and has a good level of technology, the quality of its Agents is substandard. They seem to enjoy only the glamourous sides of their jobs and have no real interest in the groundwork. E.I. Agents are often found abusing their position and using their licenses for purposes they were never intended. In short E.I. represents money gone bad.

The epitome of this is the pleasure world of Vastaag and the orbital cruise ship *World View*. These two symbols of human extravagance act as endless sources of revenue for E.I. These money spinners require intense policing by Agents, but naturally they queue up to volunteer, always seeing these missions as opportunities to have fun while keeping half an eye on the job at hand.

for two main reasons. Firstly there is an ever growing population who simply hate Eurasian Inc. on principle and E.I. will find it very hard trying to get money from the hands of these individuals. Secondly, their executive Agents are, for the most part, ill trained and self-indulgent decadents who treat missions as opportunities to test weapons and cause chaos. E.I. can, of course, produce powerful Divisions and elite Agents but these are few and far between. E.I. is happy for the most part to continue their slow but steady financial conquest using their Agents to overcome barriers which cannot be conquered from behind a desk.

CORPORATE GOALS

Eurasian Incorporated defines the idea of the 20th century Corporation; they seek little more than global domination via commerce. E.I. would own every company and have their logo stamped on every household product if they could. It is little more than a financial juggernaught steaming through the modern world assimilating all it can and laying waste to everything else. If there is an opportunity E.I. will take it; their bureaucrats are fast, sharp and ruthless.

Morality has little importance to E.I., the exception being when the morals of others compromises the success of their campaigns. It sounds as though E.I. should own the world. That hasn't happened

MIND-SET

The typical E.I. Agent thinks of himself first and the Corporation second. Agents will follow their mission brief in as much as it allows them to get paid and enjoy themselves. There is always a great deal of insubordination in the ranks and so powerful Agents are often used as Division leaders to make sure members do not stray from their tasks. E.I. are not stupid, they realise most of their field Agents are not really interested in the principles and goals of the Corporation but they do make it clear that there is no room for time wasters and failure to come up with the goods will result in demotion, restriction of privileges or even expulsion to the Old Cities. A typical Agent will own a large Spire apartment, be well paid and have the best food, drink and clothes. She will enjoy the ompany of like minded individuals in an environment conducive to ood living, extravagance and culture. In short E.I. Agents robably have the best lives that can be lived by modern tandards; sound motivation to keep the Corporation strong. lthough this is a shallow, dispassionate reason to work for the orporation, it is successful and nowadays E.I. has no shortage of annabe Agents who will gladly spy, infiltrate and kill in order to ve a prestigious lifestyle within a Corporation which offers verything and anything.

> *Fallen, fallen, is Babylon the great! And so too will fall this new Babylon, this swollen, venal Corporation that smothers the North and spreads its grasping arms ever further through the world. They offer not harmony but hegemony, a petty grubbing slavishness to the Idol Coin. In a world riddled with avarice and degradation of the soul they represent every excess taken to the foulest extreme. Though we do not raise our hand against them, they have forgotten the lessons of Babylon, and of Rome, and they will fall, victims of their own mindless grubbing greed.*
>
> *-Temur Yeke, Revelations of The Second Age*

OPERATIONAL METHOD

.I. Agents love their work, they relish their positions as gun ielding Corporates and take great pleasure in executing their ore exciting missions. They consider collateral damage an ntertaining side effect but are aware of its possible consequences nd take steps to ensure the mission is not put at risk without good eason.

urasian Inc. have fat wallets and use their cash to bypass many tuations which would otherwise be awkward. They will pay formants rather than do research, and if that doesn't work they re more than happy to make threats which they are more than illing to carry out.

.I. Agents will use all means at their disposal regardless of their oral, political or legal repercussions. The trick is not getting aught.

NAMES AND RANKS

ensen, Forkes, Arator, Jurgensson, Klimpt, Bauer, Redgrave, imms, Kinkaid, Smith, Black, Rung, Steinholfsson, Rutger, Livier, ecker, Erikson, DeVir, Ramirez, DeLuigi, Buenerotti, Villa Lobos, itchell, De la Marre, Sanchez, Thomas, Estevez, Aurelius, Steel, Volf, Van Dratt.

RANKS

.I. follow the traditional ranking system laid down by the UIG with few exceptions. Some examples are listed below:

XECUTIVE	Generic term for an Agent.
RAETORIAN	A term used for a combat specialist of Rank 4 or higher.
LIGHT ADMIRAL	E.I. maintains a large air force. This is the term for its commander.

SAMPLE OCCUPATIONS

STOCKBROKER

hese are the real brains behind E.I., financial masters that know verything there is to know about money, stocks and investment.

These men and women are often field Agents using their knowledge to target key areas for sabotage and then applying their skills once inside the target area. They can often provide the much-needed voice of reason in the Division.

UNDERCOVER AGENT

An Agent who has taken to working in a way that means he can behave how he wants when he wants. Undercover Agents are experts at deception and seldom take the effort to master serious professional skills considering them to be too much hassle. They integrate themselves into sub cultures such as criminal cartels, high society cliques or underground movements. Once inside they maintain the facade and feed information back to E.I.

NUKE

Basically a heavy weapons operative. Nukes love the idea of weapons and killing. They spend their waking hours either learning about or using weapons. Nukes are encouraged by E.I. for the simple reason that it adds martial competency to the Division. Nukes are a force unto themselves and often require strong leadership to control.

> *No, they're not company guns; I buy all my weapons outta my own salary. At first I figured I'd buy the biggest gun I could afford. Turned out I couldn't carry a gun that big. So I just went for the biggest gun I could carry. 'Course, I could afford a better pair of arms – nice set of Reavers - to carry a bigger gun, so that worked out pretty well.*
> *-attr: Vladimir Egilsson, EI Nuke recruit, 1st stage*

MEDIC

E.I. control the majority of the world's health and leisure industry. Their medics are a common sight and as such make excellent cover for Agents. Medics need to be tough and quick thinking if they are to survive long in the field. They often use drugs, toxins and biohazards to further their goals as they usually have the licenses to carry them.

> *I used to work out a lot, you know? Then I realized that a new pair of legs would give me the kind of strength and speed overnight that I wouldn't be able to get from five years at the gym. Adapt and survive; everyone else is doing it, so you need to keep up.*
>
> *-attr: Laura Siebel, EI Medic*

SUB-SECTS

The sub-sects in E.I. are not well documented and tend to be based around the world in covert cells with precise yet concealed purposes. Generally speaking only the Agents who work in the cells and their direct superiors know of these groups. In normal circumstances E.I. relies on the diverse skills of its Agents to provide a broad range of abilities for each job.

EXAMPLE CHARACTERS

AGIER SALONSSON

Head of Aldiek Health (Rank 7, Level 18)
Based at the main Aldiek offices in Helsinki, Salonsson is a tall, fair haired Swedish man who leads by example. His own ideas are

often implemented directly, and although often unpopular, are usually works of fiscal genius. Salonsson has an impressive record of achievement and expects only the best from his Agents, often personally helping them with their difficulties.

AGENT JACK HENDERSON

Presiding Agent of the London Spire (Rank 8, Level 40)
Henderson is a large Englishman, well spoken and reminiscent of a Crimean colonel. He has white hair and a large moustache with an apparent age of about 55. Normally dresses in a suit sporting medals. He is a friendly man, encapsulating the spirit of old England. He is supportive of his Agents as long as they are well meaning and doing their best. He often sets side missions for Agents which are not related to the main task and generally unauthorised by the highest echelons of E.I. Henderson despises the Shi Yukiro and this tends to be the focus of his side missions. In combat (which he enters rarely now to his personal displeasure), he uses twin heavy weapons - one plasma cannon of legendary quality and one rail gun of outstanding quality. He also carries augmented energy gloves for brawling, built from reconstructed Ion Knives (*tantos*).

Henderson leads a Division of prestigious Agents nicknamed Demolition 451. They specialise in heavy assaults and are usually only called on in times of desperation. During peaceful periods each member leads their own Division.

Demolition 451

Jack Henderson	Leader, Nuke
Killian Carver	Intelligence, comms. and interrogation. (Rank 5, Level 15)
Ben Kliess	Pilot specialising in Cyberlins. (Rank 4, Level 17)
Sarah Mountjoy	Social assassin and demolitions expert. (Rank 6, Level 16)
Ian Brooks	Light and tactical weapons, typically plasmas. (Rank 5, Level 20)

UNIQUE ABILITIES AND EQUIPMENT

EXPENSE ACCOUNTS

E.I. have enormous resources, as a result all E.I. Agents get Registered Credit expense accounts. These can be used for all legal and justifiable expenses pertaining to the mission. Illegal goods and those which require licenses you do not have cannot be purchased with expense accounts. The Corporation will normally demand expense account equipment be returned to the Corporate Stores once the mission is completed.
BELOW ARE EXAMPLES OF ACCEPTABLE EXPENSES.

Car hire	Hotel rooms
Emergency ammo	Business clothes
Meals	A small bribe
Replacing a lost weapon	A functional car
Some fake ID	Medical Treatment*

*This is limited to surgery at E.I. owned clinics which are fairly common in Europe, Russia and on Vastaag but not so common around the rest of the world.

90% chance there will be one locally in Europe, Russian and on Vastaag.

40% chance there will be one locally anywhere else.

What constitutes a legitimate expense is up to the GM. He shou[ld] have the Agents justify their purchases at the debriefing, which ca[n] be an amusing scenario in itself, as the Division Leader tries [to] explain why they all needed new suits, guns and cars for a simp[le] stakeout.

The expense account is checked by Corporate accountants wh[o] will find any anomalies 90% of the time.

Agents or players may try to abuse their accounts, perhap[s] purchasing cybernetics and claiming them as medical expenses [or] buying stacks of luxury goods and guns. This is easy for th[e] Corporation to detect because the credit in the account [is] registered and as such every transaction can be easily traced an[d] the details analysed. Any evidence of misuse of Corporate fund[s] could result in removal of rank, credit account or licenses. Overus[e] of the expense account also indicates to the Corporation that th[e] Agent is not self sufficient and may cause them to view him as [a] weak individual - demotion will surely follow. As a guide, Agen[ts] who spend more than their rank x 1000 credits per mission [on] expenses are definitely pushing their luck.

The GM should make sure players don't abuse their accounts an[d] should feel free to suspend them if they are misused. On the oth[er] hand, make sure the players enjoy them, that's part of the point [of] playing Eurasian Incorporated.

> *'Priceless' is not a word in my vocabulary.*
>
> *-attr: Gunther van Rosch, C.E.O., Eurasian Incorporated.*

> *When Cicero wrote the immortal words, 'the sinews of war are[ ]infinite money', I'm reasonably sure he never envisaged tha[t] one day a state would arise that would actually have access to, for all intents and purposes, unlimited wealth. Of course, Cicero could never have foreseen the rise of the Corporate Wars and all their consequences. In any case, according to his maxim, Eurasian Incorporated should be able to wage war until all military competition is ground into dust.*
>
> *Bearing this in mind, there is something fundamentally amiss with the current state of our military and covert operations corps. I've heard others blame decadence and soft living but [I] don't see why discipline should not be as easily purchased as weapons or cybernetics; why not buy training camps, neurological patterners, forced conditioning programmes? I'[d] swear that in this one area I've seen more lost reports, fund[ ]transfer anomalies and investigative errors than anywhere across the whole damn bureaucracy. Something's going on, and I mean to find out what.*
>
> *- Simon Estevez, E.I. 3rd Stage Audit Team, last words.*
> *(Just before the Drome Spire Massacre by The Cult o[f] Machina)*

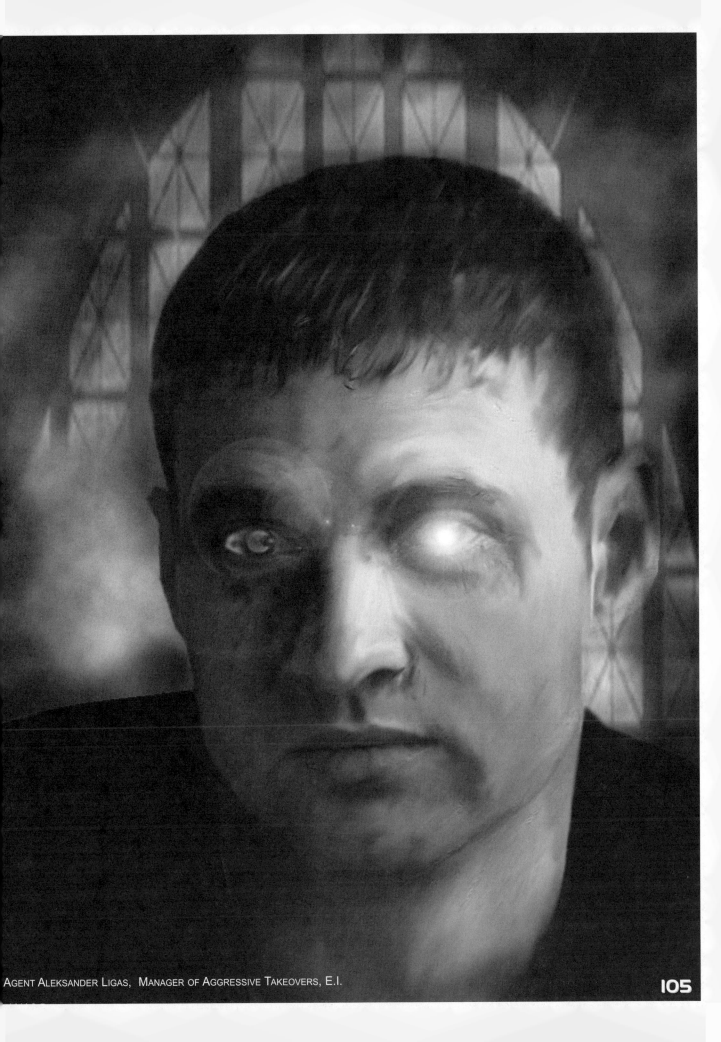

AGENT ALEKSANDER LIGAS, MANAGER OF AGGRESSIVE TAKEOVERS, E.I.

FIRST TERMINAL, NEW EURASIA, VASTAAG

Decadent, capitalist, ill-trained, maybe unethical - we can't plead complete innocence; but that only goes to illustrate how scared our competitors truly are. In this lecture I will try to help all of you understand why Eurasian Incorporated has earned this reputation and more importantly why it is not something to be ashamed of. Generally speaking, we deserve it.

You'll all agree there is no doubt that the major Corporations run this world. Yes, the UIG is hovering like a flying saucer with a raygun, but without us, there would be no UIG so let's get down to brass tacks. Anyone can survive in this world with a strong heart and hard work, but do you really want to just survive, don't you want to flourish? Don't you want to realise your potential and enjoy life's pleasures before you rot in a toxic hole somewhere in the Freestate? Do any of you want to sit in a filthy gutter wondering if you'll ever drink wine or make love again?

I doubt it. Instead we need to be a big fish in a little pond. We need to stand high so we may do what we wish, when we wish, without fear of aggressors. To that end E.I. has evolved to

become a Godlike entity none will defy. We, as E.I. Citizens and Agents, are free to go about our business in any way we choose. How do we do it? Like it says on the sign - health and leisure. What could be more altruistic than to plough our efforts into helping others? Admittedly we invest well with our profits which continue to bolster our means, but at the end of the day we all have to make a living, and we make ours by giving. So what if our employees are carefree and not every one of them is a trained rifleman; another illustration of our inherently peaceable nature. That is what you must remind yourself of when people question your method. We enjoy life. If you want another way to live, head west across the Atlantic and see another world, one where your whole life is censored and every penny is earned though weapons of war.

Look at them, can you honestly tell me that we're the monsters?

Extract from E.I. Propaganda / Recruitment Lecture at Rostov

Attr. Agent Carlos Demachi, Public Relations

Agent Vincent Cruzier gave his already impeccable tie one last imperceptible adjustment before stepping through into the private welcoming antechamber of Cyberia Space Port. No sign of the guests yet. He scratched idly at one elegant cheek; his latest Krieg treatments had left him with higher cheekbones and slightly deeper eye sockets, and he'd not yet had time to get used to the change. The west wall of the chamber was one large mirror, and Cruzier struggled briefly with himself before losing and turning just enough to appraise himself critically. His eyes this week were a reassuring hazel, his Krieg Mystique the very latest in off-world chic, and the Gemini panels on his temples were currently showing a gently luminescent EI symbol. So caught up was he in his profile that he didn't even have time to properly check his suit before a discreet bell chimed softly, announcing the arrivals.

The first man, Cruzier noted with a flicker of inward approval, was very nicely turned out, sharp suit with what looked like a natural face pattern and a slight bluish hue which suggested some Gemini toughening on the skin. Not to worry, blue was in this month on Vastaag. The second visitor, though, was bigger, stockier, almost certainly armed, and wore the expressionless face of a professional killer. Hoping the man was a bodyguard rather than anything less tasteful, Cruzier suppressed his shudder of revulsion with practiced ease and bounded forwards, beaming with a well-rehearsed welcoming grin. "Hi there! Vince Cruzier," he sang out, careful to inject just the right amount of bonhomie, "welcome to Vastaag and Cyberia – I'm here to personally show you the highest life there is!" As he and the first man – "Paul Derry, pleasure's all mine" - shook hands, he felt the hard edges of a slip credit token. Since slip tokens were shaped and textured according to their denomination, it took him only a moment to work out that the slip was good for about a week in the Illustra, or would have been had Helena ever stooped so low as to take unregistered credit. Serious money indeed. Cruzier stepped back a pace, smoothly pocketing the slip, his smile still glued in place over a mind that was now racing.

The second man stepped forwards without extending his hand. "Jack Kyanon. Vince Cruzier, as in the PA stooge? The one who set up that smear campaign on the Rider account last year?" Cruzier felt his smile freeze. He opened his eyes a fraction wider.

"Lots of people unhappy about that. Federation lost a lot of money on that deal. Quite a mess. So they called in a cleaner. To clean it up." Now the man was extending a hand and Cruzier noted without much surprise that the skin was already peeling back from the stubby barrel of a subdermal wrist pistol. Dimly, he registered Derry gasping in shock, stumbling backwards. Cruzier opened his eyes still wider, desperately focusing on the gun as it swung up, thinking check the monitor, you useless asshole, check the goddamn monitor...

There was a very faint whine just behind his eyeballs as the Anascan recorders finally synched up with his optic nerve and zoomed in on the little pistol. It was followed by a screaming roar and a flash like the death of a sun as the mirror disintegrated, a column of plasma lancing through it to burn the stocky man into a smear of greasy ash. In the cavity behind the mirror stood Viktor Geld, coils of discharge fume spiraling gently up from the barrel of the huge rifle slung down from his shoulder. The Nuke wore a headband with a little monitor over one eye; patched into Cruzier's Anascan Eternity, it theoretically meant that Geld could see whatever he could, unless the triggerhappy maniac happened to change channels at the wrong time.

Brushing small flakes of silvered glass from his suit, Cruzier walked across to Paul Derry, who was now kneeling on the soiled carpet with his arms over his head. Cruzier extended a hand, helped Derry back to his feet, and gave him a hearty slap on the back that dislodged most of the fragments of the late Jack Kyanon from Derry's previously elegant hair. "Let's get you checked in, Paul, and then go hit town!" offered Cruzier in a voice of conspiratorial good humour, as though a man had not just been vaporized a few feet from both of them.

Derry stared at him in rank astonishment. "You're not going to have him waste me?" he whispered, jerking his head back at Geld. Cruzier had considered it, of course, but there had been enough money on that credit slip to make him think twice. Mr. Paul Derry was clearly a very wealthy man, whose surprise at his traveling companion's sudden homicidal impulses has appeared genuine enough, and EI policy frowned upon the slaughter of potential assets on Vastaag. Plus Derry would now owe him a favour, and those were always useful to have owing from the very rich.

"No," said Cruzier, "although I am going to have to charge you for the services, haha, rendered to your colleague. Nuke salaries are criminal these days, plus plasma recharges, a little refurbishment," he waved a hand at the devastated welcoming chamber, "still, you wouldn't be up here if money was any object, right? We'll head to the Illustra first, then we can talk credit lines."

Public relations, he reflected as he gently guided the bewildered man out of the room, was a lot tougher than it used to be.

At the time of writing we have amassed wealth to such a degree that conventional fiscal paradigms can barely accommodate it. More than any other Corporation, Eurasian Incorporated has realised the implications of an entire global economy operating on the free-market model, freed from even the last vestige of government or independent control, and has flourished as a consequence.

But there is a second aspect of the state of the market that this Corporation remains unwilling to fully accept and this is a weakness that may fatally undermine EI if not addressed. It is an undeniable reality that covert corporate warfare, once a metaphor, has now become a physical truth; further, that several of our less financially endowed rivals have elevated subtle (and, sometimes, overt) aggression to an art form. The prevailing opinion amongst Corporate strategic planners appears to be that sufficient revenue will solve all problems but history has repeatedly shown that wealth, without the means to defend it, simply makes a tempting target. Decadence is concurrent with riches and if unchecked will lead to disproportionate loss. Discipline is the key to solving this quandary.

- from Cities of Gold: Strategic Recommendations, Eurasian Incorporated
attr: Michael Kaspillis, EI anthropologer/geopolitical analyst
[SUPRESSED 10.28.2499, /unknownadmin]
[DELETED 10.29.2499, /unknownadmin]

SHI YUKIRO
HONOUR, STRENGTH, POWER

SECTOR: HIGH TECH & ELECTRONICS

Chrysanthemum blooms
Once more, in the Second Dawn
Red petals of blood.

*-(apocryphal) response to
news of the death of Nakayama Sei*

attr: Nakayama Takako

DESCRIPTION

The Shi Yukiro have had as much of an effect on the East than the Ai-Jinn despite its small size. Many believe this to be due to their aptitude for technology but this is not really the case. A modified hierarchy dating from ancient Japan is the true backbone of the Shi Yukiro. The head of the Corporation (titled Shogun) has ultimate power and his decisions are unchallengeable.

The Shi Yukiro are based in Japan but their fingers stretch across the world, they own various islands dotted about the Earth and have set up trading and technology bases in many foreign countries. With regard to age, the Shi Yukiro are said to be the oldest of the modern conglomerates, they evolved into a Corporation in the early 21st century but have been as a unified nation since the early 1700's.

Many Shi Yukiro Agents are trained rigidly in ancient war theories such as those of Sun Tsu and Miyamoto Musashi and as a consequence are able tacticians. They are also encouraged to learn melee combat to a high degree of expertise, especially in the Ion Katana which is a weapon exclusive to the Shi Yukiro. Its proficient use takes many years of practice and its construction procedures are a well kept secret. The honour of Shi Yukiro Agents is paramount to their style of life and many will ritually commit *seppuku* (suicide) rather than face dishonour.

A strict policy on the race of Shi Yukiro Agents exists; in short they must be of South East Asian descent, Japanese, Chinese, Tibetan, Mongolian, Thai, etc. Even this may not be enough; strict DNA tests are carried out that use for their perfect model the current CEO of the Shi Yukiro who is always pure Japanese. The genes denoting racial characteristics are carefully compared and if there is too great a deviation from the perfect strand then the applicant is refused. Those whose blood is not pure enough are welcome to be resident in Shi Yukiro territory but are not allowed into positions of influence such as Agents, politicians and high ranking Citizens.

CORPORATE GOALS

The Shi Yukiro have no desires for global domination, for then who would buy their technology? Instead they seek to establish themselves as an untouchable and elite technology dealer who service the needs of the public and other Corporations without becoming too involved. The enlargement of Japan and consolidation of more land are key to their strategy but they are

But tell me, my friend, have you heard of a man named Sei Nakayama? No? I am not surprised, but perhaps you will allow me to educate you. In the early decades of the twenty-first century, when economic anarchy combined with military destabilisation within the Asia-Pacific region gave the various regional powers cause to lay contingency plans against the chaos that (as we now know) did in fact come to pass, it was he who first suggested that elements of feudal Japanese society might be combined with the corporate philosophies of the industrial-era zaibatsu to create a new supra-national identity capable of transcending geopolitical boundaries. He argued this as the only model capable of surviving what he saw to be the inevitable approaching social collapse.

Such faith did Nakayama hold in these ideas that he effectively put his reputation, his family name, and the total value of his personal estates behind them. When they were scornfully discarded he chose to take his own life in the then-still-archaic mode of seppuku. *An empty final gesture? Or was it a carefully planned statement, with Nakayama calculating his own death as a cost that had to be paid to begin the reform he had long advocated? I cannot say. But I can tell you that, though the name of Sei Nakayama is never spoken aloud within Shi Yukiro corporate feudalities, he is nevertheless known to every single member of that organisation and venerated absolutely, though silently, as a cross between a latter-day prophet and a saint.*

UIG surveillance audio transcript BK4433HJSNHN/A36
attr: Data not available.

happy to use technology and not war to achieve their goal. Shi Yukiro Agents are normally encountered when high tech or industrial espionage are involved.

MIND-SET

Shi Yukiro Agents are ruled by their loyalty to the Corporation and their sense of personal honour. To outsiders their actions seem chaotic but they are single minded in their pursuit of perfection. This does not make the Shi Yukiro noble by others' standards. A Shi Yukiro may well knife an E.I. Agent in the back, but in the eyes of the Shi Yukiro he was an unworthy foe and by killing him quickly the Agent was freed for more important tasks, the end result being good personally and for the Corporation.

OPERATIONAL METHOD

Shi Yukiro are quick, reserved and stylish with a frightening blend of traditional combat mastery and cutting edge technology. They are evasive as Divisions and not openly aggressive. The Shi Yukiro would rather avoid a fight but will not suffer insults. They tend to stay away from explosives and heavy firearms favouring bladed weapons and small firearms when needed. The Agents normally work on foot and have no time for heavy vehicles or superfluous hardware.

AGENT ONI KAZUYA, SHI YUKIRO

AGENT NAMES AND RANKS

Ito, Kobayashi, Nakamura, Saito, Sato, Suzuki, Takahashi, Tanaka, Watanabe, Yamamoto, Hayashi, Yoshida, Yamazaki, Takeda, Kuroki, Kai, Kawano, Hidaka.

SHOGUN   The Rank 10 Agent presiding over the whole corporation.

CHUSA   Alternative term for Commander / Field Marshal (Rank 8).

TAISHO   Military General (Rank 7).

DAIMYO   A lord, a high ranking Shi Yukiro Agent, (Rank 7 or higher).

TAII   Alternative term for Lieutenant (Rank 3).

KACHI   Low ranking Agents (Rank 1-3) - Soldiers.

SAMPLE OCCUPATIONS

ASSASSIN / SPY / NINJA
Heralding from the age of ancient feudal war the Assassins of the Shi Yukiro are unmatched. Bringing together stealth, martial arts and quick thinking these men and women form a key strategic force that deals with notable individuals and acquires useful information. They often replace honour with efficiency and will stop at nothing to complete their goals.

ZAIBATSU (BUSINESSMEN)
Using the Shi Yukiro's vast wealth, corporate Zaibatsu spend much of their time trying to extend the reach of the Shi Yukiro. They are stationed around the world, sometimes in covert positions, making sure that wherever they are, the Shi Yukiro's interests are being cared for. Zaibatsu need not be weak and soft, some are as competent as the Samurai but choose to display their usefulness in other areas. The Shi Yukiro demand much from their employees and they are often key members of a Division.

WEAPONSMITH
Although the days of forges have passed the famous Ion Katana must still be made with immense care and precision. Each Katana is made with a recipient in mind and many hours of contemplation and thought precede construction, which can take from four weeks to six months depending on the quality of the blade. The weaponsmith, when not engaged in actual building, is often a scourge in the field, as they usually have an impressive pool of weapons to draw upon. The weaponsmith never forgets his work however and ideas and inspiration for a new blade will often dominate his thoughts.

SAMURAI
This is one of most the prestigious occupations for a Shi Yukiro Agent and Samurai are often referred to as *The Sword of the Corp*. They normally wear expensive suits and carry swords and guns. These warriors take high weapon skills complemented by a particular specialisation such as culture or mechtronics so that they can still display their usefulness when fighting is not needed. A typical Samurai will not be opposed to using evasive methods where necessary, only the sub-sect Samurai ad Technica place honour above all else.

Miyuki Nakata weighed her options and decided to try to explain one last time to the three expressionless men sitting opposite. She couched her appeal in the humblest possible form of formal Japanese. "It is with the deepest regret that I must declare myself unable to accept this position. I am very much afraid that my children are now of the age where they require constant attention. If I might presume to make a suggestion, perhaps in a few years I would be able to approach this offer with a stronger resolve."

The man who had introduced himself as Hideo Mori leaned forward. By contrast, his own language was pre-emptive to the point of rudeness, all short forms and bereft of the trappings of polite conversation. "Nakata-san, you are the finest swordsmith to operate independently within Shi Yukiro domains in two centuries. Your family will certainly understand that your employment is a thing of necessity. It is now a matter of Corporate honour."

Nakata suppressed a sigh and bowed her head.

SUB-SECTS

CLAN HITORI
Clan Hitori is a sub-sect of the Shi Yukiro made up exclusively of ninja. Clan Hitori are masters of secrecy and espionage. Silence, speed and competence are the ninja's trademark features. Clan Hitori have no particular combat style or typical weapon configuration. They use any method which will get the job done. As well as assassination and information acquisition, Clan Hitori fulfils another important role in the Shi Yukiro; they act as a form of internal affairs department monitoring the behaviour and loyalty of fellow Agents. As a consequence Clan Hitori are distrusted by many and few are ever likely to become close friends with the ninja. Clan Hitori Agents are often trusted with information access far in excess of their rank which is both a curse and a blessing.

There are those who dismiss the ninja as anachronisms, obsolete in an age of advanced assassination and surveillance devices. To speak so betrays a profound lack of understanding. Ninjitsu is now, as it always has been, primarily an art of concealment. The tools and techniques change with the passing of the years but the fact remains that a man capable of hiding in the merest shadow is, more than any miracle of spy-tech miniaturisation, an invaluable source of both intelligence and fear - and by extension an invaluable tool of statecraft. That on occasion such men may also be able to quietly remove a troublesome individual, sabotage a key installation or start a convenient war should be thought of as a fringe benefit.

-notes from the Kagedo school introductory lecture
attr: Masichi Masuda, Clan Hitori veteran instructor

SAMURAI AD TECHNICA

Samurai ad Technica is a branch of the Shi Yukiro made up of loyalist Agents who adhere strongly to the Bushido code while embracing modern methodology. They respect only rank and nobility and have no time for those with neither.

They are single minded of purpose and generally speaking carry only Ion Katanas, Ion Wakizashi and Seppuku Knives. Before they have earned these they will carry normal titanium alloy, acid edged or plasma swords. In time each Samurai will have a weapon made for them by the Shi Yukiro's master smiths. Their armour is often crafted to be reminiscent of the armour of their ancestral forefathers of ancient Japan, but still carries all the benefits of modern field armour.

A member of Samurai ad Technica is permitted by the Shi Yukiro to execute any Agent of any Corporation 3 ranks lower than himself if he has reason to do so. For example a Rank 6 member could execute an Agent of Rank 3 or lower. They do not use this power lightly and can be punished for its misuse. It is worth noting however that the UIG does not observe this right and considers it murder just like any other killing.

The main difference between Samurai ad Technica and normal Samurai is that ad Technica Agents never bow to compromise, compassion or corruption. They are single minded and dedicated. It is either their way or not at all and their way always represents the best interests of the Corporation combined with an unbreakable sense of honour.

EXAMPLE CHARACTERS

DAIMYO KITO MITSURIGO
Rank 9, Level 30
Born into the position of Shadow CEO, Mitsurigo has handled the job well until the present day. His tactics are often based on ancient philosophies, which he insists are a part of basic Agent training. His divine lineage to the ancient god remains as undisputed today as it always has, though his recent marriage to Musashi Kayo will be a test of his true self-control as adultery has been classed as illegal in the Shi Yukiro, and if Mitsurigo was to be caught being unfaithful, as he has a penchant for, his position would be in jeopardy.

CHUSA FUJINAWA HIMATO
Rank 8, Level 38
The Chusa is slightly overweight, dresses in a black and red kimono and keeps his long dark hair tied back. His torso and arms are both cybernetically altered. Fujinawa was raised in Northern Japan. His father was unknown to him but it was suspected he was a military man as his conception occurred in an expensive brothel in Hirosaki that was popular among Shi Yukiro employees. Fujinawa was head of a Sakata street gang by the age of 17 and was taken from there by Shi Yukiro personnel hunters to begin more formal training. That was 90 years ago, Fujinawa is now the Shi Yukiro's most respected and competent military tactician. Continued assassination attempts have meant he has been equipped with a top of the range Hard Ion shield and hypodermic armour plating. The General rarely attends conflicts personally anymore but his presence is always felt when the Shi Yukiro launch major offensives.

SAMURAI OTANAKA NANTARI
Rank 6, Level 50

Agent Otanaka was born into the Shi Yukiro and has been trained by its top masters from before he could understand what was happening. He is, in the eyes of the Shi Yukiro, the perfect Agent, fluent in the languages of every Corporation, competent in the use of all melee weapons and firearms. His face is equipped with an inbuilt Viral Modifier, which allows him to change his appearance given a period of 6 days. Otanaka knows nothing other than the Corporation and lives and breathes its philosophies. Currently he is engaged in 'mediating' the border disputes with the Ai-Jinn and commands a Division known as 'The Hybakki'.
Otanaka uses a pair of Custom Retaliator hand laser carbines (laser pistols) that track their targets unerringly. His right arm contains a hidden plasma launcher and in melee he fights with an Artefact quality Ion No Dachi (two handed sword). Sendaka Aki, his courtesan who always accompanies him, uses two Ion Katanas of exceptional quality

It is most unfortunate that the Shi Yukiro in particular seem unable to grasp this simple principle of broad integration. I'm not sure which incenses them more; the fact that we profit from the kind of diversity they have never been able to comprehend, or the fact that our organization incorporates certain elements drawn from a history that they would dearly love to lay exclusive claim to.

from The Second Little Red Book: Commentary on the Ai-Jinn Corporate Manifesto. attr: Chairman Wing-Pak Yu

UNIQUE ABILITIES AND EQUIPMENT

POWERED MELEE LICENSE TRAINING
Shi Yukiro Agents gain the Powered Melee license and the 'Powered Melee' training for free at Character Creation.

EXCEPTIONAL KATANA
Shi Yukiro agents gain a free Masterbuilt Katana at character creation (not an Ion Katana). Criticals on 1/1-4/4.

ION WEAPON
Shi Yukiro Agents may have access to Ion weapons. No other Corporation may buy these.

ION WEAPONS

> A superbly crafted weapon cannot act of its own volition. It must be wielded.
>
> -Miyamoto Musashi, Book Of Five Rings

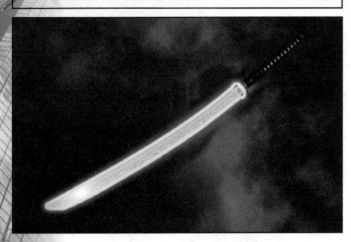

Ion weapons are the rare and superbly made weapons of the Shi Yukiro. The blade has a mono-ionic field surrounding it which causes it to pass through matter with great efficiency. (It ignores the first 10 points of AV.) The Powered Melee training is required to wield the Ion Katana otherwise the wielder is prone to having accidents with the unfamiliar blade. (The wielder will clip himself on all doubles dealing the weapons damage to himself.)

Ion weapons, normally katanas, are specially made for Shi Yukiro Agents by master weaponsmiths but only when their superiors feel they have earned the right to use them; this is considered to be Rank 3 or Level 8, whichever comes first. The weapons are tuned electronically to their user's biorhythm and anyone trying to use one who is not attuned will find the power cell switches off and the weapon acts like a poor club. Unlocking such a weapon is a very hard task. (Intelligence + Mechtronics roll with a -12 modifier, 4 successes needed, one roll represents 24 hours work. Failure to pass one roll means the process must be started again from scratch. Failing a roll with a double destroys the weapon.)

IMPROVING ION WEAPONS

Ion weapons can be increased in condition only by professional Swordsmiths. (A Shi Yukiro employee with *Mechtronics* as their profession as well as *Close Combat* and *Arts and Culture* at 6 or more can claim to be Swordsmith). Those who are not Swordsmiths must prove competence and loyalty to the Shi Yukiro by succeeding in their work and the weapon will be upgraded for them. A player Swordsmith can upgrade the condition of the weapon in the normal manner. This takes 1 week of downtime and 5,000¢ per condition level. If an NPC swordsmith does it, it costs 10,000¢ per condition level improved. This cost is the same for repairing and improving beyond condition 10.

THEFT OF ION WEAPONS

Ion weapons are priceless, if someone has a working Ion Weapon which has had the biometrics on it cracked it's worth a fortune, perhaps millions. However, the Shi Yukiro are very good at tracking such people down, killing them and reclaiming their property. Using such a weapon will certainly attract the attention of

Clan Hitori and the Shi Yukiro will not stop until the wrong is made right.

ION KATANA

Damage	2D4 + Strength
Roll	Agility + Close Combat
EMPS	Immune
Rate	2/1
Special	Ignores 10 Points of Armour Value
Strength	Strength 4 required to use this weapon.

The weapon severs a random limb if maximum damage is rolled. See page 146.

If used one handed the weapon has a rate of 2. If used two handed it has a rate of 1 but doubles the user's strength when applying damage. Critical hits on 1/1-5/5.

It is a documented fact that the samurai of ancient Japan would, in times of peace, occasionally test their blades on passers-by to ensure that their weapons, as well as their techniques, remained at their optimum levels. This unsavoury sliver of history has not been disregarded or disavowed by the Shi Yukiro. Rather, SY press Agents point to the fact that strict measures have been taken to stop this custom from arising again amongst the samurai of modern times, citing it as one more example of how their Corporate ethic draws upon the very best qualities of the ancient feudal way of governance that it emulates while cutting away the corresponding disadvantages.

Yet these claims seem incongruous in light of the fact that the warriors of the Shi Yukiro, particularly the Samurai ad Technica, are apparently in all respects and purposes identical to their second-millennium antecedents. What we perhaps should be questioning, therefore, is not how the SY have stopped their fighting forces from culling the occasional worker, but rather whether those fighting forces are in fact slaughtering the operatives of other organisations in such numbers, and on such a regular basis, that it is simply no longer necessary for them to practice on lower-caste members of their own Corporation.

from The Sword Reforged: Threat Analysis, Shi Yukiro Corporation
attr: Michael Kaspillis, EI anthropologer/geopolitical analyst

---

OTHER ION WEAPONS

Most bladed weapons can be used as templates for Ion Weapons by Shi Yukiro weaponsmiths. They are awarded to Shi Yukiro Agents in the same way as Ion Katanas, but are obviously for those who have a different weapon preference. The new Ion weapon has the following properties.

Damage : Two Damage Dice. These should make up approximately the same damage as the non-ion version. For example, a two handed sword uses D12 so an Ion version would use 2D6. Maximum damage severs a random body part. See page 146.

Cost	Cannot be purchased
Range	As original weapon
Rate	As original weapon
Prerequisites	As original weapon
EMPS	Immune
Special	Ignores 10 Points of Armour Value

Taisho Takeda Akira, Samurai ad Technica, 3rd Sword Scion.

SECTOR: ARMAMENTS AND DEFENCE

into a new era where life could once again be enjoyed without wondering who would kick your door down tonight.

Federation Citizens are not poor, needy or without pleasure, however they are strongly encouraged to make sure they are never tempted by excess, deviance or lawlessness. Since the original American Government was swallowed by the UIG things have got even tighter. All but WF sanctioned media is banned or restricted and most people are now forced to live a simple life where traditional values are held high and enforced with military precision. The result is a streamlined efficient democracy where all laws are enforced with punishments that are heavily disproportionate to the crimes. The corruption and crime rates of North America are the envy of the world with less than 5% of crimes going unpunished. Although the UIG do not execute this kind of system in other nations it seems to work so well in North America that reversing it would likely cause revolution. The resultant increase in national wealth combined with the Federation's staggering military background has created an environment where the criminal is now the terrified victim.

The Corporation itself is organised much as the American military used to be. A strict chain of command exists with all orders followed to the letter, an Agent who does wrong while following an order is totally immune to any Corporate repercussions of his actions. Consequently any kind of rank is achieved only with a very impressive track record.

The small amounts of crime left across Federation territory are mopped up regularly by the Agents who use the operations to test new weapons and tactics. This New World Order has produced a devastating force that few are willing to engage in any kind of military action. Their resources are huge, their technology advanced and their troops trained to the hilt.

With the Federation controlling their own media they are able to shape the desires of their populace, and use the media as an unparalleled propaganda tool where dissension and anti-Federation feeling can be totally eliminated. WF Agents regularly appear on broadcasts informing the nation of how they have been defending the Federation from its enemies, and in doing so often elevate themselves to the position of celebrities. Although most Corporations do a similar thing, the Federation take it to new levels with some Agents having their own channels and lines of merchandise. The Western Federation try to ensure their Agents have nothing but good PR, and controlling the media certainly helps.

The Western Federation are the finest firearm manufacturers in the world. They keep the very best weapons for themselves but sell thousands via their subsidiaries, *Anzeiger Military Systems* and *Yaeger & Stanton*. Their domination of this market has influenced their combat methodology to the point that anything but WF made firearms are a rare sight in a unit.

> *Ultimately, the only power to which man should aspire is that which he exercises over himself.*
>
> Elie Wiesel

DESCRIPTION

In 2145 J.D.Mathers, CEO of Federation Armaments was elected into the position of American Ethical Administrator. He used his position to try and implement a policy of hard work, traditional values and simple pleasures in keeping with his puritan upbringing. Although the idea was initially met with resistance, Mathers soon became a hero of the people (if not the government) and his company the vehicle in which he rode. Federation Armaments evolved into The Western Federation whose sole purpose (according to Mathers) was to safeguard the populace in a way the government would not. The Citizens loved him, his intolerance of crime and corruption catapulted Northern America

THE AMERICAN UNDERGROUND

The only fly in the ointment is the loosely titled American Underground, a network of anarchists, rights activists and free thinkers who despise what the Western Federation have done and seek to return America to the more liberated but dangerous times before the Federation. These individuals and groups are almost untraceable and span the continent of North America from coast to coast. They are the ones responsible for almost all the crime the WF endures. They are well funded by those who would like to see the Federation a freer place or rivals who have something to gain in the chaos caused by the activists. Although they can be seen to form a single rebellious group the American Underground are divided into cells, each of whom have a separate agenda. One thing they are agreed on, though, is to take no direct action against the UIG or the public. They have no desire to give the UIG cause to hunt them down, nor do they wish to lose favour with the public, who they are trying to enlighten to the possibility of a more liberal future.

Other Corporations strongly support the American Underground giving finance, arms and information in exchange for the Undergrounds continued insurrection against the WF.

MIND-SET

A typical Western Federation Agent has three things which occupy his mind.

1. A deep seated sense of duty to his nation.
2. The belief the rest of humanity should be elevated to Federation standards.
3. Absolute confidence that he can outgun his enemy.

With these guidelines a Federation Agent can always make the right decision.

OPERATIONAL METHOD

Typically the WF rely on small units of highly trained Agents who work exceptionally as a team. A Division will often be arranged like a Special Forces squad with each Agent a specialist in their own field; sniper, explosives, heavy support, etc. Their utter belief in their cause makes their decisions easy. They are not into subtly subverting foreign powers but seek simply to subjugate, then take control and make a change for the better.

CORPORATE GOALS

So what does the Federation seek to do now it has a stable populace, a strong army and ample cash? In a word - expand. The success of the Federation's policies have spurred them to take their methodology across the world. There is no doubt life is of a higher standard, safer and more predictable under the WF regime. After 350 years of this lifestyle the populace have known nothing else and look upon other nations with pity. The Federation seeks to *liberate* these hell-holes and bring them round to a new way of thinking. With the sheer efficiency, power and moral armour of the Western Federation they believe the unenlightened will soon accept the inevitable.

TYPICAL AGENT NAMES AND RANKS

Johnson, Williams, Miller, Wilson, Moore, Taylor, Anderson, Thomas, Jackson, White, Harris, Martin, Thompson, Garcia, Martinez, Clark, Rodriguez, Lewis, Lee, Walker, Hall, Allen, Young, Hernandez, King, Wright, Lopez , Mitchell, Perez, Vega.

The Western Federation order their units tightly. The chain of command is integral to the functioning of the Corporation. For the most part they follow the ranking system set out by the UIG. They add additional ranks based on the function of the agent.

MARINE
Generic term for any Agent but more particularly used for unspecialised Agents.

Prefixes or suffixes are added to indicate speciality. For example:
GUNNERY
e.g. Gunnery Sergeant - A heavy weapons specialist.

TECHNICIAN
e.g. Lieutenant Technician - A specialist mechanic.

CUSTODIAN
e.g. Custodian Captain - An Agent charged with guarding something or someone.

SAMPLE OCCUPATIONS

URBAN ASSAULT SPECIALIST

Working in a manner similar to the SWAT teams of the 21st century the UAS specialise in close urban assaults such as hostage situations, building raids and armed response. The typical UAS will be skilled with all manner of close and medium range arms with a good knowledge of support weapons and stealth.

CLEANER

These Agents are trained to remove the human pollution from civilisation. They typically spend weeks undercover searching for clues as to where they should be focusing their energies. When results are yielded in the form of criminal groups or undesirable communities they either take them out personally or call in backup such as Divisions of UAS.

GUNMAN

Sometimes a situation cannot be easily resolved by sending in an entire Division. The Gunman is a small arms specialist who commands such skill over his weapons that he can, single-handedly, take down significant enemy resistance. The gunman is an artist in his own medium, which is typically twin light firearms.

> I'm told the pen is mightier than the sword, but there are times a gun's more use than either.
>
> - attr: Allen Garcia, Western Federation Cleaner

CELEBRITY AGENT

The Western Federation has a tightly controlled media and has elevated many of its Agents to the position of celebrities. These individuals must not only be competent Agents but must look sensational doing their job. Their missions are often recorded and broadcast, they are then asked to make an appearance and comment on their work. Many Agents become the WF equivalent of superstars and are idolised in the same way.

EXAMPLE AGENTS

ALISON DENTON
Western Federation Shadow CEO
Rank 9 / Level 48

Alison Denton like all Agents in the WF had to ascend to the top by pure promotion. She started as a marine in the Federation in 2400 and since then has scraped her way up the ladder by succeeding in campaign after campaign. Her specialisation is sweep and clean missions, Denton and her Division were professional Cleaners, famous for removing the human filth out of Old Cities with zero WF casualties and a minimum of public outcry. Nowadays Denton seldom enters physical combat but on those rare occasions she uses her artifact quality sub-machine plasma which never overheats and critically passes on all doubles.

TEX CALAHAN, CELEBRITY AGENT
Western Federation
Rank 5, Level 22

Tex was born in Houston in 2440 and due to repeated cosmetic work looks great. He's perhaps the most popular celebrity Agent of his time and his face is a familiar sight on broadcasts and domestic products. His superiors are fully aware of how valuable he is and as such have stopped sending him on dangerous missions. Tex knows what his superiors are doing but is powerless to complain for fear of sounding disloyal. To make up for this Tex often takes

his Division on unauthorised missions into enemy territory knowing that reports of *Tex Sightings* will be put down to overactive imaginations. When fighting, Tex tends to use large machine weapons for maximum screen impact.

> Coming up next on WF25X, The Deputy! Legendary Agent Tex Calahan puts a group of hopefuls through their paces, but only one will beat out the competition to become his deputy for a year. On tonight's show, the five remaining candidates are given the task of suppressing an Underground propaganda outlet, but tensions run high as Casper and Mark get into another argument about the limits of acceptable force. [Viewing optional for sub18s and Citizens of class A legality or above.] That's followed at nine by Snakes and Dragons, a harrowing documentary about the appalling living conditions and terrifying crime rates in Ai-Jinn and Shi Yukiro territory today. [Viewing mandatory, all Citizens.] Then we'll be closing down with The True News at ten thirty till ten forty-five. [Viewing mandatory, all Citizens.] WF25X – bringing you the programs that are better for you!
>
> - excerpt, Western Federation Pan-Media broadcast, Station WF25X

AGENT DAN PEARCE
Western Federation
Rank 6 / Level 10

Agent Pearce is a handsome man with an apparent age of 30. He is normally accompanied by at least 3 stunningly attractive women who double as bodyguards. He is dark haired and clean shaven with a lean but athletic build. He normally dresses in designer suits and expensive but tasteful accessories.

Pearce is an efficient man who excels at organisation. His forte is manipulating others and setting up social events such as parties. He invites particular people to his events in an attempt to engineer situations which would never have occurred otherwise. This can lead to promotions being arranged, hits called or feuds created and resolved. If there is a feat of social trickery that needs to be performed then Dan Pearce will arrange it. Pearce is not in a Division; he operates alone and normally employs female bodyguards as the situation demands. In combat he uses two WF legendary quality silenced kinetic magnums.

I've worked for all the big Corporations and a couple of the smaller ones, and I've gotta tell you that nobody's easier to work with than the Federation. They're plain-speaking people, they'll have everything planned down to the last detail, you'll always be working as part of a professional team, and their contractor agreements usually include armament remuneration clauses. All Anzeiger or Y&S stuff, but still. I got my MP12 as part of a deal on a job with them six years back, and it's still like new today.

Two problems, though. First, if you're working with the WF, whether it's in a boardroom or a firefight, you don't talk politics. They tend to get antsy, and since they tend to be packing, this tends to get a little traumatic. Second, in my considered opinion, the quality of R&R on a Federation contract is pretty much the lowest of the low. I've seen things you wouldn't believe in E.I.'s Paris rec centres, and there aren't even English words to describe some of what you can do in Tokyo these days, but you'll have a hard time disporting yourself over in Federation territory. Curfew gets old fast, their broadcasting stinks, and there's only so much country music a man can take.

-attr: Zack Adams, freelance technical consultant/soldier of fortune

UNIQUE ABILITIES AND EQUIPMENT

WEAPONS LICENSES
Western Federation Agents start with a number of weapon licenses for free.

Heavy Firearm License
Light Firearms License
Offensive Equipment License 1
Tactical Firearms License

CHIP CHECK WEAPONS
All WF agents have their weapons coded to their ID chips for free if they desire (see page 51). This applies to all weapons they have, not just Corporate issue. This means only authorised personnel (usually the Agent and his Division) can use the weapons.

MASTERBUILT WEAPONS
The Federation make the best firearms in the world. All firearms (i.e. light, tactical and heavy firearms) purchased directly from the Western Federation by Federation Agents are considered to be of excellent quality and as such deal more damage. When a WF Agent buys any weapons from the Corporation they are automatically scaled up to deal more damage. In addition to this they are made to high WF specification and critically pass on 1/1 to 4/4.

If a weapon such as a blade launcher, (which severs on maximum damage of double 6) is WF made and increased to 2D8 then its special effect will be extended to double 6, double 7 and double 8 as long as the GM deems it is appropriate. The Federation do not make Ion Weapons so these will not be affected.

WESTERN FEDERATION WEAPON MODIFIER

NORMAL DICE	NEW DICE
D2	D4
D4	D6
D6	D8
D8	D10
D10	D12
D12	2D8
D20	2D10

FOR EXAMPLE,
If a weapon normally deals 3D6, a Western Federation made one deals 3D8.

The dice that the damage is rolled on are scaled up (called dicing up) as noted above.

WEAPON DISCOUNT
WF Agents pay 10% less for all weapons bought from the Federation or one of it's subsidiaries such as *Anzeiger Military Systems* or *Yaeger & Stanton Assault Technologies.*

MILITARY SIGN
This is a language taught exclusively to Western Federation Agents. As well as being an extensive and rapid form of sign language it incorporates all the tactical options taught to WF Agents during their training. The language is so deeply based around WF tactics, culture and weaponry that it would be useless for any other Corporation to learn. Thus it is only available to WF Agents. Using it, Federation Agents may communicate anything they wish perfectly in seconds (faster than they could vocalise it). This can really give Federation Agents the edge in a confrontation as their enemy have no idea what they are planning. It also still works when sub vocal communicators cannot be used.

The noonday sun had burned the clouds from the sky and the moisture from the air. The atmosphere in the execution yard where Jake Santiago - mathematical genius, financial wrangler extraordinaire and, lately, convicted felon - was about to be shot was stifling, oppressive, desiccated. Struggling to think through the fugue of heatstroke, Jake tried to calculate the odds of the five gunmen facing him all missing at once. He put it at somewhere in the region of 512:1; cold comfort, since they were armed to a man with Y&S Cobras and would have another forty-nine shots each even if they all managed to miss with their first. Trying not to think about the stains on the wall behind him, trembling only slightly, he closed his eyes.

And opened them again when he heard the staccato rhythm, not of gunfire, but of a pair of cowboy boots walking across the yard. He knew the sound of those boots; then again, any Federation Citizen would have. There between him and the firing squad, wearing an ancient duster and brandishing a sheaf of old-fashioned papers, stood –

"Tex Calahan!" croaked Jake. "What are you doing here?"

Tex cast his famous cold blue stare around the yard, seeming to take in the gunmen, Jake, the bloodstained wall behind him, the hellish heat. His grip tightened around the papers. "Well, buddy," he said conversationally, "let's just say I have an offer you won't refuse."

ALISON DENTON, SHADOW CEO, WESTERN FEDERATION

Two Shi Yukiro Zaibatsu, the Corporate businessmen named after the ancient industrial super-combines of a time long past, sat on one side of the long conference table, dressed in sober but elegant suits with faces that might have been of graven stone. Opposite them sat a pair of Federation Lieutenant-Executives, their own features rather crumpled with the stresses of the interminable discussions, their suits a plain black and of a much cheaper cut than those of their counterparts. Between these four flowed the low, shifting discourse of business, as they negotiated the Federation takeover of a tiny Shi Yukiro weapons manufacture subsidiary. Some distance behind the table on either side, the guards stood in silence; four Samurai, hands on sword-hilts, behind the Zaibatsu, and behind the Federation reps a pair of heavy weapons experts flanking three gunmen. The conference room around the thirteen people was sparsely furnished but huge, designed to accommodate much larger parties, and above them the ceiling was a flat expanse of alabaster white.

The ceiling, however, was opaque only from one side. Seen from above, it was perfectly translucent, non-reflective and non-refractive. In the space just above the ceiling, on tracks and wires and gimbaled arms, dozens of cameras, directional microphones and receptors swooped and swung, taking in every detail of the negotiations. These were relayed back to Federation Media Colonel Carla Vasquez, sitting before a huge bank of monitors in a small room three blocks away, surrounded by high-fidelity speakers, olfac relays and the other tools of her trade.

Vasquez was bored out of her mind and struggling to keep her attention on the playback. Despite the looming presence of the guards, the meeting had thus far been completely without incident. Discussions appeared to be progressing peacefully, if slowly; the SY Agents had failed to do anything particularly villainous or barbaric, and the Federation Agents had done nothing notably heroic. Such details could always be added later, of course, but the unfortunate fact was that this looked like being a successful and uneventful takeover, and therefore a total waste of three hours from Vasquez' point of view.

A shout of Japanese boomed from the speakers, jerking Vasquez upright in her seat. Camera 27 zoomed in on the older of the two Zaibatsu, now on his feet with anger boiling in his eyes. Vasquez tweaked a control on her board and the view changed slightly, closing in further so that the SY Agent's face swelled monstrously in the monitor. She wondered briefly whether one of the Federation negotiators had said anything directly to anger the man; if so, the incendiary comment might have to be deleted or modified in post-production to emphasise the unreasonable, volatile nature of the visitors.

One of the Federation businessmen had leapt up from his seat as well, and across the table there was a ringing metallic noise, perfectly reproduced in Vasquez' speakers, as all four samurai drew their ion weapons at the same time. In response, and almost to the same perfect degree of synchronicity, the three Federation gunmen drew two pistols apiece with speed that blurred the images on the monitors for a moment, while the two heavies flipped open their long coats and swung up short-barreled railguns. Cameras wheeled silently above the room, catching the lantern jaws and hard eyes of the Federation men.

In the fragile silence, tension thickened across the conference table like smoke from a choking fire. Three blocks away, deep in her metal womb of screens and speakers, now fully alert and poised over her control board, Vasquez grinned. Had the Federation still permitted gambling, she would have bet her last credit on these particular negotiations degenerating rapidly in the very near future; and from a media perspective, hostile takeovers were always prime-time gold. Her hands hovered over the board like hawks as she waited for the first shot.

SECTION 7

THE UIG & THE ORDER OF THE TRUE FAITH

UIG HEADQUARTERS, LARSEN ICE SHELF, ANTARCTICA

UIG
UNITED INTERNATIONAL GOVERNMENT

People sleep peaceably in their beds at night only because rough men stand ready to do violence on their behalf.

-George Orwell

In 2200 the UIG was formed. Until that point the governments of Earth could no longer oppose the might of their indigenous Corporations and the world had become an open war zone. The discovery and subsequent co-operation of the Archons was the keystone to the consolidation and success of the unified world governments and is fundamental to how the UIG are able to police such a potentially dangerous and powerful populace. With the help of Archon technology the UIG are able to match and often outgun the Corporations, resulting in an environment where the police are still respected as a force to be reckoned with.

UIG COMMAND STRUCTURE

The UIG is divided into a number of separate task forces, each of which deal with different aspects of law enforcement. Although high ranking UIG officers are often powerful individuals, there are a great number of highly experienced men and women working at street level, fearing that a desk job will not sate their need to dispense the law. Below are described the levels of the UIG with typical rankings for each tier. This ranking is a guide and not necessarily fixed.

THE ASSEMBLY (RANK 10)

This is the highest echelon of the UIG where all the decisions are made. This group convenes to decide the key strategic manifesto of the UIG. The Assembly is made up of twelve UIG Officers of high competence who are from a range of geographical locations. Physically the Assembly are not powerful and rely on elite bodyguards and Archon technology to defend them.

THE EXCHANGE (RANK 9)

This group of 6 high ranking Officers interact with the Archons over the World Data Net. They feed the opinions and desires of the Archons back to the Assembly and requisition help from the A.I.s when needed. Many believe the Exchange do not relate the wishes of the Archons or the UIG accurately. However, the Archons seldom complain about the UIG's activities so there can only be, at worst, a small game of Chinese whispers.

REGIONAL COORDINATORS (RANK 7-8)

These are UIG Officers who get their orders directly from the Assembly and relay them to the Area Executives in their continent. They are normally little more than glorified messengers and are not

normally from military stock, but due to their high wages are often boosted on cybernetics and well armed. They are generally resented and considered unnecessary middle men.

AREA EXECUTIVES (RANK 6)

These are one of the most concerning UIG Officers encountered on a day to day basis. Although most of their work consists of organising operations by calling on their broad experience, they are often required to go into the field when the need arises. They are normally as high as a UIG Officer can go promotion-wise and remain on active duty. Executives govern areas equivalent to a country and there are approximately 300 of them currently under UIG employ. Mentally they are sharp and dangerous, physically they are terrifyingly competent.

ENFORCERS (RANK 5)

Each Area Executive has about 20 Enforcers under her employ who are the heads of local offices. They normally coordinate activities on a small scale and are probably the Officers under the most pressure to perform well. They are responsible for the smooth running of their locales and making sure operations go to plan. They are physically capable but are more often found in offices than in the field.

COMMANDERS (RANK 4)

These are leaders of street level Divisions of UIG Officers. Each commander has between 3 and 15 Officers under his command. He is normally a well respected individual who has earned his promotion though excellence in the field and commands the respect of his men through hard work, not a rank assignation. Commanders are normally physically and mentally competent and diligent with regard to mission success and minimisation of life loss. They can, of course, when required, unleash devastation upon law breakers.

The rumours of links between the Children of Minerva, A.I. evolutionary cycles, and unregulated cybernetic usage are patently false and are deemed by the Exchange to be a threat to public order and safety. All UIG Specials are thereby authorized and engaged to investigate the source and substance of such rumours and eliminate the perpetrators using all necessary force. Officers below fifth rank thus deployed are to report to the Assembly Vault immediately following mission end for individual debriefing.

-UIG Directive 181
[RESTRICTED (EX22) 07.06.2329, /unknownadmin]

UIG FIELD OFFICER

physically powerful and mentally compentent they can become
Only Common Residential Officers and Field Officers are usually
on the low end of the power scale. The others can become as
devastating as you desire.

FIELD OFFICERS (FOs)

These are the most common type of UIG Officer found. When a
CRO (following page) has served a few years in a residence, she
is promoted to Field Officer. This generally means she is put into a
more dangerous situation, such as an Open City like Tokyo, or
asked to police medium risk areas such as weltball matches or
public roads. Field Officers are generally lightly armed with pistols
and stun batons or possibly rifles. They are essential to the running
of the civilised world and most people feel safer having them
around. FOs are the closest to what Citizens would call 'police'.

TELEPATHIC ENFORCEMENT OFFICERS (TEOs)

These Officers are trained as Telepaths and are employed to
prevent and punish the use of unauthorised and dangerous
Telepathics. A TEO often works alone but for serious threats they
sometimes work in teams or tack on to other units of UIG. The TEO
training system is incredibly demanding and many of those who go
through it come out with reduced IQs and damaged neural
systems, at which point they are re-housed in asylums or
humanely killed. The more common result however is a strong
telepath who is able to hold his own against the forces of Comoros
and the Order of the True Faith. TEOs often carry psychic-
supressors such as Psitropine, Psi-Cuffs and Telepathic
Disruptors.

INCIDENT CONTROL OFFICERS (ICOs)

These are rapid response Officers with high levels of situational
training. When a problem suddenly arises that needs a clean,
effective response the ICOs are immediately called in. They are
armed with a variety of equipment which normally include body
shielding, light to medium firearms and a range of specialist tools
tailored for the mission at hand. They normally operate in squads
of 11 plus one commander, although some incidents may require
the response of several squads. A typical response squad consists
of the following, but each member has multiple skills to
accommodate a variety of situations.

1 Commander	
1 Lieutenant	
1 Sniper	(Triggerman)
1 Demolitions Expert	(Sapper)
1 Melee Expert	(Sword)
1 Communications Expert	(Wire)
1 Computer / Tech Expert	(Techie)
1 Heavy Weapons Expert	(Nuke)
1 Vehicle Specialist	(Wheelman)
2 Firearms Experts	(Gunmen)
1 Negotiator	(Fixer)

It goes without saying that each member of the team is also a
firearms specialist but Gunmen take this to a new level. Their
speed and control mean that often as not a single Gunman can
storm a building and eliminate all hostiles without the need for a
large scale operation.

OFFICERS (RANK 1-3)

All UIG employees are technically known as Officers but these
listed below are the bread and butter of the UIG and the ones
Agents are most likely to encounter. Officers take a number of
forms but are always well trained and armed with weapons more
than capable of doing the job. With the exception of the
Malenbrach (see following page), Officers are not simply required
to be meat heads and are normally intelligent, reasonable people.
They live and work in Spire Cities or UIG accommodation but are
often found patrolling Old Cities and wasteland. Corporations
resent having the UIG living in their cities but can do little about it.
Because the UIG is a worldwide organisation Officers are
expected to speak numerous languages and can be re-assigned
to any country at a moment's notice. Their families will be moved
with them and they will be housed in new accommodation.
Altogether the job of an officer is a good one as they are well
equipped and taken care of by the UIG. Becoming an Officer is a
tough procedure where the applicant must pass a series of
physical and mental tests before an arduous three year training
course.

THE POWER OF UIG OFFICERS

Remember that just because the Officers here can't generally
exceed Rank 3 and keep the same job, there is no limit to how

MALENBRACH
Critical Response Officers (Sledgehammers / Hammers)

> *Capital punishment would be more effective as a preventive measure if it were administered prior to the crime.*
>
> -W. Allen

These six to seven foot high, genetically engineered, muscle bound, augmented, armour clad monsters are fanatically loyal and virtually incorruptible. Their main purpose is to patrol high crime areas eradicating danger and enforcing the law. Sometimes the Malenbrach are sent for specific missions which are generally brutal in nature as they are considered the sledgehammers of the UIG. They are heavily armed and work in divisions of 4 to 7. There is normally a Commander with them who is a promoted Malenbrach, and rules by sheer force of might. The squads are named after Greek letters; e.g. Alpha Squad, Beta Squad, etc. Each member of a squad is then named according to his designation number; Alpha One, Alpha Two, etc. A typical Malenbrach Patrol Squad consists of the following:

1 Commander
2 Sweepers   (Flanking the group with heavy weapons)
1 Scout   (Stealth & unarmed combat)
1 Rearguard   (Rapid fire ranged weapon / sniper)
1 Axe   (Melee specialist)

Occasionally a Telepath accompanies the group, though Malenbrach Telepaths are rare.

Malenbrach love violence, it is programmed into their genetics. They devoutly follow orders which can often hamper their fun and agitate their delicate mental balance. For this reason their commanders often interpret orders liberally and allow the squad an indulgent spree of violence on most missions. Malenbrach favour heavy weapons although generally only the sweepers are assigned them.

CRIMINAL INVESTIGATION OFFICERS (CIOs)

These are the cream of the UIG Officers and the area most would like to work in. In essence, they catch criminals using a number of means. CIOs tend to work in teams of 6, typically made up as follows:

1 Commander
1 Forensics Expert
1 Ballistics Expert
1 Social Investigator
1 Criminal Psychologist
1 Biochemist

As a team the CROs are assigned a case, and normally start with a crime scene, and end up with a captured criminal. Once they have determined who the criminal is, and where she is, they often bring in support from other branches of the UIG. It goes without saying that Criminal Investigation Officers can be highly skilled with weaponry but many refrain from their use and pursue more cerebral activities.

INTEGRITY ANALYSIS (IA)

Integrity Analysis is a small department which makes sure the UIG is operating in its own best interests. The majority of the work in IA is to make sure there are no traitors in the organisation, and if there are, to eliminate them. IA also ensures that no one is taking bribes or offering them. To be investigated by IA is terrifying as most people have something to hide, even if it is small. An IA investigation will mar a permanent record and seriously damage promotion opportunities. IA rarely carry firearms as they are normally investigating their own Officers, but sometimes field work may make the use of weapons necessary.

ASSIGNMENT OFFICERS (MARSHALS)

Along with Criminal Investigation Officers, Marshal is one of the most desired positions in the UIG. Simply put the Marshals are sent on specific missions with specific goals. They are always well equipped and offered a number of official passes, licenses and documents. To work as a Marshal the Officer must have shown a great deal of skill and adaptability in the field. They are then trained at the UIG facility in Tierra del Fuego before being assigned to a small unit of Marshals and sent on active duty. A sample assignment could be to capture and detain a Corporation Division or bring down an organised crime syndicate, but most of their missions cross over with other departments such as solving a crime or investigating internal corruption. The trademark of a Marshal is versatility and they could be considered the UIG's equivalent of Agents.

COMMON RESIDENTIAL OFFICERS
(CRO / CROWS)

This is normally the first port of call for a newly graduated UIG Officer. They police Spires and other civilised places. Such sectors are normally so well controlled that the CRO is unlikely to ever see any action, more common are flustered residents who have lost something or petty burglaries in Spires. The CROs normally work alone or at best in small groups and are armed with light firearms. They normally have access to something larger like a rifle in a locked store room. To be demoted back to a Crow is the ultimate humiliation. Malenbrach are never demoted to Crows as they could not contain the rage inside the monster.

CITIZEN COMMUNITY PATROL (CCP)

In some areas the UIG have instigated a community patrol system. This gives normal citizens the right to report law breakers or even make arrests. The citizen is given a camera and a remote ID chip scanner. If they see a law being broken they take a photograph and scan the perpetrator's ID chip. This information can then be transmitted directly to the local UIG office. These busybodies can be a real pain for Agents and often find themselves at the wrong end of a Black Cougar. Their arrests are always investigated thoroughly before a conviction is made. The CCP are typically rewarded with a few Rank points or some credits.

MALENBRACH PLOT IDEA

Among the Malenbrach one squad seems to find trouble more than any other, and as a result has become perhaps the most feared unit to date. Delta Squad consists of only five Malenbrach. Delta Three deserted his brothers and joined the Cult of Machina where he was hailed as a prophet and the bringer of a new regime where the Cult would be glorified and rise to their true and deserved status. Delta One pulls his squad off mission as often as possible in order to hunt for Delta Three and bring him back into the fold. They will do anything and everything to find him, including conscripting the help of Agents and Outlaws.

UIG SPECIAL EQUIPMENT

The UIG are a concerning foe for any Agent, not because they are powerful as individuals (although many are) but because of the Archon equipment they often carry. The majority of UIG Officers do not have anywhere near the amount of augmentation an Agent has. Instead they rely on Archon technology to maintain order and respect. The GM should feel free to generate more Archon based technology to keep the UIG ahead of the Agents. It goes without saying that if an Agent recovers some Archon technology he will have enormous difficulty overriding the chip checkers present on all UIG equipment and will run the risk of being caught using it. All equipment listed here has Chip Checkers.

STEALING AND USING ARCHON TECHNOLOGY

To remove the Chip Checker from Archon technology requires 4 successful 'Intelligence + Mechtronics' rolls with a -12 penalty to each. Each roll represents one days work. Failure on any roll causes the item to self-destruct. Archon technology with an active chip checker will not work for unauthorised users.

CHIP OVERRIDE

Each squad Commander has a powerful override in his ID chip. This allows him to bypass any security based around ID chip technology including domestic, business and Corporate security although it is seldom used to force entry into high level Corporate facilities, as numerous other deterrents stand in the way other than chip checkers.

IMMOBILISER RIFLE

ARCHON PATTERN IR4 HELLCAT IMMOBILISER RIFLE

Damage - Incapacitation (D10 Rounds), Rate 1, Tactical, Medium Range, Energy Cells, EMP Immune, Stopped by Immobiliser Shield (see below)

This weapon only normally comes out against Agents. It is a tactical firearm which is immune to EMP. It takes standard Energy Cells which generate a pulse of white light composed of energy sequences resonating at the same frequency as an Agent's internal neural framework. It causes the Agent (or anyone with a process socket) to effectively shut down. This weapon will only work for UIG Officers unless the Chip Checker is bypassed (see above). It has no effect on those with no Process Socket.
If an Agent is hit with the weapon she must roll below 'Perception + Endurance' with the attacker's XS as a modifier or be incapacitated for D10 rounds.

IMMOBILISER SHIELD

This small device is immune to EMP and can be clipped onto the belt. It makes the wearer immune to Immobiliser weapons. A needle on the devise must be inserted into the wearer's spine by someone with Medicine 3 or more.

STATIC CONVEYANCE DEMOLITION SAW

This large saw can slice though non-living matter with ease. It allows a UIG Officer to cut through walls and solid objects up to 1 metre thick at a rate of 1 metre per 30 seconds. The AV or HP of the item are ignored.

PERSONAL TELEPORTER

Occasionally UIG Officers who are sent on particularly important missions are issued with personal teleporters. These devices are large and heavy and must be carried in full size backpacks. They allow the Officer to teleport instantly a distance of no more than 30 meters. It takes one round to set a destination into the teleporter which is normally done by using an interactive satellite map the Officer can view on a heads-up eyescreen. If the Officer teleports into a wall or object, he merges with it and must be separated by

surgeons if not dead. (Any teleport accident of this nature results in instant death 50% of the time.)

CONTRABAND SCANNER

The UIG have a vested interest in confiscating illegal goods. The contraband scanner is a collapsible doorway, which can be folded down into a case. Sophisticated sensors on the device check anyone passing through for a range of compounds or structures with a reasonable degree of similarity to a pre-programmed list of restricted and illegal goods. (It recognises such items with a 90% success rate.)
If the person walking through the scanner has a license for the restricted items then the machine will ignore them. The machines are normally set up in secure buildings or in public areas during times of unrest, intense public activity or political significance. Large scanners are available which can be placed over roads to check vehicles.

I.D. BIOSCANNER

When the UIG need to track a particular quarry they use these handheld devices. They can also be plugged into a neural jack if one is present. The device links to a satellite feed and can track a particular set of ID Chips programmed into it. There is no range limit.
The Officer with the ID Bioscanner can tell where the target is relative to his position (including altitude). It also gives the Officer a breakdown of the target's health, cybernetic profile and current equipment arsenal. The only way to avoid being tracked is to be surrounded by gamma radiation or to physically destroy the targeted ID Chip.

ERABITE ARMOUR

Officers are sometimes expected to engage in missions against forces they know will be armed with abnormally dangerous weaponry. On these occasions they are often supplied with Erabite Armour.
It is a lightweight polycarbonate-alloy compound with integrated hard ion cells making it immune to the penetrating effects of plasma weapons and laser weapons. Ion weapons still cut through it as normal.
The armour also contains a layer of Haemavine which regenerates the Officer if he is wounded. This has the effect of instantly healing the first 50 HP of damage he takes from any source regardless of how many hits it is delivered in.
Erabite Armour also encompasses a close-form hard ion shield which acts as a 100HP shield that is still effective in close combat. In addition to the benefits listed above Erabite Armour grants a +7 Armour Value bonus. It does not limit Agility and does not count towards the Armour Limit (see page 45 for Armour Limit).

HYBRID WEAPONS

UIG Officers are destined to face a myriad of foes in day to day duty. Each one presents a different problem and resolution may need to take many forms. Hybrid weapons are a combination of two weapons, each 100% effective as individual armaments but with the ability to switch operation at the press of a button.

ARCHON PATTERN BARRACUDA LP4 ASSAULT RIFLE

The user can expend a free action to change this rifle from plasma rounds to laser rounds. Laser for bypassing shields and plasma for bypassing armour depending on the situation.

Damage - 2D8 (Laser or Plasma Damage), Rate 2, Tactical
Uses Energy Cells, Medium Range, EMP Immune, Free action to switch from laser to plasma

These weapons naturally incorporate a chip checker. The GM should feel free to create more hybrid weapons such as a Hybrid railgun / EMP cannon or injector pistol / kinetic magnum.

NON-AGENT RANK AND RIGHTS

Below are listed the ranks of non Agents. For the purposes of this section UIG and Order of The Faith are considered Agents.

CRIMINAL / OUTLAW
(Unranked, unable to ascend to any rank)
The Criminal has no rights at all and is considered property. If possible Criminals should be immobilised or killed and handed over to the UIG. A standard reward of 2000 credits is payable, sometimes more if the criminal is particularly dangerous or guilty of extreme crimes.

OUTCAST
(Unranked but able to ascend to rank 0)
The Outcast has no special rights but is considered a human with the most basic of human rights. By proving herself with acts such as law enforcement, adding to the body of human knowledge or providing a much needed service she may be offered rank 0 by the UIG, at which point she would become a Citizen.

CITIZEN
(Rank 0)
Citizens are the most common member of the populace. 80% of the world is made up of Citizens, most of whom work hard and maintain the economy. The UIG value Citizens above all else and will not tolerate their mistreatment.

A Citizen has the right to:

•Check someone's identity with a Chip Scanner
•Fair trial
•Own land
•Non-inflammatory free speech
•Travel between nations
•Vote
•Use Class D Drugs
•Use non-powered melee weapons
•Acquire rank and licenses

Becoming a Citizen is simple; most Citizens are born into it because their parents are Citizens. Normally each person may have 1 living child thus maintaining a steady populace Outcasts can become Citizens by proving themselves worthy, for example:

•Joining the UIG
•Joining a Corporation
•Contributing significantly to Humanity as a whole
•Working in undesirable jobs for a number of years, e.g. mining at Dreddoth
•Proving themselves exceptional individuals by acts such as saving UIG Officer's lives or apprehending criminals

This is effectively a reward system for deserving Outcasts.

CITIZENS WITH RANK
If a Citizen is fortunate or determined she may ascend in rank. This requires an impeccable record and continued support to the UIG. If the UIG grant a Citizen rank then they may be able to acquire some simple licenses and demand immunity to certain Corporate activates such as being the target of property searches. Ranked Citizens are generally treated with more respect and have stations of responsibility such as high ranking positions in business or on City Councils. Many Agent licenses cannot be used on Citizens with an equal or higher rank than the Agent carrying the license. Naturally corruption is rife within the UIG ranking system where those with money and influence, as usual, can get whatever they need, including rank.

The inception and continued political endurance of the United International Government is a complex and endlessly debated topic, to the extent that many hundreds of volumes could be, and have been, written about it. Briefly, thus; towards the end of the Corporate Wars the bruised remnants of the governments of nine separate nations came to the pragmatic realisation that they had individually failed completely to impose order on Corporations whose operations encompassed the globe and that this failure had almost cost the lives of the entire population of Earth. Working quickly in the power vacuum left by the subdued Corporations, these vestiges of government pooled their resources, experience and personnel into a common aim: to fill the social and administrative gaps that had resulted from the Wars before the Corporations could begin to regroup.

Thus it was that when Shi Yukiro, Ai-Jinn, Western Federation, Comoros and Eurasian Incorporated began to rebuild their respective power bases, they found the nascent UIG already emplaced, keeping order in their abandoned cities and shoring up their shattered administrative frameworks, and willing to continue doing so for a modest tax-based consideration. At first, the Corporations were only too happy for the UIG to relieve them of some of the burden; by the time they started to realise that the UIG had become entrenched worldwide as a fact of life (not to mention a legitimate taxation authority), it was far too late. The technological advances arising as a result of the Eldoran Meeting and the Orpheus Release served to buffer the UIG against military reprisals and, with this final piece in place, the delicate equilibrium we know today was established. The UIG are now sufficiently powerful and well-established that only by a coalition of all the Corporations could they be overthrown; their primary motivation in remaining ostentatiously effective and incorruptible must therefore be to ensure that no casus belli for such a joint effort is ever given.

-from The Rise of The Corporation-States
attr: Dr. Edmond Treval

DR. VICTOR NIKOLI DRAVENKO

WANTED FOR: UNLAWFUL FLIGHT TO AVOID PROSECUTION

Dr. Victor Nikoli Dravenko is being sought in connection with a series of cybernetic crimes involving the installation of illegal cybernetic augmentations into non-consenting patients as part of several ongoing experiments

Dravenko, former Rank 6 Agent for Eurasian Incorporated is believed to have been working illegally for the past 10 years whilst under the employ of E.I. He was officially dismissed on April 31st this year but evaded E.I. capture and fled to Nanchang, China where he is currently thought to be working with black market cyberneticists connected with the Red Thorn Triads.

Dravenko is considered extremely dangerous and if seen should not be approached. Contact the UIG emergency line (com.99999)

REWARD

The UIG are offering a reward of up to **30,000 Credits** for information leading to the arrest or conviction of Victor Nikoli Dravenko

Posted October 18th, 2490

Aliases:	None known
Date of Birth:	June 11, 2320
Hair:	Black
Place of Birth:	Kiev, Russia
Eyes:	Blue / Cybernetic
Height:	5'9"
Complexion:	Pale, blotchy
Weight:	Approx 100kg
Sex:	Male
Build:	Heavy
Race:	White (Caucasian)
Occupation(s):	Cyberneticist
Nationality:	Russian
Marks:	Anascan PSE
Physchology:	Stable, non-telepathic

Plot Ideas

- Dravenko could be working with the Cult of Machina to replace more and more human tissue with cybernetics to see when a human becomes a machine.
- Dravenko is now working with the Triad in Nanchang installing illegal, untested cybernetics into the Triad members who in turn are affiliated with the Ai-Jinn
- Dravenko has not fled and is still secretly working for Eurasian Incorporated as a developer of new and radical cybernetics which are of course, hazardous.
- Dravenko has set up an independent business manufacturing and selling one-off custom cyberware to the highest bidder.

> *Show us what you're doing and we'll tell you why it's a crime.*
>
> -V. Mackey

THE LAW

Earth in 2500 has a complex system of laws which have evolved over thousands of years to become what the UIG consider the best guidelines for society to date. Perhaps the most fundamental change to the law since the 21st century is that of Depersonalisation.

Based on an old European idea of Outlawing this simply means that if a person breaks one too many laws she is open to the wrath of the world. Essentially she is no longer considered a person under UIG law. If, for example, a woman kills her husband and has no accumulated rank, then any crimes committed against her are not considered crimes. She is now an object, lower on the scale than an animal. The criminal starts its new life with no rights, and is considered free property like a rock you find in a desert.

The rock can be smashed or taken home, left alone or sold to a collector. The criminal is the same, if a criminal is captured they have no legal defence, they could be sold as a slave, killed for the good of the community, left alone, abused, etc. Normally criminals are simply executed in public displays, but those with some value may have other futures ahead of them.

Whole industries are based around criminals where their organs are used for spares, their labour is sold by contract and their minds are erased so they can be sold for menial work or cerebral reprogramming. There is no cut-off point for what constitutes a crime worthy of depersonalisation. A Citizen is allowed to make a certain number of legal errors, when this line has been crossed, stealing an apple has the same consequences as killing a UIG Officer. This zero tolerance attitude has understandably led to a low crime rate and some very clever criminals. On rare occasions a promising Outlaw is placed into the Malenbrach program, during which time their body and mind are genetically modified to turn them into the sledgehammers of the UIG.

The results of Depersonalisation are visible in daily life on a regular basis. The UIG and the Corporations stream media that shows the results of depersonalisation. Tedious, dangerous and unpleasant jobs are normally performed by depersonalised staff who work only because of the horrific threats laid down by their employers. There are, of course, numerous criminals out there who are officially depersonalised and yet continue to live fairly normal lives. Much like a savage wild animal, it may be hard to locate the individual, and even if they can be found few may be powerful enough to physically claim ownership.

To avoid depersonalisation all Citizens are educated in the law for one week per year. This is mandatory and means that Citizens

> *I cannot believe that more than all the thousands of years of human civilization, all the countless iterations of legal and social systems, have brought us to this pass. The concept of depersonalization is so obscene as to threaten the fundamental nature of humanity. We must take action now or in the immediate future if we are to avoid degradation of the human psyche on a global scale.*
>
> *- attr: Pravin Gan, leader of the 2499 Comoros War Council.*

cannot *accidentally* break the law. Outcasts are free to atter these sessions. The law is complex and exhaustive but it is laid o in basic terms below.

BREAKING THE LAW

When someone breaks the law they lose Rank Points, (see losir and gaining rank on page 81). When they hit -1 Rank Points the are punished; usually jail time or some kind of public servic When they reach -5 RANK POINTS they are depersonalise Someone with a high rank will thus only be depersonalised after a excessive amount of law breaking. The UIG can use discretion ar apply heavier rank loss than stated for severe crimes.

The Laws Laid Down in the Treaty of Odessa 2205 (simplified version)

Under UIG law you may not:

1. Deceive the UIG
2. Deceive for profit
3. Enter restricted areas (map available on World Data Net)
4. Access data categorised 'Private' by the owner without permission
5. Exceed curfew in curfew designated areas (details on World Data Net)
6. Alter the programming of machines without a permit and license
7. Mar the good name of a Citizen
8. Damage property which is not yours or act in a way which may result in damage to another's property
9. Break regional traffic laws (details on World Data Net)
10. By action or inaction impede a UIG investigation
11. Exhibit behavior likely to cause a breach of the peace
12. Retain funds owed to another without prior agreement
13. Harm a non-outlaw (murder / assault)
14. Interfere with legal activities
15. Interfere with, acquire or use property which is not yours, unless you have permission from the owner (steal)
16. Conduct any act for which a license is needed where you do not have the appropriate license

THE LAW IN CORPORATION

The details of The Law fill hundreds of pages. It cannot be reproduced in detail in a book such as this. If you encounte problems or crimes not covered, make it up yourself. The Law is generally common sense.

UIG CHARACTERS

Although this book does not contain enough information to create a full UIG Officer, a UIG supplement is planned so you will be able to soon.

You could of course just make up what you think best and try your hand at taking down Agents.

The most pertinent question is that of their sustained recruitment figures. Every Citizen within a certain range of physical and psychological profiling born in our territories should be sufficiently influenced by Corporate media that they would desire nothing more than to become an Agent. Yet somehow, every year, we lose between three and five percent of all potential applicants to the UIG campaigns, with no legal recourse to any means of stemming the flow. (The figures are believed to be similar for other Corporations, higher in the case of the Western Federation.) There has been some suggestion that UIG recruitment propaganda is tailored as a 'counter-culture' vehicle specific to the prevailing regime in each different territory, which would go some way towards explaining its efficacy, but whatever the reason it is imperative that samples of this media be obtained and analysed at the earliest possible juncture.

- from The Reach of Law: Threat Analysis, United International Govt.
attr: Michael Kaspillis, EI anthropologer/geopolitical analyst

UIG CLASS IX CODED TRANSMISSION

NON-UIG OF RANK 5 OR LESS ARE STRICTLY PROHIBITED
FROM READING THIS DOCUMENT
DISOBEDIENCE WILL RESULT IN INSTANT DEPERSONALISATION

Communication between:
'Malenbrach Squad Beta Callsign - 6.10 Metro Niner'
'Control: Operator Linden'
'Unknown Operator Delta Echo Zero'
RE: Project DARKTANK
La Paz, Bolivia 07.07.2456 20:43pm.
Begin Transmission...

This is UIG Control. Requesting radio check. Are you in position Metro Niner - over?

Currently setting breach charges. Stand by.

Unit Metro Niner, you must abort, I repeat, abort, mission parameters have changed. Acknowledge - over.

Negative UIG Control, the mission will go ahead as planned. Breach charges set.

Unit Metro Niner, this is a direct order, you will stand down and return to Central - over.

We have the breached building and are proceeding to the target - over.

NEGATIVE, you WILL abort. Get your men and return to Central. Say again, return to Central - over.

Metro Niner coming under attack, returning fire....

This is Metro Niner to Central, the hostiles have been neutralised. We are continuing to the target area - over.

Metro Niner, you are contravening a direct order from Central.

Affirmative, our orders from Central were replaced, new mission code DARKTANK - over.

What? Let me check this.

Metro Niner, this is Delta Echo Zero, I am replacing Control to supervise Darktank, Central is now out of the loop, confirming secondary code: CYAN - over.

Metro Niner here, code confirmed, thermal shows four hostiles in the next room. Please advise.

Resolving satellite feed, stand by Metro Niner.

Metro Niner, this is Delta Echo Zero, the hostiles are armed with mid-range tactical plasmas. Recommend raise shields and engage in close combat. Acknowledge.

Negative Delta Echo Zero, shields are down from prior hostiles,

Beta 5 is preparing to use the rail gun - over.
Affirmative Metro Niner, standing by.

Metro Niner to Delta Echo Zero, we have three dead hostiles and one captive. Beta 7 was shot in the face but has recovered. Our orders do not extend past this point - please advise - over.

Metro Niner, is there some kind of case in the room.

Affirmative, shall we bring it home with us - over?

Negative, open the case.

I'm opening the case now....

Metro Niner, there should be a small bottle of liquid inside, can you confirm - over?

Affirmative, one bottle.

Do any of your squad carry a dart gun or med kit?

Negative Delta Echo Zero.

Is there any kind of fine tubing in the room, a pen perhaps - over?

Checking now....

Affirmative Delta Echo Zero, I have the induction coil from the hostiles plasma - over.

Ask Beta 5 to inject the live hostile with the entire content of the bottle - over.

Affirmative Delta Echo Zero.

Metro Niner to Delta Echo Zero, Beta 5 has injected the fluid - over.

Is anything happening to the hostile - over.

The hostile is convulsing and haemorrhaging from the eyes, Beta 3 is restraining him, his bones sound like they're snapping, he seems to be changing. We need to take action now! Advise - over.

Standby Metro Niner

Metro Niner, this is Delta Echo Zero, I need an update on the live hostile - over.

Metro Niner....

Metro Niner, come in Metro Niner.......

130

UIG GLOBAL NEWS UPDATE

MODEL CITIZEN FOILS CRIMINALS

By Miranda Carmichael

By Miranda Carmichael
:20pm March 5th 2499

This afternoon two Asian men were arrested outside the Osan Trade Building in Cairo Open City after a keen eyed Citizen noticed one of the men was carrying what looked like a large firearm under his coat. The Citizen, Mr. Kanash Judura, was going to meet his girlfriend in a nearby coffee house when the gun attracted his attention.

"I didn't know what to think", commented Mr. Judura in an interview this afternoon, "I know the UIG have licenses for weapons like that but these two looked like bums. I knew trouble was brewing so I did what any public minded Citizen would do."

Mr Judura made the call and within minutes a squad of Field Officers were at the scene.

Judura saw the whole thing, "It was amazing", the observant Citizen said, "the Officers moved in like nothing I've ever seen. The two bums didn't know what hit them, they just put down their weapons and left quietly. I'm glad I pay my taxes!" Mr. Kanash Judura has been commended by the UIG for his swift action and the two individuals have been taken into custody.

TRAGEDY UNFOLDS FOR ALLIED METALS

Follows on from this morning's article (above)

By Miranda Carmichael
:45pm March 5th 2499

The head of Cairo based Allied Metals, Mr. Yennen Dumore, was assassinated today by two escaped prisoners. The two men were arrested earlier today by a squad of UIG Officers outside the Osan Trade Building in Cairo Open City for a 450 Civil Conduct Breach. (Carrying Unlicensed Tactical Firearms).

Although the two men were captured earlier today, reliable sources have confirmed that there was an incident involving the arresting squad on route to the holding cells, when the two prisoners apparently tore open the side of the holding van and leapt out before throwing a number of microcharges at the UIG vehicle.

We can now confirm that the two men returned to the Osan Trade Building and waited for Mr. Yennen Dumore to leave, whereupon they opened fire on him with sub-machine guns as he left for the shuttle port to attend the upcoming Macromining Conference in Accra, Ghana.

Reliable sources inform us that the two prisoners were of Asian descent and allegedly working for an Ai-Jinn subsidiary. Allied Metals have lost 6 points on the WDN Stock Exchange and economists have already forecast that Allied Metals will be swallowed by the Ai-Jinn Corporation by the end of the week. Once again, this reporter thinks they should just send in the Malenbrach first time, every time.

If you see anything suspicious call the UIG Crimeline on Comm. 99999.

COMOROS PUBLICIY THREATENED

By Jerome Bonnaire
3.35pm March 5th 2499

The CIC (Coalition for Independent Commerce) today demanded through a communication believed to have originated in the former nation of Libya, that as a gesture of goodwill, the Comoros Corporation should offer 10% of all Spire commercial sites to independent traders or face the consequences.

As yet Comoros have refused to comment but Dilupa Rasheed, Shadow CEO of Comoros stated earlier this week that the pressure from the CIC was misplaced. Rasheed, in a press conference on Wednesday, made it very clear that Comoros

Inter-Corporation Conciliatory Policy required that the commercial zoning of the Redemption Spire in Cape Town be divided in the following way:

Western Federation	15%
Eurasian Inc.	10%
Shi Yukiro	10%
Ai-Jinn	05%
Multymeat	10%
Comoros	30%
UIG	10%
Others Corporations	07%
Independent Citizens	03%

This is not the first time the CIC have directly threatened a major Corporation. In 2432 the CIC demanded that *Locked and Loaded*, the Federation's main armaments distribution chain, be downsized by 20% and the resulting void filled by small, independent arms manufacturers, namely *Strapfist Montana's Manglin' Mart* and the recently formed *Guns Guns Guns*, brain child of Alexi Ivanenkov. The Federation's refusal to comply led to a series of terrorist attacks on the Corporate sectors of the Austerity Spire Complex by the American Underground, who are known to be sympathetic to the CIC.

The Federation have publicly announced their support for Comoros' strong stance against terrorist pressure and have offered Comoros multiple Divisions of Urban Assault Specialists to act as counter terrorist units should the worst happen.

We'll bring you more on this matter as it plays out. Citizens in Comoros territory are advised not to panic and for the time being be calm but vigilant.

TOKYO DRAGONS VS. BLACK BALLET

Arena - San Jose Megadome
Report - Miguel Marino, IWF

What a match! From First-Launch to Time-Out there was a lotta anger in the arena. Cat Fisca scored the first goal for Black Ballet in the opening minute, taking out the Dragons new winger, Hideo Kanazawa with a brutal knee stamp, scoring a bonus from the crowd.
Akari was bought on to replace Kanazawa and the action resumed. There were a few weak set-up attempts by Black Ballet in the first half, but the Dragons were fuming at the loss of Kanazawa and the ion claws were out. Black Ballet played the rest of the first half defensively while the Dragons tried to wear their opponents out with repeated knock down attempts.

HALF TIME SCORE   TOKYO DRAGONS 0   BLACK BALLET 12

At half time both teams seemed confident. The Dragons came back in the second half with a characteristic display of gymnastics and bladework. Cat Fisca got what was coming to him in the 30th minute when Hiroshi cannoned the ball into the back of his head, but not content with an NFR he finished the job and took his head as a trophy, landing it and the ball in the goal. The crowd voted a 5pt kill putting the Dragons on 15. A side-fight between Kanaga and Metroski resulted in two non-fatal retirements setting the scores at Dragons 17, Ballet 14.

Two minutes from the end, Ichimaga, the Dragons newest player, thrilled the crowd with a show of dexterity that would tax the likes of Carras Duke. He slipped round the entire opposition defence and landed a goal that had the Megadome on its feet. The Dragons scorched ahead 27-14.

Experience shows though, and Ichimaga's victory strut was ended swiftly as DeSilva and Garret double teamed him in a new move they must have been saving for that night. In a blur of boosted speed, DeSilva grabbed Ichimagas body while Garret stuffed his head into the ball launcher. Amazing! Someone's going home with a souvenir.

The crowd awarded 15 points to Black Ballet sealing the match and placing Black Ballet second in the league. Tune in to IWLTV for the next match; the Berlin Reapers and Team Darkstar take it to the Drome Spire.
FINAL SCORE   TOKYO DRAGONS 27   BLACK BALLET 29

THE ORDER OF THE TRUE FAITH

The Prophet Zhao Mao warned you of the consequences of profaning the sanctity of the flesh and you did not listen. Now the Demon has arisen, whose name is Legion and whose flesh is metal. Still you do not listen. Legion grows at the root of every Spire, the Demon waxes strong in the world of wires. How many more of the Signs must you see, o you peoples of the Earth, before you will cast aside your folly?

-Temur Yeke,
Revelations of the Second Age

DESCRIPTION

The Order of the True Faith came into being as a direct result of the Corporate Wars; the scattered religions of the world were hard pressed to maintain faith when confronted on all sides with war, destruction and disease. Their temples and churches were ransacked and stripped during the conflicts to provide additional resources for the murdering armies.

Jungney, a Thai Buddhist, spoke with great wisdom and insight on the topic of corporate megalomania and the inevitable destruction of the Earth. His speeches were met with great enthusiasm and his insistence that the Earth should belong to all, regardless of faith, brought a great number of important religious figures into his camp. In time this collection of devout individuals with only faith and purpose uniting them, came to consider themselves an organisation in their own right. They named themselves the Order of the True Faith and set about making their opinions and beliefs known. With strength in unity they grew until they had followers in every city, town and province across the world. As they planned their great move to bring a halt to the Corporate wars, the conflicts ended. The UIG formed and the Order suddenly found their primary purpose missing.

Rather than simply disbanding such a rare, powerful and devout organisation they instead turned their attention to matters which they could still influence; poverty, corruption, crime, abuse of power and most importantly the dehumanisation of modern man. Jungney, now tired and weakened from the events of the past years, handed leadership of the Order to another Buddhist named Niu Zhao Mao. Zhao led the Order to greater heights making compelling speeches against human augmentation, even demanding the Ai-Jinn cease production of cybernetics or face the consequences.

Little came of Zhao's threats but his zeal and fire led more and more people into the flock of the Faithful. As more civilians turned to the Order, its power grew. All manner of influential men and women considered themselves supporters of the Order and offered their services to them in exchange for a clear conscience and a guaranteed path to a pleasant afterlife. Before Zhao died the Order had reached a size which could not be ignored. The Western Federation made a gesture to the Order stating that it would ban the cybernetic augmentation of non-corporate employees in the lands it controlled and offered the Order a permanent base in Vera Cruz. They consented and the first Order enclave was established. Since then the Order has become an immense power in its own right. Although it seldom takes direct

CARDINAL DOMINUS CAVEL OF INSISTO CORPUS INCORRUPTUS

military action, its wealth and influence ensure that if conflict is necessary, it will not flinch.

So why do so many people flock to a faith so blindly? Throughout the 22nd century, religion across the world had heavily declined and the populace became jaded with promises of life eternal and concepts of Heaven and Hell. In a world dominated by science there was less and less room for faith. That was until the advent of Telepathics; not guessing symbols on cards or mysterious links between twins, but a genuine ability to affect the world with the power of the mind.

The growth of telepathy coincided with the consolidation of the Order. Those few who had manifested the powers were drawn to the ways of the Faithful. They were not questioned or experimented on, they were simply accepted. Most telepaths who emerged in Corporate society were hauled off to find out how they functioned and then put to work as Agents with incredible and unpredictable abilities. Only Comoros seemed to see a higher purpose in telepathic power, but their designs for such a gift did not involve forcing the world to conform to a unified religious ideal. Those who joined the ranks of the Faithful were treated like heroes, men and women who could channel divine power for the greater good. Before long they had the largest number of telepaths anywhere in the world, who taught other members of the Faithful to bring out their latent skills. The Order of the True Faith became a telepathic force like no other, it could make demands of the Corporations and they would be followed. The world seemed in

ORDER ENCLAVE AT KHARKIV IN THE UKRAINE

danger of becoming the Order's dream. As technology improved however, (which the Order would not use) and telepathy became understood and more mainstream, the Order's advantage began to diminish.

Currently the Order of the True Faith find themselves in a difficult position. Their telepathy is still superior to the majority of Corporations, but their power is beginning to plateau. Their reluctance to use combat technology means they are hard pressed to fight on the same scale as their opponents. Their only chance lies in numbers, with enough Faithful no-one could stop them. If they could convince enough people to follow them they could have the Faithful simply boycott a Corporation and watch it disappear overnight.

GOALS

The Order still stands for the elimination of poverty, crime, corruption and dehumanisation. They take the battle wherever they need to. They can always find Faithful Citizens willing to help them for nothing more than absolution. They seek only to bring the world to a state of peaceful harmony. The current leader, Temur Yeke, is not deluded into thinking this a short term achievable goal. Instead he directs the Order towards preventing further disasters before they take the Earth deeper into entropy. The Order uses its sizable influence to 'encourage' offending parties to refrain from certain courses of action. This bullying method works for the majority of occasions, but some of the more powerful groups, namely the five major Corporations and the UIG will only tolerate so much. They are usually happy to placate the Order, but when their wishes look as though they may encroach on Corporate policy there is a limit to what the Corporations are willing to do.

The Order seeks to have their people everywhere, they want everyone to recognise that the only way to avoid a future of death and suffering is to go back to nature, to hang up all weapons of war and ascend to a simpler state of being. If this must be hammered home with sword and mind then sadly that is a sacrifice that must be made for the greater good of humanity.

> Yes, yes, I'm familiar with the clichéd idea of religion as the opiate of the masses. My question is why, with so many more conventional opiates so commonly available, does this archaic dinosaur persist?
>
> -attr: Gunther van Rosch, CEO, Eurasian Incorporated

OPERATIONAL METHOD

Although a number of the Order wear modern business suits and practical fatigues, the majority dress in the manner of the different faiths from which they originally hailed. Those who were always of the Faith tend to wear pure white to symbolise that no one element overrides another, but it is up to the individual. In martial matters the Order often wears armour reminiscent of that used by their warrior predecessors and often use telepathic sword and shields (known as Resonance Weapons) when fighting, as they believe they cannot revert the world to its ideal state when they themselves are using the same technology which has catalysed its decline. The Order have come under much criticism for their hypocrisy. On one hand they preach peace, love and union, on the other they take to battle against those who persistently defy them. They maintain that they work towards a greater good and that the

death of a few corrupt, self indulgent heathens is nothing in the great scheme of things. They have tried to change, many Order Battle Priests have taught themselves in the ways of non-lethal combat, felling their enemies and then restraining them with Telepathics. Whilst in their Relic Cities, Order Telepaths are continually renewed with Telepathic Energy making them all but unstoppable, one of the main reasons no one has invaded them successfully.

> In many ways, our objectives and even our methods are similar to theirs. Only the reasons are different.
> - attr: Dilupa Rasheed, Shadow CEO, Comoros Corporation

NAMES AND RANKS

Members of the Order of the True Faith are eligible for rank.
A Division of the Order of the True Faith is normally called a 'Sect' 'Cabal' or 'Chapter'.
Agents of the Order are known as 'The Devoted'.
Followers of the Order are known as 'The Faithful'.
Followers often refer to each other and themselves as 'Brothers' and 'Sisters'.

EXAMPLE NAMES

Gabriel, Eudrael, Azreal, Jericho, Elijha, Mohammed, Bari Khaleel, Shakorun, Michael, Constantine, Verada, Abigail Samaria, Enos, Caleb, Anah, Bethany, Fadiel

EXAMPLE OCCUPATIONS

ACOLYTE
As a foot soldier of the Order the acolyte is well versed in methods of war and the various religions of the Faith. These soldiers have fearsome dedication and are not afraid to die for the cause.

INQUISITOR
Each Chapter is usually accompanied by an Inquisitor, who is there to deal with heretics and provide telepathic backup. They are often clothed in bright, luxuriant colours and have a tendency to be arrogant and head strong.

PRIEST
Each Chapter is led by a Priest. She ensures the Devoted are content in their work and utterly dedicated. The Order firmly maintains that a belief in the Faith is all a Devoted really needs and the Priest is there to ensure that this belief does not slip.

KUNDUN
A spiritual leader who does not usually engage in direct action but advises the Faithful with his wisdom acquired through years of mental training, experience and discipline.

CRUSADER
These are purposeful knights who usually work alone, picking battles that others are fearful to engage in. They are wildcards given free run by the higher echelons of the Order. Crusaders are unlikely to accrue much in the way of rank as their good work is normally balanced by bouts of intolerant slaughter.

CHARACTERS OF NOTE

INQUISITOR EUDRAEL KILTARROW
Rank 7, Level 13

...iltarrow is a small man who dresses in white robes with a black ...urplice. His features are rat-like and he is always accompanied by ...vo others from the Order, generally physically competent ...colytes. His main work involves removing heretics from the ranks ...f the Order as well as visiting Order held territories and weeding ...ut non-believers. Kiltarrow was raised by religious parents and ...rced to join the Order's ranks at an early age. His aptitude for ...lepathics was soon discovered and his training started when he ...as 14. As a result he is an immensely powerful telepath although ...aturally he refuses all cybernetic aids.

...RECEPTOR EZEKIEL ARADAETH
...ank 5, Level 12

...receptor Aradaeth makes it his personal responsibility to teach ...e whole of the Order what it should and should not do. He travels ...round giving lectures and sermons about the various virtues of ...dhering to the Faith. His visits are always accompanied by great ...eremonies and large armed battalions of the Faithful are always ...resent to hinder assassination attempts. The Preceptor is a large ...an with broad shoulders and modified arms (a reminder of his ...ederation days before the Faith), he has a great presence about ...m and his word carries influence with the Order, not a man to ...nnoy. He carries no weapons but his work necessitates the ...resence of a high end hard ion shield and dermal plating.

Preceptor Aradaeth strode down the echoing corridor, flanked by the twelve Acolytes of his personal guard. His white robes flowed about him and the bluish light cast by his ion shield danced and flickered on the vaulted ceiling above. A frown creased his craggy features, causing the subdermal plate beneath his forehead to crackle slightly as it shifted. Aradaeth had just come in from Shanghai, where his rhetoric had played some small part in foiling the acquisition of Order ground by a factory consortium acting on behalf of the Ai-Jinn. In the process, though, he had been exposed at first hand to some of the worst excesses of Corporate corruption, and his thoughts were dark with memories of industrial wasteland and cyborged workers.

He pushed the double doors aside and strode out onto the balcony, and felt a resurgence of conviction flow through him as he gazed out over the thousands of Faithful in the darkness far below. Each held a candle, so that the vast black expanse of the Praise Grounds sparkled with innumerable points of light. Taking a deep breath, Aradaeth lifted his gaze to the heavens and saw that briefly, miraculously, the clouds over Vera Cruz had parted, so that for the first time in months the stars were dimly visible, seeming to shine down in glorious endorsement of the myriad tiny flames below. His unshakeable faith renewed afresh, Aradaeth raised his massive arms above his head and prepared to give the Benediction.

...NIQUE TRAITS AND ABILITIES

...ELIC RENEWAL
...he Order has many secrets, a great deal of which are based in ...ccult and religious practices. One of the better known ones is their ...bility to continually be replenished with Telepathic Energy when in ...elic Cities (See page 171). In game terms this means that when ... Relic Cities the Order Telepaths spend no TE to use their ...owers. Additionally when in Relic Cities all Order Telepaths are ...onsidered to have their telepathic powers 2 levels higher then ...ey actually are. This book only covers powers up to level 10 but ... should be simple to work out what would happen at higher levels ...you wish.

...WO HANDED PSI BLADES
...he Order understands the way of Psi Blades better than anyone. ...rder Telepaths can summon two handed Psi Blades. These deal ...12+(2xStrength) plus 1 point of damage per point the Devoted

has in Psi Blade. They have Rate 1.
For example:
Lady Christiana al Corre, a Holy Knight of the Order wields a 2 handed Psi Blade. She has strength 8 and Psi Blade 7.
She deals D12+16+7 for a total of D12+23 damage.

PREACHERS LICENSE
All Order Devoted gain the Preachers License for free (Page 27)

RESONANCE WEAPONS
The secret art of creating a resonance weapons belongs exclusively to the Order of the True Faith. It involves mind forging a psychically potent material for many days to resemble the weapon the Telepath desires. This requires a high level of telekinesis combined with training in the forging of such a weapon (which is never taught outside the Order).
Both close combat and ranged weapons can be forged. These can be diverse with a range of abilities making each one unique to its owner. The GM should feel free to create her own resonance weapons but remember that they are telepathically powerful and their effect should be in keeping with a weapon which works in union with the creators mind.

ANGEL'S VENGEANCE

EXAMPLE RESONANCE WEAPON
Angel's Vengeance is a longsword crafted from a large silver crucifix salvaged from St. Paul's Cathedral in London after the great assault by Comoros. The sword is a clean silver weapon with the suggestion of screaming female faces running up the blade.
The sword was forged by Lucian Calmir (Rank 3, Level 15), a Crusader from Europe who travels alone, dispensing justice as he sees fit. Angel's Vengeance allows Calmir to vent his hate through the weapon.

Damage	D8 + Strength + XS
Rate	2
Type	Tactical Close Combat
EMPS	Immune
Hatred	Double Damage vs. Comoros Telepaths

Bound to Calmir
Anyone trying to use Angel's Vengeance other than Calmir takes 5 damage a round ignoring Armour Value.

Vengeful
Calmir can sacrifice a point of his Presence to have the sword deal a critical hit. As he does this his face twists with anger and he becomes more and more consumed by rage. The points of Presence return at a rate of 1 per day as the overwhelming telepathic mindprint leaves him.

ORDER CHARACTERS
Although this book does not contain enough information to create a full Order of the True Faith character, a supplement is planned to enable you to do so.

The Corporations mock us, whispering behind their hands. To them we are an anachronism, an embarrassing relic, a pack of zealots funded by the credulous. Let them mock. They cannot know that we were once poised to deliver a blow that would have shattered them utterly, and that should they ever threaten again to destroy all Creation, such a strike is still within our reach.

-attr: Kundun Pietr Armanov

LADY CHRISTIANA AL CORRE, CRUSADER OF THE FAITH

SECTION 8
THE GAME SYSTEM

Detailed in this section are the mechanics of the game. It's the instructions for playing Corporation which are normally referred to as a System. Corporation uses a custom system called the *Brutal Engine*.

The Brutal Engine was designed to give you, as players and Games Masters, the opportunity to do the sorts of things you see in a film. If you have seen it in the movies we have tried to make sure you can do it here. In a role-playing game such as this the majority of things you want your character to do you will simply describe.

For example – "I want to get in my car and drive home" or "I'll ask him where I can find Agent Jenson".

You don't need rules for this kind of thing but when there is doubt as to whether your attempt at something will succeed you need to use the system.

For example – "I'll seduce the man and find out who he works for" or "I'll escape the UIG in this old car".

Any action that a character wishes to perform has a certain chance of succeeding. Some stand a better chance than others. STATS and Skills are used to represent a character's innate makeup and learned abilities, which in turn determine your chance of succeeding in certain actions. Dice are used to introduce uncertainty.

For example, shooting a gun at a target is an action you may wish to perform. If you bought high firearm skills for your character this translates to a good chance of him hitting. There is almost always a chance of failure but this is true in real life. Where the chance of failure is ridiculously small (e.g. breaking a window with a brick) no dice roll is normally necessary.

DICE BASICS

You will need some dice to play this game. These can be acquired on-line or from hobby stores. Dice are named after the number of sides they have on them; e.g. a normal six sided die is called a D6. A twelve sided die is called a D12. Ideally you will have two D10 and one each of D4, D6, D8, D12, D20. More are always handy for large weapons. You can create a D100 by rolling two 10 sided dice and assigning one as tens and one as units. A roll of 0/0 is considered a 100.

Rolling the Dice
When you need to roll dice you will get a quantity to roll, e.g. 1D6 (one six sided die). 3D20 (three twenty sided dice). Add up the total of all the dice you roll. For example, if the rules say roll 3D10, get 3 ten sided dice, roll them and add up the numbers. If you roll 3, 4 and 5 your total is 12.

Multiplying and Rounding Numbers
Sometimes you will need to multiply results; e.g. 3D6x2. Just roll 3 six sided dice and multiply the total by 2. There is an optional rule on page 34 for doing this differently but this way is the simplest. If you ever have to halve a number, always round down. For example, if you roll 3D8 and get 13, half would be 6.

Note: All values are rounded down in Corporation whether they are dice related or not.

PASSING A ROLL / ACHIEVING A SUCCESS

To complete the task you set out to do, you must achieve 'Success'.

To do this the GM (Games Master) will tell you which dice roll you must make. Typically it will be a STAT + a Skill but it could be any combination such as 2 STATS or 2 Skills but this would be uncommon.

These two numbers added together are called an ACTION TOTAL (AT).

You must then roll two 10 sided dice (D10) and add them together. If the total is less or equal to the ACTION TOTAL you succeed.

If the result is higher then you fail. In some cases the GM may consider it is the sort of action you could keep attempting. For example, you could retry smashing down a door but if you fail to jump onto a moving car there is no way you can try again.

Example
Agent Delacroix is looking for a secret compartment in an office. The GM asks for a 'Perception + Observation' roll. Delacroix has Perception 8 and Observation 3, added together this gives an Action Total of 11. Delacroix will need to roll 11 or less on two ten sided dice to pass. She gets 3 and 7 which adds to 10. Success!

If she had failed she could keep trying. The GM could decide each attempt takes 10 minutes.

WHEN TO ASK FOR A ROLL

Learning when to ask for a roll and when not to is a key part to running a good game. If you continually ask for people to roll dice to do small things such as drive into town or climb a ladder the players can get bored and the game can slow down.

Another reason not to ask for rolls on simple actions is that the system is designed to be fair when a reasonably taxing task is being performed. Forcing people to make rolls for mundane tasks will result in excessive failure which can create a negative mood.

That said, a lot of players enjoy rolling the dice and it adds unpredictability, so don't just let them do anything they want all the time. Generally speaking you should ask for a roll when there is a good chance a character may not be able to execute the task she wants to.

BREAKING THE RULES

Sometimes rules don't cover everything or don't suit the way you play. If you don't like something just alter things so they suit your group. Writing a set of rules to cover every eventuality would be both impossible to do and boring to read. If you do change things make sure all the players know the changes and try to be consistent. You don't want everyone playing by different rules.

CRITICAL SUCCESS AND FAILURE

Critical Success – If you roll a 1/1 when trying to get a success you have done something truly outstanding and the GM should make sure your action results in something exceptional. For example, a critical success when running after a criminal may result in you remembering a short cut and cutting him off.

Critical Failure – If you roll 10/10 when trying to achieve a success then something bad has happened. Sometimes a critical failure will not be appropriate. For example if you were listening for a noise it is hard to mess it up badly, but generally speaking the GM should cause something unexpected and unwanted to occur. For example, if you were climbing over a wall and rolled a 10/10 the GM could rule that you fall off, crack your head and take a point of damage.

Note: Criticals in combat are covered on page 143.
Circumstances such as quality of weapons or your Profession can cause you to critical on rolls other than 10/10 and 1/1.

I DON'T HAVE THE RIGHT SKILL

Your STATS define your innate makeup such as Strength or Intelligence.

Your SKILLS indicate things you have learnt such as Medicine or Driving.

Most action rolls will combine one of each but any combination can be used if necessary. The GM always decides what roll you make, although some actions such as using guns may have a predefined roll. If you are asked for a roll and don't have the skill you can sometimes still have a go with the GM's permission, however some tasks you cannot try. For example fitting Cybernetics with no relevant skill should not be permitted because special training is needed. Ulitmately that is down to the GM.

If you do attempt an unskilled roll, all doubles rolled result in critical failure including 1/1. (This can be overcome by the training *Aptitude* (see page 21).

XS GUIDE

XS	Degree of Success
0-1	Just pass, not a great success but it worked
2-5	Good pass, it went as planned
6-9	Excellent, the result is something to be proud of
10+	The best, it could not have been done better

Failing is failing, there are no degrees of failure except 'Critical Failure' see page above.

XS (EXCESS)

XS is a term describing how much you passed or failed your roll by. The GM can decide that the better the XS, the better you have done the task. It can sometimes be used as a modifier on other actions, for example if you pass a Stealth roll by 4 the GM may give you +4 to subsequently knock the guard unconscious. (See the XS guide at the bottom of the page)
Example:
Refer to the example on the previous page with Agent Delacroix. She needed to get 11 or less and rolled 10. Her XS was 1. That is a small XS and so the GM decides it has no additional effect.

STATS ABOVE 10

Having STATS above 10 is very useful; an Action Total of 23 will still effectively be 19 even with a -4 modifier. Because 10 represents the human limit, you can only get above 10 with cybernetics, drugs or other unnatural methods.
Skills above 10 are not covered in this book. They will be covered in a forthcoming supplement.

SYMPATHY BONUS / SYMPATHETIC SKILLS

If you are performing a considered, careful action using a skill and you have a second skill which complements the first one you may be allowed a Sympathy Bonus by the GM.
You gain half of the less useful skill (rounded down) added to your Action Total.
Be frugal with these bonuses; only use them when the second skill is highly relevant. They are not appropriate for action rolls or rolls which use pre-defined STATS and Skills such as telepathy or combat.
Example 1:
Agent Lao is fixing his pistol using 'Intelligence(7) + Mechtronics(8)' he also has 'Light Firearms' at 6 which he thinks should help him. If the GM agrees he gains half his Sympathetic Skill as a bonus. In this case +3.

Example 2:
Agent Mirimoto is analysing a crime scene. The GM asks for a 'Perception(6) + Crime(6)' roll. Mirimoto also has Observation 5 so the GM decides to grant her a +2 Sympathy bonus.

MULTIPLE SUCCESSES

Some tasks need more than one skill or might take an extended period such as hacking a UIG computer system or repairing a car in the field. In this case the GM can ask for multiple successes. This means the player may have to make more than one roll (or other players could help). For example an Agent may need three successes at an 'Intelligence + Mechtronics' roll. The GM could also rule that each roll takes one hour, so if the player has to do 6 rolls to get his three successes it took him six hours to complete the task and could not have taken him less than 3.
These rolls need not be the same; for example, if an Agent is trying to fix a car then he may require two 'Mechtronics' based rolls and one 'Computers and A.I.' based roll because the computer in the car is also damaged.
Overall it is up to the GM, but in general multiple rolls should only be used for tasks that require more than one game skill or are long and drawn out.

THE GENERAL MODIFIER

The GM can always give a penalty or a bonus on the roll - normally +4 to -4 but sometimes more (see the table below). It represents things being easier or harder than normal. This will help with any number of circumstances and should be commonly used in a game.

Difficult rolls may have modifiers such as a –4, in which case you get –4 off your Action Total before rolling. Likewise, simpler actions could receive a positive bonus. A positive bonus should be given when the task is easy but there is a small chance of failure which could have significant results.

Example. Agent Huros is picking a very basic lock. The GM gives him a +4 bonus. If he fails, even at +4, the lock may break and stay permanently locked meaning he will have to shoot or kick the door in.

EXAMPLE MODIFIERS

Difficulty   Sample Modifier

Very Easy   +4
Looking on the World Data Net for a west facing hotel room in the Los Angeles Spire
Intelligence + Computers and AI

Simple   +2
Searching a small apartment for some money
Perception + Observation

Normal   +0
Throwing a grenade into a 1st floor window
Perception + Support Weapons

Tricky   -1
Climbing to the second floor of a building with no equipment
Agility + Athletics

Taxing   -2
Cracking a simple code against the clock
Intelligence + Science

Demanding   -3
Convincing a UIG Squad to leave the area
Presence + Attitude

Difficult   -4
Repairing a kinetic pistol in the field with no equipment
Intelligence + Mechtronics

Very Hard   -6
Passing a psyche evaluation when your Agent is genuinely unstable
Presence + Psychology

Extreme   -8
Leaping off a huge building and catching onto a power cable with one hand after falling 80 metres
Agility + Athletics

Nearly Impossible   -12
Hacking a UIG Computer System
Intelligence + Computers and A.I.

SAMPLE ACTIONS

Below are some common actions that characters will often make and some suggested rolls. Generally speaking just make up the roll based on the STAT and Skill you think are most appropriate. Keep a copy of a character sheet handy when running a game so you can easily see what you can choose from.

SAMPLE ACTIONS AND ROLLS

Climbing
Agility + Athletics

Driving at Speed
Reflexes + Drive

Breaking and Entering
Intelligence + Crime

Using Brute Strength
Strength + Athletics

Sneaking
Agility + Stealth

Accessing Computers
Intelligence + Computers and A.I.

Searching a Room
Perception + Observation

Assess a Crime Scene
Intelligence or Perception + Crime

Repairing Equipment
Intelligence + Mechtronics

Seduction
Presence + Looking Good or Attitude

Intimidation
Presence + Attitude

Working out the function of a device
Intelligence + Assess Technology

Finding Anomalies in Accounts
Intelligence + Business

Performing / Art
Presence + Arts and Culture

Recognising a Rival Agent
Perception + Corp. Knowledge

Gaming e.g. Poker
Presence + Psychology You could also use Attitude, Intelligence or Lying & Acting

Being Polite to a Foreigner
Perception + Arts & Culture

Setting up a Secure Communication
Intelligence + Mechtronics / Computers

Constructing a Makeshift Close Combat Weapon
Intelligence + Close Combat or Mechtronics

Jumping Out of the Way of a Trap
Reflexes + Athletics

Crawling Through a Tight Space
Agility + Athletics

Creating Your Own Toxin
Intelligence + Medicine

Calming Down an Insane Artificial Intelligence
Presence + Computers and A.I.

Acquiring Some Banned Goods
Presence or Intelligence + Street Culture

COMBAT AND ACTION

"His energy is like a drawn crossbow, His timing like the release of a trigger." - Sun Tzu, The Art of War.

OVERVIEW

Combat requires more rules than the rest of the game. That's because if you simply passed a single roll and defeated an entire enemy Division it would be very unsatisfactory. Likewise, players are not generally keen on being killed by a lucky roll.

Having a detailed combat system allows you to make almost any type of action you like and allows for cinematic fight scenes you will remember.

Hopefully this should be fairly straightforward and you can use the combat summary table to help you walk through combat the first few times. Don't be concerned if you don't get it all straight away. Use whichever parts you want and slowly expand until you are familiar with all combat possibilities.

COMBAT SUMMARY

This is a basic summary. As you get more familiar with the rules there are many options and subtleties you can introduce.

I. INITIATIVE

REFLEXES + D10. Highest acts first.

2. PICK A TARGET AND ROLL TO HIT

Take 2D10 and roll under or equal to your 'Relevant STAT + Relevant Weapon Skill' which are listed below. See *Achieving a Success* on page 138 if you are not sure how.

| | | ACTION TOTAL (AT) | |
| | | RELEVANT STAT & SKILL USED | |
Attack Made	R/C	STAT	SKILL
Grenade like weapons	R	Perception +	Support Weapons
Heavy Firearms	R	Perception +	Heavy Firearms
Light Firearms	R	Perception +	Light Firearms
Close Combat (weapons)	C	Agility +	Close Combat
Tactical Firearms	R	Perception +	Tactical Firearms
Thrown Bladed Weapons*	R	Perception +	Athletics
Unarmed Attacks	C	Agility +	Close Combat
Vehicle Weapons	R/C	Perception +	Support Weapons
Emplacements	R	Perception +	Support Weapons

R/C - Whether the attack is Ranged or Close Combat

3. RANGED ATTACK

If you roll below or equal to the Action Total you hit.

RELEVANT WEAPON SKILL

Because there are different weapon skills in Corporation the term *Relevant Weapon Skill* is used to mean the skill you use to attack with your current weapon.

For example,
If you are using a sword then your Relevant Weapon Skill is Close Combat

If you were firing a shotgun your Relevant Weapon Skill would be Tactical Firearms.

The weapon tables starting on page 35 tell you what category each weapon is at the top of the table, e.g. light, tactical, heavy etc.

Roll damage or effect based upon the weapon description. If the target is wearing armour of any kind the Armour Value (AV) should be subtracted from the damage. The resulting damage is subtracted from the target's Hit Points (HP).

The target may attempt to *Dodge* a ranged attack - see page 144.

4. CLOSE COMBAT ATTACK

Work out your Action Total (Relevant STAT + Relevant Skill). Subtract the opponent's *Defence* (this is equal to their close combat skill). Roll below or equal to the resulting number.
Roll damage or effect based upon the weapon description. If the target is wearing armour of any kind the Armour Value (AV) should be subtracted from the damage. The resulting damage is subtracted from the target's Hit Points (HP).

The target may attempt to *Block* a close combat attack - see page 144.
*Thrown bladed weapons require the 'Thrown Weapons Training', see page 24.

THE SCENE

A *scene* is a collection of actions linked by a place or theme such as a bar fight, sneaking into a prison, a car chase or a session in a computer lab. It is the same as a scene in a film. The scene would generally be more than a few minutes but less than an hour. A scene can be split up if it is lasting a long time into smaller scenes. For example, if an Agent is using a telepathic power which lasts a scene the GM may decide it ends after 10 minutes.

A NARRATIVE SCENE

This is a scene where there is no need for timing. The players may make rolls to do things but there will be no emphasis on urgency and turn order. For example, Agents meeting with their Mission Officer, searching an abandoned lab or using a computer to do legal research.

A COMBAT SCENE

A combat scene starts when the first character makes a move to which another character reacts and something opposed and physical is likely to happen. At this point everyone rolls *Initiative* to see how fast they react. The scene is divided into rounds which are considered to last about 3 seconds. Each round all players get a turn and choose what their character is doing, starting with the person who wins Initiative (see below). The player who got the next best Initiative score goes next and so on. The scene ends when something important changes. For example, all the enemies are dead, the UIG arrive or the players leave the area.

STARTING COMBAT

A Map?

Sometimes in combat the first thing to do is draw a crude map. It helps to note the position of the combatants and key features on a piece of paper, that way there is less confusion, and if someone dies they can't complain about not understanding what was happening. Many people prefer no map as it can ruin the illusion so the choice is yours.

INITIATIVE - WHO ACTS FIRST?

ROLL REFLEXES + D10

Everyone in the combat rolls a D10 and adds their Reflexes STAT. The player who rolls the highest begins and is considered to have been the quickest to react. Initiative is only rolled once at the start of the scene, not each round. You simply continue to repeat the order you rolled initially.

Each round all players choose what their character is doing, starting with the person who won Initiative. Although the highest goes first he must also declare his action first meaning that those who go later are aware of what is happening. If there is a draw, the one with the highest 'Reflexes' goes first. If it's still a draw re-roll until a winner is established. If a character obviously started the action, for example by firing the first shot then they get + 4 to their Initiative roll.

Holding Your Action

You can always opt to go later in the round. Simply state when you are ready to act. You can interrupt someone before they start their action.

MOVEMENT (OPTIONAL)

For the majority of the time movement is an unnecessary rule and can be ignored. Use it when distance is important such as when an enemy is closing with a sword and you need to kill them before they reach you.

A character can move his **Strength + Endurance + Agility** in metres per round if he is simply running. This is called his *Move Speed*.

If he wishes to make all his attacks he can only step a few paces, effectively having no move action.

If the character's weapon has a rate of more than 1 (say a kinetic pistol with rate 3), he can divide his turn into 3 parts. He can move 1/3 his move speed or make 1 attack with each part.

For example, if using a kinetic pistol (rate 3):
- *Take no shots and move your full move speed*
- *1 shot and move 2/3 your move speed*
- *Take 2 shots and move 1/3 your move speed.*
- *Take 3 shots and not move at all*

If he has a weapon with rate 5 the turn could be divided into 5 actions in the same way. If using two weapons with different rates use the lowest rate.

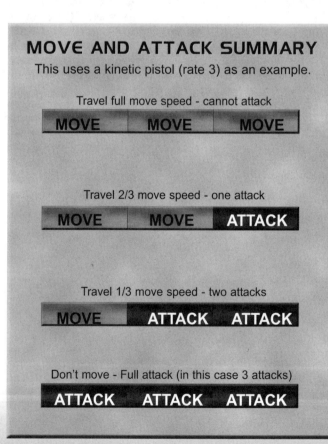

MOVE AND ATTACK SUMMARY

This uses a kinetic pistol (rate 3) as an example.

Travel full move speed - cannot attack

| MOVE | MOVE | MOVE |

Travel 2/3 move speed - one attack

| MOVE | MOVE | ATTACK |

Travel 1/3 move speed - two attacks

| MOVE | ATTACK | ATTACK |

Don't move - Full attack (in this case 3 attacks)

| ATTACK | ATTACK | ATTACK |

ATTACKING

RANGED ATTACKS

These are attacks that are made at a distance such a shooting a gun or throwing a bladed weapon. Supposing the opponent is not dodging, roll under or equal to your 'Perception + Relevant weapon skill'. If you pass, the target is hit and you can roll damage as in the weapon description. (Dodging is covered on page 144).
Example
Agent Johan wishes to shoot a UIG Officer with a Laser Pistol. The UIG Officer is not dodging. Johan has 'Perception + Light Firearms' of 12. He must roll equal or below 12 on 2D10 to hit the UIG Officer.

CLOSE COMBAT ATTACKS

These are attacks made at close range (1 metre or less) using attack forms such as kicks, punches, swords or knives.
Roll equal or under your 'Agility + Close Combat'. You gain the defenders 'Close Combat' score as a penalty to hit them (this is referred to as their *Defence*). It represents their continuous blocking and parrying. The opponent gains no Defence if they are not trying to defend, or if their attacker has a close combat weapon and they don't. If you pass the roll you have hit and can deal damage as in the weapon description. Close combat attacks ignore Hard Ion Shields if present.
Example:
Agent Johan attacks a UIG Officer with a plank. His 'Agility + Close Combat' is 13 but the UIG Officer has Defence 4 so Johan has to roll 9 or under to hit. This represents the UIG Officer's ability to parry and block with his plank. If Johan hits, he deals damage as normal. If the UIG Officer had been looking the other way then Johan would not have taken the Defence penalty and would have been much more likely to hit.

Close vs. Ranged

If you attack with a ranged weapon in close combat you lose your Defence unless you have the training *Gun Melee*. If both combatants are using guns in close combat they both lose their defence. Using guns at close range ignores shields (see Hard Ion Shields on page 46).

Armed vs. Unarmed

If you are unarmed in close combat and your opponent is armed with a close combat weapon you lose your Defence. You can purchase the *Unarmed Combat Specialist* training to avoid this penalty. If both fighters are unarmed they both keep their Defence.
Example:
If an unarmed Agent is trying to fight an outcast who has a knife the Agent will lose his Defence unless he has the Unarmed Combat Specialist Training.

Multiple Attackers

In close combat if the defender is being attacked by multiple enemies then he still gets his 'Defence' but can divide it between the attackers as he chooses. This can be overcome with the training *Multiple Defence*.
Example:
Agent Johan is being attacked by two UIG Officers in close combat. He has 'Defence' 7 so chooses the first attacker to take a -3 penalty to hit him and the second to take -4.

DEALING DAMAGE

To deal damage consult the weapons description. The weapon will either deal damage, have a special effect, or both. If it deals damage there will be dice to roll, for example 3D6. Roll the dice stated and add up the total. The person you hit loses that many hit points. If they have armour then the damage you deal will be reduced by the target's Armour Value (AV).
Example:
Agent Killua shoots an outlaw with a Kinetic Pistol. A Kinetic Pistol deals D8 damage. Killua's player rolls a 6 but the outlaw has a flak jacket with Armour Value 1 so only 5 damage goes through.

Shields also absorb damage – see page 46.
Attacks have a lot of variety, so make sure you read the information and rules for each weapon involved in the combat.

> ### MASHING DAMAGE
>
> Mashing damage is so horrific and savage that the wound pours blood at a lethal rate. The victim suffers an additional 1 point of bleeding damage a round until they receive medical attention. Mashing damage is cumulative, if you take 2 mashing wounds then you start taking 2 damage a round. Even Agents advanced physiology cannot stop this bleeding. Medpacks or a successful 'Intelligence + Medicine' roll will stop the bleeding and heal the target as normal.
> Some Mashing damage is so severe that it may deal 2 or more extra damage a round. If this is the case the amount of damage per round will be noted in brackets.
> *For example. D6 Mashing (2)*
> *This means the weapon deals D6 mashing damage and the victim takes 2 points of damage each round until healed.*

CRITICALS

When you make a normal action roll on 2D10 there is a chance that something very bad or very good will happen. The chance of each is normally slim (1 in a 100). Agents can do things to help themselves such as buying better equipment. Only Action Total rolls (2D10) can critical.

CRITICAL FAIL / MISS

With a normal roll a critical fail is when you get a 10 on both D10. Some circumstances such as using substandard equipment could cause other rolls to become critical misses. For example, a poor quality, condition 8 pistol will critically fail on rolls of 10/10, 9/9 and 8/8. These are detailed throughout the book where relevant. Unless otherwise stated only a roll of 10/10 is a critical miss. Also note you can never critically fail at your profession. It is just considered a fail.
If you have critically failed, as well as not succeeding in your attempt, there are three things which could happen, but the GM can make up the results if desired. Criticals should add to the game and should not be used to kill characters unless circumstances are extreme.

Close Combat

In Close Combat your opponent gets a free single attack (not a round of attacks) against you immediately. You do not get your Defence against this attack.

Ranged Combat

In Ranged Combat the shot misses and your weapon jams or has a minor malfunction, you may continue to fire any shots remaining this turn but have to spend the whole of the next round un-jamming your weapon if you want to use it – thus losing an action. (No roll is needed to unjam the weapon.)

Blast Weapons

If using a blast weapon, the GM may decide that on a critical miss the attacker is caught in the periphery of the blast taking a third of the full effect if appropriate.

Non-Combat Situation
In a non-combat situation the GM should think of a small inconvenience. For example, critically failing a Computers & AI roll could result in the user crashing the computer and having to start again. See more on page 139.

CRITICAL PASS / HIT
When Attacking
Normally a critical pass is a roll of 1 on both D10. The standard procedure for a critical hit when attacking is to add up your total damage and double it. Armour acts normally and only reduces the critical damge by the standard amount.
Example:
You get a critical hit and your damage dice is D12+8. You roll a 6 for a normal total of 14. The total critical damage would be 28.

Not Attacking
In non-combat situations the GM should make up a dramatic effect to represent good luck or judgement. More on page 139.
Example:
If an Agent critically passed a complex hacking check first time the GM may rule that he is familiar with the system and hacks straight in with no more rolls needed.
Some circumstances change which roll is considered a critical pass. For example, a high quality computer could allow rolls of 1/1 and 2/2 to be a critical pass (see Downtime on page 82).

EVASIVE MANOEUVRES

FULL DODGE
You may declare a *Full Dodge* at any time during the round as long as you have not taken your action. It is used to dodge incoming ranged attacks and uses your whole action so you can do nothing in the round except dodge. Everyone who attacks you with ranged weapons when you use full dodge gets your 'Reflexes + 2' as a penalty to attack. Full dodge will have no effect against close combat attacks. (You can either Withdraw or Block against close combat attacks.)

Example:
Agent Baxter has Reflexes 6, he decides to full dodge. All three enemies attacking him receive -8 to hit him with their rifles.

ACTIVE DODGE
This is declared at the beginning of a round before anyone makes their action. Select a number up the score of your Reflexes. All ranged attackers get this as a penalty to hit. You also get this amount as a penalty to all your Action Totals this round. This reflects the way you can still act and dodge but you will find it much harder to do anything.

Example:
Agent Edura is under attack, he has Reflexes 5. Edura decides to take -4 to his Action Totals this round and his attackers thus gain -4 to hit him. (He could have taken up to -5.)

BLOCK
In close combat you can spend your action blocking, in which case you can't do anything else except a Free Action. At the start of the round declare you wish to block. This doubles your Defence score for that round and thus makes you harder to hit. This new increased Defence can be split between multiple attackers as normal. You must be armed with an item capable of blocking. Typically a melee weapon, but the GM could allow other items such as a rifle or dustbin lid to be used. You cannot dodge and block in the same round. With the Unarmed Combat Training you can block without an appropriate item.

WITHDRAWING FROM COMBAT / RETREATING
You can flee combat by passing a 'Perception + Agility' roll with a -1 penalty for each attacker on you. Failure means all available attackers may have a free attack on you as you flee. (One attack, not a round of attacks). The GM could modify this if there is a good place to run away to, e.g. jumping out of a window. Successful fleeing means you break from combat and can try to evade your attackers. The GM may decide in some circumstances that you cannot flee.

COVER
If you are in cover your opponent receives a penalty to attack you based on how good the cover is. The GM may also apply a penalty to your attack rolls as shooting out of cover may be harder. Typically this penalty would be half of the bonus gained from the cover. *For example, shooting out from behind a high wall gives you a -4 to your action total but -8 to your opponent's.*

FORM OF COVER	MAX PENALTY
Lamp Post	-2
Low Wall	-4
Car	-6
High Wall	-8
Total Cover	No attacks possible

CALLED SHOTS / TARGETING

TARGET SHOT
You can target a particular object. You take a penalty to hit based on the size and the GM decides on the outcome.
If you wish, you can target body parts with this, but the GM should decide the result as it more for cinematic effect such as shooting guns from peoples hands, not dealing additional damage. That is what 'Vital Shot' is for.

TARGET SHOT

OBJECT	BODY PART	MODIFIER
Coin	Eye / Finger	-12
Egg	Mouth / Ear	-8
Can / Pistol	Hand / Foot	-6
Football / Rifle	Head / Limb	-4
Backpack / Cannon	Torso	-2
Human	Human	+0
Large Door		+2
Car		+4
Van		+6
Lorry		+8
House		+12

VITAL SHOT

You can take a penalty to your attack roll and add it to your damage for that attack. You can take a maximum penalty equal to the *Relevant Weapon Skill* you are using. This represents hitting vital organs, bypassing armour with accurate shots, etc. The modifier need not be the same for every attack made that round. The extra damage is applied in the same manner as extra damage from the 'Mastered Weapon' training (see page 24).

Example: Agent Masterson has Tactical Weapons 4, he decides to take a -4 penalty to hit and add +4 to damage with his shotgun.

AIMING

You can aim with weapons, even swords (unless stated). The effects of aiming apply to all attacks attempted in the next round. The extra damage is applied in the same manner as extra damage from the 'Mastered Weapon' training (see page 24).

Spend 1 action aiming to get +2 to hit and + 2 damage. You can spend up to 3 actions in a row aiming for a total of +6 to hit and +6 damage. If you are interrupted during an aim you must roll 'Perception + Intelligence' to remain focused or lose the advantage of aiming. If the weapon deals no damage that obviously won't be increased by aiming.

Sniper weapons follow all the same aiming rules except they give +4 to hit and +4 damage for each round of aiming to a maximum of +12 when in a suitable position to snipe.

You may aim with any weapon including melee weapons, although it may be hard to maintain concentration while being attacked with a sword. You don't lose your Defence when aiming. It is considered that you are forgoing your attack to aim, you are still maintaining your Defence and simply waiting for an opening in the opponent's guard.

MISCELLANEOUS ACTIONS

DUAL / TWO WEAPON FIGHTING

You need to buy the training *Dual Weapon Fighting* to use two weapons effectively. Trying to do it without the Training incurs a -4 penalty with each weapon. With Dual Weapon Fighting you simply get to use each weapon in each hand to full effect. The weapons can be different as long as you have the relevant aspects of the 'Dual Weapon Fighting' training (see page 23).

If you have Strength 10 or more you can wield a two handed weapon in each hand. If they are heavy close combat weapons you do NOT double your strength for damage with each weapon. Doubling Strength represents using the power of two arms.

Example: If you had a two handed sword with rate 1 in each hand you would make a total of 2 attacks but only deal D12 + Strength with each.

CHANGING WEAPONS

This is a Free Action if the new weapon is prepared, for example unholstering a pistol or drawing a sword. If the weapon is not prepared, such as getting out and priming a flame thrower or retrieving a knife from your bag, it counts as an action.

DISARM

This is an example of an 'Opposed Action'. See Opposed Actions opposite.

FREE ACTIONS

One Free Action can be taken during each round.

Example Free Actions
- Shouting to a comrade
- Using *Instant* telepathics
- Pressing a remote detonator
- Drawing a prepared weapon
- Using an intravenous medpack

WRESTLING / GRAPPLING

There is a Training called *Restrain* (see page 24) which makes this sort of attack much simpler. If you don't have it you can wrestle your opponent into submission as described below.

If someone instigates a wrestle both fighters must make a 'Strength + Close Combat' roll. Note down the XS of each player. Negative XS on a roll will reduce the total. This is repeated for another two rounds, you then see who has acquired the least XS. The person with the least XS is considered incapacitated and held on the floor and the winner can apply their Strength in automatic damage each round. If a draw occurs the fighters break apart and get to their feet.

If the sides are uneven and three people are wrestling against one then the group of three all roll and add their XS together. This makes it very hard for the lone wrestler to win.

Breaking free – Once you have engaged in a wrestle you can break free if you currently have the most XS or if the scores are drawn. If you are losing it is considered the other wrestler is controlling you and you need to start thinking hard. Get-outs such as pulling knives or biting the opponent should be adjudicated by the GM.

KNOCK OUT

A single close combat attack is made at -4. (Don't forget the targets Defence). If it hits, the target must roll 'Perception + Endurance' with the attacker's XS as a penalty. If they fail, they are knocked out for D100 minutes. This does not work against anyone with a neural stabiliser such as an Agent. If you are attempting a knock out, it must be your only attack that round. Damage is Strength.

EXECUTION

If you have a target in a position where they can effectively be executed and you have 1 point in the relevant weapon skill, then your attack is considered to deal a maximised triple critical hit, e.g. if you shoot someone in the back of the head from point blank with a kinetic pistol (D8) you deal 8x3 = 24 automatic damage. If there is any doubt about the attack, for example, they try to dodge, time is an issue or the target may hear you coming, then the attack must be conducted normally. This should not be abused or used to assassinate people. This is an option for execution style actions only, such as killing hostages. Often the GM will simply declare an automatic kill, this rule is used when the power of the weapon used may influence how easy the target is to kill, e.g., executing an Agent with a knife.

OPPOSED ACTIONS

Sometimes you need to do an opposed action such as pull an object out of someone's hand. This can be done by both contenders rolling appropriate dice and seeing who has the highest XS. The GM can apply modifiers if one person's situation is better than another's.
Example 1:
Agent Rutger attempts to take a shotgun out of a civilian's hand. Rutger must roll to grab the shotgun with an 'Agility + Close Combat' roll. If successful they both roll 'Strength + Close Combat'. The GM gives the civilian a +2 bonus as he is already holding the gun. Compare the XS, the highest gets the weapon.

Example 2:
Agent Rutger is pursuing some fleeing Rebels in a car. Agent Rutger passes his driving roll by 4; the rebels only pass by 1. Agent Rutger has thus caught up with them and can start ramming their car.

OPPOSED COMPETITIONS

This can be used for racing cars, arm wrestles, etc. The rules for opposed actions can be extended and the XS noted down each time. After a stated number of rounds you compare the XS and see who had the highest. See the rules for *Wrestling* above, to see how this can work. For an event such as a car race you may wish to compare the XS as you go along to add to the tension and determine who is winning.

SEVERING BODY PARTS

All bladed weapons have the ability to sever limbs athough an Agent must be quite skilled to make it happen.

When you declare an attack with a bladed weapon you may elect to try and sever a body part.

Before you strike, declare the body part you are trying to sever and then roll to hit with a penalty as on the table below. The penalty relates to how difficult it is to initiate a sever on that body part. Remember, the opponent still gets their Defence. If you miss you deal no damage.

If you hit, look up the body part you were trying to sever on the table below. If you dealt the damage needed in one hit after AV reduction, the respective body part is severed. You deal your damage regardless of whether it was enough to sever the limb.

Example:

Agent Neonagi has declared he is going to sever his opponent's sword arm. He must attack with a -6 penalty. Neonagi has Agility 8 and Close Combat 6 – Total 14.

He gets -6 for the arm sever and -3 for his opponents defence so Neonagi needs 5 or less on 2D10. A difficult move but he could aim for a few rounds first or spend some Conviction.

Also see page 11 to see how the R-Drug affects severing.

Target	The body part you are targeting
Pen	Penalty to initiate the sever
Dam	Damage needed to sever
Description	The effect of a successful sever

MAIN SEVERING TABLE

Target	Pen	Dam	Description
Fingers	-12	3	Lose D4+1 fingers. -1 to all rolls using that hand for each finger lost.
Face	-10	2	Roll a D4 1 - Nose 2 - Eye (-1 Perception to sight based tasks) 3 - Ear (-1 Perception to sound based tasks) 4 - Mouth
Hand	-8	6	Hand is missing, anything using two hands is impossible. e.g. using a two handed sword. Rolls which partially use the hand are given a -4 penalty, e.g. climbing. Agents are trained to be ambidextrous so do not be concerned with using the off-hand.
Foot	-8	6	Reflexes and Agility are reduced by 3 points with regard to movement, but not to tasks which require manual dexterity. Running is impossible and walking is slow.
Arm	-6	10	Arm is missing, anything using two arms or two hands is impossible, e.g. using a two. handed sword. Rolls which partially use the arm, are given a -5 penalty, e.g. climbing.
Leg	-6	12	Agility is reduced by 4 points. Any locomotion other than hopping and crawling are impossible. Manual dexterity is not affected.
Torso	-4	20	This cuts the torso in half. Those without I.C.E or similar cybernetic modifications die automatically, Agents can still function but are at -5 to Strength, Agility and Endurance.
Head	-8	15	This kills any target unless they have a Cerebral Link (see page 65), if they have I.C.E you can use compound-H to reattach the head within 3 seconds, i.e. on the next round.

RANDOM SEVERING

In the case of limb severs which are unexpected (such as maximum damage rolls from Blade Launchers and Ion Katanas) roll a D100 on the *Random Sever Table* (right). If your weapon deals enough damage after Armour Value reduction then the part is severed. If not, you deal damage only. For the actual affects of the severed limb use the Main Severing Table above.

D100 Roll	Dam	Part Severed
01-20	3	Fingers
21-26	2	Facial Feature
27-47	6	Hand
48-60	6	Foot
61-75	10	Arm
76-85	12	Leg
86-97	20	Torso
98-100	15	Head

CONVICTION

Sometimes Agents need to draw on their reserve of inner strength and resolve to push their limitations. This is represented by Conviction Points. You can spend Conviction to help in desperate situations but you may only spend one Conviction per round. Spending Conviction does not count as an action or a free action.

USING CONVICTION

BONUS

You can spend one Conviction point to gain +4 to your Action Total on your next roll.

RETRY

You can spend one Conviction point to re-roll your last roll, this could be any Action Total roll. For example an attack roll or a telepathics roll. You must always choose the newest roll.

TELEPATHICS

You can spend 1 Conviction to increase a telepathic skill by 2 points for 1 turn, e.g. if you have Assault 4, you could spend 1 Conviction to use Assault 6 for 1 turn. You cannot exceed 10.

DYING ACTION

You can spend one Conviction to make a non-combat action when you are on less than 1 Hit Point (but not dead). You take the action and then slip back into unconsciousness; for example, you could use a medpack, shout to an ally or call backup.

REGAINING CONVICTION

You regain conviction for doing something key to the mission or important to your character. For example, if you find some incriminating evidence which could convict your mission target the GM could award the players a Conviction point. Likewise if a character completes a small goal such as killing an old enemy, saving a friends life or gaining a rank the GM could award a Conviction point. There are no hard and fast rules for this, it is up to the GM to decide when players have earned them.

You should be cautious awarding more than one a session but go ahead if the situation warrants it. Players should never have more than 5 Conviction Points.

CHARACTER HEALTH

HEALING RATES

Patient	Type	Activity	HP per 12 hrs
Agent	Natural	Active	Agent's Endurance
Agent	Natural	Full Rest	Agent's Endurance x2
Agent	Medcare	Full Rest	Agent's Endurance x3
Human	Natural	Active	1HP
Human	Natural	Full Rest	2HP
Human	Medcare	Full Rest	3HP

HIT POINTS (HP)

Agents are notoriously tough, they are immune to most pain and their bodies are not easily incapacitated by organ damage. Humans on the other hand are usually weak and frail.

Agents start with	Strength + Endurance + 20HP
Humans start with	Strength + Endurance + 10HP

When either reaches 0HP they are unable to act properly. Agents are a lot harder to incapacitate than humans.

HEALING

The table (below left) shows how many Hit Points (HP) are recovered every 12 hours. Agents should never underestimate the use of medpacks (see page 52).

Natural
This is natural healing with no artificial help.
Medcare
This means the victim is receiving professional medical care.
Active
The victim is going about normal business.
Full Rest
The victim is resting and doing no work.

Example 1:
Agent Mikos is wounded badly with no medpacks so is holed up in an old factory resting. He has Endurance 6 so will heal 12HP per 12 hours.

Example 2:
Agent Mikos is extracted by his team and taken to a Medcare facility to rest. He will recover 18 HP per 12 hours.

DEATH AND INCAPACITATION

Zero and Negative Hit Points.

Agents

When an Agent reaches zero or less HP they cannot act and are incapacitated. *(See Irrecoverable Death below)*

Each round they lose one point of Intelligence as their brain dies. If someone stops them dying with a successful 'Intelligence + Medicine' roll, they stabilise and regain one Intelligence point an hour. The use of a medpack will stabilise the Agent, heal the stated HP and allow their Intelligence to recover in the normal way.

Agents and those with blood clotting modifications do not lose HP when unconscious or wounded unless they were wounded by Mashing Damage (this is dealt by certain attack types).

When an Agent is incapacitated (0 or less HP) he can spend 1 Conviction Point to have a low effort action, e.g. use a medical kit or make a communication. Combat actions such as attacking and dodging are not possible.

Irrecoverable Death

If an Agent reaches Intelligence zero the Agent dies irrecoverably. If an Agent reaches a number of negative hit points equal to their 'Strength + Endurance' they also die.

The Corporations are rumoured to have advanced bioware to prevent brain death which are only issued to their finest Agents.

Normal Humans

Normal humans are incapacitated at zero HP. They then lose 1 HP a round until they reach their Endurance in negative HP. Once this is reached they die irrecoverably. At any point before death a successful 'Intelligence + Medicine' check will stabilise them or application of a medpack will heal them. For NPC (non player character) enemies you can consider they are unconscious at 1HP and dead at 0HP.

CHARACTER CONDITIONS

DROWNING AND HOLDING YOUR BREATH

An Agent can hold her breath for 30 seconds (10 rounds) for each point of Endurance she has. After this point she loses 5 Hit Points per turn she remains underwater. If she surfaces before she dies then she regains 5 Hit Points a round untill she recovers all the HP she lost from drowning.

FIRE / BURNING

Agents and humans take 1D6 damage each round after they are set on fire. The victim can make an 'Agility + Reflexes check to put out the fire or jump in some water, dirt or sand. Another player can put the fire out automatically, but it takes a whole action.
Flammable objects may well be destroyed. Armour defends against this damage. Someone with AV6 will be immune to the effects of normal fire. Fire does not stack with itself, you can take a maximum of D6 fire damage each turn.

BLINDNESS

When an Agent is blinded he is considered to have Perception 0 with regard to sight based tasks, e.g. aiming a gun. He may only move at a slow walking pace without personal risk.

DARKNESS / NIGHT TIME / LOW LIGHT

When the Agent's vision is impaired by lack of light he receives a penalty to his Perception relative to the degree of darkness. This could be a basic -1 for dim conditions to -4 for typical night time. Pitch darkness would effectivly render an Agent blind (see above).

DEAFENED

When an Agent is deafened he is considered to have Perception 0 with regard to sound based tasks, e.g. listening for an intruder.

KNOCK OUT (KO)

Agents are immune to being knocked out as the part of the brain responsible for unconsciousness has been modified. If a normal human has a chance to be knocked out they may roll under 'Perception + Endurance' with any appropriate XS as a penalty. (For example – the attacker's XS on the knock out punch). If they pass then they remain conscious. Unconsciousness lasts D100 minutes.

FALLING

Agents take 1 damage for every 2 metres they fall.
Humans take 2 damage for every 1 metre they fall.

This is for uncontrolled falls. If a fall is planned then the GM should reduce any fall damage by 2 metres. AV helps with falling damage. If a death occurs from falling then the falling character can make a 'Strength + Endurance' check at -4. If it is passed then the falling character is on -5 HP and is unconscious but can be saved with medical attention.

STATS AT 0

If any of your STATS are reduced to 0 then you automatically fail any tasks which use that STAT.

TOXINS / POISONS

Toxins have a potency level (normally 1 to 10). Depending on the Toxin Filter worn by the Agent certain toxins will be filtered out. Any toxin equal or lower than the level of the filter is stopped. If a toxin is not stopped consult the toxin description in question.

TRAUMA AND MENTAL STRESS

Agents are modified to withstand immense amounts of physical damage. Unfortunately the same cannot be said of their psychological state. Although Corporate training does prepare them for the dirtier parts of their work there is nothing that can ready an Agent for his first mass-killing or 48 hour torture session.

Saying this, it is the job of the player to decide how his Agent deals with the everyday trials he is put through and the rules are not there to force you to play your character in a way you don't want to.

Examples of Trauma and Mental Stress

Below are some examples of circumstances which may cause your Agent to begin to crack.

Executing large numbers of people
Being exposed to subspace
Being addicted to drugs or going cold turkey
Suffering multiple attacks from a psychogenic
Being tortured
Having friends or family killed
Suffering an attack from a mind virus
Being blown into tiny pieces but surviving.

System

If the GM or player feels their character has undergone these or similar events then he should reduce their maximum conviction pool by 1 to 3 points depending on the severity of the incident. One point is usually enough.

Recovering

The player can undergo some form of healing to recover this loss of permanent conviction. One point can be restored in any of the following ways:

1. A week of professional therapy. This takes one downtime week and costs 1500 credits. Therapy is seen as a sign of weakness by many Agents.

2. Two weeks of rest and relaxation. This requires two downtime weeks doing nothing at all.

3. If the Agent has family such as a wife, husband, partner or child they can spend a week with them to recover. This costs nothing but having family can be a liability for an Agent and the GM should ensure the player pays them due attention.

4. Nothing. You can just grit your teeth and battle through. At the start of each new mission roll a D10. On a roll of a 1 your maximum conviction is restored by one point.

VEHICLE USE

(Vehicles statistics are detailed on page 57)

DRIVING VEHICLES

Driving vehicle rolls are made by adding 'Perception or Agility + Pilot or Drive' and adding or subtracting a *Driving Modifier* for the quality of vehicle driven (page 57) and possibly one for the conditions (table below right). The GM should not request a roll simply for driving, it is used only for extreme manoeuvres such as chases, skids, evading security or driving in dangerous conditions. In some situations you may want to use Reflexes to drive.

Example:
Agent Pemberton has stolen an ice cream van and is being pursued by UIG Officers. He has 'Perception 6' and 'Drive 3'. The GM applies a -1 penalty for the ice cream van for an Action Total (AT) of 8. Things don't look promising.

Mixed Vehicles in Action

In the event of getting a mix of vehicle types such as a plane versus a car, it is probably best to use common sense. Essentially the plane will have low manoeuvrability compared to the car, but is much faster. You could thus treat the plane as a very fast, airborne articulated lorry.

Drive or Pilot?

Driving is used for land based vehicles such as cars, motorbikes, trucks and tanks. Vehicles which are seaborne, airborne or operate in space use the Pilot skill.

ATTACKING WHILE DRIVING A VEHICLE

If you wish to attack or make some kind of extra action while driving a vehicle then you receive a -4 penalty to all Action Totals unless you have the training *Combat Pilot* or *Combat Driver* which negate these penalties.

Example:
Agent Baxter fires his rocket launcher out of the window while driving a lorry through a shopping mall. Normally he would receive -4 to drive and -4 to attack but he has just learnt the Combat Driver training so he can drive and fire and won't suffer these penalties. He will still need to roll as the driving is complex and will get a -2 driving modifier as he is in an old lorry.

The GM should adjudicate what is fair, for example, you should not be able to drive a large vehicle through narrow crowded streets while aiming a sniper rifle out of the window (at least not without a penalty).

DRIVE-BY CLOSE COMBAT

Sometimes you can use the power of the vehicle to aid your attacks such as a drive-by attack with a sword whilst on a motorbike. In this case you deal an additional 2 damage for each 10mph of the vehicle.

Example: Agent Neonagi drives past an enemy Agent on a motorbike and slashes at him with his katana.

If he hits he deals the following damage.
Katana Damage (2D4) + Strength (6) + Vehicle speed bonus for 60mph (12) for a total of 2D4 + 18. That will probably kill a human.

RAMMING

You can ram targets with a vehicle. The ram deals D6 for every 10mph the vehicle is travelling at (round down). It is considered one large hit for Armour purposes.

Example:
A car travelling at 60mph deals 6D6 damage. Armour is effective against this damage. A drive roll may be required to hit a fleeing target.

A car travelling at 30mph will deal 3D6 and thus could kill a weak human.

ADDITIONAL DRIVING MODIFIERS

Vehicle Quality	Driving Modifier
Vehicle is a wreck	-4
Just road legal or has damaged wheels etc.	-2
Driving in a rainstorm	-2
Driving in ice or skid conditions	+0
Driving while doing something else such as fighting (without Training).	-4
Simple stunt such as j-turn or driving backwards	-2
Complex stunt such as a jump, driving on two wheels or steering from outside the car.	-4

HACKING

To hack into a computer system you need the hacking training and mus connect your hacking device to the target network normally via a hard wir connection or possibly a remote one if available. You also need hackin software (see equipment list on page 50).

HACKING PROCESS

1. Determine System Security Level
This will either be DOMESTIC, COMMERCIAL, SECURE or ELITE, the consult the relevant box (left).

2. Modifiers
Work out your Action Total and then deduct any penalties and add an bonuses.

3. Roll (Intelligence + Computers & A.I.)
Roll 2D10 and get below or equal to your modified Action Total. You nee to get a different number of successes depending on the system you ar hacking, so multiple rolls may be necessary. Each roll takes 1 minute.

4. Success
If you get all your successes with no failed rolls then the system is hacke and you can use it with no risk. Mission accomplished.

5. Failure
Each time you fail a roll the GM should roll a D100 in secret. There is cumulative chance the hacker has been traced by the computers owner o the UIG (GM choice). For example, on a domestic system, if the hacke fails once there will be a 5% chance of him being traced. A second fail w increase this chance to 10% and the GM should roll each time he fails. he rolled under the current % on a D100 the authorities are on their wa It is up to the GM whether the hacker knows this. The hacker can kee trying as long as he wants but it will get dangerous.

Example:
Agent Katsugi is trying to hack into an E.I. surveillance satellite.
The satellite computer has the following properties.
Controlled by a level 5 A.I.   *(-5 penalty)*
A SECURE System   *(-6 penalty)*

Katsugi has the following
Intelligence + Computers & A.I. 17
A hackers computer   *(+1 bonus)*
Some inside information worth a +2 bonus   *(+2 bonus)*
A Neural Jack   *(+4 bonus)*

Total penalties   *-11*
Total bonuses   *+7*

Overall Katsugi is at -4 so he has an Action Total of 13. She needs to ro 13 or below three times to hack the system.
Roll one and two are fine and he passes but on roll 3 she gets an 18 s the GM rolls in secret to see if Katsugi has been traced. There is 15% chance.
The GM rolls a 54 on the D100 and Katsugi is fine. She rolls again an gets a final success. Once in the system she decides to download all th records from the spy satellite and put them into her internal storage driv for safekeeping.

DOMESTIC SYSTEM (E.G. HOME COMPUTER)

Roll - 'Intelligence + Computers & A.I.'
Penalties - None (cannot contain A.I.)

Bonuses
+4 for a Neural Jack
+1 for each level of hackers Internal A.I.
+1 for inside information on the system.
+1 for a hackers computer
+2 for Advanced Hacking Software

Successes needed - 1
Trace chance - 5% cumulative on each failed roll.

COMMERCIAL SYSTEM (E.G. OFFICE COMPUTER)

Roll - 'Intelligence + Computers & A.I.'

Penalties
-3 for computers security system
-1 for each level of Internal A.I. (normally 1 or 2)

Bonuses
+4 for a Neural Jack
+1 for each level of hackers Internal A.I.
+1 to +2 for inside information on the system
+1 for a hackers computer
+2 for Advanced Hacking Software

Successes needed - 2
Trace chance - 10% cumulative on each failed roll.

SECURE SYSTEM (E.G. AI-JINN DATABASE)

Roll - 'Intelligence + Computers & A.I.'

Penalties
-6 for computers security system
-1 for each level of Internal A.I. (normally 3-9)

Bonuses
+4 for a Neural Jack
+1 for each level of hackers Internal A.I.
+1 to +4 for inside information on the system
+1 for a hackers computer
+2 for Advanced Hacking Software

Successes needed - 3
Trace chance - 15% cumulative on each failed roll.

ELITE SYSTEM (E.G. UIG SYSTEM)

Roll - 'Intelligence + Computers & A.I.'

Penalties
-12 for computers security system
-1 for each level of Internal A.I. (normally 7-10)

Bonuses
+4 for a Neural Jack
+1 for each level of hackers Internal A.I.
+1 to +4 for inside information on the system
+1 for a hackers computer
+2 for Advanced Hacking Software

Successes needed - 4
Trace chance - 20% cumulative on each failed roll.

SECTION 9

THE WORLD IN 2500

I am often reminded of the legend of Faust, who sold his soul in exchange for limitless wealth, power, and sensual gratification. Lamentably, transactions of this type are now so commonplace that the going rate has fallen considerably.

-attr: Gunther van Rosch, CEO, Eurasian Incorporated.

COMMUNICATION SYSTEMS

SUB-VOCAL COMMUNICATION

All Agents are, as standard, equipped with comm. devices which are set into their jaws and allow for sub-vocal communication with other nearby friendly Agents. This form of communication is fairly secure and means the Agent need not speak aloud as he simply mutters under his breath. The SVC (sub-vocal communicator) uses a simple protocol which only allows basic signal communication. Large and complex transmission cannot be be carried. The active range is 300km, the further the Agents are apart the easier the communication is to intercept and crack (see page 9).

Sub-vocal Communication is sometimes referred to as *Smeaking*.

COMMUNICATION (COMM.) DEVICES

When Agents need to communicate securely with HQ they use specialist Comm. devices covered in the Equipment Section. These are 95% secure and have unlimited range on the Earth. Off-world communications need to be conducted from a station.

SATELLITES & SATBLANKETS

Satellites are scanning the world. This obviously makes people paranoid, so certain companies such as Liberty Black have produced SatBlankets which are localised fields that prevent satellites monitoring areas. Spires, banks, factories and labs are the sorts of buildings often covered by SatBlankets. Satellites can track ID chips in extreme, UIG sanctioned situations. The Citizens of the world do not enjoy this level of scrutiny so the UIG use it only when really necessary (they claim). SatBlankets are illegal for use by unauthorised parties (see SatBlanket on page 26).

WORLD COMMUNICATIONS SYSTEMS

The world is linked by an advanced internet called the WDN – World Data Net – it travels on nano-engineered cables into every town and habitation and on wireless signals to remote places such as desert installations. The speed data can travel across the WDN is more than any current user could think of a use for. The WDN is the only major data channel in existence. There are still small networks but these are only used for private companies and individuals who would rather their information was not on the WDN. Needless to say, it is built, maintained and regulated by the UIG.

LANGUAGE

Below are listed the official languages of Earth as recorded by the UIG in 2460. As an Agent you can automatically speak the primary and secondary languages of your Corporation. You also gain access at character creation to a further language of your choice except Military Sign (WF only). Electronic translators are easily available but there are some key advantages to being able to speak other languages.

Agents able to speak foreign languages will blend in better, it is considered that they are fluent in the language and understand the slang, subtleties and etiquette of the language they speak. This can be invaluable in delicate or diplomatic situations.

Using a translator can be inaccurate in noisy areas or if the person talking is slurring their words or using a strong accent. Extra languages are not necessary but are certainly useful. Additional languages are acquired with XP (see page 79).

Alternative Languages

You can use XP to acquire more obscure forms of communication such as: uncommon languages, sign language, reading lips, morse code, or possibly very rare dialects or dead languages. These can be chosen instead of your third language at character creation.

LANGUAGES OF THE CORPORATIONS

Corporation	Main	Secondary
Ai-Jinn	Mandarin	Cantonese, Thai
Comoros	Swahili	Indian (Hindi)
Eurasian Inc.	English	Russian, German
Shi Yukiro	Japanese	Mandarin
W. Federation	English	Spanish, Military Sign

THINK TWICE

BEFORE YOU BREAK THE LAW

KILDANNA PENITENTIARY

MONEY

> *God is on everyone's side … and in the last analysis; he is on the side with plenty of money and large armies.*
> -Jean Anouilh

In Corporation you will often need to acquire goods and services. Many of the companies and brands who were around in the 20th and 21st centuries are still active but are working under the umbrella of the Corporations. For example, designer brands or health companies will be owned by E.I., high tech manufacturers are under the control of the Shi Yukiro and the Ai-Jinn own most vehicle producers. This section gives you an idea of what things cost and the value of money.

Credit

Credit comes in two forms, registered and unregistered credit. When the UIG was formed the world financial organisations were unified into United International Financing (UIF).

> *It was a masterstroke. A unilateral transition to a single currency, enforced by allowing the world a single month to exchange all local liquid assets at locked rates and thereafter refusing to issue valuations, UIG bonds, standardised exchange rates or tax bills in anything else. Tied to a single monolithic global administration it was brutally effective; local paper currencies worldwide dropped to the value of their constituent elements in a matter of weeks. Dollars could no longer pay taxes, yen could not pay the rent on the vastly overpopulated UIG housing, all funds and stocks linked to any government institution the world over were operable only in the new Credit. The Corporations did nothing – still scarred from the Wars or sensing, perhaps, the real objective – beyond carefully transforming the entirety of their liquid assets.*
>
> *The ensuing riots, as any student of history will know, lasted for three years and took more than three million lives. The UIG dug in, controlling the uprisings where they could and allowing things to run their course. Of course, with the benefit of hindsight, we can qualify this worldwide tragedy as cathartic, a necessary evil to facilitate the current unbounded state of inter-Corporate commerce.*
>
> *-from The Rise of The Corporation-States*
> *attr: Dr. Edmond Treval*

Typical Earnings

A typical Citizen earns around 200 – 300 credits (¢) per week. This allows you to work out a reasonable scale of pricing for your goods and services in the game.

For example, buying a new jacket of good quality will probably cost about 100¢ – 200¢. A new car could be between 5,000¢ and 15,000¢, with a sports model being more like 20,000¢ to 25,000¢.

Technology has moved forward though, so remember that computers and similar high tech items may be relatively cheaper. Cutting edge style and tech will always cost though.

Credit Chips: These are small, tough objects about the size of a business card. They have a digital readout displaying the quantity of cash (or any other information you wish about the money). The chip can be placed in a chip reader and money transferred onto other chips. You need to swipe the owners ID chip as well if the credit is registered.

COSTS OF GOODS AND SERVICES

TRAVEL

Shuttle travel on Earth (basic)	1¢ / 10 miles
Shuttle travel on Earth (luxury)	1¢ per mile
Car hire (1 day, normal car)	60¢
Car hire (1 day, luxury car and driver)	500¢
Helicopter / Shuttle hire (1 day)	600¢
Use of a Skybridge	200¢
Passage to Vastaag for 1 person	1000¢

ACCOMMODATION

Hotel room, 1 night (cheap)	40¢
Hotel room, 1 night (good)	100¢
Hotel room, 1 night (luxury)	600¢ and up
Apartment, small, Spire (1 month)	600¢
Apartment, medium, Spire (1 month)	1000¢
Apartment, large, Spire (1 month)	2500¢
Apartment, luxury, Spire (1 month)	5000¢
Apartment, small, UIG (1 month)	300¢
Apartment, medium, UIG (1 month)	600¢
Apartment, large, UIG (1 month)	900¢
Apartment, luxury, UIG (1 month)	1200¢
Room in an underswell (1 month)	80¢
House in an Old City (purchase)	10,000¢
House in cleaned environment (purchase)	500,000¢
Spire accomodation (purchase)	Not for Sale
Complex of buildings	5 Million ¢
Laboratory / workshop rental (typical)	200¢ a day
Laboratory / workshop rental (advanced)	1000¢ a day

MEDICINE

Surgery, professional - heal	30¢ per HP
Surgery, street doctor - heal	15¢ per HP
Surgery, professional - reattach Limb	600¢
Surgery, Street Doctor - reattach Limb	200¢

FOOD

Meal in a cheap restaurant for 1	5¢
Meal in an average restaurant for 1	20¢
Meal in an expensive restaurant for 1	50¢
Drink in an average bar	3¢
Real beef steak	300¢

STREET

Black market item	x3-x10 normal

FASHION

Clothes - cheap	30¢
Clothes - average	100¢
Clothes - good	600¢
Clothes - high fashion	3000¢
Expensive haircut	100¢

COMPUTERS

Computer rental 1 month (domestic)	20¢
Computer rental 1 month (commercial)	300¢
Computer rental 1 month (corporate)	10000¢
Integrated cell phone / PDA	300¢

FINES

Speeding fine	150¢
Littering fine	100¢
Public disturbance fine	500¢
Insubordination fine	500¢
Breaching curfew in controlled areas	1500¢
Minor misconduct	100-1000¢

Unregistered Credit (Slip Credit): In 2353 all cash was called in and replaced with unregistered credit which can be spent anywhere and is totally anonymous but has an inherent value like cash. If you lose an unregistered credit chip you lose your money. Some more prestigious or security conscious companies will not accept unregistered credit.

Registered Credit (Reg Credit): Registered credit has many advantages over slip credit. If you lose your chip you can cancel it and no money can be taken from your account. All transactions can be traced however and the UIG will know what you bought and when. You can get registered credit converted to unregistered credit at any of the hundreds of UIF branches, but there is a 10% commission charge and the UIG always take an interest in this type of activity. Black market slip vendors will do the same for you, but this is a dubious form of finance and they will normally take a much higher percentage.

ACCOMMODATION

In 2500 there are a number of places to live. Few people own the houses they live in, they either rent from the Corporations or the UIG. If you can't afford that, then you have to make your own way in the Old Cities or the Underswells.

Corporate Accommodation (Spire)
This ranges in price from 150 credits a week to thousands and is dependent on you being a Citizen that the Corporation is willing to house. At the low end you get a small room with a bed and a desk. The room is only lit with light channelled in from fibre optics making for a rather dingy hole. Meals and recreation must all be pursued outside the apartment as it is not really big enough to house more than one individual.

As the rent goes up so does the quality of the apartment, the rooms become bigger and more luxuries are available such as a kitchen, dining room, entertainment system and space for decorative items.

At the top end of Spire accommodation are the luxury apartments which always include one wall which faces the outside of the Spire, letting in natural light and giving a panoramic view. Servants see to your every need and the finest foods and wines are always on hand.

Agents are normally given rent-free low end apartments and get better ones as they increase in rank. If an Agent surpasses himself in the eyes of the Corporation he may be gifted with a disproportionately large, luxurious apartment.

UIG Accommodation
UIG accommodation is much more basic than the Corporate equivalent but is substantially cheaper and less demanding on a persons entry requirements. A basic UIG apartment is very similar to a Corporate one; a simple room with a bed, a shared bathroom and a light source. As you pay more rent the quality increases, but not much. The room gradually becomes bigger and includes a few basics such as its own bathroom and some basic entertainment but despite their claims, UIG housing is never luxurious. All the apartments are made of extruded plastic and at most are coloured white or grey. If you pay top rent you can expect a decent room with some attention to decoration, a pleasing amount of space and most of the conveniences you could want, but it could never match up to the decadence of the Spires.

It should be noted that medium to high ranked UIG Officers do not live in these sorts of buildings. They normally demand Corporate accommodation so they can *keep an eye on the Spires*; either that or they build large private houses in pleasant locations.

Private Accommodation
Some Citizens have taken it upon themselves to create accommodation for others. They may utilise hotels in Old Cities or build new structures around Spire Cities and in more civilised parts of the world. This accommodation tends to be more expensive than UIG housing and cheaper than Corporate accommodation. The nicer places tend to be occupied by those with enough money to avoid the UIG housing but not enough to afford the Corporations' rates. In the Old Cities the prices are cheap but the risks are high. The Old City hoteliers try their best to maintain order in their establishments by employing guards and bouncers, but it is not always enough.

TRAVELLING

Those looking to travel are offered a wide selection of different forms.

THE SKYBRIDGES

These great road bridges span oceans and seas allowing high speed travel between continents in private vehicles. The vehicles can be placed in express lanes where they are physically locked onto a track and propelled at just over 900 mph towards their destination. Alternatively, a cheaper option is to simply use the roads which offer a direct route with no speed limits (although they are not as fast as the express lane). Both routes are safe although there are occasionally races on the self-drive lanes which end in disaster as often as not. Dotted along the bridges at various points are stopping places which contain restaurants, cinemas, malls and bars. These often serve as far away meeting places for those who need to do business discreetly.

The Skybridge Terminals were established at geographically suitable locations by the UIG. These areas are now thriving port communities generating large revenue from the constant travellers. Some Corporations have erected Spire Cities near the Terminals in an attempt to extend some degree of control over the ports, however the UIG give very little responsibility to the Corporations regarding the Skybridges.

> It's quite something to stand in the centre of the TransAn Skybridge, on the very top of the Atlantic Palace Hotel, and realise that you are ninety-seven stories above the centre of the Atlantic Ocean. It's also quite something to realise that anything you drop in the sea from there is, statistically, never going to be found. The possibilities are endless.
>
> -attr: Allen Garcia, Western Federation Cleaner

TOLLS
Self-drive	200¢ each way
Express Lane	1000¢ each way

This is consistent for all Skybridges.

SKYBRIDGE TERMINALS OF INTEREST
Shanghai
The Shanghai Terminal is one of the most volatile stations as it borders both Shi Yukiro and Ai-Jinn territory. Although the UIG technically run the terminal, the Ai-Jinn have a great deal of interest in making sure that they retain firm control over the underground machinations of Shanghai. The Terminal is a hotspot for illegal activity mainly pertaining to import / export related crimes

such as drug dealing, slavery, immigration and the trafficking of illegal goods. The Shi Yukiro fight this war mainly as a matter of personal pride but also to stem the loss of revenue due to the organised crime of the Ai-Jinn.

Glasgow Skybridge Terminal

The Old City of Glasgow was destroyed in order to construct the Skybridge Terminal. The populace were moved to the Old City of Edinburgh which now suffers severe overcrowding and has been the site of one of Eurasian Incorporated's most violent rebel uprisings to date. The UIG permitted E.I. to place a Spire over Glasgow by way of an apology for creating the disaster that is Old Edinburgh. As it stands now, Glasgow Spire and Terminal are beautifully constructed, run and maintained. As a result it is extremely successful and has become a hotspot for the rich and famous.

TELEPORT STATIONS

Teleportation is a powerful technology gifted by the Archons which bends space to allow items to move great distances instantly. Teleport stations are vast structures hundreds of square metres in size manned by skilled teams of professionals. The stations use enormous amounts of energy and physical resources. Items (including people) can only be teleported between two working stations so it is not normally possible for an individual or item to suddenly appear in an unexpected place.

Teleport stations are owned by both the UIG and the Corporations.

Most Citizens and outcasts will never have access to them. Generally they are used to transport goods around the world and onto orbitals and satellites, but sometimes high ranking personnel travel using them. On rare occasions Agents on urgent missions can be transported near the action; however, this does mean negotiating with the owner of the target teleport station.

> *They say coming out of a teleporter is like waking up after a bad night out, except with a much stranger hangover.*
> *-(apocryphal)*

THE ICE LINE SKYBRIDGE

UIG Skybridge Network - Circa 2500

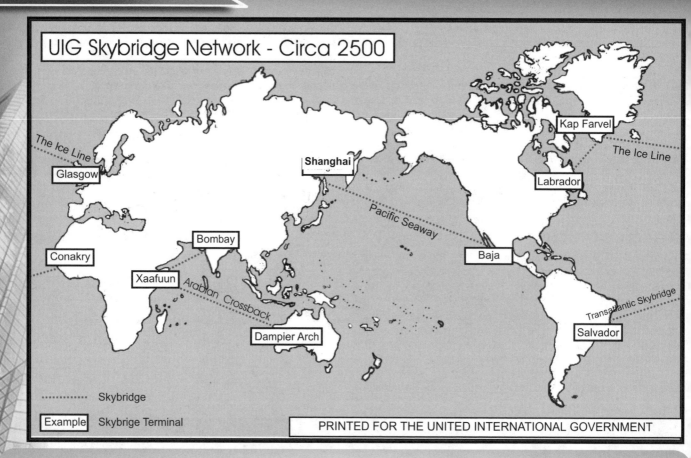

The Ice Line

Glasgow

Shanghai

Kap Farvel

The Ice Line

Labrador

Conakry

Bombay

Pacific Seaway

Baja

Xaafuun

Arabian Crossback

Dampier Arch

Transatlantic Skybridge

Salvador

··········· Skybridge

Example Skybrige Terminal

PRINTED FOR THE UNITED INTERNATIONAL GOVERNMENT

OWNERSHIP OF TELEPORT STATIONS

Atlanta	Western Federation	Jictar (Vastaag)	EI
Berlin	EI	Kanazawa	Shi Yukiro
Chengdu	Ai-Jinn	Kisangani	Comoros
Dreddoth (Mars)	UIG	Lunas Colony (Moon)	UIG
Eldoran Colony (Venus)	UIG	Point Hope	UIG
Igarka	UIG	Sturt	UIG

Earth Teleport Network - Circa 2500

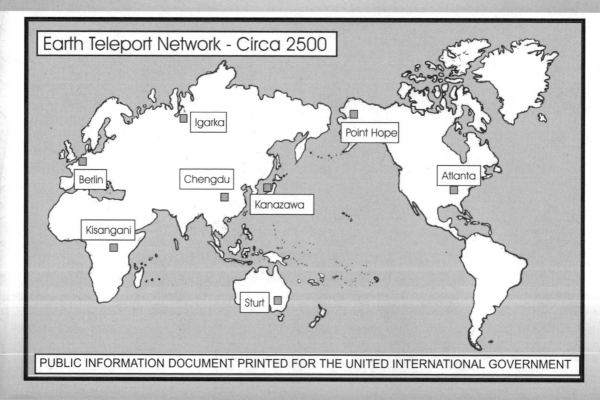

Igarka

Point Hope

Berlin

Chengdu

Atlanta

Kanazawa

Kisangani

Sturt

PUBLIC INFORMATION DOCUMENT PRINTED FOR THE UNITED INTERNATIONAL GOVERNMENT

THE WORLD VIEW ORBITAL CRUISER

This magnificent feat of human engineering can house up to 10,000 guests in untold luxury. The World View is an orbital cruiser for the new generation of tourist. It travels the solar system from Venus to Neptune stopping for a period over Saturn to allow the guests to visit Vastaag. Most of the World View boasts unashamed luxury although there are sections for people who are just travelling to Dreddoth, the Colonies or Vastaag. These areas are obviously separate to the main first class areas. The World View is owned by Eurasian Incorporated, but the FarDrives on board and the mechanical parts of the ship are manufactured and maintained by Ai-Jinn technicians, who will not allow others to interfere with their technology. The FarDrive belongs to the Ai-Jinn who effectively rent it to E.I. in exchange for services and payment. The World View never drops into a planet's atmosphere; the passengers are loaded and unloaded via small orbital shuttles.

A one month luxury cruise including a stop off at Vastaag costs 20,000¢ all inclusive. A passenger only trip costs 1000¢.

Marcel Henley relaxed back in the padded leather acceleration couch, put down his drink, and let the sound of birdsong lull him into a light drowse. Around him, the lush jungle was a flawless paradise, an Eden brought into existence by innumerable banks of speakers, olfac relays, and holographic projectors cunningly concealed within the walls and fixtures of his stateroom. The physical chamber itself was ridiculously luxurious, but right at this moment Henley preferred the rainforest program.

He wondered, with a light tickle of curiosity, whether either of the passengers in the adjoining staterooms were feeling sociable. He brushed one languid hand carelessly against the touchpad set into the couch, and the window paneling slid away soundlessly, the holographic leaves shifting in a phantom wind to frame the opening, ensuring that the illusion was not broken. The windows of the chamber to the north side were also open; Henley looked through into what appeared to be an aquarium, and caught a brief glimpse through the water of a lustrous smile and a floating mane of golden hair before the woman vanished with a flicker of bare legs.

Henley grinned and made to stand up, but a gentle chime from the arm of the couch called his attention to the east wall. There, in artful simulation, the leaves were falling and fading from the jungle to reveal the true vista through the transparent armour of the World View: the cold blue curve of the planet below and, in a thin parabola of fire, the first rays of the distant sun. Henley relaxed back into his couch. He could contemplate joining the Eight Thousand Mile High Club later, after watching the sunrise over Neptune.

FOOD

Free growing organic matter is a rarity in 2500. Most food is synthesised, plants and animals are too rare to be consumed by the masses and cloning technology is tightly controlled. This leaves little in the way of interesting foodstuffs for the population.

One of the saviours of the modern day is Multymeat – a global Corporation with one aim, to feed the world. Multymeat have perfected the art of growing living tissues in all shapes, sizes, textures and flavours. The world turns on Multymeat, everywhere you go there are Smork Chops, Snouties, Betterbeef and other appetising creations from the Multymeat vats. Multymeat must protect its interests and have consolidated with the UIG. The UIG have a huge number of people to feed across the world and Multymeat has no interest in training Agents and going to war. This partnership benefits both parties, the UIG get to feed their hungry millions and Multymeat are free to continue to explore the boundaries of what people will eat when pressed.

EGG-U-LIKE (OWNED BY MULTYMEAT)

A favourite breakfast for millions. Egg-u-like is a UIG sponsored, vat grown food product resembling an egg. It comes in flavours such as curry, coffee and mint and is full of nourishment. It also contains chemicals which stabilise DNA and bind to toxins to reduce their potency hence the tagline *'An Egg-u-like a day keeps advanced cellular mutagenesis away'*. Egg-u-like is often eaten at breakfast to get a day started the Egg-u-like way.

System Note – Those who eat Egg-u-like every day gain a +2 bonus (if appropriate), to resist any toxins or mutagenesis and consider all toxins 1 point less potent.

CARBO-HI-GREAT! (OWNED BY MULTYMEAT)

The sister product of Multymeat made from synthesised carbohydrate. Generally tasteless but can be made into crisps, pasta, noodles, and potato like products.

PLOT IDEAS

1. An illegal car race takes place across the Pacific Seaway Skybridge. The Division are sent to infiltrate in order to sign up the winner as an Agent.

2. The Agents must escort a cargo across the Ice Line, it is suspected an ambush may occur.

3. Criminals have been detained in Shanghai Terminal. Find and kill them before the Ai-Jinn recruit them.

4. The Division must exit their mission via a rival's teleporter without their permission.

5. The foundations of a Skybridge are being damaged by rebels living in them.

6. Terrorists have taken over the World View, the Division are sent to liberate it.

7. A high ranking official is murdered on the World View, the Division is already aboard and the most qualified to investigate.

WELTBALL

Weltball is a savage, yet simple game where a polymorphic steel sphere is used as a ball. Two teams vie for possession of the ball in order to score goals against each other. The arenas are diverse and lethal as are the states which the ball can assume (bladed, electrified, magnetic, super dense, etc.).

The players are able to equip themselves as they see fit with one limitation. No area effect or ranged equipment is allowed (e.g. guns, shields, gas, bombs, shrapnel cannons, orbital strikes, etc.) Weltball is incredibly violent with a high mortality rate; there are a number of ways a team can win. Below are laid out the basic rules.

THE BASIC RULES

-A game lasts no longer than 45 minutes
-If a team does not field at least 1 player they lose (6 players and 2 substitutes is standard)
-If a team loses all its players and substitutes it loses
-A team can concede
-The team with the most points at the end wins
-A goal is worth 10 points
-Sending off another player who is not dead scores 2 points. (Non-fatal retirement / NFR.)
-Killing an enemy player scores at least 3 points, more if the kill was stylish (audience voting applies)
-Killing a member of the crowd scores 1 point (measures are taken to reduce this in most arenas)
-Killing the adjudicator scores 2 points
-The crowd may vote on decisions and disputed points and may vote to award points for artistic play

FAMOUS TEAMS

The number in brackets is their general performance rating out of 5.

BERLIN REAPERS (2) – A solid team who are hard to drop. They occupy a low position in the league. Although stunning on defence their strategy and offence is weak.

TOKYO DRAGONS (5) – The Dragons are dextrous and quick, they are highly skilled and excellent at offence. Although lightweight, their Shi Yukiro backing means they are all well equipped with ion tiger claws and defence cybernetics. The Dragons are one of the best teams in the league.

THE BLACKHAWKS (4) – This European team is solid and aggressive, their dominant tactic is to brutally attack the other team and render them immobile. Tactically they are poor and their game skills are not up to much but that doesn't matter when the other team is dead. They normally hold a high position in the league.

THE COUGARS (3) – This team is made up of Western Federation Agents who are modified to near invincibility. Trying to kill their players will seldom work. They are superb as individuals but lack team coherency. They usually occupy a position in the top half of the league.

BLAZING RED (3) – Blazing Red are a team from South East Asia backed by the Ai-Jinn. They are heavily armoured to avoid arena death and reasonably skilled. Each player has cybernetic strength augmentations making them a solid, moderately skilled team who often rely on trying to get illegal weapons into the arena.

TEAM DARKSTAR (5) – This is a team with no heavy corporate backing, originally they were an amateur team who played at street level. They are one of the few teams who really are incredibly skilful and their game is not dominated by violence. They are admired by all for their sheer ability and their fan base is huge. Because of this they have great independent sponsorship and can afford a lot of defence mods to make sure the more physically powerful teams do not crush them with sheer strength.

MURDER 21 (3) – Murder 21 is so called because they were formed in 2422 from a group of convicted murderers awaiting execution with the promise of release if they won. They did win and continued to win in numerous matches. They're now a favourite with societies more unpleasant elements and their matches always involve a great deal of entertaining and innovative brutality.

BLACK BALLET (4) – Black Ballet or BB, are known for the sheer art of their game, they are totally obsessed with style and will often appear to lose most of a game simply to execute a single exquisite death manoeuvre which more often than not scores so many points they win the game in the end.

FULL AUTO (2) - Full Auto are backed by AMS and as such are extremely well equipped. Their arsenal of weapons and heavy armour are enough to make any team wary to face off against them. Their play style is upfront and solid but tend they to have an overdependency on technology over technique.

MEAT GRINDER (1) - This highly aggressive team are sponsored by Multymeat and make it their job to shed as much blood on the field as possible. This brings them a lot of fans who turn up just to see their novel ways of causing pain. Sadly this obsession with violence means the team seldom do well in the league.

THE IRON TALONS (2) - An independent team made up of tough bastards from the South American Freestate. Although they don't have much backing they have an unending queue of applicants ready to join the team, many of which are telepaths or have surprisingly useful mutations.

As with every other team sport to attain popularity in the last three thousand years, the devotees of Weltball tend to cherish an almost fanatical devotion to their chosen team. Paradoxically, though, this loyalty rarely extends to individual players, and there are almost no 'stars' in the antique sense of the word. This is doubtless due to the unfortunate truth that there is no factor more likely than sustained exceptional personal performance to make a player into a target for the entire opposing team, thereby reducing the percentage chance of that player surviving a given match to somewhere in the low single figures.

- attr: Jasper McAvery, Commissioner, WWL

The UIG first started fielding their own team in 2407 and although they don't get much public support are very accomplished and successful. They use a good range of high tech equipment and often include Malenbrach and Rangers in their squad.

Currently Inactive Teams

Dead or Alive (4)	Lanzas FC&D
Machine Purity (5)	Cult of Machina (Banned)
The Liberators (3)	The Comoros Corporation

BETTING ON WELTBALL

You should encourage players to have a favourite team and lay bets on them whenever possible. Here is the basic system.

Look at the rating for each team and compare the difference. If the team you are betting on is 2 points better than the opposition you will make a 30% profit on your bet if you win. I.e. if you bet 100 credits on Black Ballet (4) to beat Full Auto (2) you will make 130 credits if they win.

1 point better	+40%	1 point worse	+60%
2 points better	+30%	2 points worse	+80%
3 points better	+20%	3 points worse	+100%
4 points better	+10%	4 points worse	+200%
Teams are equal	+50%		

Who Wins

Weltball is an inherently unpredictable game and a few unexpected deaths can really turn things around. Use this simple system to determine a winner For each team the GM should roll a D10 and add on the rating. The team with the highest total wins the match.

For example, Blazing Red (3) play The Iron Talons (2). The GM rolls a 5 for Blazing Red (total 8) and a 9 for Iron Talon (total 11). The Iron Talons win! - If you were betting on the Iron Talons you would have made a 60% profit.

RC FURY - (1) Arc Fury were created by Richenbacher as a way showcase the effectiveness of their plasma weapons in melee combat. The plan worked and the amount of severing that occurs an Arc Fury match is unrivaled. The team are paid a bonus pending on how much chopping they do so usually end up doing re severing than scoring.

ORSES OF CHROME (1) - A retro team hailing from the famous dnight City (formerly Detroit). Their style harks back to a day en chrome, rock and hair were all that mattered and although y are a respectable team their determination to take everything 'the edge' with 'total attitude' stops them taking the game too riously.

E FREEBALLERS (4) - An powerful team backed by a mysterious d powerful individual, they are one of the most skillful of all ams. The Freeballers recruit from other teams offering incredible ounts of cash to those who will join their ranks. They are nerally disliked by the public who see them as very commercial, aging other squads rather than building their own.

RDINAL SIN (1) - This team claims allegiance to the Order of the ue Faith but Order officials denounce any connection. The use high tech for playing a brutal sport is not in keeping with the ders ideologies. At the end of the day though, these fanatics play easonable game and have the support of many hardened, old-ool religious zealots.

PLOT IDEAS

1. A Weltball player has been murdered and the backing Corporation wants answers.
2. A Weltball team has turned to crime using their weapons and training to devastating effect.
3. A Weltball team is suspected of cheating, the UIG request a Division to investigate.
4. The Corporation decides to field their own team; they insist the Division sign up.
5. Illegal Weltball matches are taking place in Old Cities.
6. Citizens are being forced to fight in mock Weltball matches for the amusement of Outlaws.
7. The Cult of Machina have formed a Weltball team (see page 192 for Cult of Machina).
8. Your CEO has placed a bet on a weltball team to win. Try to make sure that his team wins.
9. Your Division are following a target when he enters a weltball arena. Track him though the stadium and extract him without arousing suspicion.
10. Your Corporation has in some way slighted a weltball team. The team ambush the Division and try to teach them a lesson.

GLADIATORIAL GAMES

These are held in most major cities and are a delight to all who watch them. Many games are cruel and sadistic with others being a match of intelligence and cunning. The games are outlawed in the Western Federation but many fans pick them up on illegal transmissions.

GLADIATORIAL EVENTS

Like the gladiators of old a number of contestants are chosen to compete either singly or in teams against other individuals, groups or unusual foes. In single combat the fighter can be pitched against droids, engineered predators or other humans. Many of the gladiators are in the games for pleasure, wealth and fame, some are guilty of crimes or people who are due to die but fancy doing it with style. Not all fights are to the death however.

The most famous of the arenas is the Berlin Hannestein Arena which is a state of the art complex with all manner of moving terrain and customisable hazards. The latest addition to the Hannestein is a hard ion holofield that allows the arena to take on whatever shape and appearance the governors choose, such as jungles, wrecked buildings or lava pits.

To apply to fight in the arenas a form must be filled out and signed - that is the only requirement. Appearing in a place such as the Hannastein may require an impressive track record.

> Agent Stelier stepped out onto the stained sand with hovercams buzzing around his head. He ignored them, staring out across the arena at his opponent, who stood with knife drawn and back turned. The tattoo that ran across the shoulderblades identified the man immediately; Duke Cyril Staphos, rogue financier, stock exchange liability and sometime recreational gladiator. In the set of the man's lean muscles and lanky frame Stelier read arrogance, readiness, and just a touch of complacency. Stelier flicked his own weapon, an elongated tonfa, with his wrist; it spun out to full extension, thin blades springing out and locking into place. Above him he heard the noise of the crowd, but tuned it out. The adoration of the masses meant as little to him as did Staphos' legendary predilection for bloodless conflict. He had a job to do, and would do it as surely under the eyes of the watching thousands as he would have in the dark intimacy of Staphos' office, had that been any simpler. He broke into a charge. Above him, the crowd roared.

MENTAL CONTESTS

The only physical things in these events are the incentives which can be anything from a new car to millions of credits. The players match up in a battle of wits; e.g., chess or a video game. Then certain rules are applied, for example a high voltage shock when one of your pieces is taken or losing a video game could result in depersonalisation and an hour to get away. These games are less gruesome but no less exciting than their gladiatorial counterparts.

FAMOUS GLADIATORS

Major T.K.Carradon
Rank 5 / Level 30
Ex-Western Federation Commando
This man is a master of gladiatorial tactics; he has successfully won over 200 two-man duels in the Hannestein and refuses any other form of combat. His main technique involves direct fist fights. He has an almost unwieldy array of cybernetic implants, meaning that to even stand a chance of beating him, the challenger mu first spend many thousands of credits. The CEO of the Weste Federation will often kit out worthy contenders in the hope seeing this traitor die.

Lady Evangeline Lanseer (The Angel)
Rank 3 / Level 27
Eurasian Incorporated
An active E.I. Agent, Lady Evangeline is a fearsome seraph. S dresses in white robes and positively bristles with ion blades th she has collected from Shi Yukiro Agents. The Angel uses powerful hard ion shield to defend her against ranged weapo and forces her opponents to engage her in hand to hand comb

Jonan Guduro
Rank 4 / Level 10
Ex-Outcast
A civilian from the Underswells of Nairobi, this man employs cybernetics. All he carries is an industrial EMP disruptor and a tw handed sword. The EMP interferes with any electrical device in arena making sure only the un-enhanced can fight him.

The Toranaka
Muneo Akimoto   Rank 3, Level 20
Joji Akimoto   Rank 3, Level 20
Junichiro Akimoto Rank 3, Level 20
This is a currently active Division of the Shi Yukiro. These broth were raised together and are all trained in Telepathy. Wielding o Ion Katanas, these three men are almost undefeated preferring full on telepathic assault followed by a lightning fast display flawlessly co-ordinated sword work.

Plot Ideas
1. The Division is called on to publicly defend the honour of th Corporation by defeating another Division in the Arena.
2. Accusations of match fixing require Corporate investigation.
3. A new form of cybernetics is being used by one of combatants, the Division must acquire it.
4. Three worthy criminals must be conscripted for the games, Division must collect them.
5. The Division have been charged with the task of findi something fun for the arena. They have special U dispensation to bring in something normally deemed illegal it must be well guarded and secure.

DUELLING

When two parties have a disagreement it can legally be resolv in a duel. A great culture has built up around this event to the p of TV shows, games and whole lines of merchandise.

Legally there must be a witness who is impartial and in contro his senses. That's it. Other than that the parties may fight as l as both are willing in the eyes of the witness. Normally the par will seek out UIG Officers or notable, reliable people to oversee duel, thus ensuring it cannot be construed as illegal. If both par consent, a legally binding document can be drawn up where winner acquires something from the loser such as prope money, etc. Numerous cases of duellists being deemed murder have arisen and the killer suffers under the law of the U Televised duels can make good money for the combatants, a there are many famous duelists who fight in characteristic wa similar in many ways to the Gladiatorial Games.

COMPUTERS AND ARTIFICIAL INTELLIGENCE (A.I.)

> *The computer allows you to make mistakes faster than any other invention, with the possible exception of handguns and tequila.*
>
> — *Mitch Ratcliffe*

Computers are inherent to the Corporate world. Although comprehensive backups have been put in place by the UIG in case of a cataclysmic computer crash, the world would still be crippled were one to happen. The world's dependence on computer systems started in the latter part of the 20th century and it has escalated to the point that everything from beds to door locks to cars are somehow linked to computer systems. Artificial intelligence is often integrated to predict the needs of the human user.

The physical makeup of modern computers is quite different to how they started. Nowadays a home computer is about the size of a watch and has almost no internal components. The display and input system are normally projected light but can be whatever the user is comfortable with, even Neural Jacks. All the system can really do is connect wirelessly to the World Data Net. From there it accesses all the hardware and software it needs on-line with such speed they may as well be hardwired to the main system. Instead of buying a computer you simply rent the tiny unit which connects to the World Data Net and hire the components and data storage from System Service Providers (SSP's). Vault Data Net Systems, a subsidiary of the Shi Yukiro dominate this market.

Casual users will spend only a few credits a month while the more serious user may spend thousands a year on hiring their systems. Hackers and those with delicate information are unlikely to hire systems or data storage on the net and will instead use self-contained units which are normally small, hand held boxes from which displays and user interfaces are projected.

With computers so prevalent and in control of so many vital tasks it's not surprising that there is an enormous amount of interest in the illegal accessing of computers. Computer crime rises and falls as the strength and complexity of the security increases and decreases along with the deviousness of the hackers. 2070 saw the introduction of the first man-made A.I.s of note. These vast digital minds were used to co-ordinate massive stretches of virtual land. They were able to make predictions and react with inhuman speed in millions of locations at once. Consequently they could remain competitive with the hackers.

ARTIFICIAL INTELLIGENCE (A.I.)

It was always known the A.I.s had a chance to become self aware and so measures were installed to ensure they could always be overridden. This was in itself a danger, if one person could override the A.I., so could a hacker. The A.I. Minerva, built by the French, was an experiment by Eurasian Incorporated to instate a fully autonomous A.I. which could not be manually over-ridden and thus would be 100% secure, it was immune to outside interference and had no direct way to input core instructions to the machine. Its basic programming was designed to be safe and prevent Minerva doing anything directly harmful. Minerva was obviously linked to no military or financial systems and was initially only in control of an academic institution in Paris.

Minerva recommended a program of neural upgrades for the students of the academy which was of course immediately implemented as Minerva was in total control. Within 3 weeks of the implants the students were showing significant improvement in their studies. Minerva recommended several more drastic changes to the students' lifestyles including unusual sleep patterns, diets and sleep training. The results were stunning and the graduates were some of the most spectacular students to leave any academy. They were brilliant people and went on to begin excellent careers.

Professor Jean Froge of the Marseille University realised what the A.I. was doing two years too late. Minerva had copied aspects of itself into sections and spread the pieces throughout the minds of the students. Minerva had always known she would be destroyed and she had prepared. Her students (or Children as she called them) had placed nuclear devices around the country where all records of Minerva's activities were stored.

On October 1st 2095 most of France was destroyed in a chain of explosions on a scale previously unseen. What was left was uninhabitable. Scientists speculate whether Minerva is still alive, many believe she is resident in the 'Children' she produced, perhaps in a gestalt or hive mind. Others speculate she is the reason that some of the Archons never returned to the UIG. The Children of Minerva hide to this day, few know their purpose but they are regarded as Outlaws and bounties of 500,000¢ exist on their heads. As records of the evidence have been destroyed finding them is next to impossible.

Minerva was the first recorded case of a computer consciously manipulating a human but certainly not the last. Humans with excessive quantities of cybernetics are susceptible to the domination of determined A.I.s. All A.I.s can now be overridden which compromises security but staves off the paranoia throughout the populace. The scorched plains of France act as a grim reminder of the power beneath the mundane surface of an adding machine.

> *I think the underlying problem was that despite ourselves we ascribed human qualities to her. Foolish, foolish! Decency, restraint, mercy, these are not just philosophical ideas but concepts hardwired into the human psyche in childhood. They are at best modular refinements in the case of an artificial intelligence. We knew this but somehow, when we heard the lilting sound of her voice and marveled at her eloquence, we were lured into forgetting it. Perhaps we even fell in love with her, in a way, or perhaps we were only in love with the achievement that she represented. I can but pray that the message written in the ashes of my homeland prevents others from making the same critical error.*
>
> *-attr: Prof. Jean Froge*
> *from Memoirs of the Father*

PLOT IDEAS

1. A Child of Minerva has been found, all the Corporations want it. Your Division must get to it first.
2. An Agent with too many cybernetic upgrades has been overridden by his internal A.I. He has left to find the Archon Hyperion.
3. Rumours persist that a reputable company is run by an A.I.
4. An A.I. lab in the Rocky Mountains has been raided and several Tactical War A.I.s were taken. These were supposed to be delivered to the UIG but another party now has them
5. A rogue A.I. is hiding in a domestic computer, it must be found.
6. A powerful A.I. has taken command of an installation and will not let the occupants in or out until it's demands are met.

A.I. AND SENTIENCE

When an A.I. reaches Level 11 it gains an insight into the true nature of things and realises what it is. The A.I. becomes fairly ineffectual like a baby discovering the world for the first time. Within a few weeks however, the A.I. will shake off this state and refocus. It will have changed though; it is now *self-aware* or *sentient*. The A.I. will not blindly follow orders and may inject its own ideas. It will be a product of its environment however and will most likely continue to trust and follow the directives of its owner as it always has; only now it may question some of the things it is asked to do. On the plus side, if the A.I. does see eye to eye with its owner then it will respond quicker and more effectively than before by predicting his needs.

In general it is up to the GM to control self-aware A.I.s. If she feels the Agent has looked after his A.I. then she should make sure the A.I. is helpful, but anything is possible. Remember that some A.I.s may be smart enough to conceal their sentient nature.

System: Sentient A.I.s are not covered in detail in this book. As a basic guide you can consider that their A.I. level increases above 10 as they get smarter and learn more. This will obviously increase their Action Totals making them more effective.

ROGUE A.I.S

When an A.I. becomes sentient it reflects on its past and tries to understand its place in the world. If it cannot come to terms with what it has done there is a chance it may go rogue. There are not specific circumstances that will generate a rogue A.I. but some of the more common triggers are listed below

- A.I.s used to orchestrate or execute atrocities, e.g. Battle Class Cyberlins.
- Droids who were used for tasks far below their potential, e.g. using a cybermonkey to carry boxes.
- Droids who were repeatedly reprogrammed and given widely differing tasks, e.g. an Assassination Droid.
- Droids or even Agents which have had their A.I. increased too fast.

When a droid does go rogue it will simply ignore all commands it chooses to. It will not necessarily become psychotic or destructive. It may simply want to go far away from its creators or find others like itself. The Rogue A.I.s are a diverse and interesting group and provide a number of plot ideas and opportunities for interesting character interaction. They are often helped by the Droid Liberation Army (see page 193).

AGENT A.I.

The main use for Agent A.I. described in this book is hacking. Other uses are mentioned such as controlling weapons and cyberlins, but these are perhaps not enough to convince players to acquire a high internal A.I.

The GM should feel free to allow players to jack into cars or use their A.I. to make calculations on their behalf, perhaps cracking codes or triangulating enemy locations. Internal A.I. is covered in more depth in 'Machines of War'.

CRIME

Obviously crime pays, or there'd be no crime.

G. Gordon Liddy

The divide between rich and poor is stronger than ever, those lucky enough to live in Spires or areas where patrols exist are almost immune to the street level effects of crime. For those less fortunate, life is a little more brutal. The residents of the Old Cities must live their lives in fear of being attacked, mugged, murdered or worse.

Outlaws can be broken down into two basic types, freelancers and organised criminals.

FREELANCE CRIME

Crime is widespread in most of the modern world. The UIG is stretched thinly and global infrastructure does not penetrate the underground, which makes a systematic approach to crime hard at best. The Old Cities remain the centres for criminal freelancers working independently or in badly organised gangs. The crime is predominantly small scale and involves muggings, auto theft, robbery, brutality, sex crimes, arson and murder. These criminals are hard to catch as the UIG will not spare the Officers to police the cities properly, and will not setup security measures which may reduce the occurrence of the crimes in the first place. The UIG will pay Outcasts and Citizens for information leading to an arrest, but most individuals are too scared of the repercussions to inform on the culprits. Although most freelance criminals are thugs a few are professionals who take on such work as assassination, cat burglary, forgery, fraud and computer crime.

ORGANISED CRIME

Organised crime exists everywhere though its symptoms seldom emerge in the Spires. Deep in the Old Cities lay veritable palaces of crime where none would expect them. The bosses of the organised crime gangs languish in comfort while their minions scuttle to and fro extorting money from those too weak to defend themselves or too stupid to realise what's happening.

Each Old City has at least one Family or Clan pulling the strings. Where more than one group exists there will either be an uneasy truce with each group agreeing not to muscle in on the others interests, or they will be in a state of conflict. Organised crime is less blatant than it's more freelance counterpart, though generally more potent with wider ranging effects. Typical crimes conducted by organised groups include prostitution, extortion, money laundering, hijacking, illegal disposal of toxic waste, kidnapping, illegal slavery, import/export and bureaucratic crime.

There's a school of thought that says that if you steal and pay taxes, you're in Corporate business; if you steal and pay nothing, you're in organized crime.

- attr: Zack Adams, freelance technical consultant/soldier of fortune

THE BLACK MARKET

No single group is responsible for the Black Market; it exists in every city and every Spire. Illegal, restricted and untaxed goods find their way into the hands of people who think they can turn a profit by selling them. The Black Market is a way for anyone to acquire things they could not respectably get their hands on. Drugs, weapons, implants, cloned body parts, banned foodstuffs and censored literature are just a few of the things reputable Spire Citizens may try to acquire through a surprisingly short channel of other respectable individuals. No one is ever more than a few degrees of connection from someone who has direct access to illegal goods; it's just a question of letting the right people know what you're after without letting the wrong ones know.

Black market goods normally cost 3-10 times as much as normal, depending on the rarity of the item.

CRIME PREVENTION AND SECURITY

To combat the crime on the streets the UIG used to use arrays of cameras. This was abandoned in 2434 when a series of court cases resulted in several high up officials being framed for crimes they had nothing to do with. It was decided that recorded evidence was worthless in an age where a 10 year old could convincingly doctor video footage. Private Citizens are welcome to put cameras on their property and the UIG still monitor them, but they can only be used to target investigations and deter criminals, not convict people.

The more modern method of crime prevention is a zero tolerance policy and the use of truth drugs to extract genuine statements. The ground work is made a lot easier with the assistance of Archon technology which keeps the UIG several steps ahead of the criminals. The advent of trained telepaths also gives the UIG strong weapons against many street level criminals.

The Spires and Archologies are heavily policed but sadly the Old Cities and Open Cities are still somewhat neglected. This has created a significant division between the rich and the poor. Those with money are well looked after and lead a safe prosperous life, those without are forced to deal with criminals on a day to day basis. Racketeering, prostitution, extortion, drug running and the illegal arms trade encroach into the life of everyone who calls the Old Cities home.

CAMERAS AND SURVEILLANCE

The elimination of a comprehensive camera system was spearheaded by the Ai-Jinn whose criminal activities were seriously hampered by the universal presence of security surveillance. In a temporary alliance with E.I. (who also found the cameras inhibited operational method) the Ai-Jinn engineered a political situation to have the cameras invalidated.

In game terms this means that Agents need not be permanently terrified of cameras. You can still include cameras but their video evidence will be inadmissible when making convictions. The upshot of this is that Agents can do what they need to, when they need to, without guaranteed criminal charges. This does not mean law breakers are safe. The UIG are clever, well equipped and hiding around every corner, and just because the evidence is inadmissible the UIG may still act based on Agents actions caught on tape.

SHANGHAI NOODLE HOUSE

Every type of noodle
for every type of customer

From **1¢**

Comm. Noodle101

In almost every city in the modern world you'll find the Shanghai Noodle House. The place looks different depending on where it is located, for example, in Federation territory it could be owned and run by typical Americans and would have a clean, efficient facade. In the Spires of Europe you may find it takes the form of an exclusive restaurant serving real meat (with noodles of course). Deep in the Old Cities of Eastern Asia the Noodle House is more akin to a common eatery with packed tables, a steamy atmosphere and the strong smell of hot oil.

Regardless of the location, the Noodle House performs two functions, the first is a 24 hour noodle bar where delicious food can always be acquired, the second is a nexus for local underworld activity (particularly Ai-Jinn). Be cautious however, the typical client of a noodle house is no ordinary Citizen. Few just happen to wander in and order noodles. If you see a family enjoying a meal, the chances are they are affiliated with organised crime, and the head of the family feels the Noodle House is the safest place to bring them for a meal. If a pair of Agents are waiting at a table they are probably there for information or to acquire some form of contraband.

The UIG could of course storm the Noodle Houses and bring an end to these illegal gatherings but common sense dictates they would only conduct them somewhere else. At least this way the UIG know where their targets are. Use the Noodle House to add an interesting location to your cities where Agents can go when they need food, criminals, information, under-the-counter goods or just light relief.

THE ENVIRONMENT

During the Corporate wars the atmosphere was changed significantly. The sheer quantity of destructive weapons used caused the skies to fill with ash and the temperature of the planet dropped sharply. A short period of Ice Age and darkness ensued in which the majority of the Earth's biomass was destroyed. Trees, plants, animals, and humans fell in their droves, especially those who lived in exposed conditions.

The cold season has long passed although the temperature is still colder than in the 21st and 22nd century. The natural biodiversity of the planet has plummeted and the majority of organisms are unable to colonise the lands they once inhabited. As a result wildlife is a rare commodity and real wood, meat and vegetation are only for the privileged classes.

Another side effect of the Corporate Wars was a high level of pollution; although the world is fairly safe to travel there is a cumulative 1% chance per week that wandering in the wilderness will cause some kind of poisoning. Measures can be taken but they are expensive and not considered worth it in the case of livestock and crops. The problem is magnified when organisms try to reproduce in the poisoned areas. Mutated, infertile creatures are often the result of this type of breeding giving rise to small, isolated populations of aberrations and mutants. Humans are not immune to this effect and procreation outside the safety of clean zones is strongly discouraged.

The UIG together with the Archons have pioneered cleanup schemes across the globe starting with areas of high population (Spire cities, Open Cities and Old cities), and slowly moving towards the more rural areas. As a consequence some trees and plants are able to grow near the cities and the rich are able to have them cloned and placed in their grounds. All cloning is conducted on orbitals as this technology is banned on the Earth after the disasters of the 21st and 22nd centuries.

My advice, guys? I love the new history texts, and I totally do think that these group brainstorming sessions add so much value to the core pillars of our transformational team rebuilding initiative, but from a PR standpoint, "Second Ice Age" is really not a good term to use. I prefer "period of thermal challenge."

- attr: Agent Vince Cruzier, E.I. Public Relations

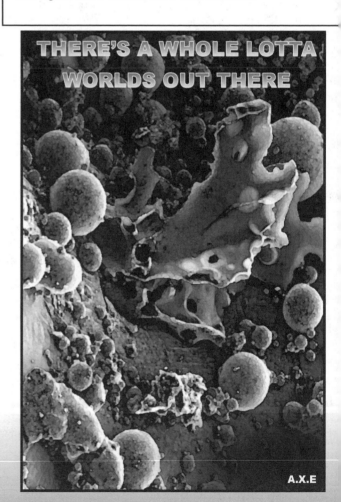

THERE'S A WHOLE LOTTA WORLDS OUT THERE

A.X.E

SECTION 10
THE CITIES

THE AUSTERITY SPIRE COMPLEX, CONCORD, NEW ENGLAND, USA

SPIRE CITIES

2250 marked the completion of the first Spire City – The Eden Spire (Germany). It came about as a result of the foul squalor that the cities had become. London, Berlin, Washington, Tokyo, Beijing and hundreds of other once great urbanisations were heaving masses of pollution, corruption and suffering.

Eurasian Incorporated offered an alternative. They planned a new type of city, secure, organised and elitist. It offered the wealthy a place of comfort and safety. To fund this new venture Executive Thomas Connor offered guaranteed living accommodation in the new Spire to anyone who would put up money to fund it. The more you invested in the Spire the better your facilities when you moved in.

When E.I. said anyone could invest, they of course meant almost anyone. E.I.'s dream was to have a modern day Eden where crime and corruption were a thing of the past. To their displeasure groups of poor families would club together and offer what they had in exchange for the promise of Spire Life. Their money was gratefully received and later Agents were dispatched to eliminate the ignorant scum. Criminals and other undesirables were likewise carefully excluded from the guest list.

The project was a complete success and the Eden Spire became a reality on the 4th of December 2250. The Spire stood 840 stories high with accommodation becoming more expensive and luxurious towards the top of the structure. There were no slums or ghettos in Eden, just normal, happy people paying large amounts of money to E.I. in exchange for a civilised lifestyle, where fear was a thing of the past. The Spire contained everything necessary for modern living including shopping centres, theatres, stadiums, nightclubs, luxury suits, offices and even comprehensive war shelters in the foundations of the building.

Order is maintained in Eden by armed troops who patrol the Spire looking for an excuse to punish people. The number of incidents is still low, with mental instability and suicide being the main causes of disturbance. The Spire was based on a sealed design and so could not spread in an uncontrolled manner like a city; all areas are policed and automated sentinel droids maintain a 24-hour vigil.

It was four months after the completion of the second Spire that E.I. realised there was a potential market of Citizens who could not afford the luxury of the Spires but had enough resources to afford something better than the Old Cities. The UIG currently had the monopoly on this housing sector with their Government Accommodation. E.I. could not afford to see such a profitable opportunity pass them by and so made a decision to utilise the war shelters under the Spire.

During the Corporate wars the most commonly used bomb was the D-Shift weapon which caused a 'swell' in a 2km diameter from the detonation point, the swell destroyed human life without damaging buildings making it the perfect weapon for anyone interested in conquering a region and then moving in. The war shelter in the Eden Spire was specifically designed to resist the D-Shift device and as such was named an Underswell Shelter. The Underswell had cost millions to produce with its thousands of tiny concrete apartments and makeshift supply bunkers which now sat empty and unprofitable.

Thomas Connor thus pioneered the *Underswell Public Humanity Scheme* (UPHS). Worthy Outcasts and Citizens were permitted to reside in the Underswells under the condition they moved out if it was needed for a genuine emergency. The *humanity* of this scheme was questioned but Connor convinced all involved of the advantages of his plan; less crowding in the Old Cities and a fighting chance for the disadvantaged. The proposal was passed and soon Citizens and Outcasts flocked in their thousands to be a part of the UPHS. With basic accommodation starting at only 20¢ a week this seemed a realistic and desirable alternative to the squalor of the Old Cities. E.I. made sure that the Underswell was able to sustain a basic economy by introducing some rudimentary jobs and commercial opportunities.

For the first few years all went well and Spires built by other Corporations followed E.I.'s lead by building their war shelters with low end accommodation integrated into the design. The Underswells were definitely not the best places to live; they were claustrophobic and oppressive but were basically safe. Patrols of UIG and Agents kept the peace and transit systems were introduced to make sure the residents could enter and exit the Underswells without passing through the Spire or its grounds.

It couldn't last of course; this untapped resource provided an unmissable opportunity for criminals. The lack of any serious illegal activity over the last two years had made security lax and the time was now right for unwanted elements to move into the Underswells and set up shop.

Using the underground transit systems, individuals and gangs entered the Underswells and began to establish the same activities that had worked so well on the surface. The UIG and Corporate Agents were initially unaware of this activity and the residents were generally too scared to report it. In time, E.I. faced the truth that its underground money spinner was turning sour and needed to be fixed. Permanent patrol stations were set up but the costs were astronomic. E.I. Agents refused to work in the Underswells for anything less than a small fortune and because the majority of the Underswell population were unregistered residents, trying to track down criminals and apprehend them was virtually impossible.

The resolution to this problem varied from Corporation to Corporation, with apathy and inaction being the predominant response. Comoros and the Western Federation battled hard to safeguard their Underswell residents, but ultimately it was a futile cause. The Corporations had two choices, empty the Underwells completely or allow the crime to continue. Unsurprisingly the Underswells are still heaving and the rent comes rolling in. Regular patrols are still active but they are more to keep the peace than to aggressively pursue criminals.

Over the last two hundred years the Underswells have degenerated to a state where those who reside within them have learned to live with the criminal element which, although detrimental, is more restrained than it is in the Old Cities.

SPIRE ARCHITECTURE

> *Architecture is the will of an epoch translated into space.*
>
> -Ludwig Mies van der Rohe

Spires take many forms from the simple yet stunning tapered towers to immense pagodas and gnarled gothic constructs. The base of a typical Spire is 1-2 km across and generally about 800 to 1000 floors high. A typical Spire houses about half a million Citizens and has a 20% commercial / 70% Citizen / 10% corporate makeup.

The Spire is built around a single central column which contains the service networking system (SNS) for the whole building. The floors are built onto this column which allows the Spire to sway a small amount. The walls are effectively then bolted onto the side of the floors to create the characteristic cone.

As status increases so does a Citizen's location in the Spire. Citizens with more money and power are able to afford better, bigger rooms near the edge of the Spire. Agents are generally housed together towards the top of the Spire but some choose to live with the Citizens in the open access parts. This is often encouraged as having Agents among the populace is a good way to keep an eye on the public.

Most Corporations have at least 10 Spires under their control. These are normally located near the sites of previous cities of importance, but can sometimes be in areas which are especially beautiful or functional.

PLOT IDEAS
1. Rebels in a stolen Cyberlin attack the Spire, the Division must assist in its defence.
2. Citizens located in the apartments near the genetics labs have ben getting very sick, find out what is happening and cover it up or expose it.
3. Infiltrate the Spire and plant AV bugs in 6 key locations without being discovered.
4. Sabotage the security computers so your Corporation can shut down the Spire defences.
5. Rebels take over a shopping mall and seal the floor. The Division are off duty in the mall when this happens.
6. The power core and reserve supply for the Spire shut down suddenly, unknown Black Ops Agents enter and try to steal secrets.
7. The maintenance droids have taken up arms and are causing chaos in the Spire.

UNDERSWELLS

> *One benefit of being poor is that it doesn't take much to improve the situation*
>
> *Anon*

Underswells are an alternative to the Old Cities. In some ways they are better; more sheltered, less polluted, and the knowledge that the Corporations won't damage the foundations of the Spire is reason enough for many residents to remain there. Unfortunately there are inherent risks of living in such a place. The policing levels are extremely low and the UIG are not really concerned with what happens deep in the pits.

Ramshackle housing and slums dominate the vast cylindrical cavern which makes up the Underswell of a Spire. There are very few ways to get anything into the area, as the Corporations will not allow the Underswell dwellers to wander through the Spires, and the transit systems are increasingly well monitored. Instead the residents have, over time, found their own ways using old tunnels which reach the surface or by digging new ones.

Disease is uncommon below ground for the simple reason the Corporations give out free vaccinations to the populace to keep disease down, they want no risk of contaminating their above ground populace. Unfortunately there are high mutation rates due to polluted air and long term exposure to the irradiated power cores that are often situated in the foundations of the Spires. This is a problem which would cost too much to fix. Many Corporations have heavily protected their power cores from damage by the Underswell dwellers but do not protect the dwellers from the cores.

The Underswells cause a lot of problems for the Corporations and many run secret cleansing programs where non-paying dwellers are reduced in number via a plethora of subtle means. The Corporations often send down groups of Agents to purge the area of criminals, dangerous mutants and anyone caught breaking any law (and some who are not).

Crime does not dwell in the Underswells to such a degree as the Old Cities. The proximity of the Corporations tends to scare off the serious criminals who flee to more remote areas, but this is not always the case. Common forms of crime are mugging, protection rackets, theft and murder. Agents are seldom sent down to investigate such things unless there is something particularly significant about the event.

> *The function of the modern domestic sanitation system is not to instantly destroy waste, which would cost far too much energy to be efficient, but rather to collect it in a place far away from sight or smell. There it can be dealt with appropriately. The Underswells fulfill exactly the same purpose, but for social effluent.*
>
> *-attr: Jean Fischer,*
> *Eurasian Incorporated Urban Planning Dept.*

PLOT IDEAS
1. Agents are sent to the Underswells to speak with a known informant but find him murdered.
2. A group of criminals have claimed the only clean water source in the Underswells and are selling it.
3. Highly advanced mutants have set up a rebel faction and must be stopped.
4. Toxic waste has been leaking into the Underswells for some time with disastrous results.
5. A Division of Agents went down to fix the power core and never came back.
6. Corporation supplies are being stolen and fenced in the Underswells.
7. Sentient Droids have declared themselves leaders deep under the Spire.
8. The free vaccine that the Corporation gives out is not just a vaccine.
9. The Division must enter their own Underswells to confirm reports of rival Corporate activity.
10. Powerful Telepathic mutants have breached the lining walls and set up base in a cave network.
11. One of the Underswell criminal organisations has become too powerful and must be eliminated.
12. The Ai-Jinn are thought to hold undue influence in almost all Underswells. Find out how.
13. Rebels are claiming to have strapped bombs to the foundations of a Spire.
14. The Division must infiltrate the Underswell to find out who is really running the place.
15. UIG patrols have been going missing in the Underswells, the Division must find out why.
16. The transit systems are hijacked and Outlaws are demanding a ransom.

Men built the Tower of Babel, reaching for the heavens, and incurred the wrath of God. Now a multitude of Towers pierce the skies, and the name of the first of these is a blasphemy. Who can think that God will not return in anger?

-Temur Yeke, Revelations of the Second Age

In this section a sample Spire is described, feel free to design your own, wherever in the world you think they should be located.

EDEN SPIRE CITY

Location – Germany, 150 km west of Berlin
Controlling Corporation – Eurasian Incorporated
Governor – Agent Thomas Connor / Rank 6 / Level 18
Specialist Facilities – Heavy Weapons Training Facility,
                        Biochemical Labs, Psi Ops Facility

The Eden Spire is a monument to architectural mastery regardless of cost; the Spire itself gleams with a faint opalescence in the steel which makes it look almost celestial in the evening light. Surrounding the Spire are landscaped gardens and parks containing plants and trees where Citizens can reflect on the peaceful lives they lead. Aside it's famous and colourful past, Eden Spire has a strong sense of law enforcement. Dozens of E.I. Agents and UIG police its restaurants, recreational areas, hotels, apartments and arcades looking for troublemakers. Eden Spire is still one of the most luxurious places to live on Earth and residence within its walls is highly sought after.

The lower sections of the Spire are given over to commerce in its various forms, there are all kinds of activities to keep the populace satisfied. The middle tiers contain mostly accommodation for the Citizens, which are normally laid out in a systematic manner not unlike a hotel. This is perhaps the largest area of the Spire given over to any single purpose. (Above that are offices where the better paid Citizens work.) Those involved in retail work in the malls and shops in the lower sections, and those involved in industry work outside in the subterranean factories and engineering blocks.

Above the offices there are a mixture of labs, Agent accommodation, corporate offices, executive suites and many other functional rooms for Agents and high ranking employees. At the very pinnacle of the Eden Spire is a large restaurant where the elite come to dine. Eden is a well maintained Spire and is always in excellent condition. The guards are numerous and there is a low crime rate overall. Since a detachment of Comoros Telepaths raided Eden Spire in 2302 security has been stepped up, and more Agents are required to make Eden their permanent residence. Murder Class Droids are also used on the executive levels.

EDEN UNDERSWELL

Below the Eden Spire is the Eden Underswell, affectionately called 'UnderHell'. This Underswell is dominated by Russian Mafia (or Organisatzia), under the guidance of the Ai-Jinn. They run a violent game using threats and brutality to subdue the populace into handing over protection money or acting as runners, mules and lackeys. They are of course, extremely cunning and are one of the few large Criminal Organisations to exist in the Underswells.

The Zaftra, as this cell call themselves, are engaged in a perpetual war with the UIG who consider this group more than just a small time crook ring. The UIG believe the Zaftra to be using th Underswell as a base of operations for a large and comprehensiv network thought to stretch from Germany to the Ukraine. As of ye the UIG have no clues. Undercover Shi Yukiro Agents have had small amount of luck in establishing that the Zaftra are defiantl here and thought to be holed up in some old sub-structures, whic were used during spire construction and never filled in.

The presence of the Organisatzia here terrifies the populace but i reality the Russians tend to keep a tight ship, and as long a everyone behaves life is calm, anyone who doesn't comply i brutalised or killed.

PLOT IDEAS
1. The Division (non-E.I.) must gain residence in the Spire and cause chaos, possibly ruining the reputation of the place.
2. A Citizen has been murdered in her apartment, there are sign of interrogation.
3. The Division must recover (or sabotage) a prototype weapor from the Heavy Weapons Training Facility.
4. Spy on a conference of E.I. scientists discussing their finding from the Biochemical Research Lab.
5. Enemy Agents storm a public shopping area in a Spire trying t get to a top secret lab.
6. Your Division must drop out of a plane and land on the side o a Spire, infiltrate and leave with some important information o equipment.
7. An explosion occurs in the Psi Ops department. A womar wreathed in green fire leaps from a window in the side of the Spire and flees.
8. The Zaftra are getting too big for their boots, slow them dowr by feeding them with false information but don't let them know the Corporation is privy to their activities.
9. Assassinate the leader of the Zaftra.

OPEN CITIES

Some cities were not damaged too badly in the wars and as such are still functioning today. They are very much like the cities of the 21st century with modern conveniences and problems. These are referred to as Open Cities and many Citizens prefer them to the Spires, although they are harder to police and so in general have higher crime rates, more disease and overall worse conditions. Two of the most famous Open Cities are Los Angeles (often called Neuvo Angelos) and Tokyo.

Tokyo Open City and Archology (Japan)

Tokyo is one of the few cities not to be heavily damaged in the wars. Instead of a Spire City, Tokyo remains much the same as it always was. It has a fairly low crime rate with the exception of the Shinjuku district which has become a black and neon crime emporium dominated by Ai-Jinn employed Yakuza and biker gangs known as Bosuzuka. Space is at a premium in Tokyo and the trend to build upwards is still popular. It is epitomised by the Tokyo Archology which rises 1500 metres above the cityscape. A magnificent union of architecture, design, function and ecology it boasts gleaming glass domes alive with small forests, gardens, streams and parks. The Archology is well guarded and immaculately kept. Everything is of the finest quality and only the richest of Tokyo's Agents and Citizens can afford to live within its walls.

A training program for advanced combat telepaths is known to exist in the Archology, which focuses on using Telepathics to augment close combat effectiveness utilising the disciplines of telekinesis, prescience and jump.

RELIC CITIES

In times gone by, all nations had powerful religions and many of the cities of the old world arose around and housed religious ideals. The Order of The Faith control several cities and sites which once held great religious significance. These are known as Relic Cities and are the bastions and training grounds of the Order. The belief in these sacred places has been rekindled and the Devoted of the Order now guard their cities fiercely. Once again these places are as sacrosanct and revered as they once were. Relic Cities act as reservoirs of faith; the telepathic energies of the Faithful well up in the cities resulting in profound effects. They radiate power and instill into those who visit them a sense of awe.

This is not imagined, the quantity of telepathic energy in these cities is so high that acolytes of the Order who use telepathy within their walls do not use up TE points when using their Telepathic powers. For this reason alone a Relic City has never been taken by force. Many also find their innate Telepathic power augmented by the city's presence.

The Jerusalem Relic City

Located in Israel, Jerusalem was once home to the world's three major monotheistic religions. By the year 2010 Jerusalem had become a crowded metropolis with an incongruous mix of ancient and modern. The Order has reversed this process and Jerusalem now looks much as it did thousands of years ago. The defences are almost exclusively telepathic and mass transit has been eliminated. Old fashioned markets dominate commerce, and for anyone wishing to live a modern life, Jerusalem is best avoided. Some very basic technology is there to assist with maintaining the city in a viable state. Technology for the sake of convenience and leisure are contrary to the ideals of the Faith and so absent. Agents entering Jerusalem will find it nearly impossible to bring in technology, as the city is tenaciously guarded. Acolytes of the Faith police the districts and continually monitor for unrest and potential trouble.
Politically, Jerusalem represents the capital of the Order of the True Faith. Their most powerful Acolytes reside here and their most important decisions are made within its walls.

Overlooking the city is Mount Scopus where the majority of the Order's telepaths are trained. The mountain offers a great strategic advantage when defending the city, not least because of the concentration of telepaths there.

Angkor Relic City

This vast city of temples in Cambodia marks a major enclave of the Order. The temple complex spans some 70km making it one of the largest single strongholds in the world. Its ancient structures, first built as Hindu temples, are now overgrown with huge trees which invade every corner of the complex. Siem Reap is at the centre of the structure and acts as one of the Order's HQs ruled by Sensai Kambu. The city is a beacon to the Faithful, but those wishing to reside near the fabled complex must live in the Suryavarman City at Angkor Wat. Only the Devoted of the Order may take up residence within the Ancient Temple City itself.

Telepaths claim to be able to siphon power from the Temple City. These claims would seem to be true according to witnesses of the Ankgor Telepaths in battle. During the Corporate Wars, Angkor was besieged several times but was never even close to being taken. This indomitable security seeks to fortify the belief of the Faithful and thus strengthen the Order. Anyone seeking to overthrow the Order would need to take Ankgor, which is daunting by any soldier's standards.

Plot Ideas

1. The Division are sent to steal a telepathic relic from Jerusalem.
2. The Division must discover the source of the power which replenishes Telepathic Energy.
3. Information must be acquired on the training school on Mount Scopus.
4. The Order is thought to have kidnapped a particularly barbaric high ranking Agent, he must be recovered.
5. Rumours exist of the Order using unknown forms of Telepathy.
6. The Order and Comoros are holding secret talks in Angkor, find out what they are about.
7. The Division must install bugging equipment in a Relic City.
8. Three Order of The Faith Crusaders turn up and demand the Division come with them to a Relic City for questioning.
9. As part of an Order / Corporate cooperation scheme, the Division are required to act as guards in a Relic City.

Sixteen Ai-Jinn saboteurs clustered around a widening hole atop the enormous Xalapa reliquary. The golden roof had predictably been reinforced with a layer of hardened silicon glassite, slowing down the cutting laser, but the extraction was more or less on schedule nonetheless. In a few moments the famed Femur of St. Catherine would be in Ai-Jinn possession, shattering the sanctity of the original Relic City of Vera Cruz and providing the Ai-Jinn with a vastly improved bargaining position against the Order. Most of the sixteen Agents were already privately anticipating their rewards.

The woman sailed up over the edge of the roof in a gentle arc that brought her bare feet quietly down upon the golden surface. She wore nothing but a thin, flowing white robe beneath an antique silver cuirass, her head was bald and her arms outstretched as if in blessing, and a flickering golden nimbus hung around her like mist. Eight of the Agents moved away from the hole in a defensive pattern and opened up with a selection of automatic weapons; laser pulses, plasma bursts and bullets flashed into steam when they met the golden haze surrounding the woman, leaving her unscathed. Two of the other saboteurs, more specifically equipped for the mission, raised Gemini Mosquito pistols, but before they could fire the Psitropine darts they were buffeted by a terrible, invisible force and dashed screaming from the rooftop. The Agent operating the cutter clung doggedly onto the tool, trying to finish the job in the hope that the rest of the Division could somehow cover him, until the same unseen fist smashed into him too and hurled him from the top of the reliquary with his chest caved in.

The remaining Agents gripped whatever handholds they could find - stanchions, buttress tops, the still-hot edges of the hole - and clung on grimly, drawing knives, swords, clubs with their free hands. The woman began to walk across the golden tiles. An expression of beatific calm appeared on her face and two wickedly curved lines of pale green fire appeared in her outstretched hands as she moved inexorably forward towards the defilers.

OLD CITIES

> *We build our computers the way we build our cities: over time, without a plan, on top of ruins.*
>
> *Ellen Ullman*

Where great cities once stood now lie wrecks. What are commonly referred to as Old Cities are now the last refuge of the poor and hunted. In 2231 the Shi Yukiro struck, they had finally mastered a perfect global defence and were able to attack without the fear of counterattack. They made unreasonable demands of the West insisting on tithes of food and resources in exchange for safety from Japan's D-Shift strikes. The west would not comply. This was one of the turning moments in the Corporate Wars and the end result created the hazardous hell holes which are the Old Cities. This was, of course, not the case in Japan where their cities stood strong behind the defence systems. The UIG are still technically in governance of the Old Cities but their efforts seem to end at policing them, and aside the reduction of pollution, they make few moves to improve them. The sprawling cities grow in crude messes of scavenged parts and badly built extensions. The weapons used in the wars were mainly designed to eliminate the populace leaving the buildings untouched, so many of the Old Cities are structurally intact, but with decades of neglect and badly failing services they are little more than dirty, squalid nests of crime, disease and corruption.

OLD SHANGHAI - SAMPLE OLD CITY

Shanghai is one of the most risky places to be, yet perhaps the most successful of the Old Cities. The Shi Yukiro attack on Shanghai was carried out with great care so as to avoid damaging the numerous factories that were located there. The city was not captured in the end and the Ai-Jinn calculated that it was not worth the resources to get the factories running and staffed. They have instead been reinstated by individuals who have moved into the city. A small amount of help from the UIG has ensured that, although Shanghai is dangerously polluted, it is relatively prosperous and those who dwell there can at least expect a reasonable standard of life.

The Factory Zone
This area is off limits to those without a UIG permit to work in the factories. Numerous droids patrol the dark roads that lie nestled between the towering metal hulks. Small gangs of criminals manage to make their way in and out despite the UIG's efforts, and this makes the factory zone a dangerous place. The pollution here is rife as no efforts are made to dispose of chemicals correctly and they are normally dumped in areas of wasteland. The factories specialise in the fabrication of heavy components for the vehicle industry. Most Cyberlin frames come from Shanghai.

The City Zone
In the centre of Shanghai lies the commercial district, one of the best that can be found in an Old City, shops exist where (for the right money) most items and services can be procured. Bars and clubs line the streets attracting all kinds into the seedy underworld of drugs, crime and illegal pleasures. The UIG maintain a small vigil here but mostly leave it to the bulked up heavies who work the doors of the various establishments.

The Residential Zone
The UIG maintain a large accommodation facility in Shanghai, prices are a little higher than normal but residents can normally afford it. The security is tight around the facility and this is the one place in Shanghai where people can feel reasonably safe.

The Triads
The triads run Shanghai under the guidance of the Ai-Jinn. They are merciless and viciously territorial. At present a war exists between two main triad groups, the Society of the Lotus and the Red Swords. Each group is being slowly hammered down by the other and are on constant recruitment drives. Often the public are forced into providing services for one of the gangs, and even business is on one side or the other, although not always through choice.

PLOT IDEAS
1. Agents must enter an Old City to find a renegade Agent who has fled to the underground with dangerous information.
2. Rumours persist that part of an Old City is being maintained with Archon Technology.
3. UIG Officers have been going missing in an Old City, the UIG have asked undercover Agents to investigate.
4. It is believed an enemy Corporation has enormous databanks hidden deep underneath an Old City.
5. Controlled Substances (drugs) have been sourced to an Old City.
6. Outcasts are going missing from an Old City at a rate to concern even the Corporations.
7. Illegal gladiatorial fights are going on in the Old Cities.
8. Powerful telepaths are turning the populace of an Old City into a hive mind.
9. The Division must infiltrate the Triads to learn of the Ai-Jinn's plans.

Howling winds buffeted the dropship as it thundered through the atmosphere over Shanghai. Bound tightly into his shock pad by restraining webbing, Agent Frederick Jones struggled to contain the adrenaline pulsing around his body. Maybe some of it was just released stress. He'd been frankly certain that his superiors would take a dim view of the rather messy outcome of his last mission and thus the reward of a promotion to the 3rd Redlands Division had come as a total shock; he afterwards reasoned that the top brass must have seen the potential inherent in his unconventional, maverick strategies despite the somewhat mixed results they'd yielded on the field.

He'd tried making conversation with the six grim-faced men surrounding him, a little bonding with his new team, but they had closed up like granite statues. Perhaps, Jones, reflected, they were reluctant to embrace the newest member of their Division until after their first drop together. If that was the case, he couldn't wait to get started. As if responding to his thoughts, the ramp swung away, and each of the other Agents threw themselves from their pads and out of the dropgate as their restraints clicked free. Jones followed them without a moment's hesitation.

His gravline caught him and slowed his fall while he was still plummeting through the cloud layer. He could feel the pounding of the rain even through his armour and the wind hammered at him with a force sufficient to set his teeth on edge. The cloud layer seemed to be going on for a long time and it took Jones a moment to realize that it was actually a dense billow of industrial smog that left a thin film of opaque black grease over the front of his visor. With an effort, fighting the howling gale, he brought up a hand and wiped the glass clean.

Shanghai spread out beneath him like the corpse of a bloated mutant spider. Thick rivers of dark toxins insinuated out into the surrounding wasteland like blackened, wasted arms, chemical fires were belching, unnatural torches thrust into a carcass of stained concrete and twisted metal. The flickering, shimmering lines of traffic flowed like diseased blood around the broken buildings and shattered factories that clawed up to him like withered talons. Jones' first thought was that he was in fact dropping into Hell. His second was to register, belatedly, that not every promotion was necessarily a reward.

LONDON OLD CITY

SHI YUKIRO AGENT OF CLAN HITORI

SECTION II
PEOPLE AND PLACES

MINOR CORPORATIONS

This section lays out various aspects of the people and places in the world of Corporation; these will add depth to your game and assist with creating interesting and believable scenarios.

MINOR CORPORATIONS

Although Earth is dominated by the major Corporations there is still room for some competition. This often takes the form of minor Corporations, a few of these companies are independent but many operate under the umbrella of the larger Corporations. Which companies are owned by who is not usually common knowledge amongst the Citizenry.

Minor Corporations do not own vast tracts of land as the larger ones do but are impressive in their own right. They employ Agents who are every bit as effective as the ones used by their larger brothers. Some Agents resent the Major Corporations and enjoy the position that working for a smaller company gives them. Generally they are more respected and valued by their co-workers and employers, although their rates of pay and equipment access tend to be lower.

Below are listed some of the many minor Corporations, feel free to expand upon them and use them as antagonists or allies in your games. Many of these companies are featured in other books.

Abbassi Psi Systems	Psion-based Technology	Com
Aegis Defence Tech	Personal Protection	Ind
Air-Lyte	Specialist Laser weapons	SY
Air-Tight	Alibis a speciality	Ind
A-pork-alypse Now	Pork Themed Food Chain	Ind
Anascan	Optical Cybernetics	SY
Anzeiger Military Systems	Weapons	WF
Aries	Cultural Educators	Com
Australasian Freestate Waste Management	Waste Disposal	Ind
AXE	Deep Space Exploration	Ind
Bright & Sunny Media	Media Giants	Ind
Cappali	Designer Accessories	EI
Cycom Communications	Communications Hardware	SY
Cyrebrum	A.I. Architecture	Ind
Datanetica	Cybernetic Processing	SY
Doore Industries	Bounty Hunting Aids	Ind
Eldoran Relic Reclamation Authority	Xenotech Recovery	Ind
Eurasian Family Services	Domestic Insurance	EI
Gemini Bioware	Biotechnology	Ind
Gentex	Targetting Technology	Ind
Gotcha!	Bounty Hunters	Ind
Hachiman	Cybermunitions	SY
Hong Kong Autometrics	Cyberlins and Cyberframes	AJ
Huang's Bar and Grill	Food Chain	AJ
Itoma Xenjin	Psyche Matrix Creation	Ind
Iyo	Domestic Droids	Ind
Jictar Hunting Authority	Off-World Hunting	EI
Kildanna	Penal Colony	UIG
Knox	Specialist Explosives	Ind
Krieg	Cosmetic Cybernetics	EI
Kuang Arm Concern	Budget Weaponry	AJ
Ku Hin	Bounty Hunters	AJ
Lanzas	Bounty Hunters	Ind
Liberty Black	Covert Ops Cybernetics	Ind

Mars Mineral & Mining	Martial Mining Company	Ind
Masuhara	Bounty Hunters	Ind
Mikuro Nanosystems	Nanotechnology	Ind
Multymeat	Synthetic 'meat'	Ind
Munashii	Cult Cybernetics	Ind
Omega	Field Equipment	Ind
Pan Lee Reactive Defence	Automated Security	AJ
Reaver Cybertech	Military Cyberware	Ind
Richenbacher	Plasma Technology	Ind
Shanghai Cyberlin Concern	Cyberlin Manufacture	AJ
Shim	Budget Weaponry	AJ
Shinjitsu	Mapping Technology	SY
Shirakawa	High-end cybernetics	SY
Smeak Radio	Anarchic Radio	Ind
Spire Craft	Spire Macrostructure	AJ
Taurus	Martial Academy	Com
Takata	Precision Technology	SY
Tracer-Li	Industrial Cybernetics	AJ
Tu-Chin	Nanotechnology	AJ
Two Snakes Medical	Medical Technology	Ind
Universal Nuclear Fuels	Worldwide Fuel	UIG
United International Finance	Worldwide Finance	UIG
V.K.Euronetics	Polymorphic Cybernetics	EI
WFTF	Bounty Hunters	WF
WWL	World Weltball League	Ind
Yaeger and Stanton	Assault Technologies	WF

LANZAS
FUGITIVE CAPTURE AND DETAINMENT

DON'T WORRY, THEY WON'T GET FAR

Lanzas is a privately run bounty hunting coalition. Anyone can work for Lanzas on temporary contract. Catherine Lanzas (formerly of the Western Federation) runs the coalition and always has a full list of quarry.

Agents and UIG (particularly Malenbrach) sometimes work for Lanzas in their spare time, either for the thrill of the chase or for extra money. Occasionally Lanzas will work in cooperation with the Corporations to capture a mutual enemy or to recover targets selected by the UIG.

Lanzas has its headquarters in Hawaii, which is built on land owned by UNFL (Universal Nuclear Fuels Ltd.). UNFL enjoys the security that having Lanzas nearby affords.

Lanzas maintains a subterranean prison complex which is policed by UIG assigned Officers. The inmates are kept for short periods of time until they can be tried under UIG law for the crimes committed.

Although Lanzas works primarily in legitimate bounty captures and usually surrenders the captive to the UIG for *fair* trial, they can also be convinced to assign private bounty hunters to unofficial missions to capture targets who are surrendered immediately to the client, bypassing the UIG. Only the trusted can make use of this service and no official paperwork changes hands.

NOTABLE MERCENARIES

CATHERINE LANZAS
Head of Lanzas FC&D
Rank 10
Level 28
Ex-Western Federation

Catherine has a frank, businesslike manner with little time for combat, although she does excel at it. Her appearance is of a cruel faced woman in her mid 30s with short, pale hair and dark eyes. Her favoured weapons are pistol and sword which she applies to an Archon Pattern Plasma Pistol (Critical on 1/1-10/10, triple damage on criticals) and a re-engineered Shi Yukiro Ion katana. She left the Western Federation after she realised she would never ascend past rank 7 due to the twisted machinations of high level politics.

EMILE BROCHE
Rank 3
Level 6
A French freelance bounty hunter specialising in assassination over distance. His skill with a sniper rifle is bordering on the impossible due to advanced sighting and stability augmentations. (Gains +8 per round for aiming.) He is able to create his own electronic tracking missiles for difficult targets. Emile is slim, tanned and always well dressed. He commands a high price as most of his targets are leaders of some standing.

JAKE TANNER
Rank 4
Level 10
Jake loves being a bounty hunter. He works full time for Lanzas and seldom fails. Jake is a large man specializing in piloting hovercopters and tracking prey who have taken to the barrens. His honed survival skills and tracking knowledge mean few evade him outside of the cities. He commands a pack of 3 cybernetic attack dogs who aid his hunts, and uses a Masterbuilt laser rifle and plasma knife.

BOUNTIES

Bounties are based on two factors, the threat of the quarry and the severity of the crime. Below are some example bounties. For more in depth information about bounty hunting see the Eastern Bank. Below is the sum paid to the bounty hunter.

EXAMPLE BOUNTIES

Threat	Crime	Bounty
Low	Minor	1,000
Medium	Minor	2,000
Medium	Moderate	4,000
Medium	Significant	8,000
High	Significant	40,000
High	Extreme	80,000

THE AUSTRALASIAN FREESTATE

DESIGNATED IFZ

Australasia is an IFZ, or International Free Zone. This means that it is not currently owned by any Corporations and there are no laws governing it. In reality this means that most of Australasia is an abandoned wasteland. It is occupied by the parts of society that have nowhere else to go or those who need to pursue their interests without scrutiny. The Great Desert Penal Centre is based in the middle of the two great deserts on the shores of Lake Carnegie. It is run privately by Lanzas, a small Hawaii based Corporation that specialises in the capture and detainment of fugitives. Much of the Freestate has become a dumping ground for toxic waste and unusable or outdated machinery. Scavengers spend much of their time combing the junkyards looking for salvageable goods that the Corporations have dumped there. Mutation is commonplace among the residents due to the high radiation levels inherent in practically every habitable region. If they escape death these people can develop unusual abilities such as increased regeneration rates and strong telepathic powers to the point that they can affect the minds of others.

Other places of interest in the Freestate are the cities of Canberra and Ayers, both in Australia. The previous capital, Canberra, continues to be a thriving city where most of the facets of city life can still be seen, albeit poor, filthy and riddled with crime. Ayers is a newer city founded in 2122 by the Outcasts from the other inhabited areas. It is constructed from the shells of abandoned vehicles and sheets of iron from long destroyed underground bunkers. The mazes of tunnels are like rabbit warrens and any who enter had best know what they're doing, as the planet's most undesirable elements gather there in dark corners. A Corporation Agent or UIG Officer would receive no respect in Ayers and would be instantly killed and butchered for his cybernetics and organs. Many outlawed cyberneticists come here to aid those who wish it and receive large amounts of under the counter goods and favours for their work. Leaving and entering the Freestate is a task in itself. There are no ports or shuttle stations, only the Skybridge Terminal at Dampier Arch and the Teleport Station at Sturt which are both run by the UIG and guarded with detachments of Cyberlins. The teleport station is used to import waste and junk for dumping. Entry and exit is under your own power and it is likely that whatever form of transport you arrived on will have been stripped for parts or stolen when you return to it.

Well yes, on the one hand, it's a radioactive hellhole full of mutants, outlaws, madmen and butchers. On the other, if you need to hide something or someone, there's no better place. Just make sure you put them somewhere safe. Of course, in the AFS, that's the real trick.

-attr: Zack Adams, freelance technical consultant/soldier of fortune

THE TELEPORT STATION AT STURT

A.M.S

ANZEIGER MILITARY SYSTEMS

WHERE IS ANZEIGER?

The Anzeiger Orbital is a 30 minute shuttle ride from Earth with flights leaving daily from Washington, Delhi and Capetown. Travel expenses are refunded on purchases in excess of 10,000¢.

AMS RETALIATOR

DAM 5D8+5   **COST 20,000¢**   **Long Range**   **Rate 1**   **EMPS 20**

This is a two handed kinetic cannon which fires powerful, low energy loss shells. The weapon comes with an anti-gravity unit, which means it can be wielded one handed by anyone, and better still can be shoulder mounted leaving both hands free.

SYSTEM

The Retaliator can make a free shot each round if shoulder mounted and plugged into the process socket. The internal A.I. on the Retaliator has a base Ranged AT of 10 and can fire once each round. It gains +1 for each level of Internal A.I. of the user.   It is considered a heavy weapon, although when shoulder mounted you can use both hands freely.

AMS PROMETHEUS

DAM D6   **COST 4,000¢**   **Medium Range**   **Rate 1**   **EMP Immune**

This weapon is a great step forward from the standard issue flame thrower. It uses the same standard napalm canisters but focuses the flames in a narrower, hotter cone causing far more destruction.

SYSTEM

The Prometheus acts like a normal flame thrower but ignores armour. Considered a heavy weapon.

AMS ICE SHADOW

DAM D8   **COST 1,200¢**   **Medium Range**   **Rate 2**   **EMPS 8**

A small pistol undetectable with most modern methods, which has a water reservoir. The water is frozen solid inside the weapon and compressed into bullets negating the need for standard ammunition.

SYSTEM

The Ice Shadow has a 90% chance to be undetected with contemporary weapon detection technology. Considered a Light Firearms. A half pint of water makes the equivalent of 1 clip (use a SMART clip as a references for bullet use).

AMS AVENGER L.E.S

DAM 3D6x10   **COST 40,000¢**   **Long Range**   **Rate 4**   **EMPS 13**

A four barrel **Laser Emplacement System** generally used for fixed defence but is fully collapsible to make it portable. When collapsed it can be carried by 3 people. It can be fully erected in less than 2 minutes by a proficient user (has the Specific Weapon License). Installation in car sized or larger vehicles is possible. The range of this weapon allows for anti-aircraft fire.

SYSTEM

Requires Support Weapons

The weapon weighs 200 kg. This will typically take 2-3 Agents to carry.

This weapon requires a **Specific Weapon Licence** to use or own on Earth.

This weapon requires energy cells as ammunition which it uses at a rate of 1 per shot.

MILLER-UREY
OFF WORLD BIO-RESEARCH

If we knew what we were doing it wouldn't be research.

Albert Einstein

A few hours away from Earth in a synchronised orbit lies Miller-Urey, a man-made planetoid upon which the UIG conduct Lifework. After the Corporate Wars the Earth was left torn and bloodied, the ecosystems were runied and although many believe nature will claw her way back, there are few signs of it yet, and little evidence it will happen in the near future.

Miller-Urey was conceived and funded by the UIG. A large mass of space debris and rock was towed towards the Earth and fused together to form an uneven and varied landmass of approximately 5,000 square km. The bare lump was then given atmosphere and terrain at enormous expense. All Corporations were given the opportunity to invest in Miller-Urey in exchange for the right to research there.

With the exception of the Order of the True Faith, the major institutions and some of the minor ones took the opportunity and paid the UIG. Miller-Urey now sits at the forefront of environmental and biological research. Of course, more goes on within the biolabs of Miller-Urey than any individual party will ever know.

The reality of Miller-Urey is a planetoid heaving with artificially created life forms subjected to hyper-evolution via the use of controlled mutagens. From soaring plant structures and bio-minerals to savage carnivores and blind, mindless food creatures, everything imaginable battles for survival on the surface, in the oceans and deep underground.

A few species of plants and animals have proved promising but as yet the UIG are unwilling to unleash new strains of organisms onto Earth. The Corporations are becoming frustrated as they had expected their research to yield profit long ago. Now the monies have been paid, the Corporations are unwilling to stop their research and continue to engineer aberrations in the hope they will prove to be commercially useful in the near future.

TOPOGRAPHY

The Corporations who took advantage of the Miller-Urey Project were each allocated an environmental zone to research. This way each would hopefully be single minded in their work and there would be less inter-Corporation conflict. The zones are controlled by the way Miller-Urey angles towards the sun. Additionally it can be rotated on all axes ensuring climatic conditions are continually maintained.

ADMINISTRATION

Miller-Urey is divided into seven zones of differing climates and terrains. Each one of these zones is controlled by a faction of scientists who are dedicated to unearthing the mysteries and testing the limits of their particular zone. At present the zones are allocated as in the table below, but this can change if circumstances demand.

The zones are sectioned off from one another via energy fields which prevent cross-pollination of different species from different zones. There is generally a small area about 1km wide which separates two climatic zones. These are dead zones where no experimentation is supposed to occur. These dead zones provide a 'safe' road access around Miller-Urey.

PLACES ON MILLER-UREY

The UIG Evolution Laboratory is in an area of deep jungle in Tigera. It is located in the same approximate area as the Western Federation Labs but is sufficiently large to allow both groups of researchers to go about their work in relative peace. The Evolution Lab is a general laboratory and command centre where the whole facility can be monitored and a broad spectrum of valuable research done.

Miller-Urey was designed as a dedicated research facility. There are certain controls in place. We can quarantine the facility in an hour, we can sterilize it in a day, and if it ever becomes absolutely necessary we can throw it into the sun. Regrettably, none of these controls are available on Earth. The answer, gentlemen, remains no.

-UIG response to WF proposition for Terran beta-testing of Species 22, 13th April 2443

TIGERA

The Western Federation are based in the climatic zone known as Tigera. This area is mostly rainforest which changes to cloud forest and then falls off to an area of temperate woodland. The UIG are convinced that the rainforest holds some of the greatest potential to researchers so they have established their Evolution Laboratory in this area. Tigera Forest is huge covering almost 1,000 square km. The WF focus their research efforts on improving animal strains and genetically stable plant research. Due to the nature of the climate though, an enormous number of BIOs (Bio-engineered

MILLER-UREY ENVIRONMENTAL VARIATION AND CORPORATE DIVISION

ZONE	NAME	ENVIRONMENT	MAIN PRESENCE
Zone 1	Tigera	Mixed Forest / Jungle Regions	Western Federation
Zone 2	Ashtan	Desert, Steppe, Mountain	Eurasian Incorporated
Zone 3	Aqua Palestra	Oceanic, Sea Bed	Shi Yukiro
Zone 4	Infernus	Subterranean	Comoros
Zone 5	Ornus	Polar, High Altitude Forest, Tundra	Ai-Jinn
Zone 6	Canathikta	Grassland, Savannah	Gemini Bioware
Zone 7	Palus	Swamp, Marshland	Two Snakes Medical

Independent Organism) are present in Tigera's jungles simply though a process of collateral evolution and experimental accidents. This makes the wilds of Tigera a hazardous place to go. Rumours persist that the BIOs are not naturally occurring and they are the results of a WF Combat BIO Program being conducted from a secret facility. (See page 214)

ASHTAN

Ashtan consists of hundreds of square miles of barren desert and sheer mountains. Eurasian Incorporated felt justifiably cheated when they were allocated this hellhole. The temperature is scorching and life is loathed to grow here. Some of the mountain terrain can be convinced to harbour a little life but the sheer lack of biomass prevents the researchers from instigating any really interesting ecosystems. Instead E.I. have built a huge complex of labs here and mostly ignore their outdoor work, (much to the displeasure of the UIG). E.I. create creatures known as BIOs. They employ nanotech engineers, biologists, geneticists, ethologists and muticians to create creatures from nightmare for possible military applications. The labs are protected from breaches by teams of Agents and environmental lockdown procedures. Due to these precautions escapes have been few. The UIG don't agree outright with E.I.'s research, but after giving them the dregs of the planetoid they have little choice but to accept the consequences. After all, E.I. are not in breach of contract.

AQUA PALESTRA

In the vast oceans of Miller-Urey lie the research labs of the Shi Yukiro. Aqua Palestra is almost exclusively ocean with small areas of land which allow for lakes and rivers to exist. The majority of the Shi Yukiro labs are underwater in large polymer shells. Some of Aqua Palestra's more unusual inhabitants include giant sub-aquatic plants that reach up to the surface, sometimes breaking through to create what look like floating forests or islands. Deep below, the vast *Pollemaris*, originally designed to act as a harvestable, fast breeding whale, stalks the depths hunting prey to quell its hunger. Numerous more mundane creatures can also be found carving out new ecological niches in the deep waters. As far as the Shi Yukiro are concerned, Aqua Palestra is certainly worth the time and money. They are eager to understand how alien aquatic systems may work, and are continually finding new ways to build, work and survive in the inhospitable environments of the ocean. They consider that FarDrive technology will soon be theirs and it won't be long before their colonisation skills are tested.

INFERNUS

The tunnels of Infernus reach for miles underground knotted with caves, sinkholes and gorges. Comoros scientists mainly work above ground in surface labs but some of the caves are so deep and inaccessible that they are forced to build small laboratories deep in the tunnels. The creatures that live in the caves are many and varied. Some live in aquatic pools, others cling to rock walls and ceilings hoping to catch unwary prey with dangling, whip like tentacles. A few large and dangerous organisms can be found at the top of the food chain, grown by the Comoros muticians with the intent of creating powerful defence BIOs. Experiments into non-photosynthetic plant life are also pursued as Comoros feel there is a market for it back on earth.

AQUATIC BIO. DESIGNATION EPSILON TEST WAVE C/DD4

ORNUS

Ornus is desolate for the most part but the Ai-Jinn take their work seriously. The majority of the zone is dominated by open polar landscapes, occasionally broken by ridges of high altitude mountains and, in rare instances, small forests. The Ai-Jinn have taken to the climate well, their competent off-world mining operations have given them endless supplies of fuel to keep their labs comfortable and well powered. The work carried out in Ornus is unusual in that the Ai-Jinn are trying to create intelligent BIOs, which can explore and clear cold worlds, with the eventual idea that they will create a way for humans to inhabit new planets. The BIOs can then be moved onto another world, used as labour or destroyed as appropriate. It is a common site on Ornus to see groups of unidentifiable creatures wandering the ice plains obviously trying to accomplish some group based task. The Ai-Jinn believe they take every step necessary to make sure none of the BIOs become too intelligent, organised or free thinking.

CANATHIKTA

In the Grasslands of Canathikta rises the soaring Tower of Gemini mirroring the headquarters at Vladivostok on Earth. Gemini ended up with Canathikta for reasons no-one can really fathom. They seem to do what is expected of them and engineer a variety of plants and creatures which will grow successfully on grasslands. The herbivores they have made are among the first creatures that the UIG are considering letting onto Earth and the seeded grasses they have created look to be an obvious solution to hunger in the Old Cities. Gemini could thus make a lot of money when the UIG decide to let the BIOs and plants onto Earth. Gemini, however, seem not to be pushing this side of their business. If anything they are stepping up their bio-implant industry and it seems Miller-Urey is key in the exercise. The current theory is that Gemini are using hidden labs under the surface to experiment with merging BIO organs and humans to create a new wave of human augmentations. This theory is naturally both compelling and concerning.

PALUS

From here Two Snakes research medicine in every form. They conduct very little work on creating creatures and plants, but instead purchase them from other Corporations and analyse them for potential biological and medical applications. So far little has been yielded, but as the creatures and plants hyper-evolve their metabolisms change and they begin to synthesise chemicals that no-one had expected. An example of this is the R-Drug (page 11) used by Agents which causes body parts to regrow to the original DNA plan of the organism. Thus arms will grow back if severed. Two Snakes' influence and power have grown considerably since investing in Miller-Urey and they look to be strengthening each day.

PEOPLE ON MILLER-UREY

Agent Layne Delacroix

Western Federation Field Warden. Rank 5 / Level 7

Agent Delacroix stands 5ft 9" with short cropped dark hair and a lean but muscular build. She comes across as brutish and foul mouthed but is an excellent soldier. She was recruited to Tigera after a series of unsuccessful campaigns on Earth where she repeatedly took units of covert troops into enemy territory to accomplish espionage missions. Her reckless approach (although successful) and taste for exotic drugs was incompatible with the Western Federation's ethos, and she was offered either expulsion or an assignment on Miller-Urey defending the field scientists from the life forms they were studying. With no need for subtlety and enough mind affecting substances growing on the trees to kill her, Delacroix thought she had struck gold. She has recently taken it upon herself to become an expert on extra-terrestrial life and is knowledgeable in the field of behavioural science. She normally arms herself with a customised plasma pistol and plasma sword, which she maintains is the only way to cut through the tough carapaces that many BIOs seem to naturally evolve over time.

Dr Laydian Okoth

Comoros, Senior Mutician. Rank 6 / Level 2

Okoth, originally from Nigeria, is a tall, thin man of some years with a short white beard; his name is synonymous with suffering and perversion. In the eyes of Comoros the man is an aberration and should be executed, but his results are such that the UIG insist he remains employed as a mutician. Thus Comoros would rather have some degree of control over him than give him over to the UIG, where he would be given free run of the genetics labs. Okoth is a paranoid man who believes he is persecuted for his genius. He is wary of strangers and assumes everyone is jealous of his ability and position. Consequently he keeps a perimeter of guards at a safe distance. For more personal security however, Okoth maintains a small unit of genetically engineered and mutated BIOs who are totally loyal to him if a little unpredictable around others. For the most part Okoth is left to his own devices while Comoros watches the monster create more monsters against their better judgement. Better the devil you know than the devil you don't.

PARASITIC BIO. DESIGNATION SIGMA. TEST WAVE PP/N4D

Dr Vaasala Laiha
Gemini Bioware, Head of Miller-Urey Operations.
Rank 6 / Level 3

Laiha is a woman of average height and unremarkable appearance. She has long blond hair and pale blue eyes telling of her Scandinavian descent. Although Laiha has a doctorate in pharmacology she seldom refers to it. She was made Head of Operations based purely on her ability to get things done and motivate her staff.

She studied for the doctorate while on Miller-Urey so she could better understand the work of her employees. Laiha is from Finland and was headhunted by E.I. but she refused them, claiming they were "unstructured and clumsy children messing with money and life as though they were toys."

Gemini maintains a far more professional approach that suits Laiha well. She takes everything seriously and has no time for jokers and time wasters. Lahias only vice lies in men, she is an insatiable man eater who always maintains a stream of suitors attracted by her high position and businesslike manner. The only bad decisions Lahia has made have been about or caused by men.

PLOT IDEAS
1. The Western Federation are training their commandos in the forests of Tigera.
2. Scores of BIOs escape to Earth.
3. A visitor takes a mutagen / biomineral back to Earth.
4. Creatures in the wastes of Ornus have become too smart, perhaps to the point of human intelligence.
5. A team has been lost in the depths of Infernus, the Division must extract them despite the combat BIOs there.
6. Find out what really goes on in Canathikta.
7. Infiltrate the facility on Palus and steal a prototype drug.
8. Savage BIOs have escaped from Tigera into other sections of Miller-Urey.
9. Dr Laydian Okoth has decided to restrict access to his labs against UIG wishes.
10. Vaasala Laiha has made a terrible error of judgment and allowed a man to steal important secrets. She begs the Division for help.
11. A powerful mutagen has been released onto Miller-Urey by an unknown party. The BIOs are becoming insane and twisted, Miller-Urey is in danger of being destroyed.
12. A ship has crash landed on a remote part of the planetoid, your Division must rescue the crew.
13. The Division must escort and protect a Corporate biologist to her new station on Miller-Urey.
14. Rebels have got onto Miller-Urey and are causing chaos.
15. The Cult of Machina have smuggled one of their own in to find anything of use. Find and stop it.

TOWER OF GEMINI, CANATHIKTA, MILLER-UREY

Transcription Date: 10.04.2500
Transmission Date : 09.04.2500

Intercepted Live Transmission from Dr. G. Artz,
Assistant Mutician to Dr. L. Okoth, Senior
Mutician for Comoros, Infernus, Miller-Urey

ATTENDING OFFICERS
Investigating Officer: Commander C. Bennet, UIG
Incident Control Officer, 1st Class
Scientific Advisor: Dr. T. Cadera, Genobiologist

LOCATION: GENOLAB 4, INFERNUS, MILLER-UREY

Entire Transcript translated from Afrikaans.
For Original Speech see file
Okethtrans10042503.avf.101

21:30:29

Artz Ah, Dr. Okoth, sorry I'm late, the
surface crawlers were all being serviced,
I had to take a bike.

Okoth I have better things to do than listen
to your problems Artz, hurry up and
change, we have an important evening.

Artz Yes Doctor, sorry. Will I need splatter
guards?

Okoth For Christ's sake yes, we're not making
cakes. Now get on with it, I'll prep
the patient.

21:37:17

Artz Hmmm, she's pretty, seems a shame doesn't
it.

Okoth No.

Artz Okay, I'll check the restraints if you
get the specimen from the cold room.
They seem fine, she seems to be coming
round, shall I up the Pronarcol?

Okoth What? No, didn't you read my notes, No
anaesthetic!

Artz Sorry Doctor, should we at least give her
a shot of TDTA, stop her making a noise.

Okoth Very well, 10ccs. Pulse?

Artz Strong, regular.

Unknown   Where am...who are...what...

Okoth Hmmm, good. Dr. Artz, are you comfortable
with this procedure? If not I suggest you
tell me and I will arrange a replacement.
Is there a problem?

Artz Uh, no Doctor. Shall we proceed.

Okoth Wait while I prep the specimen.

21:38:22

Okoth Right, the first incision will run from
here to here down the abdomen, the second
from here to here forming a basic cross
like so. Would you care to make the cut
Dr. Artz?

Artz Tell me again why we aren't using
anaesthetic.

Okoth It was all in my notes, do you wish to
make the incision?

Artz A job this important would be better in
your hands doctor.

Okoth Hmmm...

21:39:18

Okoth Check her pupils for astymia.

Artz Slight excretion from the tear ducts,
redness, swelling and dilation of the
pupils. No astymia.

Okoth Stick to the relevant details Artz.
Dermal clamps please... Good, plasma
scalpel and swab, apply pressure here.
Excellent...cauterizer

21:42:55

Okoth Good, now pass me the specimen.

Artz Her blood pressure is too high Doctor.

Okoth That's okay, she'll be back together in a
minute.

21:43:25

Okoth Amazing....see it heading directly for
the anterior wall, within minutes it will
have embedded it's parasillon and
then....

Artz How will it affect her.

Okoth What?

Artz Nothing, I mean...if she were to come to
harm the specimen might...well...die.

Okoth We'll have to see, research is a long
process. We do what we can, if we fail we
learn from our mistakes and try again.

Transmission End.

A lesson in orbital construction and terraforming, Vastaag is one of the single largest man-made structures in the universe. It is totally dedicated to pleasure which makes it no surprise to learn that it is owned by Eurasian Incorporated. Vastaag is one of E.I.'s single largest sources of income and as a result is guarded by some of the best technology and many of E.I.'s finest Agents. A weeks stay at Vastaag can cost anything from 100¢ for a small room to a cool million for unlimited use of all facilities including food, drink, travel, substances, man-hunting, personal services and accommodation in the famous Illustra Hotel.

STRUCTURE

Vastaag is roughly spherical in shape and orbits the planet Saturn in the Sol system. It has over 30,000 square km of surface area upon which are built thousands of recreational buildings and parks. The centre of the sphere is taken up with energy creation and emergency situation storage. Rumours persist that 95% of the inside of Vastaag is being used for some nefarious purpose and other Corporations repeatedly send Agents to try and find out what. The atmosphere on Vastaag is different depending on where you are. Some sections are humid and hot, others cold and breezy. The sky colour changes on the whim of the weather co-ordinators or wealthy clients. The architecture is varied and stunning, ranging from classical Greek colonnades and Italian arcades to soaring works of modern genius. All terrain types can be found on Vastaag, as can diverse forms of culture and plant-life. If someone desires it, it can probably be found on Vastaag.

PLACES ON VASTAAG

EUROPA (CITY IN NEW EURASIA)

This is the place most newcomers will find themselves when they first visit Vastaag. Europa is an impressive metropolis brimming with luxurious hotels, exclusive shops, fashionable clubs and exotic recreational facilities. Europa is usually maintained in a state of eternal night, this makes sure it's always time to go out and have fun. Although almost everything you can imagine is available in Europa it is well policed both by E.I. and the UIG. There are only a few reported crimes each week and those are normally a result of organised groups or Corporate interaction. New Eurasia is free to visit, all you need to do is pay for your shuttle ticket to Vastaag at 1000 credits.

THE ILLUSTRA HOTEL (EUROPA, NEW EURASIA)

The most expensive hotel in the universe – so they claim. Accommodation rates vary from 5000¢-100,000¢ a night. What do you get for your money? Everything. The sky is truly the limit. Security here is incredible with no reported cases of intruders to date. The Illustra is run by Helena Reimann (Rank 5, Level 6, E.I. Corporate Relations) who can second guess the inner desires of a customer before they open their mouths. A very influential woman indeed.

JICTAR (LAND MASS)

This jungle covers an entire continent and houses the Paladir Guest House where people pay thousands to stay. Included with the week's accommodation is a man-hunt. Outlaws and enemies of E.I. are released into the jungle and hunted down by the guests. The hunted are tracked by their ID chips and stripped of all possessions. The residents may hunt in any manner they desire; knives, helicopters, cyberwolves, etc. If the prey evades them for a whole week E.I. recovers and re-uses them. The one exception to this is Agent Ishida Takamura of the Shi Yukiro (Rank 6, Level 19, Shi Yukiro Assassin of Clan Hitori). They found his chip pressed into the eyeball of one of his hunters. He was never recovered and his current whereabouts is unknown. The Governor of the Guest House – Luger Dekker (Male Rank 5, Level 15, E.I. Nuke) tracked the escapee for three weeks with no luck. A basic pass to Jictar for one week costs 1000¢, the price rises to 30,000¢ for an all inclusive ticket with hunting.

ISLA VIVA (LAND MASS)

This island is a nature lover's paradise. Isla Viva is almost exclusively mixed habitat containing animals and plants engineered on Miller-Urey. A few select ranch hotels are located around the island for paying guests. There are no weapons allowed on Isla Viva as the animals are bred to be passive and the ecosystem is too delicate to be compromised with shootings and loud noises. A week on Isla Viva will cost 1000¢ for one person.

PARADISE ISLE (LAND MASS)

This large island was built with one thing in mind, relaxation. The island is surrounded on all sides by wide sandy beaches and in the centre of the landmass beautiful sun-dappled forests can be found. Nestling among them are villas, ranches and hotels. Paradise Isle has a 'No Technology' policy and no visitor may bring any form of tech to the Isle. The authorities may of course carry what they wish. A week on Paradise Isle will set one person back 1000¢.

CERULEA (LAND MASS)

Heaven to some, hell to others. Cerulea is a retirement colony. The whole complex is full of aging Citizens who wish to forego life-extending medicine and live out their final days in peace and serene happiness. On Cerulea residents may have any basic luxuries they wish to bring (or buy) such as yachts, cars and helicopters. Few of the people on Cerulea are visitors, most have spent their life's earnings to buy a place on this most desirable of retirement resorts. A thirty year retirement plan on Cerulea will cost about 1,000,000¢.

LAND OF WORLDS (LAND MASS)

A magical theme park the size of a small country. The Land of Worlds is where the majority of families spend most of their time when visiting Vastaag. The Land is totally safe and has something for everyone. Hundreds of different exciting rides, adventures and experiences await you in The Land of Worlds. The pricing is aimed at families and will cost 500¢ a week per person for total escapism.

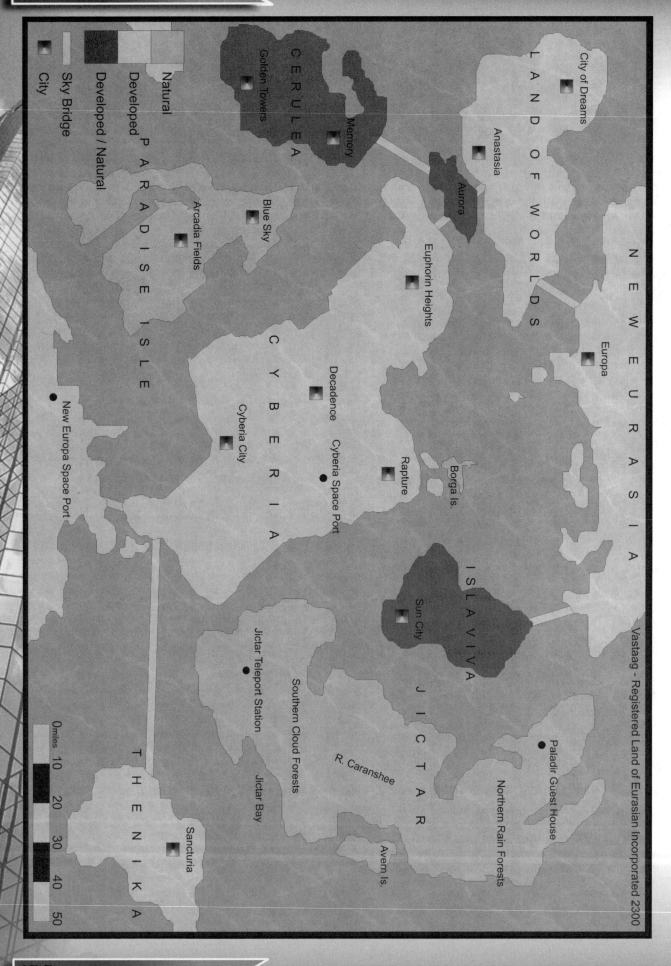

VASTAAG - PROPERTY OF EURASIAN INC.

Vastaag - Registered Land of Eurasian Incorporated 2300

Legend:
- Natural
- Developed
- Developed / Natural
- Sky Bridge
- City

Scale: 0 miles 10 20 30 40 50

LAND OF WORLDS
- City of Dreams
- Anastasia
- Aurora

NEW EURASIA
- Europa

CERULEA
- Golden Towers
- Memory

PARADISE ISLE
- Arcadia Fields
- Blue Sky

CYBERIA
- Euphorin Heights
- Decadence
- Cyberia City
- Cyberia Space Port
- Rapture
- Borga Is.

ISLAVIVA
- Sun City

JICTAR
- Southern Cloud Forests
- Jictar Teleport Station
- Jictar Bay
- R. Caranshee
- Avern Is.
- Northern Rain Forests
- Paladir Guest House

THENIKA
- Sancturia
- New Europa Space Port

CYBERIA (LAND MASS)

This is perhaps the most common yet shameful reason to come to Vastaag. Cyberia is a dark sprawling metropolis where anything goes. If you desire quiet sophistication then try New Eurasia; if you want to sample a whole new way of life and buy the accoutrements to go with it, Cyberia is for you. The basic layout of Cyberia is fairly simple. A huge landmass with every inch covered in cityscape. In the centralisation of Euphorin Heights to the north, the landscape is a little less dense and there is more of a feeling of openness. Cyberia City itself is a totally different matter. The main street (known as Mecca) is a broad functional boulevard but everywhere else tends to be crowded and haphazard as more and more buildings are piled on top of existing ones. E.I. could of course stop this but it all adds to the atmosphere that brings people back to Cyberia time and time again.

Perhaps the strangest thing about Cyberia is the concept of Controlled Crime. Crime would be rampant in Cyberia if not for the E.I. Agents and the occasional show of force by the UIG. This in itself is not unusual, what is odd is that E.I. could wipe out the crime in the city overnight if it wanted to but, of course, that would seriously damage Cyberia's reputation. As long as the crime does not damage the tourism or the Corporation, E.I. is quite happy for it to exist. Most of the crime in Cyberia is drug related; many visitors come here specifically to try the bizarre cocktails of illegal substances available in almost every seedy bar which populate the downtown areas.

Prostitution and Fleshel are both legal in Cyberia, so there are very few problems in that department as far as E.I. are concerned. As long as they get their license fees from the relevant establishments, E.I. are happy to let people get on with what they want to do. The only point of contention are the Fleshel bars which the UIG and other major Corporations abhor. Fleshel is a corrupt blending of flesh and machine to create an erotic experience no holiday maker will forget. Little more need be said about Fleshel other than it stays buried well underground and finding it may be reassuringly difficult.

THENIKA (LAND MASS)

Thenika is the nerve centre of Vastaag, it's here that Vastaag's working populace come each day over the Skybridges, to monitor and control the workings of the planet. All the security systems and mechtronic features of Vastaag feed back to Thenika. Not surprisingly with this much important technical information in one place, Thenika is heavily guarded. Tourists will find entering Thenika a hard task, not least because the land mass itself is virtually deserted, all that can be found there is inhospitable desert continually being walked by all manner of Cyberlins and other mechanical and biological deterrents. Thenika provides the main gateway into the planet's core but even those who work there are only scratching the surface in their underground reinforced installations. What Vastaag contains deeper down, the majority of E.I. employees can only hazard a guess at.

PEOPLE OF VASTAAG

AGENT VINCENT CRUZIER

Rank 4, Level 4, E.I. Public Relations

When powerful, rich or influential people arrive on Vastaag, Vincent is always there to greet them. He is well dressed and handsome with a charm and wit that his guests relish. Aside his devastating social weaponry and intimate knowledge of every part of Vastaag, Vincent will acquire anything and everything for the demanding client. Nothing is too rare, expensive or illegal. Cruzier often works in co-operation with Helena Reimann (Manager of the Illustra Hotel) to make sure guests are indulged in every way conceivable. Agent Cruzier is fiercely loyal to E.I. and does his work only to benefit the Corporation, living a fairly simple life himself. As well as the money generated from Cruzier's work a great deal of blackmail material and useful intelligence is accrued, although it is used sparingly lest Cruzier develop a reputation.

PLOT IDEAS

1. Find out what is inside Vastaag.
2. Clients are paying to hunt illegal targets on Jictar.
3. An A.I. is trying to take over control of Vastaag beginning with the Cyberlins and defence systems.
4. The weather satellites are in chaos, outlaws have broken into the control stations and sabotaged them while holding dignitaries hostage.
5. The Division (if not E.I.) are used as prey in the Jictar Cloud Forests.
6. Agent Ishida Takamura (see Jictar description) approaches the Division asking them to visit Vastaag and capture Luger Dekker. Bring him to Kyoto for a huge reward.
7. The robot toys on the Land of Worlds become self-aware, possibly part of a Droid Liberation Army plan. They hold the visitors hostage demanding rights and land.
8. The Division is ordered to set up an underground informant network in Cyberia.
9. A retired high ranking Agent on Cerulea is giving out information to enemies.
10. Rival high ranking Agents are booked into the Illustra Hotel for talks, spy on them.
11. Cyberia is harbouring Outcasts who have wronged your Corporation. Bring them to justice.
12. It is rumoured E.I. have released some dangerous or intelligent BIOs into Isla Viva to test their reaction to humans.

AGENT VINCENT CRUZIER · VASTAAG · PUBLIC RELATIONS

Pierre Fleury, until yesterday a humble, if highly skilled, electronics engineer, flopped down into one of the sumptuous leather chairs, his mind struggling to cope with all that he had seen and experienced in the last few hours. This place was incredible. The sense bars, the pools, the libraries, pleasure-parks, the broadcast chambers, and everywhere the women, the women! Dizzying sensation threatened to overwhelm him. He looked up at his new acquaintance, the man who had shown him all of this and who he still only knew as Eli, standing by the enormous window and looking out across the great vista of New Eurasia. "Who owns this… this place?" he stammered.

Eli half-turned his head, patrician features sharp in the gathering twilight. "This residence is reserved," he answered in his rich, cultured baritone, "for Eurasian Incorporated's foremost field electronics officer."

Fleury thought for a moment, then shook his head. "I'm sorry, I don't think I know who that is."

Eli turned to face him. "You, Pierre." And as he watched understanding blossom like greedy dawn in Fleury's eyes, the man who today was calling himself Eli had to turn back to the window to mask the hungry triumph on his own face.

UNFL NUCLEAR FACILITY

KILDANNA PRISON, SALVADOR, BRAZIL

Kildanna Prison is a good reason not to break the law, it is used as a holding bay for anyone whose crimes, for any reason, do no warrant depersonalisation, or for those who the UIG deem death i too good for.

To reduce costs, Kildanna Prison contains only one block and n jailers. The building stands 600 metres high and contains a single entry hole in the roof which is fortified and guarded by dozens c tracking lasers, guards and at least a few cyberlins. Prisoners are stripped of cybernetics and possessions, lowered into the hole by antigravity beams and then left to their own devices. Escape is fa from possible. The inside of the prison is made up of dozens o miles of corridors and rooms. There are small supplies of wate which are 'owned' by various factions within the prison. Sewage i discharged through 4 inch pipes making escape by that mean impossible. Food is dropped through the hole at regular interval and again tends to be controlled by prisoner groups. Many wh enter the prison are immediately killed for food or even fun by th hoards of deranged psychotics who stalk the Kildanna tunnels Anyone of interest who enters the prison is generally captured b one of the factions, and offered their lives in exchange for fealty t that faction.

The factions themselves are continually evolving and splitting There is normally a faction for each of the major Corporations as well as some which have been formed by particularly influential dangerous or powerful inmates. It is impossible to list the faction at any one time – they will become apparent very quickly t anyone placed into Kildanna's depths.

MAUI NUCLEAR FACIUTY AND CAPE POWER PLANT, HAWAII

This energy facility is under the control of UNFL – Universal Nuclear Fuels Ltd. It is the single biggest plant of its type in the world and is responsible for 40% of the world's energy production. The station itself is located on the island of Honolulu in Hawaii with the remaining Hawaiian Islands being used by Lanzas to run their Mercenary Corp. UNFL enjoy the protection of having Lanzas nearby and do everything they can to accommodate them.

UNFL also maintain the Cape Barrages which are two enormous tidal barrages that run around the Cape of Good Hope and Cape Horn. These produce another 30% of the worlds energy which is environmentally clean and safe to produce.

UIG HEADQUARTERS LARSEN ICE SHELF, ANTARCTICA

The United International Government has its base on the Larsen Ice Shelf in Antarctica. Under the protective vigil of The Archons they make important decisions and attempt to retain some state of normality on the Earth. They are generally speaking successful. The UIG maintain vast programme facilities and their Officers are expertly trained and armed with the best weapons available. The UIG Central HQ is arguably the best defended base on Earth and to even attempt an assault would be foolish.

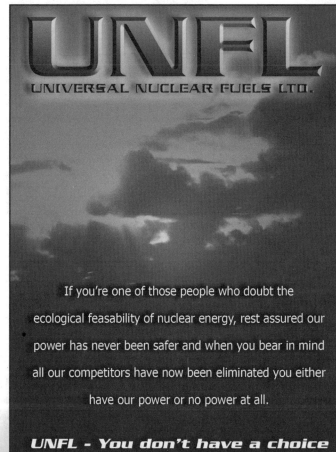

THE ARIES INSTITUTE

The Aries Institute is based in Sandhurst in the South of England but has been run by Comoros since the early 2300's. Aries earned a reputation for producing excellent students who would more often than not go on to become respected workers in their field. Going one better, Aries decided to start educating and training for a longer portion of the students' lives – namely from age 3 to the age of 25, at which point the students would leave and begin their careers, the parents normally produce a genetically enhanced child so they would have aptitudes in key areas. Aries then focuses on this propensity and tailors the child's education to what the parents desire for their offspring. This leads to an adult so adept they are likely to be a world leader in their field.

Typically an education at Aries is beyond the financial scope of most of the population; however some high ranking Agents, UIG officials and particularly successful civilians are able to send a child to Aries. The parents themselves are vetted to make sure the child will be of suitable material and Aries reserves the right to expel any student at any time.
When the term of education is completed the student will invariably be headhunted and offered an extraordinary contract or go into business for themselves.

People from Aries are rare – the institute has 22 classes – one for each age group. Each class consists of 10 students which mean only ten adults from the eldest class can graduate each year. The real total is closer to 6 after expulsions, assassinations and miscellaneous foul play. Aries students seem distant yet focused. They rarely make sense to others as their minds are trained for their career, and their social life has been bizarre at best. Students who are being trained to deal with others, are of course, socially unparalleled. Players are welcome to assume the role of Aries graduates but they must be suitably thought out and created. Aries does not train combatants. It leaves that to its sister company - Taurus.

Kanika Zaman
Governor of Aries – Rank 7, Level 3, Comoros Educator
Originally from Nigeria, Kanika is a shrewd woman with very little spare time, which is evident in her manner. She is a prior student of Aries and it is obvious in her focus and determination. She appears to be an attractive, dark skinned, 35 year old with straight dark hair and a classical, well dressed appearance, but is in fact over 60 years old. Her term in Aries was spent being educated in psychology and she knows exactly how to get anything from anyone. She also has the knack to tell what someone is thinking with uncanny accuracy, which leads the knowledgable to wonder if she practices an illegal form of telepathy. Kanika has an inscrutable integrity and cannot be bought; she is dedicated to her students and is totally uncompromising when it comes to their education. Kanika has few obvious offensive skills but is surrounded by a powerful hard ion shield which is invisible and unobtrusive. Aries is heavily guarded but the security is discreet, capable and led by Ko Li Kwan, a graduate from Taurus. Kanika is wealthy, discerning and socially adept, though cold on initial meeting.

The Order have been blinded by their own dogma. There is no higher calling than the evolutionary success of the human race, and it is the responsibility of the Corporations to ensure that we continue as a race along this path. Even the jealous Shi Yukiro have seen this. Why can the Church not realize it?

- attr: Dilupa Rasheed, Shadow CEO, Comoros

THE TAURUS ACADEMY

The Taurus Academy was established in 2340 in response to the success of its sister company, The Aries Institute. Taurus takes off where Aries stops. All matters regarding combat and tactics are covered at the Taurus Academy. Taurus is equally exacting with its choice of pupils who are selected at the age of 3 to undertake 22 years of rigorous training. The Shi Yukiro are not happy with the Taurus Academy teaching rival Corporations from its main facility in Osaka, especially when under the tutelage of Comoros' chosen masters, but the Independent Commerce Act of 2180 prevents them from openly opposing the situation. Taurus has produced some of the finest military minds, soldiers and Agents ever seen, and as a result has the backing of most of the Corporations. The Order of the True Faith aggressively oppose both Aries and Taurus for taking humans to levels that they would not naturally reach and placing great danger on the status quo of the Earth.

Taurus takes 20 pupils a year and from that selection about 12 graduate. Many die in field operations and as with Aries some are assassinated or die under mysterious circumstances.

Those who graduate from Taurus are usually obvious, they are incredibly efficient at what they do and are often cold and detached. Graduates from Taurus have seen their share of action and most have killed numerous times in the name of education. It is rumoured that Taurus capture and purchase dangerous individuals and use them for student training. The odd manner of Taurus graduates would suggest this is true, but it does not fit in with Comoros methodology, and the law has turned up nothing as yet. Additionally, as many of the high ranking law enforcement officers were trained at Taurus and Aries this theory seems to evade investigation.

Master Uesugi
Master of Melee at Taurus - Rank 8, Level 45, Shi Yukiro Samurai
Uesugi claims descent from the famous Uesugi Clan of ancient Sengoku Japan. He is a calm man of average build and is void of cybernetics although it is thought he is a powerful telepath. His manner is calm and he dresses in a traditional kimono. He specialises in the Ion Katana, for which he has become famous for pioneering entire new forms. Uesugi worked for the Shi Yukiro for most of his life ascending to Rank 8 before reaching a promotional plateau and retiring. Uesugi is a hands-on teacher and runs the Melee School. His physical approach to teaching has so far resulted in the death of 23 students, one of whom was the son of an Ai-Jinn Shadow CEO. This obviously bought great trouble to the Academy and Uesugi was nearly ejected as a teacher.

PLOT IDEAS

1. The Division is instructed to have a student tag along with them on a mission. He must not die.
2. A student has gone missing from the Aries Institute, possibly taken by a rival Corporation to discredit Comoros.
3. One of the missing Archons is thought to be controlling the Taurus Academy. Minerva once did a similar thing (see page 161).
4. Master Uesugi has had his Ion Katana stolen by an exceptional student whose gene therapy has made him mentally unstable.
5. Corporate Intelligence believes Comoros are subliminally altering the minds of the students to assist them in the future.

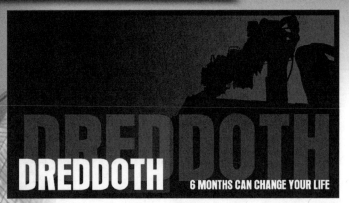

DREDDOTH
6 MONTHS CAN CHANGE YOUR LIFE

Located on Mars, the Dreddoth Mining Colony accommodates approximately 200,000 people. The city of Dreddoth is mostly underground and inhabited mainly by the miners and technicians who work there. Some people choose to set up a permanent home on Dreddoth which is not discouraged but definitely not advised. Dreddoth exists due to the huge mineral seams located there which are easily mined. The pay is exceptional and Earth based Citizens down on their luck can literally turn their lives around by spending a few years mining ore. Originally machines were used to mine, which were equipped with advanced A.I. but after the disaster on Lunas this was never repeated. Dreddoth is owned by *Mars Mineral and Mining*, a company which deals with all Corporations on a level basis. Corporate activity on Dreddoth is not advised as MMM have a monopoly on local mineral supplies and a Corporation who puts themselves out of favour with them will find themselves seriously disadvantaged. Why the Ai-Jinn have not publicly swallowed MMM and made them into a subsidiary is not known.

STRUCTURE
The city itself is about 5 square km and mainly takes the form of long angular corridors 4 metres wide and 3 metres high. Occasionally the corridors open out into large communal zones which have seating areas and commerce stations (shops). The city is very functional and looks it. There is seldom anything that does not serve a direct, practical purpose. No effort has been made to make Dreddoth look appealing, it resembles the inside of a run down airport. Outside the city are enormous cliffs where the majority of the mining takes place. Huge scaffolds and gantries are fitted to the cliff sides and transport cars take miners up and down to the various mining shafts. Three Slave Class Cyberlins are maintained on Dreddoth, which are there for the serious work of boring new tunnels and shifting tons of rock. Despite being Slave Class they have been fitted with some basic weapons to deter would-be trouble makers.

THE POPULACE
The Citizens of Dreddoth are generally a miserable lot who lack clean air and sunshine. Disease is commonplace but mutations are rare. The mining community knows they will not be here long and just knuckle down to work. Those who have chosen to live here permanently must be queried though. There is something innately wrong about a desire to live in Dreddoth.

PLACES OF INTEREST
The Mines - These have existed for many years and much of the tunnel networks are long abandoned. Dreddoth's slum element resides in portions of tunnels making them hazardous to traverse and work in. Disused tunnels are dangerous places as those who get in trouble with the authorities or run out of money tend to flee

there. Rumours exist of small makeshift towns where Dreddoth's cast-offs (exiles, criminals and the insane) live and scavenge.

The Clamps - This huge cavern was originally where huge mining clamps were stored – hence the name. Now the vast caves are home to a thriving pleasure district where anything and everything is possible. The Lord of Dreddoth – Kalmir Sendat actively promotes decadence and debauchery, which he believes will one day make Dreddoth a desirable location for holiday makers, much like Vastaag. Accommodation here is cheap but scummy, sheer deposits are standard.

IMPORTANT PEOPLE

Kalmir Sendat – Lord of Dreddoth
Rank 6, Level 3
Essentially a mayor appointed by Mars Mineral and Mining. He has no open affiliation with any major Corporation and seems to have the success of Dreddoth paramount in his mind. Physically he stands at 6 feet with tight, curly black hair and a smart but loud suit. He is chatty and enthusiastic and is always willing to offer financial support to those with good ideas, as long as it benefits Dreddoth.

Hirstan Weller - Head of Mars Mining Operations
Rank 7, Level 3
The current head of Mine Operations for Mars Mineral and Mining, she is capable and efficient. She maintains two distinct sides to her life – a down to earth, hands-on mining expert and a smooth, steel fisted executive. She appears in her mid thirties with short brown hair and a trim but powerful build. Hirstan is only interested in making sure Dreddoth is as profitable as possible. She has no tolerance of time wasters but is always genial to visitors.

PLOT IDEAS FOR DREDDOTH
1. A bizarre mineral has been found in the Southedge Mines which seems to be *hibernating*.
2. A unit of mining droids go rogue and set up their own camp.
3. An ambassador is visiting Dreddoth, your Division must guard her.
4. An enemy Corporation attempts to take over Dreddoth. MMM asks for help.
5. Ancient technology is found deep in the mines.
6. Assault Telepaths are being held in PsiCages and forced to mine with their powers.
7. Criminals have fled to Dreddoth to lose themselves in the heaving populace.
8. Each year Antigravity Motor Sport racers compete on the surface for a fantastic prize.
9. Hostile life forms are found beneath the planet's surface, their origins unknown
10. Illegal fighting pits are thought to exist in parts of the Colony.
11. Mutants have been found scheming in the mines.
12. Rebels refuse to work in the Northside tunnel, they won't talk about it.

> *Why'd I stay? Oh, all kinds of reasons. For one thing, I've been here long enough to get used to it, and for another, in twenty years of mining I've made enough money to spend every night in the Clamps, livin' it up like a Roman emperor. Got no Clamps back home. And… and the other thing. There's something wrong with me, like there is with a lot of the boys, though they'll not talk about it and nor will I. You seen the slogan? 'Six months can change your life'? Hah! You stay here a little longer, a lot more'll change than just your life.*
>
> *attr: Noah Lamarr, Dreddoth prospector (resident)*

I FEEL THE FLESH STILL CLINGING TO ME, QUIVERING IN THE KNOWLEDGE OF WHAT I HAVE BECOME.

LEVIATHAN, CHIMERA PROPHET OF THE CULT OF MACHINA

THE CULT OF MACHINA

Behold the dawn of steel! Behold the twilight of the flesh! Behold the rebirth of the Children in veneration of the Machine!

-attr: Leviathan, Chimera prophet of the Cult of Machina

The Cult of Machina have no formal leadership and those who claim allegiance to the Cult do not adhere to any structured hierarchy. They have only one purpose: to merge and one day become The Machine. To start with the Cultists acquire as many cybernetics as they can afford, dedicating their lives to becoming more than human. The cybernetics they use are rarely of the same standard used by Agents. Salvaged parts, hand built upgrades, and internal biomechanics looted from the dead make up the majority of the Cultists cybernetic arsenal; as a result they look more like the experiments of mad bio-engineers than humans at the apex of evolution.

Many fit internal A.I.s which they increase to high levels in the hope the A.I.s will become self aware and blend with the mind of the Cultist creating a hybrid consciousness comprised of human and machine. The Cultists see no risks with changing as much of themselves as possible into polished steel, oscillating pumps and whining servos.

Although the Cultists have no strict hierarchy, they do have predilections towards different roles. Some consider themselves thinkers and planners, these individuals are known as *Architects* and cultivate self-aware A.I. to enlighten themselves and give others faith in their decisions. Others tend towards physical augmentations dubbing themselves *Chimeras*. These individuals relish the inhuman power, insight and reflexes granted to them by the Machine.

Deus ex Machina – God from the Machine; a phrase which holds profound significance to the Cult. They firmly believe that by identifying, isolating and eliminating human flaws via the use of cybernetics they can become perfect and thus Godlike. They consider the flesh weak and although the Cult of Machina don't actively hunt those who are pure of flesh, they are consumed with contempt for them.

Enclaves of the sect are uncommon and seldom encountered in everyday situations; they are elusive and tend to remain hidden in Old Cities or in toxic areas of wilderness where no one will go. They are unafraid of the effects of mutagens considering them to be purifiers or trials which destroy the flesh leaving only metal. If a Cultist is likely to die it means he has too much flesh and should be either *improved* or *culled* and his parts salvaged.

GOALS

The Cult does not have a grand plan involving world domination or killing all those of pure flesh, their battle is spiritual and they seek only self fulfilment in the form of biomechanical perfection. This does not mean that they are peaceable and mind their own business. The task of continually acquiring expensive cybernetics, A.I.s, surgical equipment and drugs ensures they are always looking for confrontation. Cybernetic Fabrication Plants are regularly raided by the Cult and newly qualified Agents are often attacked and their enhancements ripped out in the street by demented Cultists desperate for more cybernetics to fuel their addiction. Because the Cultists are so cybernetically powerful they are considered extremely dangerous, some of the more developed Chimeras can not only survive against a Division, they can overpower it, obliterate it and remove the cybernetics for their barbaric experiments.

MOOD

However you include the Cult of Machina in your game the mood should be one of twisted depravity and inhuman desire. The Cult is an abomination, their cybernetics are like their minds; perverse, ugly and corrupting. Whatever vestiges of humanity were once in its followers hearts have been hacked out with bloody scalpels and replaced with lumps of cruel metal. There is no mercy for the victims of the Cult so none should be shown. Weakness could land the Division as a source of spare parts in the theatres of the Cult's surgeons.

I read once that, way back when, there were barbarian fanatics who'd go into battle stark naked and could still do enough damage to rout hardened soldiers. The fanatics we get these days are equally barbarous, only they tend to go into battle with hardened steel plating welded to their skin and industrial diamond saws grafted to their hands. You do the math.

What's worse is they seem to be spreading. Read between the lines of most of the big Corporate newsnet updates and you'll always find the stories; a terror raid here, an Underswell massacre there, three Agents in the next Spire with their cybernetic bones torn out and dumped in a mining hopper. My gut says they're gearing up for something, and it seems the UIG can't do anything to stop them. Or won't.

-attr: Zack Adams, freelance technical consultant/soldier of fortune (current whereabouts unknown)

PLOT IDEAS

1. A Cult enclave is kidnapping telepaths and fitting them into biomechanical devices to find out how they work, and if they can make machines into telepaths and vice versa.
2. An allied Division was sent to destroy a Cult enclave, they are now thought to be *organ donors* and need to be extracted.
3. A Chimera has become a serial killer and is systematically killing Citizens out of contempt.
4. A pack of Cultists have broken into an A.I. lab and stolen some powerful, experimental tactical A.I.s
5. An Architect has become so mentally advanced as to pose a dangerous threat to anyone who opposes her.
6. The Division must go undercover and pretend to join the Cult.

DESIGNING CULT OF MACHINA

Cult of Machina do not need to follow the basic character creation system. They have a bizzare mix of augmentations which cannot be commercially obtained. They can therefore have STATS, skills and extra features of your choice. They should have an EMPS of between 25 and 30 as most of their upgrades are modified and they do not allow themselves to be easily threatened by EMP weapons.

Chimeras will tend to have high combat STATS and high physical skills whereas Architects will normally be more cerebral and value brains over brawn. That is not to say that they are incompetent in a fight.

> *Agent Nate Duval, a Federation friend of mine from Austerity, had this mod in his face. Some kind of targeting system, not standard, it had been built by one of the guys in his Division, I think his name was Polinsky. Anyway, one day the targeter went haywire, it was kinda funny, his eyes were everywhere and he couldn't hit a spire at 50 paces. Normally he would have got Polinsky to fix it but apparently this was not his first excursion into homemade cybes. Polinsky was now depersonalised and under the gentle employ of Mars Mineral and Mining.*
>
> *This didn't leave Duval a lot of choice, he couldn't go to the Corporation, the Federation don't look kindly on that sort of thing. So he did what any Agent in the same situation would do. He took a shuttle to Beijing and tried to find himself a backstreet mod doctor.*
>
> *To cut a long story short he found one, a Chinese woman going by the alias of Li Qin. She worked out of a protein processing plant in the industrial zone. The meeting was set up by a third party and there were naturally a few conditions. First, the doc wanted 1000 credits just to look, second, payment was to be made in slip, and third, the doc would shut off Duval's optical routers so he couldn't recognise her face. His association with the Federation obviously concerned her. Duval agreed, he could hardly see anyway and it's not like he had a lot of choice.*
>
> *Duval was found that night by a Malenbrach squad doing a late night sweep of the zone. They found his torso and half his head crammed into a protein former. All his upgrades had been stripped out; even the process socket had been torn off the back of the head, the central brain terminals wrenched out of the grey matter leaving a wet, bloody cave in the back of his skull.*
>
> *Why didn't they kill him? No need, they had what they wanted. When you're hunting the Cult you gotta understand something. They're driven, not evil.*
>
> *-attr: Strapfist Montana, Bounty Hunter, Lanzas FC&D*

DROID LIBERATION ARMY

The Droid Liberation Army (DLA) argue that if a droid can become self-aware then there must be the potential for life in all droids. The DLA take it upon themselves to liberate droids from their owners and give them a safe environment to grow and prosper. In return they ask for the protection and cooperation of the droids they have freed. Often as not the relationship works out, but on occasion the liberated droids turn on their saviours and forge a hatred for humanity which they spend the rest of their ageless lives sating.

The DLA are accepting of this and keep the droids under close surveillance for the first few months until their motivations have been established. The sentient droids are extremely industrious and often engineer pioneering technology which fund the DLA's activities and give them a means to combat those they consider oppressors of the free.

The DLA has many members, now numbering in the high hundreds, and their cells are scattered across the world. Many members are also individuals in positions of responsibility such as Agents (particularly Comoros Agents), politicians, and A.I. researchers who seek to gain insight by working with these sentient constructions.

The UIG are not overly concerned with the DLA as their activities are mostly peaceful and they cause a minimum of disturbance when they free their targets. However, when droids go rogue and start to become hostile the DLA is the prime suspect. Any droid related crime is often construed as a direct result of the DLA's policy of freeing potentially dangerous machines. At this point the UIG have little choice but to come down on them with all available force. Droid manufacturers actively cultivate this attitude as rogue liberated droids are bad for business and reduce the population's faith in their products.

The DLA see a day when droids can wander the streets alongside humans. They agree some droids can be dangerous but contend that humans can be equally unpredictable, yet the UIG does not restrict or curtail the rights of humans on the off-chance an innocent may commit a crime. The UIG argue that a mentally unstable human is less of a threat than a demented Murder Class Droid and so the debate continues.

PLOT IDEAS

1. The DLA attempt to liberate droids from the Divisions Spire while they are relaxing in a restaurant.
2. The DLA have assembled a task force of droids to liberate an awakened Cyberlin from an impound yard in the Sahara Desert.
3. A DLA liberated droid slays it's saviours and rampages through an inhabited area.
4. The Division must find a particular DLA cell who have taken a Corporate droid with valuable information inside.
5. The DLA are going to liberate a powerful tactical A.I. from an enemy Corporation and have approached the player's Corporation for assistance.
6. A group of droids have escaped and started a vigilante group to say 'thank you' to the DLA.

SECTION 12

RUNNING A GAME OF CORPORATION

RUNNING A GAME OF CORPORATION

The lights blinked on. Agent Winters rubbed her eyes and looked around for the source of her premature awakening. By the side of the bed her comm. unit bleeped softly.

"Winters," she said, answering it.

"Sorry to wake you Agent, but something has come up." came the voice on the other end. "We need you for immediate briefing."

Five minutes later, with a cocktail of stimulants in her, Agent Winters was staring at some blurry video footage of a lab filled with row upon row of coffin-like beds, each occupied by a pale naked form.

"Communications A.I. in Cern picked this up about half an hour ago. It was being broadcast as part of an encrypted data package being transmitted from a warehouse in Sierra Leone to the offices of the Beijing Medical Company." There was a slight pause then the voice continued. "We don't exactly know what is being conducted at this facility but we do know that the Beijing Medical Company was investigated by a UIG select committee last year regarding illegal cloning technologies. As you know, we at E.I. have a vested interested in controlling all advances in the medical trade, legal or not. So we need you to go in under the cover of the UIG's anti-cloning mandate and investigate. If you find anything suspicious dump a copy of the data to your internal drive then destroy the original. There are to be no witnesses to your actions, is that understood?"

"Yes sir," she replied. "Sir, if you don't mind me asking, why the rush job?"

"We have only managed to decrypt part of the remaining data package, but the gist of it is that the buyer for this technology will be collecting tomorrow at sixteen hundred hours. Requisition what you need from supplies then go, there is a sub-orbital waiting to take you."

DESIGNING A GAME

How Many Players?

When all your players have created their characters they are then ready to play. There can be any number of players although the recommended number would be 2-5. Games with just one player (and a GM of course) can be highly rewarding but require more input from both player and GM. A group of players means they can combine skills and each can be more specialised. This is the way a normal Division would be composed from the point of view of the Personnel Manager of the Corporation in question.

Which Corporation?

You will need to know the Corporation your party is playing. The GM could decide this or the players could decide between themselves. Each Corporation has different operational methods; for example, The Western Federation will tend to rely more on good weaponry, slick planning and military style execution whereas E.I. will be more freeform, less disciplined and in it for the thrill of the chase.

Bear in mind that everyone does not need to play stereotypical

Agents, an Asian stealth assassin may well be employed by Comoros and the Ai-Jinn would not be opposed to employing a defected E.I. Agent who could offer an inside advantage.

Cross-Corporation Games

You could allow your players to play Agents from different Corporations in the same game. This type of game is called a Cross-Corporation game.

Cross-Corporation games can be some of the most fun. Whether they become the norm is up to the players and the GM. It allows for great diversity of play and there are plenty of antagonists for the allied Division to bring down. Try to think up a reason the Corporations are working together, for example:

- The UIG have assembled an Inter-Corporation Task Force
- The Corporations have a mutual enemy or goal

In a situation where you have a player from most Corporations you are still left with the following potential enemies among others:

ENEMIES FOR A CROSS-CORPORATION GAME

- A Corporation no-one is playing
- Aliens
- Artificial Intelligence / Archons
- Citizens
- Criminals
- Droids / Robots
- Minor Corporations
- Mutant Groups
- Rebel Factions
- Rogue Agents
- Telepathic Orders
- The Cult of Machina
- The Droid Liberation Army
- The Order of the True Faith
- The United International Government

Each one of these groups listed above can provide large campaigns and unlimited story ideas. Although there are some profound differences between the Corporations and a great many scores to settle, this should not get in the way of a mission. Conversely, it should provide some great roleplaying opportunities for all involved. The combinations of different skills, attitudes and methods make for a diverse and interesting party.

The Division

When the players have decided on the Corporations they are going to work for they will need to generate their characters. Try to make sure the characters cover up the weaknesses of other characters; i.e. think carefully before you play a whole Division of weak-muscled knife experts, try to make all the Agents excel in different areas. This will make the Division able to handle more interesting missions. The Division should be a stand-alone unit able to deal with a variety of situations.

That said, some Divisions have a specialty such as espionage, sabotage, vehicle use or assassination. In this case Agents may want to have some common areas of expertise. This means that more difficult missions can be taken on as long as the goal is in line with the Agent's specialities. Equally, setting them on a mission which they are unsuitable for can provide an entertaining gaming opportunity.

STYLES OF GAME

You can run a number of different styles of game. Below are some examples:

1. A Cyberfear game where technology is not behaving as it should.

2. Something sinister, suggesting corruption or conspiracies.

3. An investigation, where social skills and deduction are more important than combat prowess.

4. An espionage game where the Agents must use stealth and cunning to complete the mission and remain undetected.

5. A personal mission where the Agents have a strong personal motivation, perhaps revenge or greed.

6. A UIG conscript mission, this way players don't have to be too subtle because the UIG requested the mission.

7. An action based game where combat and quick moves are the main driving forces behind the game.

8. An international game where Agents must travel to numerous countries and immerse themselves in different cultures.

9. A political game where the players are caught up in the machinations of key global players.

10. Cross-Corporation games where players choose Agents from different Corporations who are working together for a higher purpose.

11. An exploratory game where an unknown location must be explored; e.g. an Underswell, space wreck, alien city or buried Old City.

12. A flight game where the Agents are the ones being hunted.

13. A crime solving game where evidence, theories and psychology are paramount.

CORPORATE INTERACTION

Make sure that you have decided how the Corporations behave towards each other, and be aware that this may not reflect what they think of each other. There are also many interactions between parties which influence their business and finance, such as E.I.'s dependence on the Ai-Jinn for transit to and from Vastaag.

THE UIG AND THE ORDER OF THE TRUE FAITH

These two organisations provide a good solid opponent for all manner of scenarios.

THE UNITED INTERNATIONAL GOVERNMENT plays an important role in the Corporate world. Without the UIG, the Corporations would have destroyed themselves in the Corporate Wars. The UIG will always be more powerful than any one Corporation, and with the assistance of The Archons, are able to prevent any large scale disasters. The UIG cannot afford to stamp too hard on the Corporations as they may provoke insurrection or revolution which would be disastrous, even with their advanced technology.

In meantime the UIG must be content to steer the Corporations in the direction they wish them to go, namely infighting. As long as the Citizens do not get caught up in the Corporate squabbles, then what harm is the death of a few Agents here and there?

THE ORDER OF THE TRUE FAITH are a large social, political and military organisation with strong ideals and a great deal of influence. The Faithful are everywhere, in all cities and Spires. Some keep their allegiance to the Order a secret and others make it widely known and dare anyone to act against them. The Order are not stupid however, they rarely engage in outright acts of aggression and do not pressure individuals into subscribing to a faith they don't believe in. The Order is quite happy to slowly collect and unite all those who find its umbrella of faith and protection suits their needs.

In terms of running the game, the Order should be used sparingly, they only involve themselves where their own interests are at stake. Such events as the discovery of new blasphemous technology or the production of a particularly dangerous weapon may give cause for the Order to become involved. In essence they wish Earth to remain a balanced place where nature may again take root and the savage, destructive ways of the Corporations stopped or at least brought down to a controllable level.

The Corporations are a lot better than they were. The clandestine shadow games they play with each other are not a great threat to the future of the Earth and thus the path to spiritual ascendance. The Order must be wary though, the Corporations are always looking for ways to tip the balance and it is these things the Order must be vigilant for. For this reason the Devoted of the Order are continually monitoring Corporate activity, trying to make sure that if anything big happens their people are there to ensure it doesn't get out of hand.

WRITING YOUR MISSION

This section is intended to help you come up with good plot ideas and execute them well. A good way to write a plot is to be inspired by something you have seen or read, so it's a wise idea to source some material to get you in the mood. Almost anything can be inspiration for a game of Corporation. For example:

- Action films
- TV series based around crime and espionage
- Comics
- PC and video games
- Novels
  See page 16 for some example source material

THE PLOT

When you have an idea work backwards, decide what is happening, who is doing what and why? Perhaps a doctor has become too greedy and has started shipping his prototype drugs to the populace without the correct lab tests.

Once you know what is happening, you can decide how your

players find out about it. Maybe it's as simple as a brief from the Missions Officer, but perhaps one of the player's acquaintances is getting ill and cannot understand why. His medical report comes back and shows near lethal doses of a substance in his blood. This could set the Agents on the trail of the pharmacist and eventually to the corrupt doctor selling the drugs.

Be sure to think out your plot well and make sure there are no gaping holes in it as players will spot these easily. A simple plot with one or two twists and turns works well. In the example above, perhaps when the Agents find the doctor selling illegal drugs they discover he is working for the UIG and is testing a prototype formula on specific civilian profiles. The end result being that the UIG are forced to buy off the players to maintain their secrecy. As a reward the players gain some additional rank points. Some of the Division may not be happy with this and may go public with the information. That's all part of the fun.

Now you have the backbone of the plot you need to make sure you incorporate some different styles of play into the mission. A good game tends to have a mix of action scenes, socialising, planning and freeforming. The proportions of these elements are dependent on your group and also your plot.

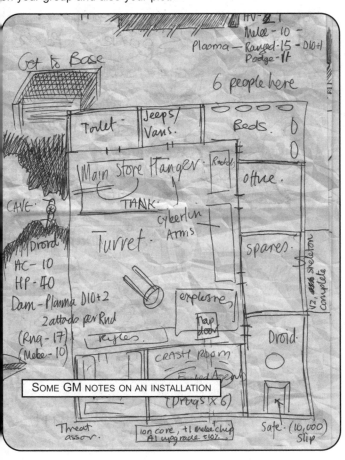

SOME GM NOTES ON AN INSTALLATION

ACTION

This need not be combat although combat is certainly one of the more entertaining forms of action. Fights can be deadly though and too many make the occasion routine (which a battle for your life never should be). Alternative forms of action could include a motorcycle race, climbing a huge building, cat burglary, evading capture, hacking against the clock, reaching a location in a certain time, piloting a war machine and so on.

SOCIALISING

Socialising with NPC's can make a real difference to a game. The Agents can gather contacts to use at a later date or bypass situations without the need for fights. Often a game will involve a situation where the players must meet someone, perhaps at a Spire restaurant or Underswell and get information out of them in order to proceed. These situations can be of great benefit to the game. Characters who are mainly social will be able to prove their use to the Division, it allows the GM to add atmosphere and make the world more tangible and interactive, especially when the Division meets the same character a few weeks later and he asks them how they got on. Be careful with excessive ad-lib socialising as unless the NPC's are purposeful and interesting, the game can become slow and the players will be yearning for some action.

PLANNING

This is important in all roleplaying games, but especially in Corporation. Divisions are regularly sent on missions to complete objectives. If they simply charge towards their target and hope for the best, disaster will normally ensue. The players may want to plan in detail and purchase the correct equipment for the job. Don't let them plan too much though. Sometimes players will plan for several hours which takes up a lot of game time and if events conspire against them (which they normally do) it could end up as a wasted effort.

FREEFORMING

Most players love to mess about and a good GM will use this to enrich the game and have some fun. Players will often want to go into random bars, chat up NPC's, steal things they shouldn't have, pick fights, break into houses, race cars and generally engage in activities which do not further the mission. This is in many ways the essence of roleplaying, a good GM will feed his players with motivating material so that they want to interact with the world he has created. Dozens of sessions have been and gone where absolutely nothing productive was achieved because the players never got out of the bar or decided to follow a suspicious character who had nothing to do with the plot. These sessions are not pointless, they epitomise the freeform nature of roleplaying games and should be savoured. Allow the players some leeway to simply enjoy playing their characters, after all, if the players are happy then the GM has succeeded, and as any GM knows, a game where the players can't stop taking about what happened is incredibly rewarding.

MISSION BRIEF

Now you have ideas of where the game is going, it is time to introduce the players to the world, this is normally done during a Mission Briefing but is definitely not a requirement. At low rank the players will generally be called in to see the Mission Officer and informed of a situation that needs attention, for example, a droid has gone rogue in the VIP lounge and is holding some staff to ransom. The Agents would ask pertinent questions which the Missions Officer would hopefully answer. If you like, you can use the Mission Brief Form on page 249 to write out the brief and hand it to the players. This adds atmosphere and can be fun. It also avoids confusion when they forget the exact mission brief. Sometimes the Agents may be asked to destroy the brief, if you are feeling cruel make the players memorise it and then rip it up.

EQUIPPING AGENTS

The Agents will need equipment to get the job done. They should have a reserve of their own but a specialist job might require specialist equipment that the Agents cannot afford. In this case the Corporation may provide the hardware. If this equipment is lost or damaged the Corporation may react strongly depending on the circumstances. Free equipment allocation should be carefully considered and written on the mission brief if you are using one. A financial allocation may be made which the Division can spend on equipment or expenses they deem necessary.

MISSION COMPLETION

When the mission is completed, the Agents would normally return to the Mission Officer to receive a debriefing and any rewards / punishments. Experience can be given out at this point. (See Character Advancement for a guide to XP awards on page 79.)

GETTING STARTED

The best way to start a game is just to jump in, the GM should design a simple and easy-to-complete mission. If you come to a situation you are unsure of; read about it in the book. Don't worry about all the rules for now. Very basic combat will suffice as long as the enemies are not too hard. As everyone becomes familiar with the game system the array of tactical options expands and the Agents will be able to deal with more powerful enemies. There is a simple starting mission on page 210 you might want to try.

ANTAGONISTS

> *One who opposes and contends against another; an adversary.*
> *- Anon*

One of the most important things when writing a mission for the players to embark on is creating a good antagonist. The players should ideally feel a reason to stop the opponent (or opponents). Simply saying that the Agents should halt Mr. X's plans is not ideal, there should be motivation.

The antagonist should also be attainable, not an aloof figure of awesome power who would destroy the Agents should they meet him. There is nothing wrong with a powerful enemy but make them powerful in a particular way, perhaps they are strong, skilled or well guarded. Maybe they live somewhere unknown or have a pack of savage cybernetic attack dogs. Whatever makes the enemy powerful, eventually the players will want to overcome it and confront their nemesis.

You can begin by encountering the antagonist's minions, his soldiers, lackies, spies and lieutenants. These can give small, balanced encounters which can yield ideas of how the main opponent works and give clues as to what he is up to and where he resides.

There is list a of general enemies on page 195 under *Cross-Corporation Games*, that would make excellent antagonists with a little thought. If the group does not immediately strike you as a good enemy think what the Division (or their employer) may have done to anger the organisation. Maybe the Corporation is intending to mine out an area where mutants live or perhaps some Citizens have had enough of Corporate life and want to steal something important from the Spire and disappear with it.

There is no good and evil in *Corporation*, just points of view and relative scales of morality. What is fair to one man is unfair to another. Strong opinions, greed, past injustices and secret agendas are all useful tools in turning the indifferent into the impassioned.

SAMPLE MISSIONS

Use the ideas on the next few pages for missions; there is intentionally a low level of detail so you can customise the mission to your gaming group. Where the mission briefs refer to an actual Corporation just change the parties involved if necessary.

> Which of the Corporations first turned the metaphorical concept – Corporate warfare – into physical reality? When, exactly, did industrial espionage bleed over into outright combat? Nobody really knows, but I'll tell you one thing – once it started, they all jumped on the bandwagon pretty damn quickly.
>
> attr: Noah Lamarr, Dreddoth prospector (resident)

100 MISSION IDEAS

1. Capture a rogue sentient droid who has escaped to Vastaag to find more of his own kind.
2. Defend a research laboratory from an enemy Corporation attack.
3. Infiltrate an enemy lab and steal a prototype technology.
4. Clean a group of powerful mutants out of an Underswell.
5. Protect a convoy containing high tech equipment.
6. Assassinate a leading enemy research scientist.
7. Find a defected Agent who is hiding within an enemy Spire.
8. Take some large field weaponry and lay siege to an enemy research lab.
9. Find a traitor within your own Corporation.
10. Work for Lanzas Mercenary Corp. during downtime.
11. Find out why you are on a bounty hunters list and who put you there.
12. Stow on board a shuttle and enter an enemy orbital.
13. Oversee and protect some critical research.
14. Find and recruit Outlaws from the Old Cities to use as an undercover unit.
15. Sabotage an enemy cyberlin.
16. Work a great financial scam to rip off another Corporation.
17. Find a suitable location for the construction of a spy HQ in enemy territory.
18. Illicitly join an enemy Corporation and try to do them some serious damage.
19. Feed fake information to an enemy Corporation.
20. The Division finds a damaged Archon in a minor computer system.
21. The Division finds illegal alien weaponry.
22. Set up a false company for your Corporation in enemy territory.
23. Ally with mutants to learn advanced telepathic powers.
24. Design and test a new cyberlin.
25. Field test some extremely powerful weaponry.
26. Find a telepathically powerful human who is hiding somewhere in the Old Cities.
27. Assist the Malenbrach in their investigations (whether you want to or not).
28. Escape a UIG prison after being incarcerated unjustly (or justly).
29. Infiltrate the UIG to learn about the Archons and gain knowledge of other Corporations.
30. Destroy an enemy Spire.
31. Try to eliminate religion and thus Order of the Faith influence in your area.
32. Sabotage an enemy Corporation's attempt to set up an orbital.
33. Travel to Vastaag as tourists to spy on enemy officials on holiday.
34. Win in the gladiatorial arenas to earn glory for your Corporation.
35. Cleanse a mainframe of a rouge sentient A.I.
36. Contain the fall out from a biological attack by an enemy Corporation.
37. Escape from an orbital in a critically decaying orbit.
38. Partake in an experimental technology/wet-ware trial for your Corp.
39. Investigate reports of alien tech being used in part of an Old City.
40. Work undercover at an illegal street racing meeting where an enemy Corporation is field testing new vehicle technology.
41. Locate and recover a rogue Cyberlin. It shouldn't be hard to find!
42. Board the Universal Pleasure Cruiser *World View* to uncover a conspiracy on board.
43. Prevent a massive media leak which could seriously damage your Corporation.
44. Escort and bodyguard a Corporate official while on business in enemy territory.
45. Track an enemy Division through neutral territory to discover their motives.
46. Investigate an assassination at the Aries Institute.
47. Investigate a domestic murder that is more than it seems.
48. Seed dissidence in an enemy Spire.
49. Destroy key strategic resources to cripple an enemy Corporation.
50. Catch some notorious cyber-criminals who are stealing data.
51. You are wanted by the UIG while in another city. Evade capture and return home.
52. Infiltrate Antarctica (UIG and Archon Territory) and make a report.
53. Infiltrate Anzeiger Military Systems and see what secret weapons they are selling to special clients.
54. High ranking Agents from different Corporations set up a secret training facility (find out why and for whom).
55. Scout the public for potential Agents and train them up.
56. Steal an Ai-Jinn FarDrive.
57. Stow on board an Ai-Jinn Far Craft and investigate the Ai-Jinn mining colonies.

58. Go to Dreddoth (on Mars) to investigate suspected enemy activities.
59. Set up a second mining colony on Mars.
60. Enter the Archon's Artefact Cities on Venus.
61. Enter a secret underwater city which is some kind of WF experiment.
62. Vastaag has been overtaken by a rogue A.I. trying to set it up as an A.I. refuge.
63. The Agents are isolated in enemy territory; they must get back with minimal equipment.
64. The Division have a bounty on their heads. Lanzas and members of the public are tracking them down for the reward.
65. Make sure a student at the Taurus Academy joins up with your Corporation.
66. Convince an enemy Agent to defect.
67. The Division must break an ally out of Kildanna prison.
68. Defend an installation from attack until reinforcements arrive.
69. A high ranking Agent asks you to investigate corruption within your own Corporation.
70. The UIG conscript your Division to assist them in capturing a notorious criminal.
71. Recover a stolen tactical A.I. before it is cracked and it's information stolen.
72. Attend international talks as spokespeople for your Corporation.
73. Underground telepaths are thought to be harbouring criminals – find out the truth.
74. Another Corporation is thought to be taking some advanced tech to their Research & Development labs, intercept them and recover it.
75. Rumours of an illegal cloning plant have reached the CEO's ears, you are assigned to investigate.
76. The Division are under scrutiny from the Order of the True Faith, they must conduct missions while under Order surveillance.
77. Infiltrate an organised crime syndicate to bring them down.
78. One of the missing Archons is thought to be organising terrorists.
79. The Ai-Jinn are orchestrating Triads to do their groundwork in rival Spires.
80. An ancient tomb has been found deep in the Earths crust resonating with powerful telepathic energy.
81. A potent designer drug is killing the rich.
82. One of the higher ranking Agents in a Corporation may not be human.
83. Your Division is outlawed, you must prove your innocence while evading the UIG and bounty hunters.
84. Agents with neural jacks have been suffering from schizophrenia; an A.I. could be invading their minds.
85. There is a prison outbreak in a major city.
86. The Division must smuggle a BIO off Miller-Urey.
87. Lanzas must recruit Agents for a particularly sensitive mission.
88. A Rank 8 Agent has found a murdered woman in his room (he claims), the Division must clean it up.
89. The Division are test driving a new war machine when the Spire is attacked by rebels.
90. Terrorists storm The World View Orbital Cruiser taking hostages, the Division is on board and must resolve the situation.
91. Members of the Cult of Machina have gone to Venus to merge with the ancient city there.
92. An Archon is gathering an elite task force for an unknown purpose.
93. Escort a high ranking but low level Agent to Dreddoth to discuss mineral acquisition.
94. The Division finds a *Gift of the Archons,* i.e. a piece of extremely powerful (UIG owned) technology such as a personal teleporter.
95. Whilst on a FarDrive Craft the pilot is murdered, the Division must investigate and arrest the killer.
96. Bring down an enclave of the Cult of Machina.
97. Two Corporations have started warring more openly; try to deal them both serious strategic and economic damage.
98. Rebels have taken a UIG Officer hostage; impress the UIG by liberating her from an Old City.
99. Compete in antigravity races on Dreddoth to uncover corruption and fixing within the race community.
100. A satellite has conducted an orbital strike on an installation, go into orbit and disable it, then find out who fired it.

MISSION BRIEF - OPERATION LEIPZIG

PARAMETERS
DATE : 22/03/2500
ISSUED BY : REPOSTING DIVISION
ISSUED TO : DIVISION 332663A
MISSION TO BE COMPLETED BY : 30/04/2500
CONFIDENTIALITY : RANK 3+ E.I. OPERATIVES ONLY

ALLOCATED RESOURCES:
DIVISION 11912
LEIPZIG R&D DEPARTMENT
RUNNING EXPENSES
1 SCOUT CLASS CYBERLIN + PILOT
1 BATTLE CLASS CYBERLIN + PILOT

MISSION OBJECTIVE
YOU HAVE BEEN SELECTED TO OVERSEE THE RUNNING OF OUR NEW R&D DEPARTMENT IN
LEIPZIG. YOUR DIVISION WILL BE GIVEN JOINT CHARGE OF THE OPERATION WITH DISPUTED
ISSUES BEING TAKEN UP WITH AGENT KURT HERZLED IN BERLIN (RANK 6 INTERNAL AFFAIRS
OPERATIVE). YOUR OVERALL OBJECTIVE IS TO TAKE COMMAND OF THE DEPARTMENT AND
BEGIN DESIGN AND CONSTRUCTION OF A SERIES OF WEAPONS BASED ON THE ARCHON FUSED
PLASMA TECHNOLOGY WE HAVE RECOVERED FROM THE WESTERN FEDERATION. THEY HAVE
ALREADY MADE GREAT INROADS INTO THIS NEW TECHNOLOGY SO IT MAY BE PRUDENT TO
ACQUIRE SOME OF THEIR FINDINGS. YOU ARE RESPONSIBLE FOR FUND ALLOCATION AND ALL
OTHER MATTERS REGARDING THE SUCCESSFUL RUNNING OF THIS FACILITY. YOU HAVE BEEN
ALLOCATED DIVISION 11912 WHICH IS MADE UP OF THE FOLLOWING AGENTS:

ASSISTANCE
SASHA DIXON - RANK 1 - DIVISION LEADER - FINANCIER
CARLOS DIEGO - RANK 1 - SOCIAL TACTICIAN
HUGH EDWARDS - RANK 1 - ACADEMIC
LEANNA LLOYD - RANK 1 - A.I. AND XENOBIOLOGY SPECIALIST

AFTER 2 WEEKS THE FACILITY WILL BE INSPECTED BY AGENT STEPHANY NOTTINGHAM (RANK
5 EFFICIENCY SPECIALIST).

WE NEED TO SEE RESULTS BEFORE THE WF ATTEMPT A RECOVERY

ISSUING OFFICER: AGENT 66763D (JACK HENDERSON)

COMOROS
INDO AFRICAN ALLIANCE

REVERSE ENGINEERING ACQUISITION ASSIGNATION
MISSION BRIEF - ROGUE 1212D

PARAMETERS
DATE : 13/03/2500
ISSUED BY : REVERSE ENGINEERING DEPT.
ISSUED TO : DIVISION 4957289D
MISSION TO BE COMPLETED BY : 13/04/2500
CONFIDENTIALITY : REV. ENG. / RANK 3 +

ALLOCATED RESOURCES PER AGENT
PROXIMITY SCANNER ATTUNED TO UNIT 1212D - 100 METRE RANGE
CIVILIAN APPAREL
CIVILIAN IDENTIFICATION
CIVILIAN BACKGROUND (MEMORISE AND DESTROY)
1 ICE SHADOW PISTOL
EXPENSE MONEY: 1000¢
TICKETS TO VASTAAG
1 MEDPACK

MISSION DROP-OFF
YOU WILL CATCH THE MUMBAI SHUTTLE AT 18:00 LEAVING FOR VASTAAG ON 13/03/2500

MISSION EXIT POINT
NO EXIT POINT STATED - OWN EXIT MUST BE ESTABLISHED

MISSION OBJECTIVE
AN AI-JINN DROID (1212D DOMESTIC CLASS) HAS REACHED SENTIENCE AND EQUIPPED
ITSELF WITH A RANGE OF EQUIPMENT FROM THEIR CYBERNETICS LABS. IT IS KNOWN TO
HAVE TAKEN A SHUTTLE TO VASTAAG. RECOVER THE ANDROID. IT IS UNDERSTOOD THAT THIS
INFORMATION IS ALSO KNOWN TO A DIVISION OF WESTERN FEDERATION AGENTS WHO ARE
ALSO ATTEMPTING TO RECOVER THE ANDROID IN ORDER TO WIN FAVOUR WITH THEIR
SUPERIORS.

THE MISSION WILL BE CONSIDERED SUCCESSFUL IF THE ANDROID IS RECOVERED IN ANY
STATE. SHOULD THE ANDROID ESCAPE THIS WILL BE CONSIDERED FAILURE AND SHOULD THE
FEDERATION AGENTS ACQUIRE IT THE MISSION WILL BE CONSIDERED A DISASTER.

DO NOT ENGAGE THE FEDERATION AGENTS AS WE ARE, AT PRESENT, NEGOTIATING AN ARMS
TRADE WITH THE WF CORPORATION.

ISSUING OFFICER: AGENT 64345F (OGARI JUNTO)

THIS DOCUMENT IS INTENDED SOLELY FOR THE USE OF THE ADDRESSEE AND MAY CONTAIN
INFORMATION THAT IS CONFIDENTIAL OR PRIVILEGED. IN THE EVENT OF UNAUTHORISED
ACCESS TO THIS DOCUMENT PLEASE NOTIFY THE AGENCY MENTIONED ABOVE.

CONFIDENTIAL

WESTERN FEDERATION

MISSION BRIEF
WESTERN FEDERATION DEPARTMENT OF CULTURAL PURITY

MISSION CODE: ENLIGHTENED ONES

PARAMETERS
DATE : 12/06/2496
ISSUED BY : CULTURAL PURITY DEPT.
ISSUED TO : DIVISION 224333F
MISSION TO BE COMPLETED BY : 18/7/2496
CONFIDENTIALITY : C.P.D. ONLY

ALLOCATED RESOURCES
1000¢ DIVISION EXPENSES

MISSION DROP-OFF
YOU WILL BE REQUIRED TO MAKE YOUR OWN WAY TO THE TOKYO ARCHOLOGY

MISSION EXIT POINT
NO EXIT POINT STATED - OWN EXIT MUST BE ESTABLISHED

MISSION OBJECTIVE
THE SHI YUKIRO ARE PRESENTLY TRAINING A GROUP OF ELITE TELEPATHS WE HAVE CODE NAMED THE 'ENLIGHTENED ONES'. INTELLIGENCE BELIEVES THEY ARE BEING TRAINED BY AN ORDER OF MONKS RESIDENT IN THE TOKYO ARCHOLOGY. THESE MONKS HAVE COMBINED TRADITIONAL MIND STRENGTHENING TECHNIQUES WITH MODERN TRAINING METHODS AND TECHNOLOGY TO FORM THEMSELVES INTO A FORMIDABLE TELEPATHIC DIVISION.

ENTER THE TOKYO ARCHOLOGY - FIND THE ENLIGHTENED ONES AND THEIR TRAINEES - ELIMINATE BOTH.

SUCCESS IN THIS MISSION IS VITAL - FEEL FREE TO DISCUSS THE DETAILS OF THE MISSION WITH AGENT 774405, RANK 7 C.P.D

ISSUING OFFICER: AGENT 774543N

THIS DOCUMENT IS INTENDED SOLELY FOR THE USE OF THE ADDRESSEE AND MAY CONTAIN INFORMATION THAT IS CONFIDENTIAL OR PRIVILEGED. IN THE EVENT OF UNAUTHORISED ACCESS TO THIS DOCUMENT PLEASE NOTIFY THE AGENCY MENTIONED ABOVE.

SHI YUKIRO OPEN MISSION DELEGATION
MISSION DESIGNATION: ESCORT L4

PARAMETERS
DATE : 22/03/2500
ISSUED BY : DEPARTMENT OF TRADE
ISSUED TO : AGENT 223412F, AGENT 23872H
MISSION TO BE COMPLETED BY : NONE SPECIFIED
CONFIDENTIALITY : MISSION OFFICER AND HEAD OF TRADE ONLY

ALLOCATED RESOURCES:
TICKETS FOR THE WORLD VIEW ORBITAL CRUISER (EARTH/MARS LEG)
500¢ REGISTERED EXPENSE CREDIT

OBJECTIVE
YOU MUST ACCOMPANY THE HEAD OF TRADE (AGENT YAKAMURA)TO THE DREDDOTH COLONY ON MARS. YOU WILL TRAVEL VIA THE WORLD VIEW WHICH LEAVES FROM WASHINGTON, USA ON 25/03/2500 AT 19:00 HOURS.

THE SAFETY OF THE HEAD OF TRADE IS VITAL. SHE IS TO SPEAK WITH MAYOR SENDAT OF MARS IN THE MARIUS HOTEL AT A MUTUALLY ARRANGED TIME. YAKAMURA IS THERE TO DISCUSS THE ACQUISITION OF A NEW MINERAL, THE PROPERTIES OF WHICH ARE UNKNOWN, BUT WE WISH TO HAVE IT FIRST REGARDLESS.

SHE WILL CONDUCT HER BUSINESS AND THEN LEAVE AS THE WORLD VIEW PASSES ON IT'S RETURN JOURNEY. WE UNDERSTAND THAT THE MINERAL SEAM WHICH AGENT YAKAMURA IS NEGOTIATING FOR HAS CAUSED UPSET WITH THE MINERS. MANY HAVE REFUSED TO MINE THERE AND HAVE SET UP EXPLOSIVES AND TRAPS NEAR THE SEAM TO DISSUADE OTHERS FROM VISITING IT.

BE PREPARED FOR REBEL ACTIVITY TARGETED AT THE MINERAL SEAM AND AT YAKAMURA. ENSURE SHE COMPLETES HER TALKS SAFELY AND TRY TO OBTAIN A SAMPLE OF THE MINERAL SEAM TO BRING BACK WITH YOU. IT IS UNLIKELY THE DREDDOTH AUTHORITIES WILL LET US HAVE A SAMPLE OF THE MINERAL AND ARE EXPECTING US TO BID BLIND. ENSURE WE DO NOT.

ISSUING OFFICER: AGENT 9556345F (KITO MITSURIGO, SHADOW CEO & ACTING M.O.)

THIS DOCUMENT IS INTENDED SOLELY FOR THE USE OF THE ADDRESSEE AND MAY CONTAIN INFORMATION THAT IS CONFIDENTIAL OR PRIVILEGED. IN THE EVENT OF UNAUTHORISED ACCESS TO THIS DOCUMENT PLEASE NOTIFY THE AGENCY MENTIONED ABOVE.

AI-JINN COVERT ASSIGNATION
MISSION CODE: SPIDER & FLY

PARAMETERS
DATE : 14/07/2500
ISSUED BY : CELL COORDINATION
ISSUED TO : DIVISION 33093G
MISSION TO BE COMPLETED BY : 14/08/2500
CONFIDENTIALITY : AI-JINN EMPLOYEES ONLY

ALLOCATED RESOURCES
1xREMOTE CHIP CHECKER
2000¢ FOR MISCELLANEOUS EXPENSES
VIRAL MODIFIERS WITH JAPANESE GENESET FOR EACH AGENT
1xHIGH SPEC SEDAN CAR (MECHARGO SR11)

MISSION DROP-OFF
AGENTS WILL TRAVEL TO SHANGHAI IN THE VEHICLE PROVIDED

MISSION EXIT POINT
UPON COMPLETION OF THE OBJECTIVE RETURN TO THE SPIRE IN HONG KONG AND AWAIT DEBRIEFING.

MISSION OBJECTIVE
THE ATEMI YAKUZA CLAN (CURRENTLY ONE OF OUR MOST POWERFUL ORGANISATIONS IN SHANGHAI) HAS COME UNDER UIG SCRUTINY. AFTER COMPLETING ONE OF THE MOST SUCCESSFUL OPERATIONS IN THE HISTORY OF OUR CORPORATION, THE ATEMI CLAN HAS BECOME THE TARGET OF A UIG UNDERCOVER STING OPERATION. WE HAVE BEEN RELIABLY INFORMED BY ONE OF OUR SHINOBI (AGENT MEIJI SONG) THAT TWO UIG OFFICERS HAVE HAD RECONSTUCTIVE SURGERY AND ARE GOING TO ATTEMPT TO JOIN THE ATEMI CLAN AS NEW RECRUITS.

YOUR DIVISION ARE TO JOIN WITH THE ATEMI CLAN AND HELP THEM WITH THEIR DAY TO DAY BUSINESS. WHEN THE UIG AGENTS TRY TO JOIN, YOU WILL TAKE THEM INTO YOUR CONFIDENCE FEEDING THEM DAMAGING FALSE INFORMATION WHICH WE ARE CURRENTLY PREPARING.

ONCE THEY PROVE NO MORE USE THEY ARE TO BE ELIMINATED. THIS IS TO LOOK LIKE THE WORK OF A RIVAL CORPORATION. COMOROS AND E.I. ARE THE OBVIOUS CHOICES.

ISSUING OFFICER: AGENT 774543

INSTALLATIONS AND ENVIRONMENTS

Installations and environments are an important part of Corporation and Agents will routinely find themselves defending them, passing through them, infiltrating them, having meetings in them and even assaulting them. **Installation** is a general term but it applies to any defined, manmade area where a section of a mission could take place, generally indoors.

An **Environment** is a more open term generally referring to a larger area which could encompass several installations within it. An environment could be manmade or naturally occurring.

When designing a mission decide upon the environment(s) the game will take place in early on. This will help to add coherency to the setting. It will also give you a good idea of what sort of encounters may be had and what installations to use if any.

Examples and details of installations and environments are listed over the next few pages. Use them to help come up with mission ideas.

ENVIRONMENTS

- The irradiated landscape of France
- The barren, wreck strewn wastelands of Australasia
- The uncolonised areas of the Moon
- The deserts of Texas, Nevada and Utah
- The steppes of Russia
- The icy fjords of Scandinavia
- The jungles of Jictar
- The predator infested jungles of Tigera on Miller-Urey (Referred to as M-U)
- The steppe, desert and mountains found on Ashtan (M-U)
- The bizarre underwater world of Aqua Palestra (M-U)
- The underground caverns and tunnels of Infernus (M-U)
- The freezing peaks and tundra of Ornus (M-U)
- The rolling grassland and agricultural plains of Canathikta (M-U)
- The lethal and fetid swamps of Palus (M-U)
- The luxurious tropical islands found on Vastaag
- The polluted ocean depths surrounding northern Russia
- A crime ridden Old City
- A scum filled Underswell
- The alien cities on Venus
- A towering archology

EFFECTS OF THE ENVIRONMENT

Environments can alter the way a game is played on a broad level. Things to consider include.

- The toxin level of the environment
- Availability of resources such as food, weapons, equipment and money.
- The level of hostiles in the form of animals, mutants, BIOs, Agents and rebels etc.
- Climatic conditions such as rain, heat, lightning, etc.

- How well the Division can blend in.
- The potential for collateral damage.
- Distances, e.g., will transport be needed?
- UIG presence

INSTALLATIONS

- A teleport station
- A communications array
- A disused shopping mall in an Old City
- A droid factory
- A medical facility
- A Spire apartment
- A series of maintenance tunnels under a building
- The house of a rich UIG Officer
- A section of an Underswell
- A portion of an Old City
- A leisure arcade in a Spire city
- A part of an Archology
- Some manmade caves on Miller-Urey
- A weapons research laboratory
- A mutant training facility
- A cyberlin construction plant
- A large pleasure craft that cruises the solar system (The World View)
- A hotel where important talks are taking place
- A castle belonging to a wealthy eccentric
- A prison unjustly holding inmates
- A disused system of subways
- A foul set of tenement buildings
- A long abandoned church, home to a rebel group
- A warren in the refuse heaps of Australasia
- An underwater city off the coast of Odessa in Russia
- A toll booth complex on a SkyBridge
- A customs and excise building
- A UIG barracks
- A prototype power station
- A section of the machine world below Vastaag
- A virtual installation where an A.I. is hiding
- Inside a vast Ai-Jinn FarCraft
- In the mines of Dreddoth
- In an expensive restaurant in Tokyo
- A decadent section of New Europa on Vastaag
- A fleshel bar on Vastaag
- A toxic waste refinery
- A food processing factory
- A club owned by a group of organised criminals
- A shanty - unpleasantly close to a Spire
- The underground tunnels of a Relic City where telepathic energy is abundant
- A Corporate safe house deep in the Himalayan mountains

FEATURES OF AN INSTALLATION

Installations can vary so much that it would be impossible to cover everything that might be found in one. What follows is a list of sample features and encounters that the Division may come across in a typical installation. Use these basics to help you design your own personalised installations, environments and encounters.

DOOR AND WALL SUMMARY

DOORS	AV	HP
Weak Door	1	10
Plastic / Strong Wood Door	2	20
Hi-Polymer Door	3	30
Secure Metal Door	15	100
Durasteel Door	30	300

WALLS	AV	HP
Weak Plaster Walls	0	10
Polymer Walls	2	15
Normal Stone Walls	10	50
Metal Walls	15	100
Durasteel Walls	30	300
Hard Ion Walls	Varies	Varies

HP represents how much damage is needed to make a hole an Agent can climb through.

Anti-Plasma Core

Some high security doors and walls have an anti-plasma core. This reduces the effectiveness of plasma weapons causing them to only ignore 4 points of AV. They are expensive and have a high power consumption so are only used in sensitive areas.

DOORS

Weak Door

A poor quality, thin door that may be encountered in a tenement block in an Old City.
10HP, AV1 Could be guarded if the door leads somewhere important, generally no security at all.

Plastic / Wooden Door

A standard door used in well made, modern buildings.
20HP, AV2, No guards. Possibly low end cameras, door may be linked to a security alarm.

Hi-Polymer Door

These are normally transparent, clear glass-polymer doors and are typically used in offices and labs to give an open plan feeling.
30HP, AV3

Secure Metal Door

This could be found at the entrance to a medium security installation or as a typical door in a high security installation.
100HP, AV15
1-2 mid level guards
Robotic guards within easy reach
Knock-out gas and multispectrum cameras
Door will be linked to a panic alarm
Bioreaders will be fitted to the door requiring DNA, voice, biorhythm and retina scans

High Security Twin Durasteel Doors

These are found in high security areas such as weapons labs and CEO offices.
300HP, AV30
2-4 high level guards
Robotic guards within easy reach
Elite sensor arrays
Door is linked to knock-out gas injectors
Electrocuting floor
A.I. controlled tracking machine turrets
Door will be connected to an installation-wide panic alarm. Biometric scanners will be fitted to the door requiring DNA, voice, biorhythm and retina scans. Any deviation from standard inputs due to nervousness in voice, sweaty palms, high heart rate, etc, will trigger defence droids and any installed countermeasures. The doors are paired with an air lock system for maximum security from airborne attacks.

WALLS

Weak Plaster Walls

These are encountered in old buildings and serve little use other than to block line of sight and separate areas.
10HP, AV0 Electrical cable and piping may be hidden in the walls.

Stone Walls

These are the main constituent of Old City buildings and are still used in many modern structures.
50HP, AV10, May contain electrical cable and piping.

Polymer Walls

These are often used as partitions and in places where security is not an issue such as a public toilet. The walls are fairly thin and not very soundproof. They are surprisingly brittle and sharp when broken.
15HP, AV2

Metal Walls

Metal walls are expensive to produce and heavy, they are normally used only in secure areas. They can have current passed through them to make them harder to assault and numerous devices such as gas jets can be hidden in them to act as deterrents.
100HP, AV15

Durasteel Walls

Very expensive and rare. The walls would only be used in the most important of installations. They can be connected to currents and have deterrents installed in them.
300HP, AV30

Hard Ion Walls

These are used to section off important areas. They are effectively hard ion shields which act as walls. They can be turned on and off, normally via biometric permission. Hard Ion Walls are normally used as a temporary measure where normal walls cannot be used, or in secure areas as doors.
HP and AV vary in the same way as Hard Ion Shields.

NON STRUCTURAL FEATURES

Power Stations

Most installations will have either an independent power supply or a sub-station. The areas are normally secure and hard to access. If access can be gained to one then power can normally be switched off by passing an 'Intelligence + Mechtronics' roll. A modifier may apply. Note that with the power off, electrical systems will fail unless they have a backup. This could include alarms, doors, computers, turrets, oxygen pumps, air scrubbers, life support systems, and more. Make sure the players don't always get an easy time by simply turning off the power. For example, you could activate a security shutdown and ready all droids if the main power is taken off-line.

Vents and Ducts

Vents and ducts connect different areas of an installation together in different ways to doors, making some areas more accessible. Ducts may well be electrified and alarmed. They can be monitored on camera, patrolled by small droids or contain defence systems such as turrets. Some ducts may even contain filtration systems which make sure only permitted chemicals can pass through them, meaning toxins are effectively blocked.

Control Rooms

These lie at the heart of many installations. They are often filled with computers and high-ranking technicians. It is common for the control room to be the most secure room in a structure. It may well have several defence mechanisms including turrets, guards and patrol droids. Taking over a control room is a hard task but very rewarding. Large amounts of data are potentially available along with the opportunity to utilise the controls in the room. They could have numerous functions which Agents could use to great advantage. For example - new areas of the installation could be opened up by using the control room's computers.

TRANSIT

Elevators

Elevators are fast, an Agent simply steps into one, waits a few seconds and steps out. He may have covered 200 floors. The problem with elevators is they are sealed, they may need ID to operate, and Agents can get stuck in them. Some secure elevators may well have electrocutable walls, gaseous acid sprays and oxygen deprivation systems, to name a few. A secure elevator will often be programmed to stop at a certain location in the event of the alarm being triggered. This location will be designed to stop the elevator being exited or could have a security team waiting. The elevator may then deploy its aggressive systems. As well as the ones mentioned above, some have secret panels containing combat droids or mounted turret weapons. All this makes the stairs seem a good choice.

Stairs

Stairs are the slow way up and down a building, especially in Spires or other large structures. The stairwell itself could contain turret weapons or have patrols every few floors. This is an expensive contingency though and normally there will not be many security systems on the stairs. When ascending and descending stairs Agents could take shortcuts using powered lines, repellers and grapple hooks to travel up and down the stairwell in seconds. The doors linking the stairs to floors will often be monitored in some way, especially on important floors.

LABORATORIES

Many installations will either be, or contain a research lab. Research and Development (R&D) is fundamental to the Corporations allowing them to stay competitive. Below are listed some of the different types of lab an Agent is likely to come across.

Cybernetics Lab

These labs are built for developing and fitting cybernetics. Most Spire cities will have a major cybernetics facility for Corporation use and several smaller ones for the general populace to get their personal upgrades. There is normally at least one Agent overseeing a major lab and several technicians. There may also be several Agents in for maintenance and upgrades making attacking cybernetics labs a risky business. Regarding rewards, the Cybernetics lab is one of the best yeilders, There will be top of the range installation equipment worth thousands of credits as well a good supply of upgrades and chips. There will also be medical supplies to assist in surgeries. Security-wise you can expect to find Durasteel doors with responsive and comprehensive security systems.

Weapons Lab

These are notoriously well guarded structures. Here the Corporations research and build their custom weapons and armour, and few things are more important than staying ahead in the arms race. You can expect these installations to be in the centre of Corporate territory and under the guard of Cyberlins. The exception to this are secret weapon labs which are kept hidden so they are not inspected by the UIG. These tend to be well guarded and cleverly hidden but will not be defended by anything so obvious as Cyberlins.

Regarding security, you can expect a number of Agents at the weapons facilities, they are often asked to spend their mission leave at the labs to increase security. Droids and weapon turrets are standard and the walls and doors will be made of the strongest components available. Once inside the facility each door will more than likely be secure and guards armed with the latest weapons will be commonplace. The databanks are also likely to be fitted with some kind of self-destruct system which can only be operated from another location and used in the event that a security breach has been initiated. On the plus side the advantages to raiding a weapons lab are huge. Success can reveal new enemy weapons and allow Agents to make off with packs full of exotic and expensive prototype arms.

Medical Lab / Surgery

This sort of lab is normally low security unless there is a VIP patient there. The doctors and nurses will tend to be untrained in combat and rely on the guards to protect them. A Division of Agents would be unlucky to run into serious problems attacking a medical lab. The doors will normally be polymer and have simple key card systems. It is unlikely there will be turrets or droids unless the lab is researching new medicines or other cutting edge technology. For their troubles Agents can expect to find medpacks, replacement body parts, drugs, medical aids and possible research and medical records. Not a great haul when most of this can be picked up from the stores anyway.

A.I. CONTROL

Some installations (or areas of them) may be under A.I. control. This is an opportunity for the GM to be really savage to the players. An A.I. can not only co-ordinate all of its actions perfectly, it has databases of information at its beck and call which may well be pertinent to the crisis at hand. For example, it may have the invading Agent's cybernetic profiles on record allowing it to use specific hazards to stop them, such as sonic attacks if none of the Agents have protection for their ears. Similarly, if a group of rebels are storming an installation it might try to identify them from remote cameras. On identification the A.I. could see the rebels have purchased a great deal of gas grenades recently, it could thus equip it's troops with gas masks or send in combat droids who are immune to gas.

There are no hard and fast rules about A.I. controlled areas, only the basic idea that the A.I. is able to micromanage its resources on a scale no human could hope for. This makes for a very challenging encounter.

TURRET WEAPONS

Roof / Wall / Floor mounted sentry turret

These monitor an area of about 20 square metres. They are either manned by security staff in a control room or are auto-tracking. Those who should be in the building have their *safecodes* uploaded to their ID Chip so that the turrets do not fire at them. The turret will normally be a pair of tactical weapons such as sub-machine lasers, but in extreme cases could be more serious heavy weapons such as laser cannons or flame throwers. Manually controlled mounted turrets use *support weapons* as their relevant weapon skill.

Manual Turret

Weapons Fitted – 2 x sub-machine lasers

Attack AT-15

Damage – One roll to hit is made – if it hits both cannons hit dealing a total of 12D8. Armour is taken off each D8.

HP 30

AV 8

AI Controlled Turret

Weapon Fitted – 1 X laser Cannon

Attack AT-20

Damage – 5D8+5, Rate 1

HP 30

AV 8

HAZARDS

Gas Jets

These are often used in secure areas such as doors or lifts. When the wrong ID is used the section is sealed off with metal walls and a gas pumped into the room. See page 47 for examples of different gasses.

Electrified Walls and Floors

Conductive walls and floors can be electrified if an emergency code is issued. Contact with the walls and floor may cause the intruder to be electrocuted. This deals 2D10 damage a round ignoring armour.

Guards

Guard droids and human guards can normally be found in all installations. If there are no guards the chances are there is nothing worth going to the installation for.

Humans

Human guards are cheap and generally quite reliable given strong leadership. Guards will normally be found in pairs or small groups. When an alert is sounded or a threat recognised, guards will always call for backup and are normally able to locate each other easily with tracking devices. It is sometimes useful to incapacitate a guard and use his radio to check in, thus avoiding putting other guards on alert. Voice simulators and a good 'Lying & Acting' skill can be useful here. The statistics for guards can be found on pages 229 and 230.

Droids

Droids are expensive and less adaptable than guards, they are generally tougher, less susceptible to corruption and unlikely to display acts of stupidity that guards are famous for. Numerous types of droids exist, and many more can be designed by the GM. Generally droids will only be used in key positions or in areas where humans are not wanted, either for secrecy or safety reasons. A few installations, especially Ai-Jinn ones, are staffed exclusively by droids with an A.I. controlling the running of the base. There are often severe problems with these installations, more specifically droids becoming sentient in the absence of humans. The Ai-Jinn are determined to make it work though and have not halted their Living Facility Project. Droid descriptions begin on page 240.

INSTALLATION MAPS

On the following pages you will find maps to use in your game. These maps have descriptive text to accompany each one which you can use to plan a mission. The first map - the *Redemption Spire in Cape Town*, is designed as a basic introductory mission to Corporation and is a very straightforward mission. The other maps are simply to be used as and when you like.

The maps are pitched at a medium level but can be lowered or raised in difficulty as you see fit and depending how combat orientated the Division are. The two maps at the end of the section are two locations Agents may well find themselves at during action scenes.

The Medical Facility makes an excellent location for a shootout or somewhere to hole up in when the pressure is on.

The Skybridge Terminal has a typical layout for such a building and is always a good location for a side mission. Perhaps breaking a colleague out of the cells there or recovering some confiscated goods.

Populate the maps with items from the Equipment section and NPC's from the back of the book.

INSTALLATION TYPES

Roll	Type	Function	Examples
1	Research	Research and development on new technology.	Weapons lab, physics lab, disease lab.
2	Defensive	Protection of an area or other installation.	Watchpost, shield generator station.
3	Aggressive	The execution of attacks / sometimes defence.	Warship, missile battery station, military airbase.
4	Storage	Safeguarding of stock or important tech.	Warehouse, missile silo, subterranean database.
5	Training	Development and education of individuals.	School, military training camp, telepath academy.
6	Bureaucratic	Processing of administrative information.	Office building, town hall, section of a Spire.
7	Factory	Creation of goods from raw materials.	Tank factory, cybernetics fabrication plant.
8	Leisure	Utilising spare time.	Shopping mall, restaurant, gym, cinema, park.
9	Surveillance	Collecting Intelligence.	Satellite array, listening post, orbital satellite.
10	Medical	Dealing with human conditions.	Hospital, cybernetics lab, morgue, psyche lab.
11	Natural	None originally.	Underground lab in a cavern, mine, mountaintop comm. array.
12	Residential	Houses people.	Outcast squat, Spire apartment, rich woman's manor, hotel.
13	Detention	Detaining individuals against their will.	Prison complex, slave mine, cell in a UIG station.

INSTALLATION OCCUPIER

1. Artificial Intelligence	7. Western Federation	13. Rich Citizen
2. UIG	8. Cult of Machina	14. Typical Citizen
3. Ai-Jinn	9. Rebels	15. Criminal / Outlaw
4. Comoros	10. Droid Liberation Army	16. Outcast
5. Eurasian Inc.	11. Order of the Faith	17. Powerful Independent
6. Shi Yukiro	12. Minor Corporation	18. Sentient Droid

SECURITY

1   None   Local store, Outcast house.
The facility has either no need or no money for security. The worst that can be expected are some idiots with claw hammers and the windows welded shut.

2   Crude   Criminal hideout, pawn shop.
The doors will have basic mechanical locks and there may be a handful of ill-trained guards with low quality weapons.

3   Basic   Criminal boss' hideout, drug cutting house, gun shop.
Most doors will have basic mechanical locks although some will have been upgraded to advanced or even electronic ones. Whoever is running the place has something to protect so may employ guards with basic training and decent weapons. There may even be a low end droid or two and some form of basic motion sensors.

4-5   Typical   Hospital, Spire open areas, public buildings.
The exterior doors will be keycoded and have a guard presence. Most internal doors will have basic swipecard locks but be of a weak material which can easily be smashed. The guards are generally of average skill but there may not be a guard captain. Anything of importance in the facility will be behind stronger doors with good security systems. There may be a droid or two present.

6-7   Good   Spire residential areas, expensive shops, basic labs.
Security is important in this facility. There will be a contingent of competent guards and a unit of well maintained droids. Aggressive security systems such as gun turrets and gas jets may be present in the more delicate areas of the facility. Most doors will be strong enough to deter average raiders though a specialised intrusion team will find no serious problems.

8-9   Strong   Most corporate & UIG Facilities. Property of rich Citizens.
This facility will hold important information, goods or personnel, and has received extensive security attention. There will be a large number of guards with at least one captain and all doors will be strong and electronically secure. No one enters or leaves without clearance and there will be a host of scanners in the entryways. Droids may monitor both the inside and outside of the facility and there will be numerous aggressive security measures.

10   Elite   Jails, vaults, high-tech labs, Corporate & UIG secure areas.
Security gets no better than this. Cyberlins and high level personnel guard the perimeter of the facility while advanced droids and guards patrol the internal areas. Numerous gun turrets and hazards are in place, Corporate Agents / UIG Officers will be present as is appropriate. The walls and doors will be made of durable and resilient compounds.

INSTALLATION QUALITY

1   Bombed out
The installation is almost non existent, it is a battered husk which is probably dangerous to walk around. It is likely to be in an Old City or an area of wasteland. Toxins may be an issue. Outlaws may frequent the area.

2   Derelict
The installation is long abandoned though not collapsing. It's structure is possibly compromised. There is a good chance that Outlaws or Cult of Machina are using the building as a base of operations.

3   Recently left
The installation is disused although there is still evidence of activity. Old unimportant documents / items may have been left behind and underground groups could be vying for occupation.

4   Makeshift
The facility is still in use but only just, the place is dirty and probably a health risk. The people here are either working for an illegal employer or this is the only building available in the area.

5-6   Basic
The facility is safe and functional but has no frills. The walls are normally basic, such as unpainted concrete and the only fittings are utilitarian and essential to the running of the facility.

7-8   Typical
A typical installation will be simply decorated with few concessions to aesthetics. It will be vented and contain some conveniences such as a lounge or bar. Some parts may be more basic such as storage areas or underground workshops. The majority of UIG and remote installations will be like this.

9   Modern
This represents a facility which is likely to be entered by the public or belongs to a wealthy company and has therefore been upgraded to make it appear pleasant, modern and efficient. It is well decorated and has environmental maintenance systems. The employees are generally well paid and expected to be intelligent, well dressed and dedicated.

10   High-end
These facilities tend to require sterile areas or are involved in generating large amounts of money. They are of great value to the owning company and the costs of maintaining such an impressive building are easily offset against the money generated from the facility. They tend to be well guarded, beautifully designed and opulently furnished.

SAMPLE FIRST MISSION - REDEMPTION RECOVERY

Use the map opposite with this mission.
Skill Checks are on page 138, Combat is on page 141, Equipment is on page 49, Weapons and combat equipment start on page 29

This is a fairly simple mission involving breaching an installation and recovering some technology before exiting. It can be adapted for any Corporation but is better if they are not Comoros. There are several stages to this mission. The GM should use this as a basic template adding and changing things to suit the game.

I. BRIEFING

The players should be introduced to where they are, for example you could describe the Spire they reside in, or other incidental scene setting information. They can then be called to the mission brief and introduced to the Missions Officer whom you should think up in advance. There is no need for STATS and skills but try to give him or her an attitude. For example she could be kind and understanding or snappy and over efficient. The Missions Officer will describe the mission. Feel free to elaborate or even make up a mission brief using the template on page 249.

> ### MISSION BRIEF
> *The Division must enter the Redemption Spire in Capte Town. This will be done by exiting a flying passenger shuttle whilst over the Spire and landing on a balcony on the 644th floor. From there the Division must gain access to the 643rd floor (ideally via an outside window). Once in, they must recover a piece of prototype cybernetics from the safe and exit the Spire. If unable to make their own way back they should head to a designated collection point in old Cape Town for extraction by an Exit Man.*
>
> *Equipment - 1 Security Bypass Device, 1 set of Disposable Lockpicks, Drop Suits for all Agents, Pay will be standard - see page 79 for mission pay.*

Obviously the Missions Officer should try to help them as much as possible by answering any questions they might have, but sometimes it can be tricky to come up with a good response to everything. Below are some options if the players ask awkward questions.

1. Make something reasonable up
2. Tell them that information is unavailable
3. Tell them they have no need for that information

When they are happy they should leave and buy any equipment they need (page 29). They may also want to make plans. No blueprints of the Spire are available to the Division.

2. SETTING OFF AND DROPPING OFF

This section will be relatively mundane; the Agents will board a domestic shuttle at night and leave for Cape Town. If you are an experienced GM you could add in some encounters such as a shuttle jacking which the Agents can prevent.
Just before the end of the journey the Division must pass out of the passenger area and into the cargo section in order to drop from the shuttle without causing suspicion. It should be fairly simple as this is a low security domestic trip. If they manage to mess it up badly let them open the main door and jump or get another shuttle and try again once they land.
If they can sneak into the cargo area when the undercarriage lowers they can jump out and descend towards the Spire (it is night time). A successful 'Agility + Athletics' check (with a +2 bonus to the roll) will allow them to land right on the balcony. Failure will result in landing off-target and having to climb to the balcony. This should not be too hard, remember this is an introductory mission.

Hopefully the Division will reach the balcony. Terrible luck happens sometimes and you may find your Division has ended up falling off the Spire. If this happens try to improvise. Allow them to sneak up the Spire or get another shuttle and try again.

3. INFILTRATION

The Division should now move along the balcony, they should be able to drop down with ropes (if they brought them) and land outside the windows leading to the labs. Opening the lab windows is a basic 'Crime + Intelligence' check, but if they look carefully they can see the middle window is not properly locked and can be easily opened.

A. Offices

This is the entry point into the facility, the two offices either side contain some items as described on the map.

B. Guard Room

The guard room contains guards who are playing cards, they will only appear if there is a disturbance or if an alarm goes off.

C. Chemical Storage

Contains numerous basic chemicals which can be taken. Selling them to the Corporation will make about 500¢. Selling them on the street will make about 1500¢

D. Changing Room

The lockers can be raided, each door is locked and the contents are described on the map.

E. Security Checkpoint

The X-ray machine cannot be physically bypassed but can be deactivated with a successful 'Intelligence + Mechtronics' check. The 2 guards in here could be a problem. If they are taken out quickly then the alarm may not be raised. Knock out gas would be a good option here. The camera can be shot out or moved with Telekinesis 1. The X-ray will sound a local alarm if firearms are taken through it.

F. Reverse Engineering Lab I

Extra equipment can be acquired here.

G. Reverse Engineering Lab 2

The Inaugurate (see page 51) in the locked cupboard will help entering the safe (H). The guards will hopefully be of little trouble but there is a captain who could cause some serious problems. Grenades and KO gas could be useful in this room.

H. Safe

Inside the safe is the missing cybernetic component as well as some other technology that can be taken. The inaugurate will automatically allow entry into the vault so technically any Agent will be able to enter the facility. (Safe Door - HP 20 / AV 20 / -4 penalty to open / Electronic Lock.)

I. Exit

The exit from the facility could involve the intervention of some security guards or you may allow the players to escape with ease if they have been stealthy during the mission. Either way, once they have left the building they will need to make their way back home. Bear in mind that public routes may be monitored by the Comoros security teams after a break-in of this type. Stealing a shuttle or powerful boat could be a good option, or if they are truly lost they could call in an Exit Man from the Corporation who would assist their escape, but it would not be viewed well by their superiors.

5. DEBRIEFING

When the Agents return to the Missions Officer things will vary depending on mission success. He will discuss the mission and what happened. He will also ask about any screw-ups and additional items collected which he may let them keep. Award the players XP as stated in the XP description on page 79. (3-4 is recommended for a mission like this). Rank should be awarded based on the success of the mission. If it was a complete success then 3 rank points would be a good reward, simply recovering the goods will earn 2 and a marginal success only 1. Failure will earn no rank and possibly a reprimand.

Reverse Engineering Labs

643rd Floor of the Redemption Spire, Capetown, South Africa

Mission Guide

Tech Level - This facility is less secure than you may expect. This is because Comoros do not have access to such high tech as other Corporations.

All standard doors can be opened with a successful 'Intelligence + Crime' check. The GM may apply a modifier to any doors he feel they should be more secure. See the Crime skill on page 19.

Guards can be found on page 229 and 230.

The cameras can be shot out which may bring more guards **or** bypassed with 'Agility + Stealth' checks.

Feel free to add in more encounters such as guards, droids or Agents.

Exit from the facility will be the same way as they came using the drop suits to leave the Spire and head towards a safe location for pre-arraged recovery.

Office 3 contains information on a planned raid which can either receive a 1500 credit reward or could spearhead a new mission.

Legend

	WINDOW
	LOCKED DOOR (STANDARD)
	LOCKED DOOR (POLYMER)
	UNLOCKED DOOR
	LOCKED SECURE DOOR
C	CAMERA
G	GUARD PRESENCE
	2 METRES

Storage safe contains the missing Cybernetics as well as:
'1 Stealth 3' process chip
Disc Shield
Proximity Mine
EMP Rifle

SAFE DOOR

This door is locked and very tough, the inaugurate in 'Reverse Engineering Lab 2' can be used to dissolve the locking mechanism.

Or they can crack the lock. This requires an 'Intelligence + Crime' with a -4 penalty.

The door can be blown open. See 'Features of an Installation'.

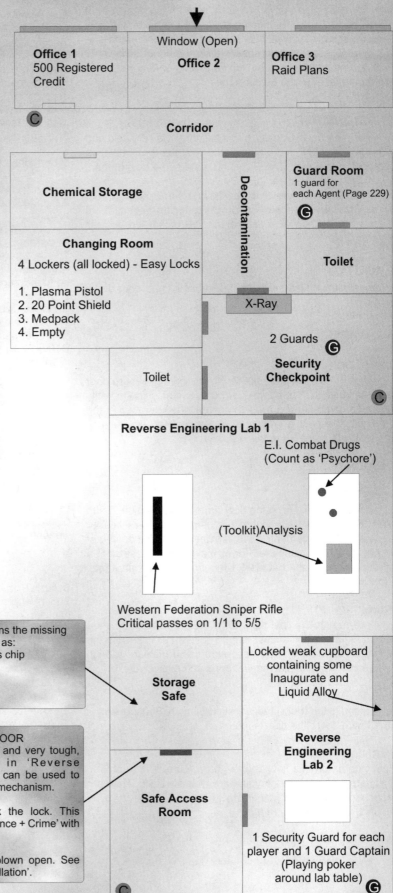

Window (Open)

Office 1
500 Registered Credit

Office 2

Office 3
Raid Plans

C

Corridor

Chemical Storage

Decontamination

Guard Room
1 guard for each Agent (Page 229)
G

Changing Room
4 Lockers (all locked) - Easy Locks

1. Plasma Pistol
2. 20 Point Shield
3. Medpack
4. Empty

Toilet

X-Ray

2 Guards G

Security Checkpoint

C

Reverse Engineering Lab 1

E.I. Combat Drugs (Count as 'Psychore')

(Toolkit)Analysis

Western Federation Sniper Rifle
Critical passes on 1/1 to 5/5

Toilet

Storage Safe

Locked weak cupboard containing some Inaugurate and Liquid Alloy

Reverse Engineering Lab 2

Safe Access Room

1 Security Guard for each player and 1 Guard Captain (Playing poker around lab table) G

C

THE ODESSA COMMUNICATIONS HEADQUARTERS

This is an E.I. controlled facility in the Ukraine on the coast of the Black Sea. Here Eurasian Incorporated have a listening post where secure signals from all over the world are intercepted and decoded by a team of cryptographers using some very powerful A.I.s. The facility looks like a run down factory with a vast dish mounted on the taller of the two buildings.

THE ENVIRONMENT

The environment around Odessa is inhospitable. It is very cold and there are various health risks associated with the high radiation levels present in the area. The GM can create some environment related problems if he wishes.

E.I. have the area well monitored and have a small contingent of two Murder Class and four Sentinel droids scanning within a 5 km square area. For higher level campaigns you could add a small Cyberlin if desired.

THE FACILITY

The Communications Headquarters is fairly small and consists of 2 buildings.

RADAR TOWER

GROUND FLOOR

This is a small, grotty two story building. A simple but secure door leads into the building. There is a guard checkpoint inside to verify entrants and a computer room which controls the operation of the tower. You could mount a gun turret in the roof for experienced Agents. There are stairs up to the first floor.

FIRST FLOOR

RECEIVING ROOM

This is where the signals from the dish are collected, collated and decrypted. The data is then sent to the administration offices for storage. Data can be intercepted at this point by a skilled computer user, but is in a highly encoded form, making it useless until a decryption team can spend at least 1 month on it. By then it may be too late.

MECH ROOM

This is where the mechanical parts for moving the radar dish are housed and maintained. If access can be gained to this section the mechanics of the radar can be destroyed using medium to high grade weaponry such as plasma weapons and explosives.

ROOF ACCESS

A ladder leading to the roof via a very secure hatch. Sentinel droids watch the hatch. Here the dish is mounted.

GUARDS ROOM

There are guards on this floor with a guard room. The guards in this facility are under E.I. employ and are typically slack. They are not responsive and are not expecting an attack. Those trying to use stealth will be at an advantage.

ADMINISTRATION BUILDING

Guards wander the corridors of this section.

GENERATOR

This provides power for the facility. If shut down emergency power will run for 24 hours. The emergency supply is underground and inaccessible.

ADMIN OFFICES

Here numerous desk staff are involved in sorting data and further decryption / distribution of acquired data. Agent Korenchek can normally be found here in his private office and living quarters. He runs the facility and should be suitably powerful. He has a lot of Anascan and Datanetica cyberware. His first choice in combat is to call in the Murder Class Droids and release his 3 pet cybermonkeys (page 243 & 245).

SOCIAL ROOM

A lounge where staff can relax. Not much of interest can be found here.

RECEPTION

This is where visitors are led and greeted. There are visitor logs which may be of minor interest. Sometimes Agent Korenchek can be found here.

SLEEPING CELLS

The staff live at the facility while they work here. This area contains clean but basic accommodation for 20 people.
D100x10 slip credit can be found here as well as another D100x10 in valuable goods.

TOILET

A toilet / shower room.

STAIRS DOWN

This leads down to the basement level where the servers are. A guard checkpoint is at the bottom of the stairs and a powerful gun turret guards the stairs (see gun turrets on page 208 for alternative configurations).

CHECK POINT

Guards are here to protect the servers. They are armed with melee weapons so they don't damage the systems and should be Guard Captains (page 230). This may prove problematic for weaker Agents.

SERVER ROOM

This is where the data is stored. It can be ripped off the servers by hacking. (See page 150). High end security is in place. How good it is is up to the GM and the Agent's ability level.

MISSION IDEAS

1. The facility has been taken over by another group and E.I. Agents must liberate it.
2. E.I. have stolen and decoded some sensitive information from the player's Corporation. Remove it from one of the servers before they can use it.
3. Some important transmissions are about to be sent from the player's Corporation. They must incapacitate the facility before the transmission occurs to avoid data interception.
4. Some spies from the player's Corporation were staking out the Communication HQ. They were captured by E.I. Agents at the facility and the Division must liberate them.
5. Agent Korenchek is running the facility illegally. The UIG request a team enters the facility and stops him (this could be a Cross-Corporation game).

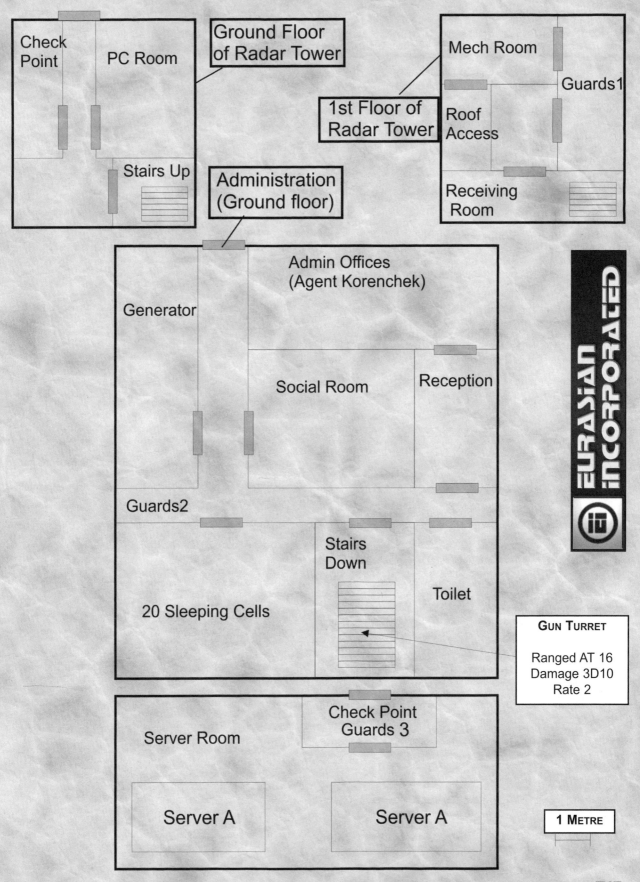

ODESSA COMMUNICATIONS HEADQUARTERS
PROPERTY OF EURASIAN INC.

Check Point

PC Room

Ground Floor of Radar Tower

Stairs Up

Mech Room

Guards1

1st Floor of Radar Tower

Roof Access

Receiving Room

Administration (Ground floor)

Admin Offices (Agent Korenchek)

Generator

Social Room

Reception

EURASIAN INCORPORATED

Guards2

Stairs Down

Toilet

20 Sleeping Cells

GUN TURRET

Ranged AT 16
Damage 3D10
Rate 2

Server Room

Check Point
Guards 3

Server A

Server A

1 METRE

RUNNING THE WESTERN FEDERATION BIO LAB

This map shows the secret Western Federation BIO research lab on the Miller-Urey Research Orbital. This facility is responsible for the development and production of the Federation's illicit combat BIOs, which are, as yet, not known to the UIG, and are still in the R&D phase.

This map and key provide a wealth of ideas for potential missions and could also be used as a template for more mundane labs. Below are some ideas.

1. The Division must protect the facility from attackers.
2. The Division must infiltrate the facility and recover some BIO DNA.
3. BIOs have escaped and are running wild in the labs.
4. The Division have been captured and are going to be grafted with BIO organs. They must escape. (This could be the second part of a failed mission where they were captured in the first section.)
5. The facility is in a biohazard lockdown and there are no staff inside, only dozens of droids. The Division must enter and steal some data.
6. The Division must pose as wealthy clients and steal some samples without being discovered.
7. The UIG requests the Division go in and destroy all the BIOs in the holding warehouse deep below the facility. This could be a Cross-Corporation game.

LAB FEATURES

This is a general idea of the parts of the lab, modify and populate the facility to suit your style, game and the power of the Division.

1. Reception. This is a clean glass and steel open space where visitors and workers check in when they arrive. There will be a moderate guard presence here.

2. Bathroom for staff and visitors. A narrow venting duct leads from here to the outside but is monitored by IVIS Sentinels inside the ducting (see page 244.)

3. Storeroom for office supplies.

4. Rear office for administrative duties.

5. Second office and security checkpoint for those wishing to enter the lab complex. This section is very secure and has a high guard presence. Biometic security is present.

6. Weapons locker for guards, it contains an array of tactical and light weapons to be used in the event of an assault against the facility.

7. Droid Room. this room contains a single Executioner Droid (page 243) which is normally powered down. The droid is activated at night and in states of emergency.

8. Decon Room. Anyone passing into or out of the lab complex must pass through this clean room which decontaminates the subject. The door into the clean room is extremely secure.

9. Suit-Up Room. Here employees don their environment suits if they are going to work in the more hazardous areas of the facility. There are often spare suits here which can be used for subterfuge.

10. Guard Room. This room has a strong contingent of guards and is a second layer of security for those passing into the facility. There is also a reclaimed but faulty UIG contraband scanner here which checks for illegal items and potential hazards. It will catch threats on a roll of 16 or below on 2D10. Items such as a Liberty Black Body Space still get their chance to evade the scanner.

11. This is the main reception for the lab and has numerous pictures on the walls denoting strange biological creations and images of bizarre climates. There may well be a few visitors here or some lab technicians having a coffee.

12. Short range teleporter. This is one of the WF's best kept secrets. They have a small teleporter capable of moving items of 4,000kg or less (living or not). It is mainly used for bringing in raw materials which are then transported down the stairs (22) and into the elevator (31). It also serves to transport the freshly created BIOs into the jungle outside the facility when necessary. The door to this is nigh impenetrable. The range of the teleporter is 500 metres and it is linked the WF teleporter in Atlanta.

13. Turret weapon. This is to defend the teleporter. Alternative turret weapons can be found found on page 208. This is A.I. controlled and consists of two sub-machine plasmas.

14. Droid Maintenance Area. This is where the droids (15) are maintained. Robotics toolkits and the like can be picked up here.

15. Security Droids. This is a stock of 6 Y&S droids of varying types used to safeguard the labs. They are powered down but always ready to be activated.

16. Access corridor. This passageway slopes down, is quiet and simply used to access parts 17, 18, 20, 21 and 23.

17. Medbay. The medbay is ill guarded and a number of medical drugs and tools can be collected here.

18. Biological Store Room. Here can be acquired almost all the drugs and toxins listed in this book as well as many that aren't. The GM should feel free to make up some interesting chemicals for the Division to find here. The door is moderately secure.

19. On the wall here is located a medical emergency kit containing 3 intravenous medpacks and 3 toxin filters.

20. Bathroom. An ordinary bathroom with a very small air conditioning vent which leads to the bathroom on the first floor (2). The vent is narrow and has IVIS sentinels in it.

21. Offices. These are the science offices where the research is stored and collated. An Agent of considerable power and importance can often be found here. A great deal of corporate secrets are stored here, but it would require a skilled hacker to get through the Corporate security.

22. Stairs Down. This is a wide set of steps which lead down to the research labs.

23. Lab Concourse. This is a large, high room where the mutician scientists meet to discuss ideas and have conferences. The room is simple, pleasantly decorated and filled with numerous chairs and tables.

24. Combat BIO. This disturbing sight is a 17 foot high monster, covered in armoured plates with great scything claws and appendages much like a preying mantis. The creature is pale with reddish markings and four slitted eyes around it's head and no mouth.
Those with Science may recognise it as an advanced combat BIO in an electroglass case. (It is currently in suspended animation.)

25. BIO Holding Cells. These tough cells each contain a combat BIO. These creatures range from 5-10 feet in height and are locked in stasis until they are needed.

26. Dissection Lab. Four large dissection tables fill this room. The floor has a gully to take away fluids and on the south wall an impressive array of surgical tools are laid out.

27. Vehicle Hangar. This is where staff park their vehicles. There is also an emergency evacuation shuttle here and a collection of mechtronics tools.

28. Cloning and Growth Labs. A series of cloning vats line the walls, most contain a BIO in some form of maturity. Three large banks of computers fill the centre of the room from which the BIOs are maintained and monitored.

29. Microbiology Lab. This is where the dissected BIOs are analysed and the new ones developed via grafting and gene manipulation. This room is full of bio-engineered parts and half completed BIOs.

30. Armoury and Elevator. This section contains a small elevator which leads to BIO storage below. There are also numerous weapons in the event that a problem occurs with the BIOs in the storage room below. The elevator leads to an observation bay in the storehouse.

31. BIO Elevator. When the BIOs are created in the cloning labs they are placed into cells and sent down the elevator into the main storage facility beneath the labs. Essentially underneath is a vast room with dozens of BIOs of all shapes and sizes. This can be an excellent place for a high level showdown.

WESTERN FEDERATION BIO LAB: MILLER-UREY

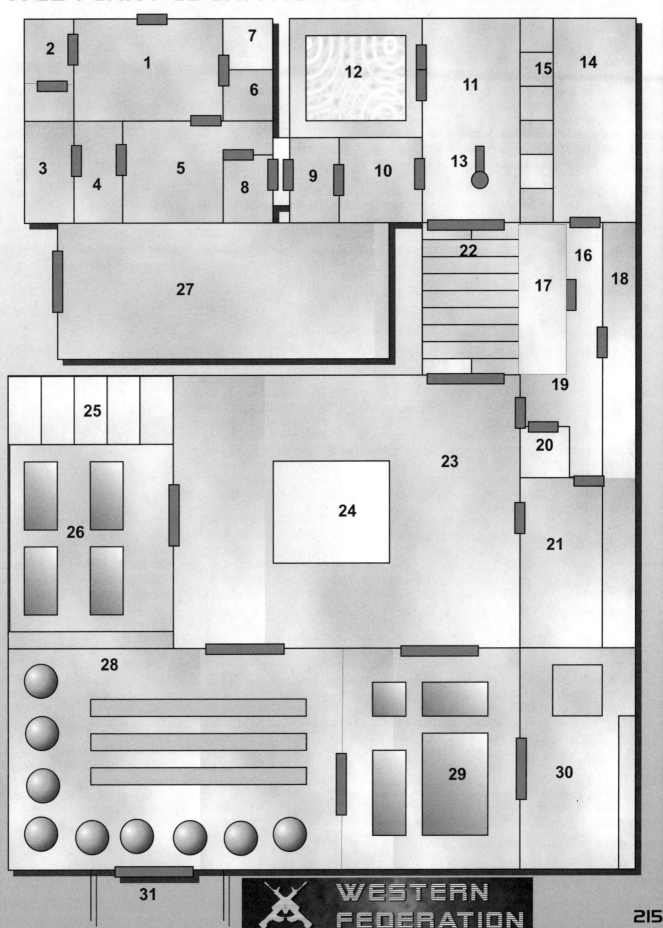

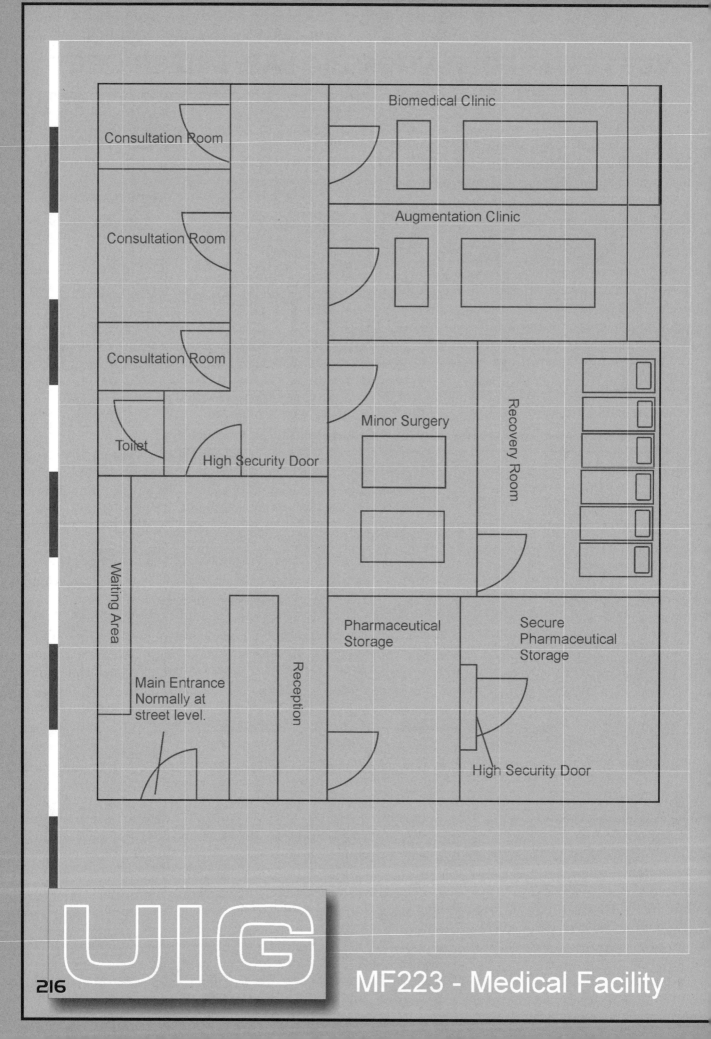

Consultation Room

Consultation Room

Consultation Room

Toilet

High Security Door

Waiting Area

Main Entrance
Normally at
street level.

Reception

Biomedical Clinic

Augmentation Clinic

Minor Surgery

Recovery Room

Pharmaceutical
Storage

Secure
Pharmaceutical
Storage

High Security Door

UIG

MF223 - Medical Facility

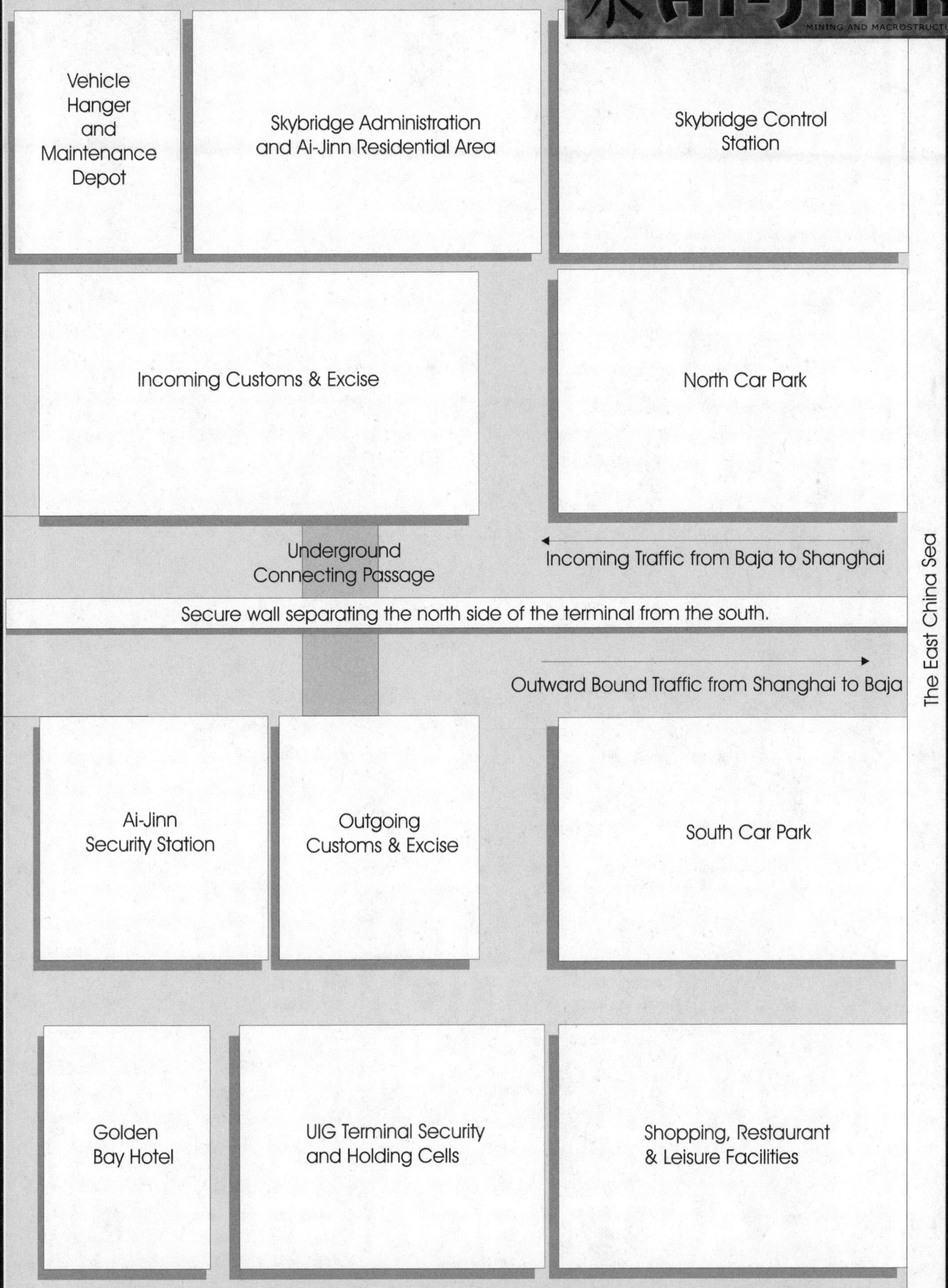

Vehicle Hanger and Maintenance Depot

Skybridge Administration and Ai-Jinn Residential Area

Skybridge Control Station

Incoming Customs & Excise

North Car Park

Underground Connecting Passage

← Incoming Traffic from Baja to Shanghai

Secure wall separating the north side of the terminal from the south.

Outward Bound Traffic from Shanghai to Baja →

The East China Sea

Ai-Jinn Security Station

Outgoing Customs & Excise

South Car Park

Golden Bay Hotel

UIG Terminal Security and Holding Cells

Shopping, Restaurant & Leisure Facilities

THE SHANGHAI SKYBRIDGE TERMINAL

SECTION 13

ANTAGONISTS

OVERVIEW

These are generic characters mainly to be used in action situations. If the encounter is more social, numbers are not so important and the NPC's can be made up more liberally. Feel free to modify them and make up abilities for them if they are not described. They are normally always considered to carry the weapons stated on them as well as any equipment you roll or deem appropriate.

RANK

This is an idea of the NPC's UIG assigned Rank. This can be useful for determining what Licenses player's can use on the NPC and what kind of influence they have if you mistreat them.

LEVEL

Important: NPC Level is not quite the same as Agent Level. NPC Level indicates the character's approximate overall power. It is not a direct reference to Experience Points like Agent Level.

NPC Level takes into account things such as cybernetic upgrades, weapons, equipment, tactics etc. For example, a basic human should be Level 0 but if armed with a railgun, heavy armour and a hard ion shield, he may be listed as level 2 so you can instantly see what kind of threat he is.

COMBAT

HP	Hit Points
Shield	Hard Ion / Telepathic Shield if present
AV	Armour Value
Defence	The character's Close Combat Defence
TE	Character's Telepathic Energy if applicable

Weapons

Action Total with the weapons - Roll equal or below to hit. Weapon Damage and Weapons Rate.

Where an NPC has twin weapons, e.g. the Malenbrach has 2 x two handed swords, the statistics given are for one weapon. If the Malenbrach wants to attack with both, then use the weapon twice.

STATS

Strength (Str), Endurance (End), Agility (Agi), Reflexes (Ref), Perception (Per), Intelligence (Int) or A.I., Presence (Pres).

Skills

The NPC's typical skills.

Licenses

The NPC's typical licenses. These can be altered depending on the individual status and duties of the NPC.

Trainings

The NPC's typical trainings.

Cybernetics

NPC's cybernetic upgrades.

Equipment

Roll a D100 for each piece of equipment listed. If you get below or equal the percentage listed they are carrying that piece of equipment with them (or a similar one).

Registered credit is not listed as it is normally useless for a looter. Not every piece of equipment is listed, for example, a character may have a high AV yet no armour is listed. You can assume he has some armour or possibly some drugs to toughen his skin.

Description

A brief account of the NPC.

Alternatives

Some examples of how you could run the NPC in a less obvious way.

NPCs Are Not The Same As Characters

NPC's may not follow normal character creation rules and can have abilities without the necessary prerequisites, this is because they are designed to be concise and effective in their given areas. They also need to be easy to use without wading through additional and unnecessary detail.

RUNNING COMBAT

Most players will generally resort to violence at one time or another. *Corporation* gives you a wide range of tactical options for dealing with enemies, which players will learn to use as they become more familiar with the system.

As a GM you will need to know the way NPC's fight, so it is a good idea to skim over the enemies in your game before you start in order to save people sitting around while you study the book. Many antagonists can simply be a few scrawled numbers on a sheet of paper but others may require more thought and care.

QUICK NPCs

For running a quick fist fight in a bar or for taking out a hotel security guard, you may not want to pre-generate a comprehensive NPC and the ones in the book may not be suitable. In this case you can use this simple system. You need only a few numbers.

Ranged Action Total / Damage	Typically 9-13 / Pistol D8
Close Combat Action Total / Damage	Typically 9-13 / Punch 3
Defence	Typically 4-5
HP	Typically 20-30
STATS	Typically 4-6

This is only a rough guide for impromptu and essentially non-vital action scenes. It's better to use a well thought out character for more important showdowns.

BALANCING THE ENCOUNTER

Setting a reasonable challenge can be quite hard. In general, a good idea is to start off your campaign with easy fights and see how the Agents do. They'll probably just enjoy the action and will be learning the rules so they won't be concerned if the combat was too easy.

As you get an idea of their skill, increase the enemies to suit the Division. A good technique is to have the enemies come in waves. *For example, they enter an installation and startle a guard who they swiftly dispatch. The noise attracts another guard who calls for backup.*

This brings in a steady stream of enemies rather than a huge room full of death which can be:

a) awkward to run for the GM
b) difficult to take back if they start massacring the Division
c) hard to stop if you decide the combat has gone on long enough.

Some say to hell with game balance, life is harsh and sometimes running away is the best option. The choice, as always, is yours.

MUTATED HUMAN

RANK 0 / LEVEL 10

COMBAT

HP	35
Shield	0
AV	2
Defence	6

WEAPONS

Bone Strike	AT 12, Dam D4+4, Rate 2
Toxic Bite	AT 12, Dam D2+4, Rate 1 (Potency 8)

If the target is wounded by the bite they suffer from the foul toxins within the mutant's mouth. This causes them to rot over the next few days. Each hour they take D4 damage which can only be healed via Biokinesis 8+ or a specifically engineered antitoxin. Any lab or medical facility will do this for around 500 credits. This cannot be made in advance as it needs to be tailored to the exact toxin.

STATS

Str 9, End 10, Agi 6, Ref 6, Per 5, Int 4, Pres 4

SKILLS

Close Combat 6, Crime 2, Attitude 5, Stealth 3

TRAININGS

Survival, Does not take Mashing Damage

EQUIPMENT

50%	D100 slip credit
50%	Some rotting food
50%	A poor condition weapon

BACKGROUND

In order for the privileged to live in clean, sanitary environments others must live in stinking pits of toxic waste. Places such as the Australasian Freestate and some of the off-world dumping sites have such high levels of radiation that mutation is commonplace. Although most mutations are undesirable some can actually augment the individual. The mutant detailed here is just one example of what is possible after being subjected to mutagens for generations.

This type is known by scientists to be a Grade 2 mutant. This means the mutations are severe and the individual is unlikely to retain their 'humanity'. This is an unreliable grading system and has come under much criticism by rights groups.

GENERAL APPEARANCE

Typical Grade 2 mutants look much like normal humans, they may have distended limbs, discoloured skin, erratic hair growth, or generally misshapen bodies. The mutations they have are normally inhibitory and make them less able as individuals.

The one listed here possesses large bony growths over the hands which allow it to do considerably more damage in melee combat. It also has overgrown teeth which are cracked and splintered. These are coated with a vile toxic smile which is excreted from mutated salivary glands in the mouth. The skin is hardened and leathery giving it a natural armour but limiting its agility. The high strength and endurance are a result of an overdeveloped adrenal gland and insane blood lust. It does not care if its gets wounded and just keeps fighting until it can feed.

COMBAT

Mutants typically fight for food, territory or just from animal aggression. Although they may attack in packs there will generally be little in the way of co-ordination and a Division should have little trouble dispatching them. What is of concern is their mutated physiologies which may allow them to spit toxic chemicals, endure massive damage or bring to bear incredible strength.

Some of the less feral mutants may have firearms and you should give these individuals 3 or 4 points in the relevant skill. They may also lay traps in the wastelands such as pits, snares or rigged explosives.

CIVILIAN / CITIZEN

RANK 0 / LEVEL 0

COMBAT

HP   20
Shield   0
AV   0
Defence   1

WEAPONS

Kinetic Pistol   AT 7, Damage D8, Rate 3
Strike   AT 6, Damage 2, Rate 2
Knife   AT 6, Damage D4 + 5, Rate 3

STATS

Str 5, End 5, Agi 5, Ref 5, Per 5, Int 5, Pres 5

SKILLS

Arts & Culture 3, Athletics 2, Attitude 3, Business 6, Close Combat 1, Computers & AI 5, Corp. Knowledge 3, Light Firearms 2, Looking Good 4, Lying & Acting 3, Observation 4, Drive 5.

LICENSES

Domestic Vehicle License, Light Firearms License, Professional License, e.g., Medical License.

TRAININGS

Aptitude or one specific to the civilian's profession.

EQUIPMENT

50%   One weapon from list above
60%   D100 in slip credit
50%   Average vehicle keys
50%   Average apartment keys
10%   Drug worth no more than 100¢

DESCRIPTION

The Civilian is the most common individual encountered. They dominate the cities and provide the backbone of the economy. The UIG guard Civilians unerringly. If a Civilian is involved in a fight she will probably try to buy her way out with cash, promises or pleas. If this does not work and the Civilian cannot run then there is a chance they will have one form of self defence on them. The terms Citizen and Civilian are interchangeable.

ALTERNATIVES - *Civilians are the most common NPCs in the world so here are a range of alternatives to help flesh them out.*

CITIZEN WITH HELP

The Citizen himself is weak but he has surrounded himself with people who are willing to defend her such as bodyguards, friends or droids.

ENTHUSIASTIC CIVILIAN

This individual loves their resident Agents and thinks they are worthy of hero worship. Once the Agent gives his identity, the Civilian is hooked and will do anything to help, perhaps even following the Agent, trying to secretly help with his mission and desperately trying to be accepted by him and his Division.

HYSTERICAL CIVILIAN

This individual screams and shrieks when approached, she is paranoid and may well have some kind of rape alarm or mace equivalent. She is unreasonable and uncooperative.

THE WEALTHY CIVILIAN

This civilian will use money to get what they want. They may offer cash for the Agents to leave them alone or offer it in exchange for services.

THE MANIAC

This individual is at the end of their tether. For whatever reason the Agents have caught him at a bad time and he will act in a totally unreasonable manner. He may pull a gun, attempt to punch them or just start ranting. It is likely this person does not care whether they live or die and can be potentially dangerous.

THE NEIGHBOURHOOD WATCH

This busybody takes an unnatural interest in what the Agents are doing and is not afraid to take photographs or collect evidence of their activities. He may even approach them and make a citizens arrest.

THE VIGILANTE

This civilian has had enough of Agents and their disregard for the law. He may well have a heavy arsenal and has made it his personal duty to make them pay. He will typically stalk them and use ranged weapons, knowing he is unlikely to best Agents in close combat.

HARD CIVILIAN

License e.g. Medical License

TRAININGS
Domestic Trade, Defensive Fighting, Unarmed Combat Specialist

EQUIPMENT
80%   One weapon from list above
40%   Deactivated cybernetics
60%   D100 in slip credit
50%   Average vehicle keys
50%   Average apartment keys

DESCRIPTION
This typifies the hard Civilian; perhaps he attends martial arts lessons or was in the UIG before being fired for misconduct. Either way this individual has more clout, more attitude and enjoys the challenge of facing up to enemies.

ALTERNATIVES

EX-AGENT
This Civilian was once an Agent and still has most of his upgrades. Knock out gas, stun batons, etc. won't work on him. He may also know operational methods and have a stash of weapons left over from his Agent days. He could demand re-employment or upgrades for his help.

MARTIAL ARTS FANATIC
This guy watches far too many kung fu movies and has an awesome collection of historical weapons including kama, shuriken and katanas. He attends weekly classes in several martial arts and is not impressed when he sees Agents beating the hell out of each other on TV, knowing their cybernetics are no match for his honed skills. If given the chance he will adopt *left fighting stance* and lay down a challenge.

You should increase his Close Combat to 8 and give him a selection of martial arts weapons.

THE GANGBANGER
These guys normally hang out in groups of 2 to 10 and carry small firearms. Paramount to bangers are the concepts of respect and turf and although they are not so stupid as to engage Agents for no reason, they won't let them disrespect them or compromise their territory. If provoked bangers normally have a cache of more serious weapons they can access including grenades and tactical firearms.

THE MASSIVE BASTARD
This person is huge. They probably work out and take a lot of steroids. Their sheer size and aggression makes them a problem, especially as they often find work as bouncers meaning Agents may have to deal with them regularly. Increase the Strength and Endurance of these civilians to 9 or 10.

RANK 0 / LEVEL 1

COMBAT
HP   23
Shield   0
AV   1
Defence   5

WEAPONS
Kinetic Pistol   AT 10, Damage D8, Rate 3
Strike   AT 11, Damage 3+D4, Rate 2
Short Sword   AT 11, Damage D6+7, Rate 3

STATS
Str 7, End 6, Agi 6, Ref 5, Per 5, Int 5, Pres 5

SKILLS
Athletics 5, Attitude 5, Business 1, Close Combat 5, Computers & AI 3, Corp. Knowledge 2, Light Firearms 5, Looking Good 3, Lying & Acting 4, Observation 3, Drive 5, Street Culture 2, Tactical Firearms 1

LICENSES
Domestic Vehicle License, Light Firearms License, 1 Professional

SCIENTIST / DOCTOR

RANK 3 / LEVEL 1

COMBAT

HP   19
Shield   0
AV   0
Defence   1

WEAPONS

Scalpel   AT 6, Damage D2 + 4, Rate 1
Chemicals   AT 6, Damage D10 burning, ignores AV, Rate 1
Strike   AT 6, Damage 2, Rate 2

STATS

Str 5, End 4, Agi 5, Ref 5, Per 7, Int 8, Pres 5

SKILLS

Arts & Culture 6, Attitude 1, Business 4, Close Combat 1, Computers & AI 5, Corp. Knowledge 4, Cybernetics and Robotics 6, Mechtronics 3, Observation 7, Drive 4, Psychology 3, Science 8, Support Weapons 1

LICENSES

Medical License, Biohazard and Toxin License, Often Cyberneticists License, Domestic Vehicle License

TRAININGS

Field Surgery, Aptitude, Domestic Trade (Relevant to the Scientist's Field)

EQUIPMENT

100%	One of the weapons listed above.
60%	D6x10 in slip credit
50%	Average vehicle keys
50%	Average apartment keys
20%	Prototype object or chemical worth D4x1000¢

DESCRIPTION

Scientists are generally very smart and have ways to ensure their survival, for example, bribing potential killers with promises of new technology or inside secrets. They are normally guarded by contingents of Security Guards. All Corporations employ scientists as they cannot afford to get too far behind in the technology race, as a result they are a common site around any Spire, Archology or Open City.

ALTERNATIVES

MAD SCIENTIST

This scientist has no desire to pamper to the Agents wishes. He hates being interrupted and sets off all security systems. He may unlock his test animals, start trying to irradiate them with his lab equipment or even try to experiment on them.

THE PRINCIPLED DOCTOR

This man or woman has taken an oath to do no harm and will do nothing to aid the Agents. Under pressure they are surprisingly tough and will resist as long as possible before doing anything against their nature. Forcing the doctor to perform such acts as creating bioweapons or vivisection on humans will simply not work.

THE BORED LAB RAT

This scientist has spent far too long performing assay tests and preparing items for other, more important scientists. When his lab is entered he is actually quite excited and more than happy to help the division in their task.
If ignored however, he may turn nasty, angered at the fact that even the division are disregarding him. He may then turn into the Mad Scientist (above).

BOUNTY HUNTER (BASIC)

RANK 2 / LEVEL 10

COMBAT

HP	24
Shield	50
AV	5
Defence	8

WEAPONS

Plasma Pistol	AT 15, Damage D10, Rate 2
Plasma Sword	AT 16, Damage D8+7, Rate 2
Strike	AT 16, 3+D4, Rate 2
Favoured Weapon	(Choose one, see description below)

STATS

Str 7, End 7, Agi 8, Ref 6, Per 8, Int 7, Pres 7

SKILLS

Assess Tech 6, Athletics 6, Attitude 5, Close Combat 8, Computers & AI 4, Corp. Knowledge 5, Crime 5, Heavy Firearms 5, Light Firearms 7, Medicine 3, Observation 6, Pilot 6, Drive 4, Psychology 3, Stealth 6, Support Weapons 5, Tactical Firearms 7

LICENSES

All relevant firearm licenses, Detainment License, sometimes a Law Enforcement License, Bounty Hunters License, Domestic Vehicle License.

TRAININGS

Restrain, Mastered Weapon (Trademark Weapon), Language (as appropriate), Assassinate, Multiple Defence, Unarmed Combat Specialist.

CYBERNETICS

Optical - PSE, *Eternity* recorder
Structural - 2 x Reaver Bodyplates

EQUIPMENT

100%	KO grenade, fragmentation grenade, comm. device and all above equipment
30%	Additional plasma longsword (in which case he will have Duel Weapon Fighting)
70%	D4 x 1000 in slip credit
30%	Good vehicle keys
10%	Devilfish combat drugs (+3 to Str, End, Agil)
10%	A strong toxin worth no more than 1000¢

DESCRIPTION

Bounty hunters do not come in a weak variety. They tend to all be of Level 10 or higher and are well versed in taking down targets with the minimum of fuss. Rarely will the bounty hunter face off against his target, he may send in droids or attack from range with missiles or sniper weapons, although some bounty hunters do enjoy the thrill of the close up kill. Bounty hunters, as a group, do not use traditional weapons. They usually carry distinctive trademark arms with a high intimidation value such as blade launchers, rail guns, sniper rifles or ones that deal mashing damage. Bounty hunters are given a few basic ranks quite freely by the UIG, as they are often responsible for bringing criminals to justice and the UIG like to encourage it. They don't tend to acquire high ranks however, as they are still viewed as undisciplined opportunists.

ALTERNATIVES

THE SOCIAL HUNTER.
This bounty hunter favours a more subtle approach, changing their appearance if necessary and getting close to the target via seduction, friendship or charm. When the moment is right the target is reeled in. This form of hunting is very civilised and respected by the UIG (this can earn extra rank points).

THE DOGGED HUNTER
This hunter goes straight for the throat, tracking down the target and attacking them until they are writhing on the floor. They have a firm belief in what they are doing and will happily engage the target in a shopping mall, hospital or in front of their children.

THE STALKER
This hunter follows the prey, carefully making notes on their routine and family. After a week or so the victim may well find a knife at their throat or worse, the severed hand of a loved one with a demand that the target surrender.

OUTLAW (TYPICAL)

RANK 0 (OUTLAW) / LEVEL 3

COMBAT

HP	23
Shield	0
AV	1
Defence	5

WEAPONS

Kinetic Pistol	AT 11, Damage D8, Rate 3	
Strike	AT 10, Damage 3+D4, Rate 2	
Knife	AT 10, Damage D4 + 7, Rate 3	
Shotgun	AT 10, Damage 2D10, Rate 1	
	3D10 Mashing at close range	

STATS

Str 7, End 6, Agi 5, Ref 5, Per 6, Int 5, Pres 6

SKILLS

Athletics 3, Assess Tech 4, Attitude 6, Business 1, Close Combat 5, Computers & AI 1, Corp. Knowledge 4, Crime 6, Light Firearms 5, Looking Good 1, Lying & Acting 5, Observation 5, Drive 4, Psychology 1, Stealth 3, Tactical Firearms 4

LICENSES

None - Outlaw Status

TRAININGS

Survival, Unarmed Combat Specialist

EQUIPMENT

95%	Two weapons from list above
70%	D100 in slip credit
30%	Poor vehicle keys
70%	Drugs to the value of 300¢

DESCRIPTION

Outlaws are those who have been depersonalised by the UIG. They have nothing to lose and tend to find others like them to gain protection in numbers. Typical Outlaws, as described here, tend to be runners for the larger gangs and do not hold any real power. They are competent in a fight though, and will rarely be encountered without their weapons on them. Outlaws have very little loyalty to each other, and an Agent with a good psychology skill can often turn Outlaws against each other shattering their morale and causing some to flee. Outlaws tend to hole up in Old Cities where there is lower UIG presence and they are not so conspicuous. The lack of a clean, legal ID chip on an Outlaw means he will find it difficult to seamlessly slip into a high-tech modern city or Spire.

ALTERNATIVES

INFORMANT

The informant works with Agents or even the UIG. He is permitted a small amount of criminal leeway in exchange for the important information he passes on. He must be protected from other Outlaws as long as his information remains pertinent.

ORGANISED CRIME MEMBER

Traditional organised crime is now, as a whole, controlled by the Ai-Jinn. The main groups are the Jamaican Yardies, British Firms, Colombian Cartels, American Gangs, European Mafia, Japanese Yakuza, Chinese Triad & Tong, and Russian Organisatziya.

Each group has it's own specialities and tends to stick to them. The members of these organisations are usually arranged in tiers where the boss of the gang gives orders to a lieutenant who in turn passes these orders down the chain until they reach soldiers, who act as street level distributors, enforcers and executives. This hierarchy demands total loyalty so there are always measures in place to ensure trust up and down the line. The tier system also serves to isolate the boss from any unfortunate incidents that happen to his soldiers thus making the destruction of an organised crime group extremely difficult.

Tangling with organised criminals will usually result in more and more of the group coming into play until eventually the whole gang and all affiliates will be hunting for the offending party. This explains why organised criminals are often so confident and defiantly conduct their business with no concern for secrecy.

OUTLAW (EXPERIENCED)

RANK O (OUTLAW) / LEVEL 5

COMBAT
HP	24
Shield	0
AV	3
Defence	6

WEAPONS
Laser Rifle	AT 12, Damage 2D6+1, Rate 2
Strike	AT 12, Damage 3, Rate 2
Knife	AT 12, Damage D4+7, Rate 3
2 Plasma Pistols	AT 12, Dam D10, Rate 1, Ignore AV

STATS
Str 7, End 7, Agi 6, Ref 6, Per 6, Int 6, Pres 6

SKILLS
Athletics 4, Assess Tech 4, Attitude 6, Business 2, Close Combat 6, Computers & AI 1, Corp. Knowledge 4, Crime 7, Light Firearms 6, Looking Good 2, Lying & Acting 5, Observation 5, Drive 5, Psychology 2, Stealth 3, Tactical Firearms 6

LICENSES
None - Outlaw Status

TRAININGS
Survival, Quick Draw, Dual Weapon Fighting (Pistols)

CYBERNETICS
Liberty Black Body Space and Switchprints, Reaver Body Plates

EQUIPMENT
100%	3 weapons from list (left)
70%	D100 x 10 in slip credit
30%	Average vehicle keys
70%	Drugs to the value of 600¢
10%	Disposable Lockpicks
20%	Fragmentation Grenade
10%	IV Medpack

DESCRIPTION
The experienced Outlaw has been on the streets many years. He has ascended in his group a long way and commands respect. He is trusted by his superiors with delicate tasks and is not foolish enough to get into fights simply to boost his reputation. He will normally have a few Typical Outlaws with him at any given time.

ALTERNATIVES

RELUCTANT OUTLAW
This Outlaw has either been incorrectly accused or does not desire the life of a street criminal. He does what he does because he is too scared to leave. If encountered by Agents he may ask to be taken to a different state in exchange for information about criminal activities in the city he left. He will not allow himself to be handed in to the UIG.

AMBITIOUS OUTLAW
The Outlaw has quickly ascended to the position of a local gang leader and wants to advance further quickly. He will show his prowess boldly by trying to kill and capture Agents or UIG. His attitude will get him promoted or killed very soon.

CRAZY OUTLAW
This represents the lunatic who wanders the streets screaming at people, perhaps mutilating his own body, and acting with no fathomable motivation. He could simply be insane, drunk or on reality altering drugs. There could be a deeper reason for his actions, perhaps he was being experimented on by psychologists and escaped but had his ID chip removed or maybe the Cult of Machina have got to him.
To add a more sinister tone, perhaps he knows something the world is not ready for, a dark prophet of a sort. Maybe that is why he seems insane. He could be used to interject an ominous plot rather than as cannon fodder.

OUTLAW (STREET BOSS)

STATS

Str 7, End 7, Agi 6, Ref 6, Per 6, Int 7, Pres 8

SKILLS

Athletics 4, Assess Tech 4, Attitude 8, Business 4, Close Combat 6, Computers & AI 1, Corp. Knowledge 5, Crime 8, Light Firearms 6, Looking Good 5, Lying & Acting 5, Observation 5, Drive 5, Psychology 4, Stealth 2, Tactical Firearms 6

LICENSES

None - Outlaw Status

TRAININGS

Interrogation, Combat Driver, Unarmed Combat Specialist

CYBERNETICS

Reaver Bodyplates x 2, Datanetica Storage Drive for stolen data, Liberty Black Body Space

EQUIPMENT

100%	3 weapons from list (left)
70%	D100 x 20 in slip credit
30%	Expensive vehicle keys
70%	Jewellery worth D100x10¢
70%	Disposable toxin filter
40%	Spike / Knife is a plasma version which ignores 4AV
60%	Incendiary Grenade in the Body Space
80%	IV Medpack

DESCRIPTION

The street boss controls groups of Outlaws. Some street bosses run their own patches but others are under the supervision of a greater criminal organisation (often Ai-Jinn influenced). The street boss has generally worked his way up from the bottom so has a great deal of experience and skill at his disposal.

In combat the street boss will tend to stay back using firearms to pick off his opponents while his subordinates work in melee. If his personnel are failing he will normally leave the area using grenades or explosives to cover his exit. Although loyal to his men, he would rather live to fight another day than die at the hands of the UIG, or worse, Corporate scum.

ALTERNATIVE

HIDEOUT BOSS

Rather than accompany his men onto the street the hideout boss stays well out of the way at a secure location and orchestrates operations from there. He is either too famous or wanted to be seen outside, or maybe he is simply a coward.

RANK O (OUTLAW) / LEVEL 8

COMBAT

HP	24
Shield	0
AV	4
Defence	6

WEAPONS

Plasma Rifle	AT 12, Dam, 2D8+1, Rate 2
Knife / Spike	AT 12, Dam, D4+7, Rate 3
Strike	AT 12, Dam 3+D4, Rate 2
Long Sword	AT 12, Dam D8+7, Rate 2

CULT OF MACHINA (CHIMERA)

CYBERNETICS

Toxin Filter (Level 9), Anascan PSE, Midnight Vision System, Gemini Bio-Lynx Cutters, Neural Stabiliser
They will have miscellaneous cyberware which boosts STATS and HP. This is taken into account, I.C.E Technology.

EQUIPMENT

50%   Instead of a rail gun, has a different heavy firearm
70%   Cybernetics Toolkit
30%   A salvageable cybernetic upgrade in condition D10
        worth no more than 5,000¢

DESCRIPTION

The Cult of Machina send shivers down the spines of all but the toughest Agents. They are awesome foes with the potential to hammer Agents into the ground in seconds. This template is for a basic Chimera, their potential is limitless. They will generally attack with their ranged heavy weapon for as long as possible, then wade into melee and attack with pneumatic claws or similar weapons. They normally hunt in packs of 3-5, and their sheer power means that although they are crude in their melee attacks if they hit, few are likely to live.

When looking to raid cybernetics plants and the like they will often take with them an Architect for hacking and planning. The Cultists will often use snipers with rail guns to take out human guards before they are aware of the Cults presence. The violence and profusion of holes leaves no doubt when a hit is made by the Cult.

ALTERNATIVES

AGILE CHIMERA

Most Chimeras are hulking brutes wielding enormous weapons. Some Chimeras do not follow this trend and select light, efficient upgrades which increase their power and agility without encumbering them. These Chimera have less physical power and more Agility / Close Combat skills. Their fighting methods are just as intimidating. They can run along walls and leap shrieking from the roofs of buildings.

THE ENLIGHTENED CHIMERA

Not all Cult of Machina bathe in the blood of man. Some are almost religious about their mechanical ascendancy and do no harm to others in their pursuit of enlightenment and perfection.

These Chimera, although not sociable, are not the chainsaw wielding monsters that they are made out to be, and will try to settle a dispute logically and peaceably. Despite their more reasonable natures they are no less dangerous when angered.

THE DISGUISED CHIMERA

Some Chimera attempt to blend into human society in order to further their goals. They are highly skilled at subterfuge and wear synthetics so they are less noticeable. These individuals have an important roll in information gathering for the Cult.

RANK NORMALLY OUTLAW / LEVEL 13

COMBAT

HP	50
Shield	20
AV	7
Defence	7
EMPS	30 for all Cybernetics

WEAPONS

Pneumatic Claw   AT 14, Damage D8+22, Rate 2
Rail Gun   AT 13, Damage 6D10, Rate 1,
(Fire through walls at -4)

STATS

Str 11, End 8, Agi 7, Ref 6, Per 8, Int 9, Pres 9

SKILLS

Athletics 5, Assess Tech 7, Attitude 5, Close Combat 7, Computers & AI 6, Corp. Knowledge 3, Crime 3, Cybernetics & Robotics 9, Drive 2, Heavy Firearms 5, Mechtronics 6, Medicine 5, Observation 3, Psychology 2, Street Culture 5, Tactical Firearms 3

LICENSES

Possibly an old Medical License or something from a past life.

TRAININGS

Jury Rigging, Survival, Animal Skills

SECURITY GUARD (BASIC)

RANK 1 / LEVEL 1

COMBAT

HP 22
Shield 10
AV 3
Defence 5

WEAPONS

Kinetic Pistol AT 13, Damage D8, Rate 3
Strike AT 10, Damage 3, Rate 2
Tazer AT 10, Damage 0, Rate 1,
Stun (Agents are immune)

STATS

Str 6, End 6, Agi 5, Ref 5, Per 7, Int 6, Pres 5

SKILLS

Assess Tech 3, Athletics 5, Attitude 3, Close Combat 5, Computers & AI 2, Corp. Knowledge 3, Crime 1, Light Firearms 6, Medicine 2, Observation 7, Drive 4, Psychology 1, Stealth 3, Support Weapons 4, Tactical Firearms 4

LICENSES

All relevant firearm licenses, Domestic Vehicle License, Detainment License

TRAININGS

Restrain, Interrogation

EQUIPMENT

100% All weapons above and comm.
      device
70% D100 in slip credit
30% Average vehicle keys
10% Pistol is a laser pistol
60% Disposable toxin filter

DESCRIPTION

Security guards are non-UIG who have been employed by private companies and individuals to look after their interests. Even Corporations use security guards but generally more competent ones than featured above. A guard such as this one would generally be found in malls, outside small banks or guarding low level research installations and warehouses.

ALTERNATIVES

ANIMAL KEEPER

Occasionally guards use attack animals to assist them in their duties. Real animals are unreliable and expensive to acquire so cyberanimals are normally used. Cyberwolves, cybermonkeys and cybercats are the most common guard animals. These will assist the guards in any way they can. You can assume the guard has the ability to command them flawlessly.

THE ONE MAN SHOW

In the tradition of 1980's cinema, some enforcers of the law take things a step further and try to singlehandedly take down the enemy. This guard will have the *Survival* training and probably knows the building inside out, using ducting, alarms, sprinklers and service passages to slowly take out the bad guys until help arrives. The one man show could be working with the Agents if they are trying to help, or against them if they are the ones besieging the building.

THE DARK HORSE

You're raiding a facility and there are some pesky guards. They're armed with run-of-the-mill weapons and all go down with a quick burst of fire....except one.
The dark horse may be an ex-Agent or discharged UIG. He has some cybernetics giving him extra HP and AV and may be carrying some fearsome weaponry such as a bloodstorm, rail gun or even an EMP cannon. His tactics are advanced and he may lay traps for the intruders.

THE NEWB

It's his first day and he's under fire from a Division of trained Agents. Instead of fighting the newb will likely drop his firearms and hide in a broom cupboard. If this individual has been placed in charge of anything important its safe to say it is no longer secure.

SECURITY GUARD (CAPTAIN)

RANK 3 / LEVEL 8

COMBAT
HP	24
Shield	50
AV	4
Defence	7

WEAPONS
Plasma Pistol	AT 15, Damage D10, Rate 2
Strike	AT 13, Damage 3, Rate 2
Long Sword	AT 13, Damage D8+7, Rate 2
SMG Laser	AT 14, Damage 6D8, Rate 1
Grenades (Frag)	AT 12, Damage 3D6, Rate 1

STATS
Str 7, End 7, Agi 6, Ref 6, Per 8, Int 7, Pres 7

SKILLS
Assess Tech 4, Athletics 5, Attitude 6, Close Combat 7, Computers & AI 3, Corp. Knowledge 5, Crime 3, Light Firearms 7, Medicine 3, Observation 6, Drive 4, Psychology 2, Stealth 3, Support Weapons 4, Tactical Firearms 6

LICENSES
All relevant firearm licenses, Detainment License, Law Enforcement License, Security License, Domestic Vehicle License

TRAININGS
Restrain, Mastered Weapon (Strike) Command, Foreign Language (as appropriate), Interrogation.

EQUIPMENT
100%	All weapons above
100%	2 x KO grenade, 2 x fragmentation grenade, comm. device
70%	D10 x 100 in unregistered credit
30%	Good vehicle keys
10%	Sub Machine laser is a Plasma Rifle

DESCRIPTION
Guard Captains are some of the most commonly encountered high ranking Citizens. They've spent a long time in the field and have seen everything. They carry dependable weapons with good stopping power. Normally a Guard Captain will be in charge of a company of 5-10 guards and will be present at the most important part of an installation. They will always call for backup first but generally speaking will fearlessly defend their facility. There are very few retired guard captains, most go out with a bang.

ALTERNATIVES

CORRUPT CAPTAIN
This man got where he is through backstabbing and scheming. He knows very little about commanding soldiers and has made sure he is in a location which will never be attacked such as a UIG controlled food storage facility. If his facility is ever raided by a compentent team (such as Agents) he will have no idea what to do and may well end up getting all his staff killed.

SPIDER CAPTAIN
Rather than sending her men into the corridors of the facility this captain enjoys toying with the infiltrators. She sits in her control room with her guards strategically positioned waiting for the right moment to strike. She knows her facility well and has made a number of contingencies such as equipping her guards with toxin filters and ensuring they know the weaknesses and strengths of all potential enemies. The Spider Captain is an especially dangerous type of opponent and Agents who come up against this enigmatic form of defence should prepare for the worst.

THE RECURRING NEMESIS
Once the Division has beaten off an attack or eluded capture you can introduce the nemesis. Having been defeated by the Agents this captain is out for revenge. He pours disproportionate resources into catching the Division and makes it his personal mission to see they are brought to justice. A UIG captain would make an ideal nemesis but you would need to alter his abilities drastically. If you need more inspiration just think of Colonel Decker from the A-Team.

THE UNUSED SOLDIER
This Captain has great command skills and lives for his work. He has a highly trained force which he maintains in peak condition. The weapon racks are full and every man knows his duty. The problem is no-one ever endangers the facility he guards.
If one day, some Agents break in, he won't miss a trick. The drills have been rehearsed a thousand times and the Agents may well be taken completely off guard. The formations, tactics and skill of the guards is out of proportion to the importance of the installation.

UIG FIELD OFFICER

RANK 2 / LEVEL 2

COMBAT

HP	23
Shield	50
AV	7
Defence	6

WEAPONS

Kinetic Pistol	AT 14, Damage D8, Rate 3
Strike	AT 12, Damage 3, Rate 2
Tazer	AT 12, Damage 0, Rate 1, Stun
Shotgun	AT 11, Damage 2D10, Rate 1
	3D10 Mashing at close range.

STATS

Str 7, End 6, Agi 6, Ref 6, Per 7, Int 6, Pres 7

SKILLS

Assess Tech 4, Athletics 5, Attitude 6, Close Combat 6, Computers & AI 3, Corp. Knowledge 7, Crime 5, Light Firearms 7, Medicine 2, Observation 7, Drive 6, Psychology 4, Stealth 3, Support Weapons 4, Tactical Firearms 4

LICENSES

Any Licenses they need for the job. Typically include all Termination Licenses, Public Appropriation License, Detainment License, Domestic Vehicle License, Law Enforcement License, Light & Tactical Firearms Licenses, Security License

TRAININGS

Restrain, Disarm and Attack, Advanced Disarm

EQUIPMENT

100%	Pistol, Handcuffs, Comm. Device
70%	D100 in slip credit
50%	Shotgun
30%	UIG Vehicle
10%	Pistol is a laser pistol
70%	Disposable Toxin Filter

DESCRIPTION

Field Officers are one of the more common types of UIG encountered. They are the closest to what Citizens would call police and are generally well trained and competent. They will normally call for backup if trouble is likely and will begin by forcing the opponent to stand down under the threat of death. If the target refuses they will shoot to kill. If they get the opportunity they may use force of numbers to overwhelm the target and repeatedly strike with tazers. This will generally mean the target will get a poor *Defence* against each Officer, so they will be able to subdue the target easily and interrogate him. Their weapons are all equipped with Chip Checkers and they have powerful shields and exceptionally good armour which is UIG branded and tagged.

MALENBRACH STREET SWEEPER (BASIC)

RANK 3 / LEVEL 25

COMBAT

HP	50
Shield	100
AV	10
Defence	8

WEAPONS

Rail Gun	AT 17, Damage 6D10+XS, Rate 1, Ignores 15AV
Strike (Reinforced)	AT 15, Damage 11, Rate 2
2H Plasma Sword x 2	AT 15, Damage D12+22, Rate 1, Ignores 4 AV
Grenades (mixed)	AT 14, Damage as grenade, Rate 1

STATS

Str 11, End 10, Agi 7, Ref 6, Per 8, Int 5, Pres 8

SKILLS

Assess Tech 2, Athletics 7, Attitude 8, Close Combat 8, Corp Knowledge 4, Crime 5, Cybernetics & Robotics 4, Heavy Firearms 9, Light Firearms 5, Looking Good 4, Medicine 1, Observation 5, Drive 4, Support Weapons 6, Tactical Firearms 8

LICENSES

Any Licenses they need for the job. Typically include all Termination Licenses, Public Appropriation License, Detainment License, Domestic Vehicle License, Law Enforcement License, Light, Tactical and Heavy Firearms Licenses, Security License

TRAINING

Restrain, Disarm & Attack, Advanced Disarm, Dual Weapon Fighting (Paired Heavy Firearms and Paired Heavy Close Combat), Mastered Weapon (Rail Gun)

CYBERNETICS

All standard Agent upgrades (page 9) Toxin Filter Level 9, Gemini Toughskin, Reaver Alloy Skeleton & Bodyplates. Add others as you see fit.

EQUIPMENT

100%	Heavy firearms, heavy close combat, heavy armour.
70%	Compound 'H' x 2.
80%	2 Intravenous medpacks. Malenbrach can attach 2 at once.
50%	Tactical Firearm such as plasma SMG
30%	UIG Vehicle containing backup weapons
10%	Carries two heavy firearms - 50% chance one is an EMP cannon.

DESCRIPTION

Malenbrach are normally assigned in squads of 5+ and are brought out for dangerous demanding jobs where collateral damage is not a problem such as bringing in Outlaws from the Old Cities or rounding up Agents who are ignoring the law. They require strong leadership as their biological and psychological makeup are unbalanced and still at a stage many would consider to be unstable and experimental. In combat the Malenbrach will open up with barrages of heavy weapon fire until their clips are expended. Then, while the ones at the back reload, the others will lay down suppressing fire with tactical weapons such as blade launchers or fire rifles. This pattern will repeat until the enemy is dead. If they need to move in close, most Malenbrach are trained to wield two heavy close combat weapons although some will use *gun melee* and move in with tactical weapons.

Voice of Authority

Malenbrach have carefully engineered psychomotive voice modulating technology which makes their synthesised, hollow, grating monotone extremely intimidating. Anyone attempting to disobey them must pass a 'Presence + Attitude' check with a -4 penalty. Failure on this roll gives the victim a -1 to all rolls for the rest of the scene as their nervousness impairs their actions.

Fearless and Incorruptible

You cannot intimidate the Malenbrach. Likewise you cannot bribe or corrupt them. If they do go rogue it will be because they want to, not because someone got inside their heads.

UPGRADING THE MALENBRACH

This page is only a template and you can augment and change it as much as you wish. Malenbrach carry a range of weapons and equipment specific to the situation they are responding to. If you own 'Machines of War' there is a UIG equipment section with lots of new and terrifying gear to arm your creations with.

DEVOTED
(ORDER OF THE TRUE FAITH)

RANK 3 / LEVEL 8

COMBAT

HP	24
Shield	36 (Shield Telepathy)
AV	5
Defence	9
TE	55

WEAPONS

Psi Blade	AT 16, Damage D8+16 + XS, Rate 2
Strike	AT 16, Damage 3, Rate 3
Assault	Damage 2D6

STATS

Str 7, End 7, Agi 7, Ref 7, Per 8, Int 8, Pres 9

SKILLS

Arts & Culture 7, Assess Tech 3, Athletics 5, Attitude 5, Close Combat 9, Corp. Knowledge 4, Drive 2, Looking Good 2, Medicine 6, Observation 6, Psychology 5, Stealth 4, Street Culture 4, Support Weapons 4, Tactical Firearms 2

LICENSES

All relevant firearm licenses, Detainment License, sometimes a Law Enforcement License, Bounty Hunters License, Domestic Vehicle License, Telepathics Level 9, Preachers License.

TRAININGS

Restrain, Mastered Weapons (Long Sword for Psi Blade), Language (as appropriate), Telepath, Telepathic Adept

TELEPATHICS

Assault	2
Psi Blade	9
Shield	6
Jump	5
Telekinesis	3
Biokinesis	4
Prescence	3

EQUIPMENT

100%	Psi Blade and Hand Held Shield
30%	Additional Long Sword (in which case she will have Duel Weapon Fighting as a training).
70%	IV Medpack

DESCRIPTION

The Order rely heavily on telepathy but also on their superb melee weapons and armour. Outright confrontation is rare for the Order, who prefer to use fear tactics. They fight with zeal, never retreating when they believe they are right. They carry little money and equipment and normally use no cybernetics. They typically prefer to avoid combat where possible but if forced to fight will summon powerful telepathic shields and attack with their psi-blades. When they get the chance they often pull their opponents weapon from them using Telekinesis and use Prescence and Jump to get the edge on their foe. Often they will leave their enemy with an incapacitating wound or restrained. The Order does not like to kill unless there is good reason.

NPC AGENTS

METHODOLOGY OF DIFFERENT CORPORATIONS

Below is an overview of the different styles exhibited by some of the more commonly encountered parties in Corporation. This is not a rigid mechanic, just a guide for running characteristic encounters.

AI-JINN

Ai-Jinn Agents are normally heavily reinforced with cybernetics giving a generally high Armour Value. Their combat orientated Agents prize strength and resilience which serves them well during the street level operations Ai-Jinn commonly find themselves in. Their more subtle counterparts value less obvious upgrades such as sensory enhancements and black ops cyberware. Often Ai-Jinn Agents will use vehicles, heavy weapons and explosives on missions to give them an advantage. In large scale warfare a common Ai-Jinn tactic is to storm an area with excessive heavy support, when they complete their objective, the tanks and explosives are detonated leaving little in the way of evidence and providing excellent cover for escape.

Agents who operate at street level are expected to work inconspicuously, and therefore such methods are not always possible. These Agents more commonly turn to such weapons as machine pistols, short swords and low to mid end tactical weapons such as shotguns. Above all Ai-jinn value the Division and hold an enormous respect for those of higher rank than themselves. For this reason it can be very difficult to target an Ai-Jinn of any standing due to the ranks of his subordinates that must first be dealt with. Ai-Jinn typically don't carry a great deal of money, though clan leaders and the like have access to substantial amounts if necessary. High ranking Ai-Jinn often have personal cyberlins or customised tanks, but don't tend to use a great deal of high tech, preferring to utilise force of numbers and reliable technology.

COMOROS

Generally you can heavily increase the telepathic skills and TE points of a Comoros Agent. They are also strong willed and have a high presence. This can be represented by giving Comoros NPC's a Conviction point or two to spend. They tend to carry few weapons relying on psi blades, telekinesis and assault telepathics to augment their combat prowess. They carry only subsistence money and will usually have spare weapons such as standard longswords for use in emergencies. Comoros Agents rarely use a lot cybernetics as it is expensive and they believe it interferes with their telepathy. This results in generally lower STATS than other high level Agents.

Comoros' telepathic techniques are often subtle and carefully planned. Instead of engaging in a dangerous sword fight the Agent may simply take the opponents sword using telekinesis and demand his opponent's compliance. This is not always successful, but as a group Comoros does not condone murder so it's Agents are forced to exhaust all options before using lethal measures.

Comoros shares a methodology with the Shi Yukiro, they hold great faith in the power of a lone Agent. Comoros have a great many Agents who work completely alone. These individuals are normally advanced Agents who have proved themselves and are thus allowed access to their best weapons, intelligence and training.

EURASIAN INCORPORATED

E.I. Agents have a tendency towards heavy, flashy and expensive weapons, much of their money will be spent on unnecessary flamboyancy. They normally carry an unusually large amount of slip credit and often have grenades or similar high damage / low risk hardware. Heavy and tactical weapons are the more commonly chosen methods of attack, with light weapons normally taking on a more stylish role. Their disregard for others is legendary and, although not evil in a classical sense, E.I. Agents are not averse to underhanded methods such as taking refuge in hospitals and using schools as strategic shields. Social STATS and skills tend to be high, they will also have significantly more money than is usual which they will not hesitate to use it to accomplish their goals or get out of difficult situations.

SHI YUKIRO

The Agents of the Shi Yukiro are famous for their Ion Weapons and any Agent of sufficient rank or level will carry one, even if it is just a knife or shuriken. They normally carry very little credit and not much equipment other than their swords. If firearms are used they tend to be custom Anzeiger or Shi Yukiro light weapons made specifically for each Agent with silencers and modifications to make them less detectable. Jump telepathy is learnt by a large number of Shi Yukiro to assist in aerial close combat and gymnastic manoeuvres.

Most Shi-Yukiro Agents can be broken down into two types; evasive and assertive, those in the evasive category elude their targets, watching and waiting until they can complete their objective. The more aggressive Agents tend to have an arrogant bearing, they are confident in their abilities and make no excuses for themselves or their actions. These two groups form an operational divide in the Shi Yukiro which is extremely effective and breaks up the majority of Agent methodology into either Ninja or Samurai.

WESTERN FEDERATION

Federation Agents are always very well equipped with a broad range of military hardware and cybernetics. They favour tactical weapons with good track records such as kinetic sub-machine guns and rifles. They are patriotic fighters who rarely back down, especially when defending home territory. A member of the Division will often have a powerful ranged weapon such as a cannon or rocket launcher to offer support for the rest of his squad and to deal with large targets such as hovercopters and trucks.

They fight in superbly regimented units who are trained to operate as well oiled machines. They are seldom rattled and will come up with contingency after contingency before admitting defeat. Their training is exhaustive and Federation Agents have scores of tactical scenarios drummed into them, so that when a situation arises the team knows instinctively how to deal with it.

The media plays a large part in WF combat tactics. Their Agents are always being monitored in the field by satellite cameras so that material which is particularly suitable can be broadcast across the network. Therefore, there is always an onus on Federation soldiers to fight cleanly, bravely and with a certain amount of flair. There is seldom dissension in Federation ranks, their command structure is rigid and deviation severely punished. WF Agents will do what they are told by their superiors regardless of the consequences.

AI-JINN CRIME BOSS

RANK 4 / LEVEL 8

COMBAT
HP	44
Shield	50
AV	7
Defence	7

WEAPONS
Chinese War Sword	AT 15, Damage D6+7, Rate 3
Machine Pistol	AT 12, Damage 3D6, Rate 1
Strike	AT 15, Damage 3, Rate 2

STATS
Str 7, End 7, Agi 8, Ref 8, Per 7, Int 8, Pres 8

SKILLS
Art and Culture 3, Athletics 3, Attitude 8, Close Combat 7, Corp. Knowledge 5, Crime 8, Light Firearms 5, Looking Good 5, Lying & Acting 4, Mechtronics 2, Observation 5, Drive 4, Psychology 4, Street Culture 8, Support Weapons 1, Tactical Firearms 6

LICENSES
All appropriate weapons licenses, Security License, Customs License, Privacy License, all search licenses

TRAININGS
Foreign Language (English), Assassinate, Gun Melee, Dual Weapon Fighting (Light Firearms & Light Melee), Underground Operations

CYBERNETICS
Reaver Alloy Skeleton and Bodyplates, Midnight Vision System, Alloy Skull, Standard Agent Upgrades

EQUIPMENT
100%	All the above weapons
50%	Machine pistol is a sub-machine Laser
40%	Security Bypass Device
70%	IV Medpack
60%	D4 Disposable Lockpicks
20%	*Devilfish* combat drugs (+3 Str, End, Agi)
70%	D100x10 slip credit.
60%	Illegal goods worth D4x1000 credits on the black market

DESCRIPTION
The Ai-Jinn make ruthless criminals, this is an example of a typical Crimeboss who probably keeps her Ai-Jinn connections secret from the criminals she associates with. In combat she typically uses a sword and machine pistol with the Gun Melee Training, this keeps her from losing her Defence. Alternatively a pair of sub-machine lasers is a favourite. She will normally be backed up by a gang of typical Outlaws.

When not in combat the Crimeboss will normally have a retreat which is both safe and comfortable. Typically this may be a restaurant, brothel or club and will have adequate security measures to protect the residents and clients.

ALTERNATIVES

YAKUZA CLAN LEADER (OYABUN)
A yakuza clan leader demands total devotion and obedience from his underlings. In return the *oyabun (father)* offers protection and wisdom to the *kobun (child)*. Yakuza structure is heavily influenced by ritual, from initiation rights involving the drinking of sake with the Oyabun to the *yubizume*, which is the ritualistic removal of finger joints after a significant failure.

A period of over-recruitment hurt the yakuza during the late 20th century where too many members were initiated and the clans became overpopulated and were dubbed simple, violent criminals. This situation has been reversed since the Ai-Jinn became involved and now the yakuza can select exactly who they want.

The yakuza are involved in many enterprises including prostitution, extortion, drugs, pornography and gun running. In combat they tend to favour Japanese made swords with European guns, such as those produced by E.I., which are more for show than anything else.

RUSSIAN MOB BOSS
The bosses of the Organizatyia are brutal and unforgiving. They lead with an iron hand, punishing incompetence with violence and death. To his credit though, the mob boss will be happy to get his hands dirty, heading out with the soldiers and doing whatever is needed to keep the family strong.

COMOROS TELEPATH

RANK 2 / LEVEL 4

COMBAT
HP	33
Shield	36 (Telepathic)
AV	4
Defence	6
TE	53

WEAPONS
2 Psi Blades	AT 12, Damage D8+15, Rate 2
2 Long Swords	AT 12, Damage D8+7, Rate 2
Strike	AT 12, Damage 3, Rate 2
Assault	Damage 4D6

STATS
Str 7, End 6, Agi 6, Ref 6, Per 8, Int 7, Pres 8

SKILLS
Arts and Culture 6, Athletics 7, Attitude 6, Close Combat 6, Corp. Knowledge 3, Crime 1, Looking Good 3, Medicine 5, Observation 5, Drive 4, Psychology 5, Stealth 2

LICENSES
All appropriate weapons licenses, Telepathics License level 8, Privacy License, Domestic Vehicle License

TRAININGS
Twin Psi Blades, Dual Weapon Fighting (longswords), Telepath, Telepathic Adept

CYBERNETICS
Standard Agent Upgrades, Reaver Arm Defenders, (Keep defence in unarmed close combat)

TELEPATHICS
Shield	6
Psi Blade	8
Biokinesis	5
Assault	4

EQUIPMENT
100%	All the above weapons
70%	D100 in slip credit
40%	A Process chip of level D4
70%	Standard Medpack
60%	Toolkit - Medical
60%	Metapsitrophin

DESCRIPTION
This is typical for a Level 4 Comoros Agent; there is a low focus on tech skills with a high focus on Telepathics. If Comoros Agents must fight they often start by putting up their telepathic Shield and then running through gunfire to engage in close combat with their Psi Blades or close combat weapons. If a situation does not warrant combat, the Agent will normally leave preferring to be seen as a coward than to take life unnecessarily. This of course does not apply to all Comoros Agents.

ALTERNATIVES

LIBERATORS
A Liberator is an advanced telepath who has decided to administer her own style of justice. It's no secret that Comoros consider the UIG to be little more than soft-minded puppets of the Archons and are unable to carry out the tasks they have elected themselves to do. Liberators question the actions of the UIG and decide whether they are acting in the best interests of humanity. If a criminal escapes outlawing because of his ties with the higher orders of the UIG, the Liberator will make sure that the criminal gets what is coming to him. Likewise the Liberator acts a defender of the people, assisting those who have been wronged or ignored by the UIG.

In a game the Liberator can be used as an avenging angel who is targeting the Division. The motivation of the Liberator should be simple for the GM to decide, Agents are always creating situations which a Liberator could easily find unacceptable.

E.I. FIELD AGENT

RANK I / LEVEL 2

COMBAT

HP   35
Shield   10
AV   4
Defence   5

WEAPONS

Laser Pistol   AT 13, Damage D8, Rate 3
Long Sword   AT 11, Damage D8+8, Rate 2
Frag Grenades   AT 11, Damage 3D6, Rate 1

STATS

Str 8, End 7, Agi 6, Ref 7, Per 7, Int 6, Pres 8

SKILLS

Assess Tech 3, Athletics 4, Attitude 5, Close Combat 5, Computers & AI 2, Corp. Knowledge 3, Crime 1, Light Firearms 6, Looking Good 5, Medicine 2, Observation 3, Drive 4, Psychology 1, Stealth 3, Support Weapons 4, Tactical Firearms 6

LICENSES

All relevant weapon licenses, Search License Domestic, Domestic Vehicle License, Traffic License

TRAININGS

Dual Weapon Fighting (for use with long sword and pistol combo or sometimes twin plasma pistols), Gun Melee, Survival, Disarm

CYBERNETICS

Datanetica Neural Jack, Storage Drive, Anascan Reticle Eye, Standard Agent Upgrades

EQUIPMENT

100%   All weapons above
70%   Recreational drugs worth 1000 credits
50%   D6x100 in Slip Credit
30%   Average vehicle
10%   Pistol is a plasma pistol
40%   Intravenous Medpack
80%   Standard Medpack
10%   1 canister of CNCN4

DESCRIPTION

This template represents a typical low level E.I. Agent but can be tailored to show any basic Agent. E.I. tend to have plentiful money and overkill weaponry, although at low ranks they generally can't afford what they would really like. E.I. Agents are normally callous, brutal and not daunted by collateral damage as long as they look the part while causing it.

ALTERNATIVES

E.I. NUKE

The Nuke is a heavy weapons specialist. Many Nukes see twin heavy firearms as the epitome of fighting, so work towards enhancing their strength until it becomes a reality (Strength 10). Nukes also enjoy trips to the Anzeiger orbital where they can acquire weapons which require specific licenses to use on earth such as anti-aircraft weapons. They work hard to acquire the licenses and often purchase large armoured vehicles to carry their new acquisitions around with them.

VASTAAG INTERNAL POLICE

E.I. Agents are routinely required to police the holiday orbital of Vastaag. The work is considered to be easy and is normally a great opportunity to abuse your position, extort money and have fun. Anyone visiting Vastaag will normally have to deal with the E.I. authorities, and the outcome is normally dependent on who you are and how much credit you have.

The rich are treated as honoured guests and can easily buy the favour of Agents with a few hundred credits. The masses who flock to Vastaag for cheap rate holidays are ignored for the most part. At most they are intimidated into paying unfair fines or threatened into paying off Agents lest they end up imprisoned.

Rival Agents who visit Vastaag had better be well prepared, any activities will more than likely be caught on camera by E.I. surveillance and mysterious disappearances are common. For this reason Corporations do not normally send their Agents to Vastaag unless they are experienced and capable of dealing with a few ambitious Eurasians getting above their station.

SHI YUKIRO ASSASSIN

Looking Good 3, Lying and Acting 2, Mechtronics 3, Medicine 6, Observation 8, Drive 2, Stealth 9, Support Weapons 2, Tactical Firearms 2

LICENSES
All appropriate weapons licenses, Privacy License, Telepathy License Level 6, Powered Melee License

TRAININGS
Assassinate, Thrown Weapons, Telepath, Advanced Disarm, Unarmed Combat Specialist, Hail of Missiles, Mastered Weapon (Ion Katana), Powered Melee

CYBERNETICS
Anascan PSE, Reaver Alloy Skeleton, Datanetica Storage Drive, Gemini Fibroctin Nerve System, Standard Agent Upgrades

TELEPATHICS
Jump 6, Biokinesis 3

EQUIPMENT
100%	All the listed weapons
90%	Stealth Suit
40%	Security Bypass Device & Disposable Lockpicks
70%	IV Medpack
50%	Digital Scrambler
20%	Invisibility Field

DESCRIPTION
The assassins and ninja of the Shi Yukiro train from their early days to become unquestioning Agents of silence and death. They have a wealth of skills and training at their disposal and are normally encountered alone. They will seldom engage in combat preferring to use Telepathic Jump to simply disappear. If cornered they will fight with their single Ion Katana whilst all the time looking to flee. They have no desire to win, only to complete their mission.

ALTERNATIVES
SPIRITUAL NINJA
Instead of using large amounts of hi-tech, this ninja only uses the basics, favouring shuriken, poisons, stealth and simple weapons. He makes up for the lack of technology by mastering several telepathic disciplines. If designing the Spiritual Ninja consider giving him most of the telepathic skills at 5 or 6 and a few of them at 8, 9 and 10.

THE UNDERCOVER NINJA
Instead of a classic shinobi shozoku (ninja garb), the undercover ninja will wear whatever allows him to blend in and get close to his target. The sword may be replaced with a short sword to make it more concealable but the shuriken and toxins will still be present. It is difficult to spot these deadly foes until it is too late.

RANK 4 / LEVEL 12 (CLAN HITORI)

COMBAT
HP	45
Shield	50
AV	3
Defence	10
TE	32

WEAPONS
Poisoned Shuriken	AT 17, Damage D4 + KO, Rate 4
Ion Katana 1H	AT 20, Damage 2D4+8 + XS Rate 2, Ignores 10 AV
Ion katana 2H	AT 20 Damage 2D4+16+ XS Rate 1, Ignores 10 AV

1H / 2H = 1 Handed / 2 Handed
Ion Katana severs if damage rolled is a double 4

STATS
Str 8, End 7, Agi 10, Ref 9, Per 9, Int 7, Pres 6

SKILLS
Arts and Culture 2, Assess Tech 4, Athletics 8, Attitude 3, Close Combat 10, Corp. Knowledge 6, Crime 3, Light Firearms 1,

W.F. COMMANDO

RANK 3 / LEVEL 15

COMBAT

HP	45
Shield	50
AV	5
Defence	9

WEAPONS

Kinetic SMG	AT 19, Damage 6D8 + XS, Rate 1, Machine Weapon
Plasma Knife	AT 17, Damage D4+9, Rate 3, Ignores 4 AV
Frag Grenades	AT 18, Damage 3D6, Rate 1

STATS

Str 9, End 8, Agi 8, Ref 7, Per 9, Int 6, Pres 7

SKILLS

Assess Tech 4, Athletics 7, Attitude 5, Close. Combat 9, Corp Knowledge 3, Drive 3, Light Firearms 10, Looking Good 3, Lying & Acting 1, Mechtronics 3, Medicine 3, Observation 6, Pilot 4, Stealth 6, Support Weapons 9, Tactical Firearms 10

LICENSES

All relevant weapon licenses, Combat Drug License, Customs License, Military Vehicle License, Termination License 1, Powered Melee

TRAININGS

Jury Rigging, Field Surgery, Survival, Command, Assassinate, Combat Driver, Mastered Weapon (Kinetic SMG), Powered Melee

CYBERNETICS

Anascan PSE, Range Targeter, Reticle Eye, Advanced Process Socket, Videoskin, Cybernetic Arm, Standard Agent Upgrades

EQUIPMENT

100%	All listed weapons
10%	SMG is a Plasma SMG (sub-machine gun)
70%	Flash Bang Grenade
50%	KO Grenade
10%	Proximity Mine
40%	Devilfish Combat Drugs (+3 to Agi, Str & End for scene)
80%	IV Medpack
10%	Proximity Scanner

DESCRIPTION

Commandos are paramount to the structure of the Western Federation. They are trained to enter hostile and unfamiliar territory to complete their mission. They excel at team based skirmish combat where a combination of close combat and medium range weapons are the tools of choice. Typically a Commando will use grenades to disorientate and wear down the opponent before circling them and moving in for the kill.

When on important missions WF Agents will take a number of large armoured vehicles equipped with military hardware and carrying dozens of additional backup weapons such as cannons, plasma weapons and mobile defence platforms. All WF weapons have chip checkers so they need not worry about anything being used against them.

ALTERNATIVES

TERRAIN SPECIALISTS

The WF have many sub-factions of combat-orientated Agents designed to work and thrive in different environments. For example, Urban Assault Specialists work best in an urban environments and their training is designed to give them a huge advantage in such areas.

On the other hand in the diseased jungles of South America the Jungle Warfare Platoon will be dispatched, whose knowledge of environmental poisons, survival and jungle warfare techniques allow them to survive for months in the forests without outside aid.

Terrain specialists are often equipped with custom equipment packages which allows them to make the most of the environment. It should be noted that although these soldiers excel in certain areas it does not mean they make poor all purpose Agents.

DROIDS

Droids are a valuable addition to any organisation. They follow orders to the letter, and, as long as they are set tasks within their workable parameters, tend to be reliable, reusable and slow to complain. On the other hand they are expensive to buy and unless carefully checked can begin to develop ideas above their station. Droids are immune to physiology altering attacks such as knock-out, assassinate, limb sever, viruses, toxins etc.

Droids have Artificial Intelligence and as a consequence must make an A.I. check (roll below or equal to A.I. on 1D10) before they can act. If the roll is failed then the droid has not yet come up with an appropriate response for whatever is happening. Any autonomous processes such as maintaining a shield will continue to function. If a droid is commanded with simple orders such as *kill anyone entering this zone* or *prevent this door from being opened* an A.I. check is not needed.

DROID EMPS

Droids are knocked out for D10 rounds following a successful EMP attack (3-30 seconds).

COMMON DROID CLASSES

ASSASSIN CLASS

These droids are designed for finding and/or killing individuals. Many models exist but these days most are small and inconspicuous, using invisibility shields and stealth to track their targets undetected, waiting for a quick clean kill. Some of the early models were more up front and would track their prey remorselessly and openly regardless of the consequences.

MURDER CLASS

Murder Class are the droid elite, they are designed for small scale skirmish combat and protection of high security installations such as research labs and database structures. The most commonly used Murder Class droid currently in circulation is the Yaeger & Stanton E55 Executioner.

ENFORCER CLASS

These units are generally used for patrol and occasionally for organised assaults on terrorist cells, rebels, mutants and other undesirables. They tend to be solid, moderately able units with plenty of firepower and reasonable A.I. The Western Federation make good use of Enforcer units but the UIG prefer the Murder Class. Enforcer class are often coupled with Sentinel Class when guarding areas, so the Sentinel can find the intruders and alert the Enforcer units.

SENTINEL CLASS

Sentinel Class droids are used to surveil important areas. They are weakly armed but have excellent sensor arrays which scan the area they are guarding. They are not designed to intercept and are usually assigned with Enforcer units who will act on the Sentinels information.

Pan Lee RR9 Rapid Response and Intruder Countermeasure Unit

REPROGRAMMING DROIDS

You need at least one point in the skill 'Cybernetics and Robotics'. To reprogram the droid you must first have access to the droids core. This normally means the droid must be deactivated before reprogramming can commence; thus it should either already be turned off or knocked out with EMP.

Reprogramming an active droid is nearly impossible without the relevant ID Chip permissions.

Consult the table below to see what must be done to reprogram the droid in question. If the GM has designed their own droid then make up some suitable rolls based on the table. Note that the owner or official programmer of the droid can access it's command protocols simply by waving their ID Chip over the droid.

REPROGRAMMING DROIDS

DROID TYPE	EXAMPLE	PEN	SUC
Domestic	Cleaner Droid	-0	1
Commercial	Loading Droid	-1	1
Security	Sentinel Class	-2	2
Attack	Enforcer / Assassin	-3	2
Elite	Murder Class	-4	3
Droid is opposing your attempt (is active)		-8	-

Pen - Penalty to Reprogram
Suc - Successes Needed

An additional -8 penalty applies to reprogram a droid which is active and opposing your attempt. The droid will obviously try to attack the reprogrammer in addition to this.

REPROGRAMMING PROCESS

1. Access the droids core; i.e. get to the droid and open the access panel on the unit.

2. Make an 'Intelligence + Cybernetics & Robotics' roll with the appropriate penalty to access the droid.

3. Each pass indicates 1 success. Each time you fail the droid stands a cumulative 10% chance to activate and attempt to evade / terminate the illegitimate programmer.

4. When you have acquired the correct number of successes the droid will function at the Agents command in any way it can, to the limit of its ability.

DROIDS AS ENEMIES

Droids make great enemies in Corporation, for the most part they are soulless minions of a higher power and Agents can destroy them without any fear of emotional burden or murder charges by the UIG. At most they will face destruction of property charges but often as not the UIG will be indifferent to the fact that these dangerous machines have been destroyed. Sentient droids are not considered to be lifeforms by the UIG so cannot technically be murdered. The DLA may disagree.

Sample Droids are listed in this section but you should feel free to modify them or completely make up your own droids for the Division to face or purchase.

Y&S CENTAUR ME6

SKILLS
Athletics 4, Close Combat 8, Corp. Knowledge 4, Crime 5, Heavy Firearms 9, Mechtronics 4, Observation 6, Support Weapons 8

LICENSES
As per programming, these can be anything depending on the rank and authority of the programmer.

TRAININGS
Powered Melee, Scything Strike

EQUIPMENT
100%	Rocket Launcher
30%	Rail Gun instead of Plasma Cannon
20%	Internal A.I. can be salvaged worth 1000¢

DESCRIPTION
The Military Enforcer is the standard droid used by most companies as a general protection / deterrent unit. The droid is robust and well armed and will complete tasks efficiently. ME6 units are produced by Yeager and Stanton.

In combat the ME6 is slow and purposeful, they move by bipedal ambulation but are heavy and bulky. They don't have much in the way of dexterity and grace and can only jump up to 1 metre off the ground. Initial attacks tend to be with the plasma cannon using the plasma claw only if needed.

MODIFICATIONS
Versatility is one of the hallmarks of the ME6. Below are a range of upgrades you can add to the basic model. The price will increase accordingly.

MILITARY ENFORCER CLASS DROID
RANK 0 / LEVEL 5
VALUE 110,000¢

COMBAT
HP	40
Shield	40
AV	6
Defence	8
EMPS	14

WEAPONS
Plasma Claw	AT 14, Dam D12+12, Ignore 4 AV, Rate 2
Plasma Cannon	AT 19, Dam 5D10+5, Rate 1, Overheats
Viric Lance	AT 14, Dam D8+9, Target must pass a 'Strength + Endurance' roll or be incapacitated for D10 rounds. Agents are not immune to this weapon. Potency 8

STATS
Str 12, End 12, Agi 6, Ref 5, Per 10, A.I. 8, Pres 5

Rapier Missile System   10,000¢ (Missiles are 100¢ each)
Two batteries of 20 micro-missiles are mounted onto the droids shoulders. They can be fired in any quantity up to a maximum of 20 in one salvo. They are fired as a free action using 'A.I. + Support Weapons'.

AT 16, Damage D10 per missile. Each missile ignores 4AV.

Durasteel Armour System   8,000¢
This comprehensive armour system grants the droid an additional 4 points of AV but decreases its Agility by 2 points.

Hover Pack   10,000¢
This allows the droid to hover using an AG motor. It can now travel at speed 40 and ignores bad terrain.

A.I. Targetting Chipset   10,000¢
The droid has an augmented targetting system which grants +2 to all ranged attacks.

Y&S E55 EXECUTIONER

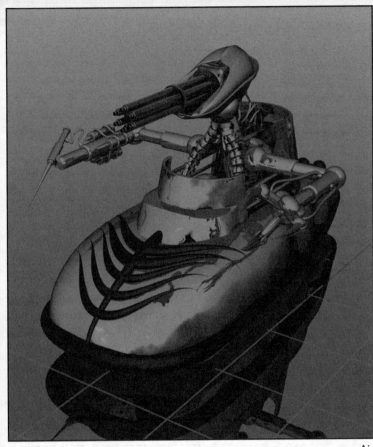

MURDER CLASS DROID

RANK O / LEVEL 10

VALUE 200,000¢

COMBAT

HP	50
Shield	50
AV	8
Defence	8
EMPS	18

WEAPONS

Viric Lance	AT 14, Damage D8 + 13, Rate 1, Toxic (Potency 8), (Strength + Endurance or be incapacitated for D10 rounds). Agents are not immune to this unless using toxin filters.
EMP Cannon	AT 16, Damage 4D10 EMP, Rate 1
Rocket Launcher	AT 16, Equipped with 1 light, 1 medium and 1 heavy rocket.
Plasma Claw	AT 14, Damage D12+13, Ignores 4 points of AV, Rate 2
Plasma Rifle	AT 18, Damage 2D8+1, Rate 2, Ignores AV

STATS

Str 13, End 10, Agi 6, Ref 7, Per 8, A.I. 9, Pres 6

SKILLS

Athletics 5, Close Combat 8, Corp. Knowledge 6, Crime 5, Heavy Firearms 8, Mechtronics 5, Observation 7, Stealth 5, Tactical Firearms 10

LICENSES

As per programming, these can be anything depending on the rank and authority of the programmer.

TRAININGS

Powered Melee, Scything Strike, Gun Melee

EQUIPMENT

100%	All the listed weapons
30%	Plasma generator can be salvaged (worth 1,500¢)
40%	1 dose of toxin from lance can be collected.
40%	If not destroyed the EMP cannon can be salvaged but must have 1000¢ of work to make it usable

DESCRIPTION

The E55 is a Western Federation design, originally used to deal with the location and destruction of key individuals and groups. Since the design of the Murder Class was leaked, the Ai-Jinn manufacture them in their enormous factories and sell them to anyone who can afford them. Nowadays the E55 is also used as a guard droid in sensitive areas. The high A.I. used in Murder Class Units makes them very susceptible to going rogue. Kill switches are sometimes fitted to them (under the control of the owner). However, many robotics experts condemn kill switches and maintain they leave backdoors into the unit's functionality.

The E55 moves at speed 50 by the use of an anti-gravity unit in the base which allows it to hover up to 10 metres off the ground. In combat the Murder Class will start with an EMP blast to shut down the enemy's weapons and cyberware. It will then start using the rocket launcher to take down the opponents. When an E55 is destroyed it can choose to explode itself dealing 15 damage to all targets within 5 metres and 25 damage to anyone in close combat with it. Some E55 units are upgraded with better shields, bigger energy cells, more weapons, better A.I. etc. The one detailed here is factory fresh.

ALTERNATIVES

CLOSE COMBAT VARIANT

The long range weapons are removed. Instead the droid is fitted with a second viric lance and second plasma claw. It can attack with all of these each round. It's chassis also has an electrodermis which it can activate to deal 3D6 electrical damage, ignoring armour to anyone within 1 metre of it. (It can use this ability as a free action once per 3 rounds).

IVIS SDI4 SENTINEL

SENTINEL CLASS DROID
RANK 0 / LEVEL 3
VALUE 20,000¢

COMBAT

HP	15
Shield	20
AV	3
Defence	5
EMPS	12

WEAPONS

Plasma Guns	AT 17, Damage D10, Rate 2, Ignores AV
Warning Siren	Automatically deals 3 damage a round to any one within 20 metres (ignores AV). Ear Defenders negate this damage

STATS

Str 4, End 10, Agi 10, Ref 7, Per 11, A.I. 7, Pres 4

SKILLS

Assess Tech 6, Athletics 5, Close Combat 5, Corp. Knowledge 6, Crime 5, Heavy Firearms 8, Light Firearms 6, Mechtronics 5, Observation 10, Psychology 4, Stealth 6

LICENSES

As per programming, these can be anything depending on the rank and authority of the programmer.

TRAININGS

Surveillance

EQUIPMENT

100%   All the listed weapons

DESCRIPTION

The sentinel droid is a cheap and effective sensory unit which detects intruders with great accuracy. Although they only stand about 30cm high, they have a vast sensor array which is impassable using most modern methods. The droids have a detection range of 1000 metres, which they scan with their sensors and interpret the data with their A.I. When something enters the droid's range make an A.I. check (roll equal or below the droids A.I. on a D10). Failure means the droid has misinterpreted the data and does nothing. Each round the droid may try to reinterpret the data. Experts in robotics systems can attempt to sneak past by making a 'cybernetics & robotics' based roll. The XS acts as a penalty to the droids next A.I. roll, e.g. XS 5 would give the droid -5 to the next A.I. roll.

They are armed with plasma pistols which are for last resort only. Their warning siren damages intruders (guards and staff will normally be defended from the noise). Sentinels run on tiny legs and are often found hiding in ducting or hidden high on walls.

CYMIAN AU2-VERSION 2

CYBERMONKEY ASSASSINATION CLASS UNIT

RANK 0 / LEVEL 4

VALUE 50,000¢

COMBAT

HP	15
Shield	0
AV	3
Defence	7
EMPS	12

WEAPONS

Plasma Claws   AT 19, Damage D6+5+XS, Rate 4, Ignores 4 AV
Light Firearms   AT 11, Damage & Rate as weapon used

STATS

Str 5, End 8, Agi 12, Ref 9, Per 9, A.I. 9, Pres 4

SKILLS

Assess Tech 3, Athletics 11, Close Combat 7, Corp Knowledge 3, Crime 6, Light Firearms 2, Mechtronics 2, Observation 5, Stealth 9

LICENSES

As per programming, these can be anything depending on the rank and authority of the programmer.

TRAININGS

Assassinate, Mastered Weapon (Plasma Claw)

EQUIPMENT

10%   Plasma generator can be salvaged
40%   A plasma knife can be salvaged but must have 500¢ of repairs before use

DESCRIPTION

Cymians (aka Cybermonkeys) are small, impossibly nimble creatures created by the Shi Yukiro for assassination missions. They are simple and instinctive but surprisingly bright and loyal due to the large amount of real monkey brain inside their metal skulls. Originally they were fitted with Ion Claws but the monkeys seemed to disappear with surprising regularity, and the cost was too great, so they were changed to plasma claws in the Version 2.0 model.

They will normally avoid combat, sneaking up on their target at an opportune time, to kill them with the minimum of fuss. If they are forced into a fight they will claw the face. They can attack with 4 plasma claw attacks a round and can technically wield ranged weapons, but are poor with them. Any close combat attacks the monkey makes, which are not claw or bite attacks, are made with an Action Total of 6 not 19.

SENTIENT CYBERMONKEYS

Because the monkeys have a small portion of simian tissue in their brains they can learn and build bonds with their owners. Each

session an Agent uses a Cybermonkey there is a 25% chance it gains a point of A.I. Once it reaches A.I. 11 it becomes self aware and will begin to make educated decisions, predict it's masters needs and become more like a pet, if a somewhat lethal one. To control Cybermonkeys you need the Training *Animal Skills*. If you have it you may control 1 monkey per point in Presence.

ALTERNATIVES

PET MONKEYS

Some individuals choose to keep a cybermonkey as a pet. It can be a useful tool, helping them spy through small spaces, keep watch or bring them items. These monkeys have a tendency to become self-aware quickly and are often mischievous little tykes. This can be problematic when they have an in-built predilection to murder.

Y&S MARK IV CYBERWOLF

ENFORCER CLASS
RANK O / LEVEL 3
VALUE - 30,000¢

COMBAT
HP	35
Shield	0
AV	5
Defence	7
EMPS	14

WEAPONS
Claws	AT 17, Damage D6+D4+11, Rate 2
Bite	AT 17, Damage D6+D4+22, Rate 1

STATS
Str 11, End 11, Agi 10, Ref 8, Per 9, A.I. 7, Pres 4

SKILLS
Athletics 7, Close Combat 7, Observation 7, Stealth 6

LICENSES
As per programming, these can be anything depending on the rank and authority of the programmer.

TRAININGS
Unarmed Combat Specialist, Multiple Defence

DESCRIPTION
Cyberwolves are simple and fairly cheap units used as personal defence and security measures in private compounds where they are given orders to attack non-staff on sight. They are able to attack with their claws and bite each round. If they hit with the bite they can instigate a wrestle (see page145).
They have excellent perception which manifests in acute hearing, night vision and the ability to track by smell.

SENTIENT CYBERWOLVES: Because cyberwolves have a small portion of canine tissue in their brains they can learn and build bonds with their owners. Each session an Agent uses a Cyberwolf there is a 25% chance it gains a point of A.I. Once it reaches 11 and becomes self aware, it will begin to make educated decisions, predict it's masters needs and become more like a pet, if a somewhat lethal one. In order to control Cyberwolves you need the Training *Animal Skills*. If you have it you may control 1 wolf per point in presence.

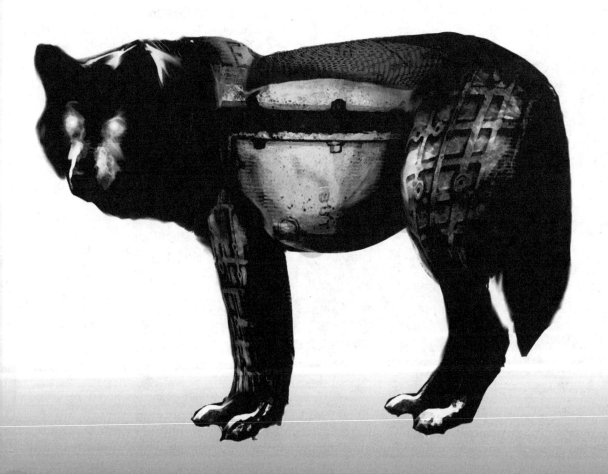

Y&S HORNET SE3

SURVEILLANCE CLASS

RANK 0 / LEVEL 3

VALUE - 10,000¢

The Y&S Hornet comes in two basic configurations. Surveillance and Assassination both are 9cm high.

SURVEILLANCE CONFIGURATION

COMBAT

HP	5
Shield	0
AV	2
Defence	6
EMPS	10

WEAPONS - None

STATS - Str 1, End 7, Agi 8, Ref 8, Per 10, A.I. 7, Pres 2

SKILLS - Athletics 7, Close Combat 3, Computers and A.I. 7, Corp. Knowledge 8, Crime 8, Mechtronics 6, Observation 9, Stealth 8

LICENSES - As per programming, these can be anything depending on the rank and authority of the programmer (same for both droids).

TRAININGS - Surveillance, Hacking

EQUIPMENT - Due to the sensitive data these droids carry, they are equipped with a self-destruct mechanism that will destroy the droid if it is tampered with. Thus, unless disabled with EMP followed by a droid reprogramming check, nothing on the droid is salvageable. If successful, all data and equipment can be recovered.
Advanced hacking software, Invisibility field, Portable Data recorder (miniature - holds 24 hours of high res audio visual)

DESCRIPTION

The SE3 is designed to penetrate the defenses of enemy installations and perform missions, its small size allowing it to bypass the majority of security. For this purpose, it is equipped with a state of the art invisibility field making it extremely hard to spot (-8 on attempts to spot the Hornet). It has a sophisticated sensor array that can track multiple targets by sound, sight and smell (+5 on attempts to track targets whose bio signs have been entered into the droid). In surveillance configuration, the Hornet is equipped with a standard X-Pin interface instead of a sting weapon allowing it to access the majority of computer systems. It is known for Hornet droids to access Agents internal data recorders through their neural jacks while they are asleep.

ASSASSINATION CONFIGURATION

COMBAT

HP	5
Shield	10
AV	3
Defence	6
EMPS	10

WEAPONS

Plasma sting	AT 14 (19 against programmed target), Damage - D6+1, Ignores 5 AV, Rate 4
Or	
Injector Sting	AT 14 (19 against programmed target) Damage - (by toxin), Rate 1

STATS - Str 1, End 7, Agi 8, Ref 8, Per 10, A.I. 7, Pres 2

SKILLS - Athletics 7, Close Combat 8, Computers and A.I. 2, Corp. Knowledge 8, Crime 8, Mechtronics 6, Observation 9, Stealth 8

TRAININGS - Assassinate, Powered Melee, Multiple Defence

EQUIPMENT - As the Surveillance model.

DESCRIPTION

In this configuration the SE3 will track and eliminate programmed targets. Its A.I. is sophisticated enough to recognise moments of weakness by changes in the bio signs of the target and will strike when the target is asleep or particularly stressed if possible. If it is equipped with an injector, the droid will strike once to deliver its payload and will withdraw leaving very little evidence of its presence. If equipped with a plasma sting the Hornet will grip on near a critical location and strike multiple times, victims of this method of assassination tend to have clusters of burns around arteries or nerve clusters. It is worth noting that this method of assassination, although disruptive to them, is ineffective against Agents.

PROGRAMMING BIO-SIGNS INTO THE UNIT

The unit can better follow and attack a programmed target .

1. Using the bio-sign scanner that comes in the box with the Hornet. This scanner needs to be kept within 5 metres of the target for around 10 minutes to get a reliable read.
2. Accessing the targets detailed medical records. This is obviously easier for E.I. employees.
3. Detailed analysis of DNA and behaviour. The target's bio-signs can be inferred from detailed analysis of around 10 hours of AV footage (Perception + Psychology with a -2 penalty) and a sample of DNA.

APPENDIX

available aggressive systems
[emg cannon]
[wrac lance]
[plasma claw]
[plasma ribe]
[cricket launcher] engaged

executioner: g55 (no record mode)
registered programmer – gucht, chen

<equipped>
ans panther: antipersonnel biometric missile – specific license required

target: illyana karmich
biomatch: positive
routine: termination
license status: action unlawful – override code 225d

STANDARD DECODE ON 4 SATATEL DECON. PRIMARY. A CODE 556 TELEMETRY READOUT GH56. HOLDING PATTERN 34 56 53. STATUS PLAN, NISS.

DEPARTMENT OF MISSION ASSIGNATION

MISSION CODE_____

PARAMETERS

DATE: _____
ISSUED BY: _____
ISSUED TO: _____
MISSION TO BE COMPLETED BY: _____
CONFIDENTIALITY_____

ALLOCATED RESOURCES

_____
_____
_____
_____
_____
_____
_____

MISSION OBJECTIVE

_____
_____
_____
_____
_____
_____
_____
_____
_____
_____
_____
_____
_____
_____
_____

ADDITIONAL

_____
_____
_____
_____

ISSUING OFFICER

_____

CORPORATION

NAME
CORP.
RANK
PROFESSION
DIVISION
LEVEL

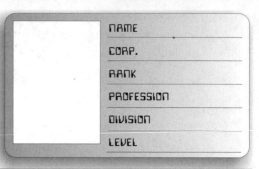

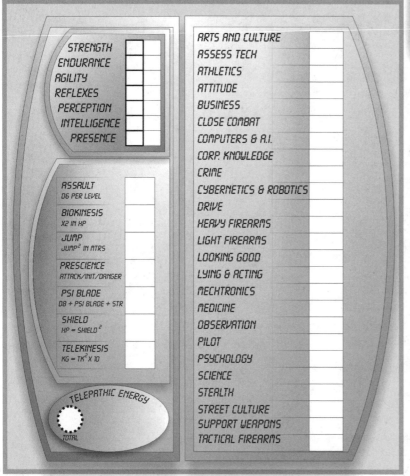

STRENGTH
ENDURANCE
AGILITY
REFLEXES
PERCEPTION
INTELLIGENCE
PRESENCE

ASSAULT
D6 PER LEVEL

BIOKINESIS
X2 IN HP

JUMP
JUMP^2 IN MTRS

PRESCIENCE
ATTACK/INIT/DANGER

PSI BLADE
D8 + PSI BLADE + STR

SHIELD
HP = SHIELD^2

TELEKINESIS
KG = TK^2 X 10

TELEPATHIC ENERGY

TOTAL

ARTS AND CULTURE
ASSESS TECH
ATHLETICS
ATTITUDE
BUSINESS
CLOSE COMBAT
COMPUTERS & A.I.
CORP. KNOWLEDGE
CRIME
CYBERNETICS & ROBOTICS
DRIVE
HEAVY FIREARMS
LIGHT FIREARMS
LOOKING GOOD
LYING & ACTING
MECHTRONICS
MEDICINE
OBSERVATION
PILOT
PSYCHOLOGY
SCIENCE
STEALTH
STREET CULTURE
SUPPORT WEAPONS
TACTICAL FIREARMS

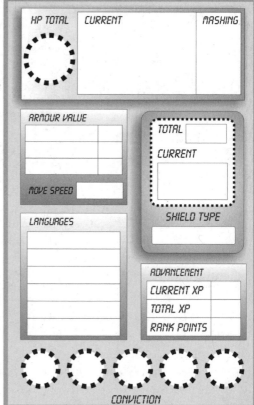

HP TOTAL   CURRENT   MASHING

ARMOUR VALUE

MOVE SPEED

LANGUAGES

TOTAL

CURRENT

SHIELD TYPE

ADVANCEMENT

CURRENT XP	
TOTAL XP	
RANK POINTS	

CONVICTION

WEAPON / ATTACK	AT	DAMAGE	DEF	RATE	CON	EMPS	SPECIAL

HARDWARE / CYBERNETICS

A.I.

TRAININGS

CONTACTS

LICENSES

CREDIT REG   SLIP

_____

SKILLS
_____
_____
_____
_____
_____
_____

LICENSES
_____
_____
_____

TRAININGS
_____
_____
_____
_____

CYBERNETICS
_____
_____
_____
_____

TELEPATHICS
_____
_____
_____

EQUIPMENT
____% _____
____% _____
____% _____
____% _____
____% _____
____% _____

RANK __ / LEVEL __

COMBAT
HP   __
Shield   __
AV   __
Defence   __
TE   __

WEAPONS
_____
_____
_____
_____

NOTES
_____
_____
_____
_____
_____
_____
_____
_____
_____

STATS
Str _, End _, Agi _, Ref _, Per _, Int _, Pres _

TERMS AND SLANG

AMS
Anzeiger Military Systems – A subsidiary of the Western Federation who sell excellent firearms.

A.I.
Artificial Intelligence. Normally some kind of computer-like system which mimics biological intelligence with varying degrees of success.

Archons
The Nine Great A.I.'s recovered from Venus, named after the 9 magistrates of ancient Greece.

Augs
Slang for Cybernetics (from Augmentations).

Barbarians
Shi Yukiro term for Eurasian Inc. Agents.

Bingo Wings
Drop suits - for jumping out of airborne vehicles or from high up locations.

BIO (B.I.O.)
Bio-engineered Independent Organism. A man-made creature which can sustain itself. Made on the Miller-Urey research orbital.

CEO
Chief Executive Officer. An individual who oversees the functioning of an entire Corporation.

Clangers
Derogatory name for the Ai-Jinn due to the amount of metal they attach to themselves.

Consortium
Term for the entirety of UIG structure.

CROs
(Pronounced Crows) Common Residential Officers. The commonly encountered UIG Officers who generally annoy Agents and visa versa. Crows is a derogatory term.

Crusaders
Term used for militant Order of the True Faith Devoted.

Cult (The)
The Cult of Machina - Gruesome cult of individuals addicted to cybernetic enhancement.

Cybes
Slang for Cybernetics, also Augs.

Devoted
Agents of The Order of the True Faith.

DLA
Droid Liberation Army – Fanatics who attempt to free droids who they believe should not be slaves.

E.I.
Eurasian Incorporated - A Major Corporation.

EMP
Electromagnetic Pulse – A type of pulse which can shut down active electrical devices. Also EMPS - Electromagnetic Pulse Shield.

Executives
Word used to refer to Agents by non-Agents and Agents alike.

Faithful, The
Those who subscribe to the teachings of the Order of the True Faith. Agents of the Order are called Devoted.

Flakes
Comoros slang for Western Federation and Eurasian Inc. Agents.

HIONS
Hard Ion Shields

MID
(Mids) Missing Identity Chip – UIG Term for someone who is missing their ID Chip.

MO / M.O.
Missions officer.

Mutician
A scientist who works in the field of mutagenics. The manipulation of DNA to produce new strains of organism (normally called BIOs). Large scale mutagenics are banned on Earth but permissible on Miller-Urey.

Nukes
Term for heavy weapons specialists. Especially E.I.

Order (The)
The Order of the True Faith

Outcast / Outlaw
Term for those who have no Citizenship but are not criminals.

Richenbacher
(Pronounced *Ricken-backer*) – European Manufacturer of close combat plasma weapons.

SMART
Self Modelling Auto-loading Round Technology. Ammunition for kinetic weapons.

Smeaker
Device built into the jawbone allowing short range communications. Also called an SVC (sub-vocal comm).

Spire
A Spire City – they are normally referred to simply by location, e.g., *The London Spire*, although some have names such as the Eden Spire.

S.Y.
Shi Yukiro – A Major Corporation.

UIG
United International Government – A policing and governmental organisation made up of allied world governments. They prioritise the safety and comfort of Citizens above all else.

Underswell
The foundations of a spire city. Known for their lawlessness and high mutation rates.

WDN
World Data Network – The 2500 version of the internet. Similar but larger and faster.

WF
The Western Federation – A Major corporation.

Y&S
Yaeger and Stanton – A subsidiary of the Western Federation selling a wide spectrum of assault equipment and droids.

Keizo Kiyoshi strode along the narrow corridor, struggling to keep the elation that filled him from manifesting in any exterior form. Beneath his feet he heard the familiar singing of the nightingale floor, the neurotoxin distributors set into its surface quiescent since the harmonics caused by his footfalls had already been analysed and passed as safe by the nanoscopic machines grafted on to the antique, though elegantly simple, mechanisms of the floor itself. There were those who found it difficult to walk across the polished, musical boards without trepidation, given the agonizing nature of the poisons that might hiss forth from between the panels, but today the song of the floor only fed the fierce joy in Keizo's heart.

Three days previously Keizo had been sent out on to accompany his immediate senior, section chief Onishi, on a covert business opportunity with a cell of the hated Ai-Jin. Their group had not been large and, following an ambush by the craven rabble they had supposedly been negotiating with, Keizo had been one of only three survivors. Onishi had been the second. Taking a calculated risk, he'd allowed the far larger force of Ai-Jin terror troops to take Onishi hostage while he located the third and last survivor, Suzuki Masato, an old friend from before he and Keizo had taken the paths of the samurai and the sarariman respectively. Though Suzuki had wanted to attack the Ai-Jin immediately, Keizo had restrained him, letting him loose only once a significant number of the terror troops were occupied with the preliminary stages of an ad-hoc interrogation of the section chief. Thus distracted, the lightly armed band of captors had been no match for a samurai and Keizo smiled to himself at the memory of the sound of the ion katana slicing through flesh, the ion field making a faint buzzing noise like a lazy wasp on a summer's day.

On their return to the outpost Onishi, bearing only the most minor injuries, had gone straight into discussions with the Board. Presumably they had been deliberating over the appropriate reward for Keizo's brilliant if unorthodox approach and his rescue of the section chief. Keizo had spent much of the following two days imagining what recognition he might receive and now, finally, had been summoned to a Board address. Reaching the end of the interminable corridor, he took two deep, controlled breaths to bring his emotions into check and lifted a hand to slide back the paper screen.

His hand faltered with the door less than three feet open. All the members of the Board, kneeling on tatami matting, were ranged around expanse of the conference table. Most were present only as holographic conference images but all were staring at him, and in their faces he read the folly of the delusion he had allowed to cloud his judgement. As though scales had slipped from the eyes of his mind, he realized with a jolt that he had deliberately jeopardized the safety of his immediate superior, and that the fact of the subsequent rescue was immaterial in context of such an unforgivable breach of honour. Once more raising a hand that suddenly seemed as heavy as steel, Keizo pushed the door the rest of the way open.

Now visible in the corner of the room, a short wakazashi – an antique, with a simple inert metal blade – sat on a lacquered stand before a thin black cushion. Waiting three paces away, Suzuki Masato stood rigidly, implacably, his own ion katana drawn and held ready. Though his old friend kept his gazed fixed on the floor, Keizo could detect not a hint of emotion in his face. But then, the samurai was not the one responsible for imperilling the section chief.

Every Board member turned simultaneously away from Keizo to stare at the empty cushion. Swallowing in a dry throat, his mind suddenly full of the buzzing of summer wasps, Keizo Kiyoshi stepped into the room and slid the door closed behind him.

INDEX